Permanent Exiles

Permanent Exiles

ESSAYS ON THE INTELLECTUAL MIGRATION FROM GERMANY TO AMERICA

Martin Jay

Columbia University Press   New York   1985

Library of Congress Cataloging in Publication Data

Jay, Martin, 1944–
  Permanent Exiles.

  Bibliography: p.
  Includes index.
    1. Sociologists—Germany—Addresses, essays,
lectures. 2. Social scientists—Germany—Addresses,
essays, lectures. 3. Criticism (Philosophy)—Addresses,
essays, lectures. 4. Refugees, Political—Addresses,
essays, lectures. I. Title.
HM22.G2J38   1985   301′.092′2   85-11364
ISBN 0-231-06072-6

            Columbia University Press
                  New York
      Copyright © 1986 Columbia University Press
              All rights reserved

      Printed in the United States of America

Clothbound editions of Columbia University Press books are Smyth-
sewn and printed on permanent and durable acid-free paper.

To Shana and Rebecca

Contents

Acknowledgments

Composing the acknowledgments for a book is always the most gratifying of the tasks in its preparation. And when the book consists of essays spanning one's career, it is even more of a pleasure. For the act of acknowledging revives strong and agreeable memories of the generosity shown by many friends, colleagues, teachers, and figures interviewed, as well as that of the academic institutions with which I have been fortunately associated. To mention the latter first, I would like to express my gratitude to Harvard University, the University of California, Berkeley, and St. Antony's College, Oxford for providing me with as stimulating and supportive a series of institutional settings as any scholar could desire. The resources of their great libraries, as well as those of the Johann Wolfgang Goethe University in Frankfurt and the Schiller National Museum in Marbach am Neckar, made my research possible. No less crucial was the financial sustenance I received from the Danforth Foundation, the John Simon Guggenheim Foundation, the National Endowment for the Humanities, and the University of California Committee on Research. I am also delighted to acknowledge with appreciation the journals in whose pages these essays first appeared: *Dissent, Geschichte und Gesellschaft,* the *Leo Baeck Yearbook, Midstream, New German Critique, Partisan Review, Perspectives in American History, Salmagundi, Social Research, Telos,* and *Thesis Eleven.* Along with the Suhrkamp Verlag, which published collections where two of the essays first appeared, they have graciously permitted republication in this volume.

The initial appearance of these essays would not, of course, have been possible without the cooperation, encouragement, and critical scrutiny of a wide variety of people, many of them the subjects of my historical inquiry themselves. Without constructing boundaries, in many cases artificial, between those who granted interviews, opened their files, read drafts, or simply gave helpful advice, let me simply thank en masse those, many of whom are alas no longer alive, whose acts of kindness left traces on the following pages: Theodor W. Adorno, Rudolf Arnheim, Bernard Bailyn, Robert Boyers, Paul Breines, Susan Buck-Morss, Lee Cooper, Gerald Feldman, Donald Fleming, Erich Fromm, Michael Timo Gilmore, Todd Gitlin, Jürgen Habermas, Irving Howe, Max Horkheimer, Norman Jacobson, Bernard Karpel, David Kettler, Paul Oskar Kristeller, Paul Lazarsfeld, George Lichtheim, Eugene Lunn, Steven Marcus, Herbert Marcuse, Paul Massing, Hans Mayer, Volker Meja, Gerhard Meyer, Sheldon Meyer, George Mosse, John S. Nelson, Henry Pachter, William Phillips, Paul Piccone, Friedrich Pollock, Reinhard Rürup, Ronald Sanders, Wolfgang Sauer, Meyer Schapiro, Michael Schroeter, Gershom Scholem, Ernst Simon, George Steiner, Richard Webster, William Weinstein, Paul Weissman, Leon Wieseltier, Karsten Witte, Karl August Wittfogel, Kurt Wolff, Richard Wolin, Lewis Wurgaft, and Jack Zipes. Perhaps three people should be singled out for special thanks: H. Stuart Hughes, who first sparked my interest in the refugees during my graduate career, Leo Lowenthal, the "permanent exile" whose friendship I consider the most valuable result of my research, and my wife, Catherine Gallagher, whose support, intellectual, editorial, as well as emotional, cannot be exaggerated.

Although the separate essays in this collection would have been impossible without the help of those named above, the book itself came into being only because of the initiative of William P. Germano of Columbia University Press, who first suggested the idea to me. I am also indebted to the Press for the scrupulous editing of David Diefendorf. The manuscript itself was prepared by the staff of the Institute of International Relations at Berkeley and the index was done by Carolyn Dean; to both I am deeply grateful.

Finally, I must acknowledge the far more intangible, but nonetheless very real help of the two people to whom this book is dedicated, my stepdaughter Shana Gallagher and my daughter Rebecca Jay. Because they were too young or yet to be born when many of these essays first appeared, I am especially pleased that they will have a second chance to come to know them. For I hope they will soon share my fascination for the remarkable generation of refugees some of whose stories I have been privileged to tell.

Introduction

"Collecting here texts published as prefaces or articles during the last decade, their author would gladly elaborate upon the life and times which have produced them, but cannot: he is too certain that the retrospective is never anything but a category of bad faith."[1] So Roland Barthes once explained in denying himself a manipulative authorial "last word" in the reception of his works. Barthes' warning is perhaps wisely heeded as a check on the temptation to rewrite the past for present purposes. But abstention is, alas, not without risks of its own. For if an author merely collects texts written over a long period of time and in very different circumstances, he courts another kind of bad faith: that engendered by the willful suppression of the original context of intellectual production and the subsequent fate of the texts in the world. Rather than effacing the productive origins and mediating receptions of separate texts to present what art historians like to call a "licked canvas," making them apparent can be an act of good faith instead.

There is, in addition, a further advantage when a historian reflects on his now historical efforts to made sense of the past. For, as I have tried to argue elsewhere,[2] in so doing, a healthy alienation effect can be produced. By juxtaposing original texts with varying focuses and written in different voices, and then adding subsequent reflections on their significance, the historian can dispell the illusion of a harmoniously smooth narrative of the past *wie es eigentlich gewesen.* Readers are thus reminded of the inevitably subjective dimension in the writing of all history, as well as of the historicity of the writer himself. It is with this goal in mind, despite Barthes' warning, that this introduction has been written.

The imperative to do so is all the more urgent insofar as my own relationship to the figures about whom I've written has often been personal as well as professional. Coming to know most of the emigrés discussed in this volume was an enormous advantage for my work, as well as a genuine privilege, although at times I am sure it affected my capacity to judge their achievements with dispassionate distance. Encountering them near the ends of their lives and often benefiting from their trust and generosity doubtless had its effects, both good and ill, on my efforts to reconstruct their pasts. Several of the essays were in fact written as memorials to emigrés whose deaths I, like many who knew them even less intimately, genuinely mourned.[3] The elegiac quality that certain readers of my first book on the Frankfurt School noted was an undeniable consequence of this personal relationship.

I never, however, intended to bury their ideas as well, contrary to the assumption of those who think historians can only look backward with nostalgia. Indeed, one of the most exciting aspects of working on the migration has been the sense of helping to rescue and make available ideas whose potential has yet to be exhausted. The German sociologist Wolf Lepenies has recently written of the temporary "storage" of controversial ideas from one discipline in the discourse of another.[4] One of his examples was *The Dialectical Imagination,* which he generously cited as the work of an intellectual historian preserving ideas that mainstream sociologists and philosophers had ignored or marginalized until recently.[5] Several other intellectual historians of my generation—most notably Andrew Arato, Paul Breines, Susan Buck-Morss, David Gross, Russell Jacoby, Eugene Lunn, Mark Poster, Anson Rabinbach, and Richard Wolin—have played a similar role. And in most cases, we have begun increasingly to draw on and criticize the ideas themselves, rather than merely record them in disinterested fashion.

Before coming to the concrete contexts of the separate essays, I must say a word about the title of the collection itself. In 1969, I published a short essay in *Midstream* entitled "The Permanent Exile of Theodor W. Adorno,"[6] which reflected on his recently and prematurely ended life and career. The phrase "permanent exiles" seemed an accurate and evocative term to describe the Frankfurt School as a whole, and so I considered it as a possible title for the book I was writing on their history. Herbert Marcuse and Leo Lowenthal, two members of the School who remained in America, agreed that it rang true and encouraged me to use it. But much to my surprise, Max Horkheimer and Felix Weil, both then living in Europe and more at peace with the contemporary world than their erstwhile colleagues, were vehemently opposed. Horkheimer, who had graciously consented to write a preface to the book, even hinted at its withdrawal were I to insist on the title. As I had another attractive alternative at hand, which I had consciously derived from C. Wright Mills' *The Sociological Imagination* (and, as it was later pointed out to me much to my embarrassment, unconsciously to a passage from Norman O. Brown's *Life Against Death*),[7] I decided to use it instead. But it has always been my conviction that the homecoming of certain Frankfurt School members to Germany did not really end the exile of Critical Theory. Nor were the other emigrés to whom I was also drawn—Kracauer, Arendt, Lichtheim, or Pachter—truly at home in their adopted country. So it now seems even more justifiable to call a book on the migration *Permanent Exiles.*

The opening essay concerns the figure who first piqued my interest in Critical Theory and its origins, Herbert Marcuse. It was delivered to the fifth annual Socialist Scholars Conference in September 1969 at Hofstra University. The meeting took place at the height of the New Left's influence in America, when Marcuse's impact was keenly felt here and abroad. Interest in his work was, in fact, so intense that the paper was published in three places, each, for reasons known only to their editors, under different titles.[8] In the last of these, a collection of essays from the Socialist Scholars conferences entitled with premature optimism *The Revival of American Socialism,* it was described with a slight touch of disdain as "an academic comment of a kind frequently presented to the Socialist Scholars Conference"[9] and contrasted with two other papers on Marcuse that linked him more directly to the practical tasks of "the movement." It was, in fact, aimed at disentangling the roots of Marcuse's ideas rather than advocating how best they might be applied under current circumstances. But it did not ignore entirely their practical implications, especially for a viable radical politics. The final, sketchy remarks on Habermas and Arendt as implicit critics of his metapolitical position were indications of this concern.

If "Metapolitics of Utopianism" was first delivered in the overheated setting of a gathering of socialist scholars straining to be socialist activists, the second paper reprinted below, "The Frankfurt School's Critique of Marxist Humanism," was called into being by a very different kind of event, the conference on Weimar Culture held at the New School for Social Research in October 1971. It was a glittering assembly of many distinguished survivors of the migration, as well as younger students of their history. Hovering over it all was the then fashionable "Specter of Weimar,"[10] as Theodor Draper called his contribution, which meant the analogy purporting to exist between its sad fate and that seemingly awaiting America in the coming years. On the program and in the audience were many emigrés like Henry Pachter, who were deeply troubled by the parallels they detected between the New Left and the irrational students who had prepared the way for Hitler by denigrating Weimar democracy.

My contribution to the conference took little note of the

analogy, which seemed to me at the time, as it does even more so now, highly questionable. Instead, I attempted to rescue the Frankfurt School from the then widespread assumption that it was another variant of Marxist Humanism. In particular, I was anxious to challenge the argument of the Swedish Althusserian Göran Therborn in one of the first historical accounts of the School that its Critical Theory was merely a "prescientific" vestige of the philosophical anthropology that Marx had left behind. In ways that would later be developed in my work on the question of totality, I began to explore the important but often misunderstood differences between Critical Theory and the Hegelian Marxism of Lukács and Korsch, to which it was often assimilated. The effort, although not without its detractors, seems to have had some impact, even in Sweden, where the article was translated in 1982 by the Marxist journal *Tekla* as an antidote to Therborn's still influential interpretation.[11]

The next essay on the Frankfurt School emerged out of a much less polemically charged context. It was solicited by Donald Fleming and Bernard Bailyn for the sixth volume of their *Perspectives in American History,* published by Harvard's Charles Warren Center. The second volume in the series had been devoted to the migration as a whole, and when it came out in book form in 1970, I had reviewed it for *Commentary.*[12] *The Intellectual Migration,* as the book was called, suggested to me a pattern of selective hospitality, depending on the emigrés' allegiance to the spirit of the *Neue Sachlichkeit,* which seemed to be borne out when I turned in greater detail to the initial American response to "The Frankfurt School in Exile."[13] The essentially depoliticizing implications of the *Neue Sachlichkeit* also fit well with another analysis by Joachim Radkau, which came to my attention when I reviewed his book shortly thereafter.[14] Radkau's general contention that the impact of the migration was ultimately conservative may have been somewhat overdrawn, but it complemented my observation about the greater success of those intellectuals beholden to the technocratic, anti-utopian values of the middle Weimar years. Insofar as a general pattern of reception is inherently problematic because of the variety of emigré experiences, such a claim can only be made tentatively, but it does suggest a hypothesis that might fruitfully be tested in other cases as well.

After *The Dialectical Imagination* was published in 1973, I began to extend my interests beyond the Frankfurt School with a new project on another refugee, Siegfried Kracauer. But as the American assimilation of Critical Theory was then gaining considerable momentum, I was drawn back into its orbit. In the fall of that year, I was invited by Paul Piccone, the editor of *Telos,* to speak at Washington University and by Jack Zipes, an editor of *New German Critique,* to do the same at the

University of Wisconsin, Milwaukee. My topic was "The Frankfurt School's Critique of Mannheim and the Sociology of Knowledge,"[15] chosen in part to accommodate another invitation by the Sociology of Knowledge contingent of the International Sociology Association meeting in Toronto.

Reaction to the article, when it was published in *Telos*, was vigorous and swift. But it did not come, as I had expected, from a defender of Mannheim. Instead, the political theorist James Schmidt took me to task in the next issue of *Telos* for having undermined Critical Theory as an inspiration for the American Left.[16] Disentangled from the overly vicious polemical rhetoric of that era, which seemed to find a special welcome in the pages of *Telos*, his critique focused on two essential flaws in my argument: the contention that the Frankfurt School's critical analysis of Mannheim's holism could be extended back to Lukács' version as well, and the claim that classical Critical Theory had failed to ground its critique with sufficient rigor. As *Telos* gave me ample time to reply in its next issue and Schmidt seems to have modified, if not entirely abandoned, his defensive attitude towards Critical Theory,[17] this is not the place to engage in yet another round of the debate. I would only say that further evidence of the Frankfurt School's hostility to Lukács' concept of totality can be found in my later piece in *Telos* on the subject, which aroused no less consternation on the part of its editors, and in *Marxism and Totality*.[18] As for the difficulty of establishing a firmer Archimedean point for Critical Theory after its abandonment of the Hegelian-Marxist belief that proletarian praxis could provide one, I would refer the reader to Seyla Benhabib's recent discussions of the issue,[19] which continue the general direction of my essay. In the 1980s it is even harder than it was in 1974 to quote, as did Schmidt, Horkheimer's uncharacteristically bold remark that Critical Theory "confronts history with that possibility which is always concretely visible within it,"[20] and then think that the problem is solved. The alternative, to be sure, is not a simple return to a traditional theoretical standpoint outside of history, as Schmidt and others claim I recommend,[21] but rather to find other ways of combining a variety of nontranscendent grounds for critique. It is because of Habermas' still evolving struggle to do precisely this that his work is so promising, especially against the backdrop of an increasingly postcritical philosophical climate that is nurtured more by hermeneutics and poststructuralism than the sociology of knowledge.

If the theoretical and practical issue of the Frankfurt School's search for a ground for its critique generated considerable debate, no less controversial has been its relation, both personal and intellectual, to what in the Germany of its members' youth was called the "Jewish question." In the secondary literature on the School, opinion ranges from those who contend the influence of their predominantly Jewish backgrounds was absolutely fundamental throughout their work to those who claim its importance was nugatory.[22] The members of the School were no less divided, as they were on the question of religion in general.[23] In *The Dialectical Imagination*, I tried to establish a balance between the extremes, but it was clear that a great deal still needed to be said about both the putative influence of their ethnic backgrounds and their own work on anti-semitism and the role of the Jews in modern society. In a short essay that appeared in *Midstream* in 1974, I tried to address these questions by situating the School in a differentiated picture of the Weimar Left's attitudes towards the Jewish question.[24] "Anti-Semitism and the Weimar Left" also highlighted some of the controversy that still surrounds the question today. Then in 1979, at the invitation of Reinhard Rürup, who was preparing a special issue of *Geschichte und Gesellschaft* on "Anti-Semitism and the Jews," I returned to the problem once more.[25] An English version of "The Jews and the Frankfurt School: Critical Theory's Analysis of Anti-Semitism" appeared shortly thereafter in the first of three, extremely interesting issues of *New German Critique* on the problem,[26] which was stirred up again in Germany by the television series on the "Holocaust."

In his autobiographical interviews, published in 1982 as *Mitmachen wollte ich nie,* Leo Lowenthal spoke at length about his own thoughts on these issues. Despite his earlier reluctance to admit the impact of his and his colleagues' ethnic status on their thought, he now acknowledged that "the subterranean influence of Jewish tradition was codeterminate."[27] The chapter in which this remark appeared was translated in a special *Festschrift* issue of *Telos* dedicated to him on his eightieth birthday in 1980. It was my great honor to serve as its editor and write a brief introduction. The latter is reprinted below less because it can stand on its own as a serious analysis of his contribution to Critical Theory than as an inducement to turn to the *Festschrift* itself.[28]

The Suhrkamp Verlag's recent decision to collect Lowenthal's *oeuvre,*[29] along with similar collected editions of Adorno and Marcuse, testifies to the still potent fascination with the Frankfurt School in contemporary Germany. Unlike in other cases where an official *Gesamtausgabe* has signaled the reduction of once lively texts into dead classics, in these, it has not. A major stimulus to the still active impact of Critical Theory has been the extraordinarily rich and voluminous work of Habermas, who continues to build on the legacy of his mentors in new and creative ways. In 1981, he helped sponsor a conference at the

Max Planck Institute in Starnberg to examine the "social scientific potential of Critical Theory." Bringing together young German scholars with others from America, Italy, and France, the conference produced a volume entitled *Sozialforschung als Kritik,* edited by Wolfgang Bonss and Axel Honneth.[30] My own contribution, like several others, was devoted to the thorny issue of the interdisciplinary nature of the *Institut für Sozialforschung*'s work. It was in large measure inspired by Helmut Dubiel and Alfons Söllner, whose two books on the inner workings of the *Institut* had uncovered a wealth of new detail absent from *The Dialectical Imagination.*[31] My emphasis, however, was on an alternative version of the *Institut*'s interdisciplinary workings from that revealed by Dubiel and Söllner, one based more on Adorno's model of totality than Horkheimer's. In subsequent work on the issue, the argument seems to have had some impact.[32] An English version appeared in the new Australian journal *Thesis Eleven,* which is emerging as one of the leading forums for work on Western Marxism in the English-speaking world.[33]

The Starnberg conference was a closed affair with only a few invited guests in attendance. The next conference to which I was invited by Habermas, after his move back to Frankfurt, was very different. Organized as well by the current director of the *Institut,* Ludwig von Friedeburg, it was dedicated to Adorno on the occasion of what would have been his eightieth birthday in September 1983. Estimates of the crowd ranged as high as 1,200 and the event was discussed at length in a dozen German newspapers. It provided remarkable testimony to the staying power of Adorno's ideas, even after the attempt made by more militant leftists to discredit them in the years after his death in 1969. Habermas asked me to speak on his American experience, as well as on the reception of his ideas in the United States. In so doing, as I later discovered, he hoped to counter the widespread assumption that Adorno was simply anti-American, an image that fit all too well with certain trends in the contemporary German political scene. In his introduction to the talk, which was included in the volume of conference essays published in record time by Suhrkamp, he drove this point home by quoting Adorno's own remark from *Stichworte:* "Arrogance against America in Germany is unjust. It only draws on the most grousing instincts, while misusing the higher ones."[34] An English version of the paper was published the following year in *New German Critique* with several footnotes expanded to accommodate the additional American literature that came to my attention in the interim.[35]

"Adorno in America" acknowledged the importance of George Lichtheim, as one of the earliest transmitters of Adorno's ideas, and those of many central European Marxists, to the Anglo-Saxon world. Lichtheim had, in fact, been very helpful when I began to do my research on the Frankfurt School in ways that I described in the memorial tribute I wrote for *Midstream* after his tragic suicide in 1973.[36] If it is true that authors normally write for an implied reader, *The Dialectical Imagination* was in large measure aimed at Lichtheim, whose work had set a standard I hoped to emulate. Part of the anger at his death discussed at the beginning of "The Loss of George Lichtheim" was, I should confess, derived from my feeling of being denied his response. But the larger reason was the general sense of abandonment by a figure who had meant so much to my generation in its struggle to assimilate the ideas and traditions he had mastered so well. When I participated in the conference dedicated to Lichtheim's memory organized by Shlomo Avineri at the Van Leer Jerusalem Foundation in June 1974, I discovered that I was not alone in this sentiment.[37]

If Lichtheim had chosen to end his life prematurely, the next emigré whose history I explored had done as much as possible to deny the inevitable closure of death. In "The Extraterritorial Life of Siegfried Kracauer," which appeared in the tenth anniversary issue of *Salmagundi* in 1975/76,[38] I employed Kracauer's desperate resistance of totalization as a leitmotif of his entire career. Together with my two later essays on Kracauer, it might be seen as a fragment of an open-ended, untotalized biography that honors Kracauer's own admonition against closure. "The Extraterritorial Life" might be understood, to use the cinematic metaphors he employed in his own ruminations on history, as an "establishing shot," while the two shorter essays are like close-ups. The discordance between them conforms to what Kracauer would have called the "heterogeneous" nature of the historical universe, which is no less disruptive of attempts to write totalized biographies than it is of general narratives.

The first of the two "close-ups" was occasioned by Leon Wieseltier's invitation to speak to the Oxford Jewish Society during the year I spent at St. Antony's College in 1974–75. In turning the talk into a publishable article for the *Leo Baeck Yearbook* the following year,[39] I was aided by the counsel of a number of expert readers, most notably Gershom Scholem, whose eight-page letter, written with the acerbity for which he was famous, saved me from many mistakes. The second essay, which was a response to Robert Boyers' request for a contribution to a *Salmagundi* issue on Adorno that never materialized, had Kracauer himself as its expert watchdog. Or at least so it seemed, as I drew on the materials he carefully left in his *Nachlass* for someone to use in precisely the way I used them. "Adorno and Kracauer—Notes on a Troubled Friendship"[40] was a particularly painful piece to write, because it involved just such a sense of being an accomplice in a posthumous act of revenge. But the important intellectual issues aroused by the dispute seemed justification enough for allowing it to come to light, despite its petty personal dimension.

The private clash between two emigrés created, to be sure, scarcely a ripple in comparison to the controversies surrounding the career of the next figure I examined, controversies which, as I soon discovered, were still very much alive. I had first met Hannah Arendt at the New School Conference on Weimar Culture in 1971 when, for reasons that still elude me, she was assigned the task of commentator on my panel. I had long admired many aspects of her work, such as her link between speech and practice, which I invoked against Marcuse in the first essay in this collection. When in 1974 *Partisan Review* invited me to write a review essay of the first book published on her, Margaret Canovan's *The Political Thought of Hannah Arendt,*[41] I eagerly accepted. As I began to reread her work systematically, however, I discovered puzzling aspects that seemed difficult to explain and even more so to defend. To make sense of them, I hit on the unifying theme of political existentialism, a movement whose dangers had been a concern of the Frankfurt School from Marcuse's 1934 essay on "The Struggle Against Liberalism in the Totalitarian View of the State" through Habermas' more recent critiques of decisionism.[42] At the time I wrote "The Political Existentialism of Arendt," to give the article its original title,[43] I was unaware of the extent of her personal as well as intellectual debt to Heidegger, which was only revealed later in Elizabeth Young-Bruehl's wonderful biography.[44] But I was convinced nonetheless that only by tracing her roots to German *Existenzphilosophie,* which Canovan had completely ignored, could her idiosyncratic political philosophy be comprehended.

Before the essay could be published, Hannah Arendt suddenly died of a heart attack. Out of an understandable reluctance to print a critique so soon after this sad event and mindful of earlier charges of bias against her in *Partisan Review,*[45] William Phillips delayed its appearance for three years and commissioned a rebuttal to run simultaneously with it. Written by an old friend, Leon Botstein, who did not allow our personal ties to dull his polemical edge, it was the first of several responses by outraged defenders of Arendt in the next few years.[46] The most heat was generated by my cautious attempt to probe the ironic relationship between Arendt, the great critic of totalitarianism, and Arendt, the bed-fellow of the political existentialists whose work "was not entirely blameless in the rise of fascism."[47] Botstein turned this argument into the alleged assertion that I believed Arendt had "succumbed somehow to fascism and was partly, by association, responsible for fascism."[48] James Knauer contended that I was claiming "Arendt's conception of politics had totalitarian implications" and Gerard P. Heather and Matthew Stolz castigated my "bizarre assertion [that] 'Hannah Arendt, nominally fleeing from fascism, first succumbed to its charms.'"[49]

Now, if I had to rewrite my essay, I would doubtless eliminate any ambiguity over the antecedent of the "it" in that last clause, but as any reader of good faith will see when turning to the sentence as a whole—which Heather and Stolz deceptively cut in half—"it" refers to political existentialism, not fascism. Although I had made this clear in my reply to Botstein,[50] the message had somehow not gotten through. As for the more serious issue of situating Arendt in the ambiguous context of political existentialism itself, one critic, Stan Draenos, has argued against it because "the overriding, governing motif of Arendt's thought is not political action at all, but rather her notion of 'the world.'"[51] "The world," according to his interpretation, is not comparable to Heidegger's use of the term, because it is severed from his fundamental concern for Being. But, as Mildred Bakan has recently and correctly emphasized,[52] Arendt's use was virtually the same as Heidegger's when he spoke of *Dasein* instead. Although it is certainly true that Arendt did not swallow Heidegger whole, as her interesting critique of his treatment of the Will in *The Life of the Mind* demonstrates,[53] it is clear that no appreciation of her work can ignore the extent of her debt. Indeed, it is only by acknowledging the power of his hold over her that we can begin to understand her apologia for his notorious political "error" in 1933, which a recent critic has denounced for having "evaded the moral problem that such involvement posed."[54]

One final point concerns the issue of Arendt's categorical separation of "the political" (a concept she shared with another political existentialist, Carl Schmitt)[55] from society, economics, and philosophy, which I found a troubling dimension of her work. Paradoxically, some of her defenders deny that the separation was really all that strict, whereas others hold on to it as a bulwark against the polluting effects of philosophical or social concerns.[56] This is not the place to marshall yet another round of citations from her work or that of other critics, except to say that it was perhaps because of her willingness to make bold if ultimately questionable distinctions that she still continues to fascinate as well as dismay many of her readers. One might even say, to play on the famous aphorism of another refugee towards whom she bore little good will,[57] in Arendt only the exaggerations are true.

The paths of emigrés often intersected, so it is no surprise to learn from Young-Bruehl's biography that in 1940 Arendt's second husband, Heinrich Blücher, was interned in a barn in the French village of Villemalard with Henry Pachter. Although Pachter and the Arendt-Blüchers remained on good terms during their subsequent exile in America, they were not always in agreement—Pachter, for example, holding very different views on the connection between Heidegger's politics and his philosophy.[58] Pachter, in fact, was rarely in agreement with anyone, as I discovered in my own encounters with him. Nonetheless, or perhaps because of his pugnaciously independent streak, he was a figure of great importance for many younger scholars interested in the migration. It was therefore with no hesitation that I accepted Robert Boyers' request to reflect on Pachter's significance after his death in 1980 for *Salmagundi,* a journal he did so much to encourage during his lifetime.[59]

In that essay, I recalled Pachter's curmudgeonly attitude toward the pretensions of his fellow refugees. As a sobering check on the idealizing tendencies of students of the migration, perhaps my own included, his debunkings were unquestionably healthy. But I would still want to reaffirm my conviction that the emigrés' place in the intellectual history of the twentieth century is undoubtedly secure. There is, to be sure, the danger of which H. Stuart Hughes has recently warned:

as a younger generation of Americans who had no direct knowledge of the emigration came of age, its lessons began to be forgotten. Witness the current recrudescence of positivism in social science. Witness the renewed tendency to slice up the study of society into clearly demarcated disciplines and subdisciplines.[60]

But whatever the loss of direct influence produced by the passage of time, the migration continues to be the center of an ever-growing interest on the part of historians. The fiftieth anniversary of the Nazi seizure of power, in 1983, saw a flood of conferences and new books, as well as the founding of a full-fledged Society for Exile Studies, directed by John Spalek, complete with its own journal, *Exilforschung: Ein Internationales Jahrbuch*[61]

It is, however, vital to emphasize that historical interest need not betoken the loss of contemporary relevance. Not only are many of the ideas introduced by the refugees far from exhausted, so too the emigré experience itself is still worth pondering. For those of us lucky enough not to be living through truly "dark times," to cite Brecht's famous phrase, studying the histories of this extraordinary group of men and women provides a powerful reminder of the ways in which intellectuals can transcend the most pernicious attempts to silence them. As the surviving remnant of a people whose incalculable misfortune still defies adequate understanding, the emigrés—especially, I would argue, those who remained in some sense permanent exiles—were the precious repository of a now moribund culture. As they progressively leave us, it becomes ever clearer that theirs is a legacy we can scarcely afford to squander in the years to come.

Part I
The Frankfurt School

1.

The Metapolitics
of Utopianism

T he rise of Herbert Marcuse from the relative obscurity of his first sixty-five years to a position as one of the media's favorite seducers of the young has not been without its costs. The dissemination of his ideas has brought with it their inevitable dilution. Through what the French, in a delightful phrase, call *"la drugstorisation de Marcuse,"* he has himself become something of a commodity. No article on the New Left is complete without a ritual mention of his name: no discussion of the "counterculture" dare ignore his message of liberation. What is by and large ignored, however, are the roots of his arguments, which are too deeply embedded in a tradition alien to the thinking of most Americans to make painless comprehension likely. It is far easier, after all, to read the unfortunate essay on "Repressive Tolerance" than to wrestle with the conceptual subtleties and stylistic impenetrability of *Reason and Revolution.* As a result, Marcuse is still to a considerable extent *Cet Inconnu,* as the French journal *La Nef*[1] subtitled its recent issue devoted to him. A complete exploration of the foundations of his thought is of course beyond the scope of this essay. A beginning, however, can perhaps be made by probing one aspect of his thinking which is increasingly come to the fore in recent years: its utopian dimension.

As has often been observed, Marxist theory has steadfastly refused to offer a blueprint for postcapitalist society. The historicist strain in Marx's own thinking was always in tension with his implicit philosophical anthropology. Occasional attempts to describe "Socialist Man" by his successors have usually been thwarted by the recognition that he

First published in *Radical America* (April 1970), 4 (3); *Dissent* (July-August 1970), 17 (4) and *The Revival of American Socialism: Selected Papers of the Socialist Scholars Conference,* ed. George Fischer (New York, 1971).

will have to define himself in a process of self-creation which cannot be described in advance. Few Marxists or neo-Marxist thinkers have been as sensitive to this historicist ban on posting a normative human nature as those of the so-called "Frankfurt School" of the *Institut für Sozialforschung,* with which Marcuse was associated during the 1930s.

The *Institut's* reluctance to suggest anything which might be taken as a universal view of man's essence even prevented it from accepting without reservation the anthropological implications of Marx's *Economic and Philosophical Manuscripts* when they were recovered in the early thirties. It is not insignificant that Theodor W. Adorno, Marcuse's former *Institut* colleague, chose music, the most unrepresentational of aesthetic modes, as the medium through which he examined bourgeois culture and sought traces of its transcendent negation. In recent years, Max Horkheimer, more than anyone else responsible for the genesis of the *Institut's* "Critical Theory," has come to believe that this refusal to picture the "other" society beyond capitalism is not unrelated to the Jewish ban on naming or describing God.

Whatever the source of the taboo, only Marcuse of the major figures connected with the Frankfurt School has dared in recent years to break it. Only Marcuse has tried to speak the unspeakable in an increasingly urgent effort to reintroduce a utopian cast to socialist theory. *Eros and Civilization* was his first attempt to outline the contours of the society beyond repressive domination. The *Essay on Liberation* goes even further in explicitly stating the need for a new philosophical anthropology, a frankly "biological foundation" for socialism. The desired transition, he argues, is from Marx to Fourier, from realism to surrealism.[2] The failure of socialism, he seems to be saying, has been the failure of imagination.

By consciously donning the utopian mantle, Marcuse has invited the scorn of "realists" in both the socialist and capitalist camps. Nevertheless, by doing so he has helped give substance and direction to the inchoate yearnings of those dissatisfied with what they see as the present Hobson's Choice between authoritarian socialism and repressive advanced capitalism. While his critiques of both these current societies are well known, the utopian alternative he has projected has been comparatively ignored. Only its psychoanalytic elements—the goal of a society freed from historically grounded "surplus repression" and the "performance principle" (a kind of generalized Protestant Ethic)—have been discussed with any rigor. Far less attention has been paid to its philosophical sources. Only by examining these can the political implications of Marcuse's vision be adequately understood.

Those familiar solely with Marcuse's writings in English are often surprised to learn that before joining the *Institut* in Frankfurt in 1932, he spent several years with Martin Heidegger at Freiburg. During this period, he attempted to reconcile Heidegger's existential phenomenology with historical materialism,[3] anticipating in a sense what Merleau-Ponty and Sartre were to try to do after the war. The details of his attempt need not concern us now.[4] What is important to note for our purposes is that, as Alfred Schmidt has suggested, Marxism served him as a "positive philosophy" answering Heidegger's question, "What is authentic existence and how is authentic existence possible?" To Marcuse, man can exist authentically only by performing radical deeds, only by engaging in self-creating *praxis.* Man is only man as autonomous subject, never as contingent predicate. The Marxist "fundamental situation," he argued, is that in which the historically conscious man performs radical acts in order to live authentically.

Although abandoning much of Heidegger's terminology and moving away from his ontological approach to history during his tenure at the *Institut,* Marcuse has never fully relinquished his own conviction that the free man is the man who can create himself through radical *praxis.* It might be added parenthetically that Heidegger's influence has persisted in another way as well. Marcuse's much debated attitude toward technology—he has been accused of being everything from a romantic Luddite to a technological determinist—owes much to Heidegger's hostility to the technological logos, which he interpreted as a falling away from the basic insights of the pre-Socratics, a process which began centuries before technology itself achieved its domination over nature and man. In *One-Dimensional Man,*[5] Marcuse openly appropriates a passage from Heidegger's *Holzwege* to attack the "technological a priori."

Still, it would be a grave error to dismiss Marcuse as an existentialist decked out in Marxist trappings, as have some of his critics on the left. Whatever his indebtedness to Heidegger, he has never abandoned his belief in the necessity of rational theory or his conviction in the validity of values beyond experience. Indeed, among his most devastating critiques is an attack on the pro-Nazi political philosopher Carl Schmitt's antinormative political existentialism.[6] (There is, of course, no necessary connection between the philosophical positions collectively known as existentialist and their political counterpart, although in the sad case of Heidegger, his Nazi sympathies cannot be totally disassociated from his philosophy.)

If there is a leftist parallel to Schmitt and his decisionism, it can be found in those who would collapse theory into an unmediated *praxis.* The most recent manifestation of this basically anarchistic position is the "Weatherman" faction of the Students for a Democratic So-

ciety. Although Marcuse has always warned against the complete separation of theory and *praxis,* at no time has he advocated action as
sufficient in itself. The goal may be the unity of thought and action, but
at this moment in historical time their relationship is necessarily problematical. To declare their unity as already existing is to fall prey to ideology. It is only as a utopian hope that the coordination of self-creating
action and rational theory should be understood in Marcuse's work.

If one element of his utopian vision is a stress on radical
praxis as authentic behavior, there is another, more important strain.
Here his distance from existentialism of all types is plainly evident. This
is especially clear when compared with the position taken by Sartre in
one of the classic existentialist texts, *Being and Nothingness.* The relevant issue here is the possibility of the reconciliation of opposites which
anyone who works within a Hegelian framework must confront. In *Being
and Nothingness* the dialectic of opposing forces remains inevitably
truncated; the redeeming power of synthesis is ultimately denied as a
possible end to the historical process. For-Itself and In-Itself, Sartre's
variation on the theme of subject and object, cannot be reconciled.
"Conflict," he writes, "is the original meaning of being-for-others."[7] The
familiar aphorism of Sartre in *No Exit* makes the same point: "Hell is
other people." Here it might be added that Marcuse's former colleagues
at the *Institut für Sozialforschung,* Horkheimer and Adorno, reluc-
tantly reach similiar conclusions in their later work. *Negative Dialektik,*
Adorno's philosophical testament, stresses nonidentity and the importance of negation as the last refuge of freedom. "The totality," he wrote
elsewhere, "is the untrue." And in the 1960s, Horkheimer returned to
an early interest in Schopenhauer and his pessimistic denial that the world
can be made rational.

Marcuse, on the other hand, disagrees both with the gloomy
reduction of man to a "useless passion" in *Being and Nothingness* and
with the stress on the nonidentity of subject and object in the work of
the other leading figures of the Frankfurt School. So often taken to task
for his "pessimism," he maintains a belief in all his work that true reconciliation, however frustrated in the false harmony of contemporary
society, is indeed a possibility. This is not to say, of course, that he believes the synthesis has already been achieved, as Hegelians of the right
have always assumed. Firmly grounded in the Marxist tradition as he is,
Marcuse is quick to point out that social conditions, behind the façade
of one-dimensionality, are still fundamentally contradictory and antagonistic. Class conflict may not be the form in which contradiction now
manifests itself, but no universal class has emerged in which all antagonisms have been dialectically resolved. Integration, as he has used it, does

not mean true harmony. On the other hand, he does believe that for the first time preconditions do exist, created paradoxically by the technology whose other effects he so dislikes, which make the prospects for reconciliation favorable. With the end of scarcity, so runs the familiar argument from *Eros and Civilization,* man's need to repress himself for the sake of productive work is no longer binding. Utopian possibilities are no longer chimerical.

What then does Marcuse mean by reconciliation? What is this true harmony he so fervently seeks? Here more than anywhere else he reveals his roots in the German Idealist tradition. One might even venture the observation that he has succumbed to the lure of Greece and its alleged cultural serenity, which had such an enormous influence on German philosophy during its classical period, as E. M. Butler has shown in her masterful *The Tyranny of Greece over Germany.* The image of the Greeks, which was so powerful, was not that of a nation of tragedy writers, but rather that of a people in a state of pre-alienated wholeness which Winckelmann introduced to the German mind in the eighteenth century.

In his essay "Philosophy and Critical Theory," first appearing in the journal of the *Institut* in 1937, Marcuse wrote:

Under the name of reason [philosophy] conceived the idea of an authentic Being in which all significant antitheses (of subject and object, essence and appearance, thought and being) were reconciled. Connected with the idea was the conviction that what exists is not immediately and already rational but must rather be brought to reason. . . . At its highest level, as authentic reality, the world no longer stands opposed to the rational thought of men as mere material objectivity. Rather, it is now comprehended by thought and defined as a concept. That is, the external, antithetical character of material objectivity is overcome in a process through which the identity of subject and object is established as the rational, conceptual structure that is common to both.[8]

Here then is the belief that identity between thought and being—and Marcuse clearly means being-in-the-world, social relations—can be established on the basis of a shared rationality. At no time, however, does he imply that the individual should be sacrificed to the whole in the name of an hypostatized objective reality. In his article "On Hedonism," written for the *Institut* in 1938, he stresses the function of hedonistic philosophies in preserving the claim of personal human happiness against the demands of overarching totalities such as the state. Here the stress on sensual gratification which was developed in his postwar work on Freud exists in embryo.

Marcuse has, however, always been careful to avoid advocating simple sexual freedom as the answer to social repression, as Wilhelm Reich on occasion did. "The bogey of the unchained voluptuary," he wrote, "who would abandon himself only to his sensual wants is rooted in the separation of intellectual from material productive forces and the separation of the labor process from the process of consumption. Overcoming this separation belongs to the preconditions of freedom."[9] The end of the dichotomy between internalized, spiritualized culture and material, sensual activity in the "real" world is thus part of his utopian vision. The stress here on reconciling production and consumption foreshadows his later use of Schiller's "play drive" in *Eros and Civilization.* Art and technology must ultimately converge; the logos of gratification must be joined with a technology freed from its project of domination.

In Marcuse's thinking, the driving impetus toward harmony is further demonstrated in his treatment of time. In *Eros and Civilization,* he stresses the function of memory, of "re-membering" that which is asunder, as a vehicle of liberation. To forget is to forgive the injustices of the past. "From the myth of Orpheus to the novel of Proust," he argues, "happiness and freedom have been linked with the idea of the recapture of time . . . remembrance alone provides the joy without the anxiety over its passing and thus gives it an otherwise impossible duration. Time loses its power when remembrance redeems the past."[10] And in his later essay, "Progress and Freud's Theory of Instincts," he more explicitly outlines a utopian idea of temporality. "Time would not seem linear, as a perpetual line or rising curve, but cyclical, as the return contained in Nietzsche's idea of the 'perpetuity of pleasure.' "[11]

There is more than a little of the tyranny of Greece, or at least the Greek idea of cyclical time, in all of this, not to mention the influence of one of Marcuse's colleagues at the *Institut für Sozialforschung,* Walter Benjamin. In his "Theses on the Philosophy of History,"[12] Benjamin developed the ideal of *"Jetztzeit"* (Nowtime) as a mystical explosion in the continuum of history, a kind of Messianic time qualitatively different from the empty, linear, unfulfilled temporal experience of ordinary men. Marcuse has always been fond of quoting Benjamin's observation that in 1830, the revolutionaries of Paris shot at public clocks to make time stop. The implications of this way of thinking would seem blatantly eschatological. But Marcuse, when questioned on this point, has denied any eschatological intentions. History will go on, he has said, short of a nuclear disaster.

And yet, it would go on in a way very different from the way in which it has been experienced until now. What will be particularly absent is conflict, strife, striving, in short, all the things which have characterized Western history for millennia. In his own words, Marcuse desires the "pacification of existence." Gratification and sensual receptivity are the traits of his new aestheticism. Unlike Marx, or at least the mature Marx, Marcuse believes labor can be abolished. Because Marx was more pessimistic on this point, he never believed that the complete identity of the production and consumption processes could be achieved. Indeed, Marx did not even fully accept the Hegelian notion of identity of subject and object to which Marcuse seems to have returned.[13]

The only place in his writings where Marcuse displays similiar caution is in his critique of Norman O. Brown, whose mysticism demands the total negation of the *principium individuationis.* "Eros lives in the division and boundary between subject and object, man and nature," he admonished Brown; "the unity of subject and object is a hallmark of absolute idealism; however, even Hegel retained the tension between the two, the distinction."[14] Elsewhere, Marcuse supports an identity theory which, although demanding the preservation of the individual, is scarcely less utopian than Brown's. It is not insignificant that Ernst Bloch, whose animistic belief in the resurrection of a new natural subject marks him as a leading identity theorist, embraced Marcuse at a conference in Yugoslavia in 1968 and welcomed him back to the ranks of the utopian optimists of the 1920s. Indeed, it would be tempting to say that Marcuse has surrendered to what Freud called the "Nirvana Principle," the yearning for the end of tension that is life, if Marcuse were not so sure that life with a minimum of tension is a possibility.[15]

These then are the two strains in Marcuse's vision of the liberated society: first, the stress on radical action, on the deed, on self-creation as the only mode of authentic being; and second, the unity of opposites, the true harmony of pacified existence, the end of conflict and contradiction. The one theme is basically active, one might even say Promethean, to use Marx's own favorite metaphor; the other rather more passive, Orphic in the sense Marcuse interprets Orpheus in *Eros and Civilization:* as the singer of joy and fulfillment. And both, he has cogently argued, are denied and frustrated in the contemporary world of repressive capitalism and authoritarian socialism.

Whether or not the two strains are compatible is a problem Marcuse does not seem to have worked out in any detail. It might be said that radical *praxis* is merely the means to achieve the revolutionary breakthrough leading to the pacification of existence. This fails to work, however, because of Marcuse's insistence that self-creating action is the only true authentic mode of being. Another possible solution would be to divide him into an "early" and a "late" Marcuse, as is sometimes done with Marx, with the result that a Heideggerian Marcuse is somehow supplanted by a Hegelianized one under the influence of Horkheimer and the *Institut.* Besides being too schematic, this solution fails to do justice to the mixture of both strains in his work. It seems perhaps best to leave this problem by saying that Marcuse, like so many other thinkers of stature, has unresolved tensions in his thought. As to be expected, the political implications which can be drawn from these conflicting tendencies are no simpler. It is to these that we now turn.

In his treatment of Heidegger's concept of authentic existence, Marcuse was critical of the abstract, undialectical quality of his teacher's idea of history. Not everyone, he argued, was in the position to perform the radical acts constituting authentic behavior. At this stage in man's development, Marcuse claimed, only the proletariat is the true actor on the historical stage because of its crucial role in the production process. To ignore the importance of class differences would be to retreat into Idealism. Heidegger's indifference to the real course of history was not unrelated to the *völkisch* ideology of the national *Gemeinschaft* transcending social contradictions.

Since 1928 much of course has happened to dilute the revolutionary potential of the working class, especially in the America to which Marcuse fled in 1934. To the consternation of those who still romanticize the proletariat, he was among the first to face the implications of its integration. Although he has recently seen evidence of cracks in the one-dimensionality of the system in student protest and the rumblings of what Marx would have dismissed as *Lumpenproletariat,* at no time has he mistaken these forces for a new proletariat or a new historical subject. As a result, he has been the frequent target of other theorists on the left who see the stirring of new "negative" forces in society such as the alienated "new working class" of white-collar workers and technicians. Whoever may be right, it is important to note that Marcuse has always identified the doers of the authentic deed with a specific historical group. To ignore the historical element in his "existentialist" stress on *praxis* is thus to falsify his analysis. Although Marcuse has often been accused of anarchism—such disparate thinkers as Hans Heinz Holz and George Lichtheim have leveled this charge against him,[16] and indeed there is an anarchistic element in his work in the healthy sense of distrusting rigid organizations—it would be a grave error to interpret him as an advocate of indiscriminate activism or political decisionism. That wing of the student movement which takes his name as a justification for such activity is misapplying his teachings, at least insofar as they neglect his stress on present historical possibilities.

And yet, a plausible interpretation of Marcuse on just this level does exist. If the so-called existentialist element in his utopian vision ought not to be interpreted as a justification for the indeterminate negation of the system, what of the other central theme in his work, the yearning for harmony and reconciliation of dialectical contradictions? Here the implications are far more problematical. In his analysis of Marcuse's aesthetics,[17] Herbert Read has argued that the achievement of a rational society would not end the need for art, as Marcuse has implied. If in our own irrational society art provides *une promesse de bonheur,* a promise of unfulfilled happiness, as Marcuse has argued, there is no necessary reason to suppose that a new society, however rational, would satisfy all of men's needs or end all his fears. Above all, the mystery of death and the arbitrariness of suffering would make human existence a continuing subject for the aesthetic imagination. The eternal return is forever bisected by the linear time of mortal men who are born and must ultimately die.

If Marcuse is too quick to assume art would be overcome in a rational society, so too, and this is a vitally important point, is he overly hasty in assuming politics would be overcome in a grand synthesis of differences. The vaunted American system of pluralistic politics may indeed be a mask for manipulation and special interests, as he has always argued, yet pluralism as such is the very essence of politics. The belief that political conflict is an epiphenomenon of economic and social contradictions is a fallacy which ought finally to be laid to rest. What the Czechs were trying in part to say, before they lost the chance to say anything at all, was that politics in the sense of readjusting priorities and working through the competition for power does not end when an economy is socialized. Furthermore, the expectation that international tension would end when the entire world becomes socialist is a hope which drowned in the waters of the Ussuri River with the Sino-Soviet clash.

Thus, in positing a utopia of identity in which all contradictions are overcome, Marcuse displays that basic hostility to politics which has been the curse of too many German thinkers for too many years. Its effects spill over into the only type of political action he sanctions today: the Great Refusal, a complete rejection of the mechanics of political change presented by the system. Although in large measure a response to the sadly true observation that the system all too often fails to do what it promises, it is also a reflection of his more basic rejection of politics as such. The inevitable result of this attitude, if apolitical quietism is to be avoided, is what the French call *une politique du pire—* the apocalyptic hope that out of total chaos will come total change. Metapolitics rather than true political activity becomes the only authentic mode of revolutionary behavior. In the end, it is perhaps all reducible to that "aestheticization" of politics against which Walter Benjamin so earnestly warned.[18] Paradoxically, the radical optimism of Marcuse's utopian vision is the dialectical counterpart of the resignation about the possibilities for change within or growing out of the system which has earned him so much abuse from liberals and the orthodox Left.

It is thus ironic that the existentialist strain in Marcuse's thinking, which is sometimes cited as the source of his anarchistic impulses, is less influential in promoting antipolitical politics than is the Idealist strain. It is almost as if Marcuse has forgotten his tempering of the ahistorical element in Heidegger's thinking in his belief that the metapolitical utopia is just around the corner. To reify the status quo and reject any medium of real change except the sudden and total collapse of the system is to jump out of history. It is no accident that Marcuse has taken more and more in his recent work to quoting that other great defector from the mundane course of history, Friedrich Nietzsche.

Perhaps the most unhistorical element in his work is the notion that the abolition of labor and its replacement by play, in Schiller's sense of unrepressed sensuousness reconciled with the "order of freedom," would be the hallmark of the new age. The end of scarcity, a task which is by no means as easily accomplished as he believes, is a thin reed on which to base the end of social, political, and psychological contradictions. Here, curiously, Marcuse shows himself both beyond Marx and beholden to him. He transcends Marx's relatively cautious stance, as mentioned before, by arguing that labor can indeed be abolished. Yet, by giving so much weight to that abolition, he reveals his indebtedness to Marx's conviction that labor is the basic human life activity. Play, it might be argued, is really on the same conceptual axis as labor, if at the other end.[19]

Marcuse's interpretation of Hegel is itself colored by his acceptance of the Marxist centrality of labor. In *Reason and Revolution* he wrote: "The concept of labor is not peripheral in Hegel's system, but is the central notion through which he conceives the development of society."[20] What Marcuse was perhaps forgetting in his desire to demonstrate the closeness of Marx and Hegel has recently been shown by the most gifted second-generation student of the Frankfurt School, Jürgen Habermas. Labor, Habermas has argued in his article "Arbeit und Interaktion,"[21] was not the only category of self-creation in Hegel's thinking. An alternative mode existed in symbolically mediated interaction, i.e., language and expressive gestures, which at least in his early work Hegel did not see as identical with the dialectic of labor. To Marcuse, however, Hegel was saying that "Language . . . makes it possible for an individual to take a conscious position *against* his fellows and to assert his needs and desires against those of the other individuals. The resulting antagonisms are integrated through the process of labor, which also becomes the decisive force for the development of culture."[22] Thus, in Marcuse's thinking, the problems of symbolic interaction are contained within the larger framework of the dialectic of labor and the production process. This permits him to give so much emphasis to the utopian possibilities liberated by the abolition of human toil. What he therefore neglects to note is, as Habermas has put it, "Freedom from hunger and toil does not necessarily converge with freedom from slavery and degradation, because an automatic developmental connection between labor and interaction does not exist."[23]

The link between Marcuse's hostility toward politics and his neglect of the problem of symbolic interaction should not be missed. As Hannah Arendt,[24] among others, has so often pointed out, speech and political *praxis* are inseparable. The abolition of labor, even if it were as easily attained as Marcuse thinks it is, would therefore not put an end to all contradictions. Symbolic interaction and the politics with which it is so intimately tied would continue to express the sedimented antagonisms of the past.

Nationalism, for example, is likely to frustrate hopes for reconciliation of particular and universal interests in the future, as expectations of an internationalist proletariat were frustrated in the past. And, of course, at the center of the national question is the irreducible fact of linguistic differences. This is a reality which Marcuse's utopianism fails to acknowledge, thus allowing him to maintain an implicit faith in the possibility of a Benjamin-like "explosion in the continuum of history." The political imperative which follows from all of this is the cul-de-sac of apocalyptic metapolitics which is really no politics at all.

2.

The Frankfurt School's Critique of Marxist Humanism

One of the most significant intellectual legacies of the Weimar period resulted from the challenge presented by a number of young thinkers to the prevailing orthodoxies of Marxist thought. Revived scholarly interest in Hegel[1] contributed to the reexamination of old shibboleths, as did other purely intellectual stimuli, but the major impetus doubtless came from the crisis within the socialist movement itself. Schematically put, the crisis resulted from three unanticipated developments in the convulsive history of Europe in the years after 1914: first, the craven collaboration in national war efforts by socialist parties pledged to international class solidarity; second, the pathetic failure of German revolutionaries after the war in contrast to the unexpected success of their Russian counterparts; and third, the meteoric rise of fascism as a competitor for the right to succeed liberal capitalism. With the organizational ruin of the Second International came the collapse of its theoretical underpinnings. Nowhere was this change felt more severely than in the country whose socialist party had been the central supporter of the International—the newly created Republic of Germany.

The story of how in the early 1920s, Georg Lukács and Karl Korsch began the process of dismantling the orthodoxies of prewar Marxist dogma has been told too often to need recapitulation here. Suffice it say that their seminal work, in *History and Class Consciousness* and *Marxism and Philosophy* respectively, in combination with the rediscovery of Marx's early manuscripts in the late twenties, nurtured an alternative direction in Marxist thought which continued to develop well

First published in *Social Research* (Summer 1972), 39 (2).

after the demise of Weimar. Known at various times as "Western Marxism,"[2] "Para-Marxism,"[3] and perhaps most frequently as "Marxist Humanism,"[4] this new trend was quickly declared anathema by the official guardians of Marx's legacy, both in the East and West. Neither the Social Democratic nor the Communist parties of the Weimar period were prepared, for example, to accept the role of consciousness in the dialectical process assigned by Lukács, Korsch, and their successors. Nor did concepts like reification or alienation enter into the popular discussion in a meaningful way. Instead, the gap between the outmoded theoretical baggage of the older generation of Marxists and the practice of at least some of their successors continued to widen (e.g., the voluntarism of Leninist revolutionary activity combined with the retention of a mechanistic and deterministic materialism on the level of theory).[5]

In fact, not until the period after World War II did Marxist Humanism, stimulated by its uneasy integration with existentialism in France and popularized by a number of German refugees in America, become a significant force in some socialist movements and widely known in academic circles.[6] Within the exile community in this country, the members of the *Institut für Sozialforschung* who are the subjects of this paper have often been cited for playing a crucial role in this process of dissemination. The reasons for this are not difficult to discern. The Frankfurt School, as the *Institut's* inner circle around Max Horkheimer became known, did in fact reject the monistic materialism, copy-theory epistemology, and reliance on "scientific" laws of historical development held by more traditional Marxists. They were furthermore very much taken with the notions of reification and commodity fetishism which Lukács had done so much to revive. They were also convinced that the social totality, rather than the socio-economic substructure alone, was the proper sphere for the radical social theorist to investigate. And finally, they frequently stressed individual gratification as a legitimate moment in that totality in a way that distanced them from the older Marxism which permitted the negation of the individual actor in the name of impersonal socio-economic forces, and from its newer Stalinist preversion.

For these and other reasons, it might be argued that the Frankfurt School can be placed squarely in the camp of the Marxist Humanists. This certainly has been the prevalent interpretation of its work. Daniel Bell, for example, in his well-known article on "The Debate on Alienation,"[7] written in 1959, cited the *Institut* for its contribution to the discussion of Marx's early writings and the accompanying interest in alienation. A decade later, George Lichtheim titled an essay he wrote on the Frankfurt School for the *Times Literary Supplement,* "From Historicism to Marxist Humanism."[8] And more recently, in a lengthy critique of Horkheimer and his colleagues in the New Left Review,[9] Göran Therborn characterized them as "historicist humanists" and called the epistemological basis of their theory a "metaphysical humanism."[10] To Therborn, who is a follower of Louis Althusser,[11] the implications of this position are plainly disastrous. "There is no room," he wrote, "in the historicist conception of history for social totalities as structures of irreducible complexity, or for a discontinuous development of those complex structures. Society is always reducible to its creator-subject, and history is the continuous unfolding of this subject. At every given point in time, society is a unique manifestation of Man."[12] As others have also charged,[13] Therborn saw the Frankfurt School as a regression to the pre-Marxist Young Hegelians who reduced social criticism to philosophy. "They substitute for real history a construction derived from a philosophy of history, the 'history' of Man's alienation or reification or—in Frankfurt School vocabulary—the 'dialectic of the enlightenment.' "[14]

Whether or not Therborn's critique of Marxist Humanism as such is valid is not the point at issue here, however, as a discussion of Althusser's "scientific" Marxism would lead us too far afield. What I would like to focus on instead is the legitimacy of his characterization of the Frankfurt School as a variant of Marxist Humanism, which, as we have noted, is shared by other commentators such as Bell and Lichtheim. What I will argue is that only in the broad sense that its members consistently opposed Stalinism can their position be called Humanist, whereas, understood more precisely, it served as a critique of both "scientific" and "humanist" Marxism.

To begin, it is necessary to make clear which members of the Institut für Sozialforschung are being discussed here, as a broad spectrum of viewpoints was sheltered at various times under the Institut's several roofs. This was especially true during the years after its creation in Frankfurt in 1923. Carl Grünberg, its first active director, came from the world of Austro-Marxism. Adherents of the German Communist Party such as Karl August Wittfogel, Julian Gumperz, and for a brief time Richard Sorge, espoused a more orthodox Marxist-Leninist line. Karl Korsch, although never a fully integrated member, participated in the Institut seminars, bringing with him his mercurial left-oppositionist views. The economically orthodox position of traditional Marxism was represented by Henryk Grossmann, an expert on crisis theory.

At the other end of the spectrum were several younger entrants into Institut affairs, who joined in the years immediately preceding the emigration in 1933. Erich Fromm presents the clearest case of an Institut figure who can be placed among the unqualified exponents of Marxist Humanism. In all of his writings on socialism, most explicitly in *Marx's Concept of Man*[15] and the volume of essays he edited entitled *Socialist Humanism,*[16] Fromm has demonstrated how thoroughly he believes that Marx's work can be grounded in his early writings. Ever since the twenties and his association then with Martin Buber, Franz Rosenzweig, and others in the so-called *Frankfurt Lehrhaus,* Fromm has accepted the necessity of a philosophical anthropology as the starting point for any social analysis.

Herbert Marcuse, who joined the Frankfurt School shortly after Fromm in 1932, is somewhat more difficult to categorize, although his opposition to traditional, "scientific" Marxism was clear from the beginning of his scholarly career. In his days as a student of Martin Heidegger in the late twenties, Marcuse also displayed a considerable interest in anthropological questions and in his teacher's distinction between historicity *(Geschichtlichkeit)* and mere history. Significantly, Marcuse greeted the recovery of the *Economic and Philosophic Manuscripts* with enormous enthusiasm in an essay he contributed to *Die Gesellschaft* in 1932.[17] His second major study of Hegel, *Reason and Revolution,*[18] which he wrote after several years as an *Institut* member, was one of the first extensive presentations of the contents of Marx's early writings to an English-speaking public. During his years with the *Institut,* which extended into the early forties, Marcuse admittedly lost much of his Heideggerian concern for questions about man's ontological reality. Still, in later works such as the *Essay on Liberation,* recent critics have been quick to find residues of his pre-Frankfurt School attitudes.

Marcuse's mature stance towards Marxist Humanism has, however, been more skeptical than Fromm's. As he wrote in 1965,

The objective identity of socialism and humanism is dissolved. It was never an *immediate* identity: it was real to the extent to which the objective condition was seized and transcended in the consciousness of the historical subjects and in their action. This mediation is supposed by the overwhelming power of technical progress welded into an instrument of totalitarian domination. . . . With the passing of the objective conditions for the identity of socialism and humanism, socialism cannot be made humanistic by committing socialist policy to the traditional humanistic values.[19]

Marcuse's growing skepticism about the efficacy of merging humanism and socialism, which distanced him from Fromm, was certainly shared by several of his other colleagues at the *Institut.* Here I am speaking primarily of Max Horkheimer, the *Institut*'s director after 1930 and the chief architect of its "Critical Theory";[20] Theodor W. Adorno, who joined officially in 1938, but was a close associate during the previous decade; Leo Lowenthal, the managing editor of the *Institut's* *Zeitschrift für Sozialforschung;* and Friedrich Pollock, Horkheimer's associate director and the *Institut's* administrative head. It was their work which constituted the core of what later became known as the Frankfurt School. Marcuse, of course, made significant contributions to the genesis of Critical Theory which should not be ignored. In understanding how the Frankfurt School differed from Marxist Humanism, however, it is more useful to concentrate on the work of Horkeimer and Adorno, who more unequivocally repudiated the anthropological elements in the humanist tradition.[21]

Adorno's role in this repudiation seems to have been crucial. In fact, if one had to pick a date when the Frankfurt School distanced itself irrevocably from Marxist Humanism, it would have to be either 1938, when Adorno emigrated to America, or 1939, when Fromm departed from the *Institut* to pursue his own clinical and scholarly interests. Fromm's severance of his ties with Horkheimer and the others followed a number of years of growing estrangement. Although personal difficulties complicated the picture, the primary reason for the break was a widening disagreement over the meaning of psychoanalysis. To Fromm, Freud's libido theory and biological determinism (i.e., the metapsychological instinct theory) were incompatible with his more optimistic reading of Marx. To Horkheimer and Adorno, on the other hand, the libido theory, despite its tendency to hypostasize an immutable human nature, expressed something very crucial about man's relationship to society, which Fromm and other so-called neo-orthodox revisionists like Karen Horney had misunderstood. What this insight was I will explain in a few moments, when other aspects of the Frankfurt School's critique of humanism have been clarified. Suffice it to say for now that Critical Theory's interest in psychoanalysis served a dialectical purpose in relation to the question of humanism: it brought it closer in the sense that it drew attention to the legitimacy of individual, personal gratification as against the claims of the totality, while at the same time distancing it by undermining the humanists' attempt to read society as a manifestation of the creator-subject, man.

Before expanding on the role psychoanalysis played in leading Horkheimer and his colleagues away from humanism, other more obvious aspects of their critique should be spelled out. As Alfred Schmidt has noted,[22] the Frankfurt School shared Marx's disdain for the abstract humanism of Feuerbach and was closer to the "real humanism" which Marx offered as an alternative in *The Holy Family.* "Real humanism" challenged the static implications of Feuerbach's anthropology by making de-alienated man an historical potentiality rather than an inherent reality. The Frankfurt School's castigation of latter-day philosophical anthropologists such as Max Scheler rested on the same premise.[23] The ultimate function of the phenomenologists' search for an eternal human essence, so Horkheimer and the others contended, was the reconciliation of man to his present, irrational condition. Talking in broad generalities about a shared human nature was thus worse than sentimental: it was objectively reactionary.

Here the members of the Frankfurt School shared that disdain for bourgeois humanism which informed such modern classics of Marxist literature as Brecht's *Die Massnahme* and Merleau-Ponty's *Humanism and Terror*. They drew back, however, from fashioning their critique into a defense of Stalinism, as Brecht, Merleau-Ponty, and others like them, each in his own way, had done. The crucial difference came as a result of their questioning the assumption that the proletariat represented, even potentially, a truly universal class in whose name abstract, bourgeois humanism might be transcended. Whereas more orthodox Marxists had scorned the bourgeoisie's claim to universality, the Frankfurt School came increasingly to question the possibility of universality itself. This led it away from socialist as well as bourgeois humanism in a way which will become more apparent when we return to its incorporation of Freudianism into Critical Theory.

Before leaving the Frankfurt School's critique of philosophical anthropology, however, it should be noted that it was very closely related to another element in its theoretical position: a strong distrust of anthropomorphism. One of its key criticisms of idealism was leveled against the implicit, and sometimes explicit, notion that consciousness could create the world. Horkheimer and his colleagues saw the *ego cogito* from Descartes to Husserl as an organ of that domination of nature by man which was at the root of the dialectic of the enlightenment. The Frankfurt School certainly did not encourage passivity or resignation, yet at the same time it was highly skeptical of man's ability to create the social world *ex nihilo*. Therborn's allegation that to the Frankfurt School "society is always reducible to its creator-subject, and history is the continuous unfolding of this subject,"[24] is manifestly untrue. In the *Institut's* earlier days such a state of affairs was seen as a desirable goal, but never a reality. In its later years, especially after Adorno's arrival as a full-time member, it was understood to be no more than a utopian dream.

Although the Frankfurt School's critique of anthropomorphism appeared most strongly in its discussions of idealism, traces of it can be found in its treatment of dialectical materialism as well. To Marx and all orthodox Marxists, man's most characteristic activity, his means of self-

realization, was labor. The labor process was understood to be constitutive of the totality of human existence, including the cultural sphere.
It was this priority of labor which made the derivative character of the
superstructure a necessary component of Marxist thought.

Within the *Institut für Sozialforschung,* the self-evident nature of these assumptions was the source of considerable debate. Marxist stalwarts of the old guard such as Henryk Grossmann and new entrants like Franz Neumann upheld Marx's belief in the centrality of labor.
Marcuse, both in an article he wrote before joining the *Institut*[25] and
in such works as *Reason and Revolution,*[26] also accepted this position.
Fromm, who was later to rechristen Freud's "genital character" as the
"productive character,"[27] expressed special interest in the problem of
alienated and de-alienated labor (although as a neo-Freudian, he argued
that both love and work were aspects of productivity).

Horkheimer and Adorno, on the other hand, were far less
certain about labor as the sole mode of human self-realization. As early
as 1934, in the volume of aphorisms entitled *Dämmerung,* which he
published under the name Heinrich Regius, Horkheimer called the centrality of the dialectic of labor into question. "To make labor into a transcendent human activity," he wrote, "is an ascetic ideology. . . . In that
socialists adhere to this general concept, they make themselves into car-
riers of capitalist propaganda."[28] In the writings of Horkheimer and
Adorno, the alienation of labor plays a relatively minor role. By *Negative Dialektik,* his last major work, Adorno was expressly critical of the
way in which Marx's early writings had been used ideologically by humanists like Fromm.[29] Although they did not deny the special role of
the economy, and by extension the labor process, in capitalist society,
they never de-historicized labor into man's "ontological" activity. Accordingly, they were reluctant to accept the merely reflective character
of the cultural superstructure posited by more orthodox Marxists. While
never minimizing the important influence of socio-economic factors on
cultural phenomena, Horkheimer and Adorno always avoided reducing
the latter to mere epiphenomena of the former. Jürgen Habermas's recent systematization of this insight into the separation of the two dialectics of labor and symbolically mediated interaction[30] owes much to
the Frankfurt School's earlier qualms about the traditional Marxist interpretation of the labor process.

Perhaps the major reason why Horkheimer and Adorno shied
away from the orthodox view was that they detected elements of the
domination of nature by man in the apotheosis of labor. A similar fear
prevented their full acceptance of the socialization of the natural world
which Marx had so often celebrated. It has sometimes been noted that

one of the ironies of the *Communist Manifesto* is its unconcealed admiration for capitalism's ability to dominate all aspects of human existence. The overcoming of natural relations by social ones, albeit reified ones, was understood by Marx as a necessary prelude to the realm of freedom in which man would consciously control his social destiny. Lukács continued this theme in *History and Class Consciousness* when he wrote, "To the degree to which capitalism carried out the socialization of all relations it became possible to achieve self-knowledge of man as *social being.*"[31] In his polemic against the pseudodialectical naturalism of Engels, Lukács was anxious to demonstrate the uniquely social status of capitalism, despite its seeming to be a "second nature." He was furthermore interested in demonstrating that socialism would be the consummation of this process of socialization. In so doing, however, he tended to obscure what inevitably lies beyond man's control, remaining in the sphere of the natural even after the realm of freedom might be achieved.

The Frankfurt School, in contrast to Lukács, was far less sanguine in viewing the capitalist socialization of the world as a forerunner of socialist freedom. Instead, its members questioned the manipulative, instrumental attitude towards nature which this implied. Man as the measure of all things meant the denigration of nature into an external other. The complete socialization of the world, which was really the materialist version of anthropomorphism, could only lead to the return of repressed nature in distorted and unforeseen ways.[32] Humanism, in short, represented a kind of species imperialism which would ultimately work to the disadvantage of man himself.

By refusing to rest its entire theoretical position on the foundation stone of labor and by rejecting the total socialization of the world as a desideratum, the Frankfurt School expressed perhaps its key anti-metaphysical insight: the rejection of identity theory, whether idealist or materialist. By identity theory they meant the belief that the ultimate oneness of subject and object, essence and appearance, particular and universal underlies the contradictions of the apparent world either inherently or potentially. Critical Theory's rejection of this assumption was the primary reason why it cannot be included among the variants of Marxist Humanism. One of the basic tenets of that position, as has often been noted,[33] was the substitution of Hegel's "Absolute Spirit" and the vulgar Marxists' "socio-economic substructure" by "man as the sole creator-subject of the social world." Nowhere is this more clearly shown than in *History and Class Consciousness,* where the proletariat functions as the universal class, at once the subject and the object of history.[34] Lukács—who later repudiated the book for reasons which were in certain ways questionable—was at least correct in pointing to the hidden idealism at the root of his reinterpretation of Marx.

Horkheimer and Adorno, on the other hand, were hostile toward identity theory from the beginning. (Marcuse, it might be added, was far less so.)[35] In his contribution to the *Festschrift* for Carl Grünberg in 1930, Horkheimer made clear his rejection of Hegelian metaphysics because of its overemphasis on totality and its concomitant tendency to denigrate contingency as ultimately insignificant. Adorno's study of Kierkegaard,[36] written for his *Habilitation* in 1931, attacked the Danish philosopher for smuggling in a secret identity theory behind the guise of his anti-Hegelian subjectivism. All throughout their earlier work, in which the dialectic of totality and moment is stressed, the negativity of that dialectic was always acknowledged. Adorno's celebrated statement in *Minima Moralia* that "the whole is the untrue"[37] was anticipated on numerous occasions in his and Horkheimer's previous writings.

It was this rejection of identity theory which underlay their hesitation about reducing culture to a function of the priority of labor. It was the same premise which allowed them to forswear the radical essentialism of those who would deny the reality of the contingent world.[38] It was the same insistence on the inevitably unreconciled negativity of the dialectic which made the de-alienated, universal, species man of the humanist vision no more than a utopian dream in their eyes. In short, for all its fury against the reification and alienation fostered by capitalism, the Frankfurt School could not join the Marxist Humanists in positing a world entirely free of those conditions. As Adorno once wrote in an essay on Aldous Huxley, "humanity includes reification as well as its opposite, not merely as the condition from which liberation is possible, but also positively, as the form in which, however brittle and inadequate it may be, subjective impulses are realized, but only by being objectified."[39]

The source of the Frankfurt School's dislike of identity theory and, by extension, of its humanist expression, is difficult to establish with complete certainty. Horkheimer's philosophical interest had been first aroused by Schopenhauer, whose pessimistic denial that the world could become rational or that will and idea might be reconciled made a lasting impression on his thinking.[40] Adorno's early training in atonal music during his days in Vienna as a student of Alban Berg perhaps contributed to his distrust of premature harmonies. In fact, his overriding interest in aesthetics may have meant that he saw reconciliation as a cultural rather than a social potentiality—although he frequently berated other cultural critics for isolating the two spheres. Whatever the initial source, the Frankfurt School's growing interest in psychoanalysis in the 1930s intensified its movements away from identity theory and Marxist Humanism.

Although Freudianism has often been acknowledged as an enrichment of their Hegelianized Marxism, few commentators have seen its central role in the evolution of Critical Theory. This is not surprising in that the *Institut*'s true attitude towards orthodox psychoanalysis remained obscure until the publication of the heavily Freudian *The Authoritarian Personality* in 1950.[41] Several years before, however, Horkheimer had admitted to Lowenthal that "we really are deeply indebted to Freud and his first collaborators. His thought is one of the *Bildungsmächte* [foundation stones] without which our philosophy would not be what it is."[42]

That psychoanalysis functioned in the Frankfurt School's philosophy to distance it from Marxist Humanism may seem paradoxical, as Erich Fromm was the primary exponent of its merger with Critical Theory in the 1930s.[43] In later years, when he became one of the most vociferous champions of Marxist Humanism, Fromm saw no conflict between that position and his revised Freudianism. His task in reconciling the two, however, was made much easier by the jettisoning of several key Freudian concepts, including the libido theory, the Oedipus complex, and the biological determinism of the instinct theory. In fact, Fromm's humanism could only emerge full-blown after he had freed himself from those "pessimistic" elements in Freud's psychology.

This appraisal of the counterhumanist function of psychoanalysis in the Frankfurt School's work will probably seem even more curious when measured against Marcuse's later treatment of Freud in *Eros and Civilization*,[44] which claims to be an extrapolation from orthodox Freudianism rather than a revision. Despite their obvious differences, Marcuse's use of Freud equalled Fromm's in arousing cries of protest from anti-anthropological critics. One of their number, Neil McInnes, has recently gone so far as to accuse Marcuse of reviving idealism in his rendering of Freud:

Eros is just a reincarnation of the universal class, of the essence of man and the *Gattungswesen*. Its Freudian dress keeps slipping, to reveal such familiar avatars as "the integral satisfaction of total man," "the complete individual," "the metaphysical plenitude of total man," and the "realized concept of man." This resuscitation, from young Marx and Hegel, of the unitary theory of mind involves a serious retrogression from Freud, since Freud destroyed the monolithic notion of personality by showing the fact of conflicts between motives. Instead, Marcuse revives the legend that all motives really seek the same thing—"gratification, fulfillment, peace, and happiness." This accords well with absolute idealism (all particular motives subserve the whole mind, just as all particular individuals must

serve the totality of society) but it does not accord with the facts, which indicate
that men and motives want different things, to the point of acute conflict.[45]

       Whether or not McInnes's characterization of Marcuse's use
of Freud is entirely accurate, it would be misleading to assume that Marcuse, or Fromm before him, spoke for the other members of the Frankfurt School on the question of psychoanalysis. Both Horkheimer and
Adorno had been interested in Freudian theory since the 1920s. In 1927,
Adorno, with Horkheimer's encouragement, wrote a lengthy study of the
relationship between psychoanalysis and the transcendental phenomenology of one of his teachers, Hans Cornelius.[46] In the following year,
Horkheimer underwent a brief analysis with Karl Landauer, one of Freud's
own pupils. Its purpose, he was later to recall,[47] was more to learn the
theory from the inside than to cure any serious neurosis. In 1929, he
persuaded Landauer to form the Frankfurt Psychoanalytic Institute, which
brought Erich Fromm, his wife Frieda Fromm-Reichmann,[48] and Heinrich Meng to Frankfurt. Of these, only Fromm maintained a connection
with the *Institut für Sozialforschung* after 1933. As noted earlier, his
relationship with Horkheimer and the other members of the *Institut*'s
inner circle soon grew seriously strained, resulting, at least on the theoretical level, from his abandonment of Freud's theories of the libido
and the instincts. Although in the early thirties Horkheimer had reacted
warmly toward Fromm's attempts to integrate psychology and sociology,[49] by the end of the decade he was becoming increasingly wary of
what he viewed as the overly facile way in which Fromm was effecting
that integration. The rejection of the libido theory, he argued, was tan-
tamount to the impoverishment of depth psychology itself. "Psychology
without libido," he wrote Lowenthal in 1942, "is in a way no psychology. . . . Psychology in its proper sense is always psychology of the individual."[50] The libido, which implied a level of human existence beyond immediate social control, was an indispensable concept for the
prevention of the premature reconciliation of society and individual.
Fromm and other so-called neo-Freudian revisionists[51] like Karen Horney were ultimately ideological in their attempt to sociologize psychology and psychologize sociology. Similarly, Fromm's notion of a "social
character," which he had developed during the thirties,[52] was a misleading representation of the condition of modern man. "The stress on totality," Adorno wrote in 1946, "as against the unique, fragmentary impulses, always implies the harmonistic belief in what might be called
the unity of the personality and what is never realized in our society. It
is one of the greatest merits of Freud that he has debunked the myth of
this unity."[53]

In short, Horkheimer and Adorno came to admire Freud not because psychoanalysis could provide a model for a universal human nature, but because its asocial, biological premises expressed, at least metaphorically, one aspect of the nonidentity of man in an unreconciled totality. "In an antagonistic society," Adorno was to write in 1955, "each individual is nonidentical with himself, both social and psychological at once, and, because of the split, maimed from the outset."[54] Moreover, although it was never spelled out explicitly, the Frankfurt School also seemed to appreciate in Freud an awareness that the socialization of the world, which both Marx and Lukács had celebrated, could never fully eradicate the natural side of men.

In fact, they came increasingly to see Freud as a bulwark against the false identity which threatened man in the postwar period (false in the sense that the rational reconciliation of contradictions had not really been achieved either in the still capitalist West or allegedly socialist East). In a tangibly antagonistic society, men may have been maimed, as Adorno had argued, but at least the tension produced by their self-contradiction prevented them from accepting this condition without protest. In what Marcuse was later to popularize as "one-dimensional society,"[55] this was no longer the case. With the increasing liquidation of subjectivity, a kind of identity had been achieved—but it was one which was a mockery of the dream of classical idealism and Marxist Humanism.

What perhaps most distinguished the Frankfurt School in the postwar era from its Weimar days was a growing suspicion that the dream had itself contained the mockery. As Horkheimer wrote to Lowenthal in 1950:

Included in dialectics is what brings it to sublation (*Aufhebung*). Since, however, sublation presupposes spirit and with it subjectivity, the process which goes beyond the spirit must contain the raw destruction of the moment instead of its preservation. That is the meaning of the anxiety that mankind might be at its end. We must work on the analysis of this anxiety, not in the psychological, but in the philosophical and social-theoretical sense. It could be that everything which until now has passed for spirit carries something of infantilism . . . [there is] in our anxiety an element of children's cries. We must only guard against its mollification by the chastening voice of the father.[56]

The yearning for a nonantagonistic society in which this would not be the case was never, to be sure, explicitly abandoned in their work. De-alienated man in a rational society was never completely laid to rest as an assumed desideratum. Yet, in the later writings of Horkheimer and Adorno, that inherent caution which can be noted from the beginning became far more insistent. This is most clearly shown in Horkheimer's recent return to his early interest in Schopenhauer, an interest sparked by Schopenhauer's rejection of Hegel's identity theory and optimism about the inexorability of human progress. For both Schopenhauer and Horkheimer, positive reconciliation, as well as the Marxist Humanist dream of a species man, was ideology. As Horkheimer wrote in the 1960s,

Hegel's teaching shows that the positivity that distinguished him from Schopenhauer cannot ultimately stand up. The failure of a logically stringent system in its highest form in Hegel, means the logical end of attempts at a philosophical justification of the world, the end of the claim of philosophy to emulate positive theology. All these attempts rest directly or indirectly on the idea of the world as the work or expression of true mind. But if the world, in its essence and in its actual condition, is *not* necessarily connected with mind, philosophic confidence in the very existence of truth disappears. In that case, truth can be found only in perishable men themselves and is as perishable as they are.[57]

In short, to Horkheimer and Adorno (although the latter's interest in Schopenhauer seems to have been less intense), in contingent man, not species man, lay the real locus of human freedom.

This has certainly taken us a long way from the heady optimism of *History and Class Consciousness* or, for that matter, from the generally hopeful tone of the Frankfurt School's decade in Weimar and first years in New York. During that time, the shadowy presence of what might be called a negative anthropology in its work was enough to sustain a certain measure of revolutionary confidence. When in later years the sobering implications of Critical Theory's stress on nonidentity were worked out against the backdrop of an increasingly quiescent proletariat, this confidence dwindled to insignificance. Without a "scientific" Marxist belief in the automatic heightening of capitalism's structural contradictions or a humanist Marxist faith in the assertion of universal man as the creator of history, Horkheimer and his colleagues were at a loss to identify the agency, if any, of social change. Marcuse's pessimism was similar, but his seems to have been tempered by a continuing confidence—at least on the theoretical level—in de-alienated, species man as an historical possibility, however remote.

In the course of this mounting skepticism, it has seemed to some observers that the Frankfurt School had retreated to the higher ground of cultural elitism and contemplative philosophy, that nonidentity was a cover for the return to bourgeois liberalism, and that theory became a substitute for *praxis* instead of its prelude. No one, however, who has really immersed himself in Critical Theory would be satisfied with such formulations of the School's position. For, if Horkheimer and his colleagues refused to negate contingent man in the name of universal man, they were equally reluctant to absolutize the solitary individual at the expense of his social side. Absolute isolation and absolute solidarity, to phrase it differently, were equally anathema. The individual was always to be understood as mediated through the nonidentical totality, never as an end-point in himself. In emphasizing the negative moment in the dialectical process, they fostered a critical awareness which both scientific and humanist Marxism seemed to lack. And in so doing, the Frankfurt School preserved the hope of a more truly human society inhabited by concrete men rather than by the abstract subjects of the humanists, with whom they have so often been confused.

3.
The Frankfurt School
in Exile

"E migration is the best school of dialectics," Bertolt Brecht wrote in his *Refugee Dialogues.* "Refugees are the keenest dialecticians. They are refugees as a result of changes and their sole object of study is change. They are able to deduce the greatest events from the smallest hints—that is, if they have intelligence. When their opponents are winning, they calculate how much their victory has cost them; and they have the sharpest eyes for contradictions. Long live dialectics!"[1]

Although the members of the Frankfurt School were rarely in agreement with Brecht on the meaning of dialectics, or much else for that matter, their experiences in America tended to confirm his point. Max Horkheimer and his colleagues were indeed sensitive to the rapid transformation of circumstances during the sixteen-year tenure of their *Institut für Sozialforschung* in America. Unlike Brecht, however, they saw these changes to be of such magnitude as to modify and in some ways render obsolete the Marxism they had brought with them from Frankfurt. Having the requisite intelligence, they were often extremely sensitive to the implications of the smallest of those hints the cultural outsider is likely to note in an alien environment. As for calculating the costs of their opponents' victories, no one who has read Theodor Adorno's *Minima Moralia*[2] or Horkheimer's *Eclipse of Reason*[3] can doubt their acute awareness of those costs, even after the primary opponent, Nazi Germany, had been defeated. And finally, the Frankfurt School's collective eye for contradictions had to remain especially sharp because of the fear of its members that the manifest traces of social antagonism were becoming decreasingly apparent in what Herbert Marcuse was later to call a "one-dimensional society."

First published in *Perspectives in American History* (1972), vol. 6.

In other ways besides those suggested by Brecht, the Frankfurt School's dialectical skills were honed during its members' stay in America. Most important of these for our purposes was an increasing emphasis in their work on one aspect of dialectical thought, what might be called its antithetical as opposed to its synthetic impulse, an emphasis that led in subtle ways to a serious tension in the *Institut*'s[4] work. The result by the 1940s was a growing distance between the *Institut*'s theoretical position, known as Critical Theory,[5] and, first, its members' attitude toward political practice and, second, their estimation of the proper role of empirical social research. It is to this tension that we must turn before considering the more general issue of the *Institut*'s impact in this country. For only by understanding the internal strain which developed in the *Institut*'s last decade in America can its uneven public influence, and especially its paradoxical and crucial relationship to the New Left of the 1960s, be grasped.

Even after this is done, however, no attempt will be made to give an account of the Frankfurt School's influence that could claim to be exhaustive, for to do so would require, among other things, an exercise in multiple biography of the hundreds of scholars who at one time or another and in one capacity or another passed through the *Institut*'s doors. Such a list would include Paul Baran, Gerhard Meyer, M. I. Finley, Ernst Schachtel, Olga Lang, Paul Honigsheim, Paul Massing, Jay Rumney, and Herta Herzog. They and others like them doubtless helped to disseminate certain of the Frankfurt School's ideas to a larger audience than would have been possible through the writings of the more permanent members alone. How thoroughly they incorporated those ideas into their own thinking and with what fidelity they transmitted them, however, can only be conjectured without a range of biographical research whose dimensions would be staggering. Instead, we will concentrate on the more general reception of the Frankfurt School's own work. At the same time, it must never be forgotten that the *Institut* was a functioning, if limited, teaching body for a number of its years in this country, as well as a supporter of numerous refugees whose work was influenced by their association.

I

Before embarking on a discussion of either the tension in the *Institut*'s work of the forties or its American impact, the general outlines of its history should be clarified. The *Institut für Sozialforschung* was founded in Frankfurt in 1923 as an independently endowed institute for the interdisciplinary investigation of social phenomena. Its major benefactors, a wealthy grain merchant, Hermann Weil, and his left-wing son, Felix, were generous enough to allow the *Institut* an independence which it zealously guarded during all its subsequent history. In the beginning, the *Institut* was unapologetically Marxist in orientation. Carl Grünberg, its first active director, had been a major figure in the world of Austro-Marxism and the editor of the widely respected *Archiv für die Geschichte des Sozialismus und der Arbeiterbewegung,* which continued publication until 1930. Under his direction, the *Institut* concentrated on the history of the labor movement and rarely ventured into the theoretical revisions of Marxism which would characterize its later years. Many of the more important figures in the *Institut's* Weimar years were orthodox Marxists like Karl August Wittfogel and Henryk Grossmann. Relations with the Marx-Engels Institute in Moscow, then directed by David Ryazanov, were extremely warm during Grünberg's directorship and the *Institut* helped gather materials for its massive archive.

At the same time, an undercurrent of disenchantment with the theoretical assumptions of Grünberg's work began to develop within a younger faction of the *Institut's* staff. Philosophically trained, interested more in aesthetics and psychoanalysis than economics, they found a leader in Max Horkheimer. Leo Lowenthal, Friedrich Pollock (whose interest in economics was the exception to the rule), and Theodor Wiesengrund-Adorno, not officially on its staff until 1938 but a close associate for the previous decade, were its members. They were joined by Erich Fromm and Herbert Marcuse shortly before the *Institut* was forced to flee Germany. Thus, when Horkheimer succeeded Grünberg as director in 1930, he had a core of supporters who helped turn the *Institut* in a different direction. In the pages of their new house organ, the *Zeitschrift für Sozialforschung,* which began publication in 1932, Horkheimer and his colleagues spelled out the tenets of Critical Theory and demonstrated how they might be applied in a number of different areas of research. With the unfolding of their ideas in the next decade, most of which was spent in exile, what later became known as the Frankfurt School began to coalesce. Columbia University, where the *Institut* was generously received in 1934, after a year in Geneva, proved a secure and supportive environment in which the *Institut's* work could be pursued. During the thirties, new members like Franz Neumann, Otto Kirchheimer, and Walter Benjamin (who contributed to the *Zeitschrift* from Paris) brought their special talents to the *Institut,* as older ones such as Erich Fromm, Karl August Wittfogel, and Henryk Grossmann either left or were given less central roles in its work. In the forties,

Horkheimer, Adorno, Pollock, and, for a brief time, Marcuse left for the West Coast and a number of members entered government service during the war. This meant a loss of the *Institut*'s cohesion, which perhaps contributed to that tension in its work to which allusion has previously been made. After the war, Horkheimer slowly and with some reluctance began to accept the blandishments of a new German government anxious to attract the *Institut* back home. Finally, in 1950, he capitulated and brought to a close the *Institut*'s American period, at least as an institution. Although Adorno and Pollock accompanied him, a number of their former colleagues, including Marcuse, Fromm, Lowenthal, Neumann, Wittfogel, and Kirchheimer, chose to remain in this country. Any history of the *Institut*'s American experience must take into account their continued impact in the years after the *Institut* officially returned to Germany. Because of limitations of space, however, we will concentrate on the influence of only those members most closely identified with Horkheimer as genuine adherents of the Frankfurt School: Adorno, Marcuse, Lowenthal, and Pollock.

Before attempting an estimation of their influence in this country, we must return to the question of America's impact on their work, to the strain in the relationship between Critical Theory on the one hand and political practice and empirical work on the other. From the beginning, Critical Theory had contained an inherent tension between, first, its insistence on the interrelatedness of all social and cultural phenomena, a holistic stress which derived in large measure from its Hegelian and Marxist roots, and, second, its apprehension that too great an emphasis on unity and coherence either on the level of theory or in social relations themselves, would only undermine the possibility of a true reconciliation in the future. The former impulse manifested itself in a number of ways: the interdisciplinary nature of the *Institut* itself, the desire of its members to combine theoretical and empirical work, and, finally, their frequent assertion that theory and practice, although problematically related, ought never to be fully separated. On a theoretical level, it meant the insistence that the social totality must be taken into account in any analysis of one of its aspects. If not, the result would be an overemphasis on one facet of the whole, a fallacy known as "fetishization" which blinded orthodox Marxists, with their overemphasis on the economy. It also meant interpreting the present not only historically, but in terms of its future potential as well. In all of this, the impulse was toward interrelatedness, if not outright unity. *Sozialforschung* differed from sociology precisely in its concern for the dialectical totality. The separation of "is" and "ought," which characterized ostensibly value-free, bourgeois social science was anathema to the

Frankfurt School; as Horkheimer made clear in his most explicit methodological statement, "Traditional and Critical Theory" of 1937, Critical Theory did not seek truth for its own sake, but sought to effect social change instead. The implicit goal was that synthesis of contradictions in a socialized society which had motivated Marxists of all kinds for generations.

There was, however, a second impulse in Critical Theory, even in its earliest years, which went in the opposite direction. Here the fear of fostering a premature reconciliation of contradictions which would be ideological in Marx's sense led Horkheimer and his colleagues to stress discontinuities and disharmonies wherever they might be found. On the level of theory, this meant emphasizing, against Hegel and other believers in the underlying identity of subject and object, that they were still nonidentical. The most important advocate of identity theory in the Marxist camp in the interwar period had been Georg Lukács. In *History and Class Consciousness* (1923), he had described the proletariat as both the subject and object of history which needed only to become conscious of this role to throw off its chains. The Frankfurt School, in contrast, came increasingly to look askance at this equation, questioning the traditional Marxist belief that the workers were the "universal" class whose victory would end the contradictions of capitalist society. Instead Horkheimer and his colleagues began to fear that the historical moment for this event had passed without the opportunity's having been seized. Accordingly, they stressed the need to preserve negative, critical social and cultural forces wherever they might be found. Although a holistic approach was to be retained, the whole had to be understood as a disharmonious force-field of both affirmative, status-quo-oriented elements and their negative contraries. Not surprisingly, Horkheimer and his colleagues rarely chose to express themselves in systematic fashion, relying instead on aphorisms, short essays, and critiques of other positions. A fragmented totality could only be explored by a correspondingly incomplete style.

On the level of politics, the second impulse in its work meant a refusal to sanction the obliteration of the individual in the name of a collectivity, without, however, making the bourgeois notion of individuality the end point of political practice. It also implied a frequent affirmation of the right to personal gratification in the movement for social emancipation in contrast to those who preached revolutionary asceticism.[6] And finally, it fostered a recognition that the unity of theory and practice was still a goal, not a reality. Theory was understood to be the senior partner in the relationship; as Marcuse wrote, speaking for the entire Frankfurt School, "theory will preserve the truth even if revolutionary practice deviates from its proper path. Practice follows the truth, not vice versa."[7] In the 1930s, when Marxism was being reinterpreted as a form of pragmatism by Sidney Hook and others, the Frankfurt School remained convinced that theory, although inevitably related to social conditions, contained truths that could not be measured in terms of their instrumental value in the present society.

In the following decade, the balance between these two impulses in Critical Theory underwent a decided shift in the second direction: toward a greater stress on nonidentity, on the individual, although interpreted problematically, as the refuge of emancipatory forces, and on the need to preserve the truths of theory against the half-truths of political practice. As Adorno was to warn at the end of the decade in *Minima Moralia*, "the whole is the untrue."[8] Dialectical thought's most urgent task was the preservation of the contingent and particular against the eternal and allegedly universal. The possibility of a true reconciliation of subject and object could be maintained only by saving the subjective moment of freedom in an administered society whose objective sway was threatening the very existence of subjectivity itself. With the increasing absorption of social and political forms of negation, the Frankfurt School began to focus its hopes on cultural phenomena, although here too, as we shall see when discussing its critique of mass culture, it was far from optimistic. "The task of art today," Adorno argued, "is to bring chaos into order,"[9] a stress opposed to the Frankfurt School's earlier belief that the vision of harmony contained in aesthetic form was a foretaste of the social reconciliation of the future.

This increased fear that negation was being systematically eliminated from culture and society meant a critical change in the *Institut*'s attitude toward political activism. One of the key assumptions of Marx's thought had, of course, been the equation of the proletariat with the universal class whose triumph would insure the social realization of a basically Hegelian idea of substantive rationality. In the twenties and thirties, the Frankfurt School, while never affiliating itself with any faction on the left had maintained an uneasy hope that this equation might still be valid. During the early years of the war when Horkheimer had just arrived in southern California, he wrote an essay entitled "Autoritärer Staat," which was included in the *Institut*'s memorial volume to Walter Benjamin after his suicide.[10] Over six thousand miles from Europe, isolated as never before from events on that continent, he speculated on the fate of the working-class movement. His distance from the circumstances he was describing manifested itself in an analysis which vacillated between extreme pessimism and occasional flashes of desperate hope. To Horkheimer, Friedrich Pollock's concept of state capitalism was the appropriate model for understanding the authoritarian states of the present era, including the Soviet Union. Here, it might be added parenthetically, he quarreled with three recent additions to the *Institut,* Franz Neumann, Otto Kirchheimer, and A.R.L. Gurland, who still believed that fascism was basically an expression of monopoly capitalism. The different implications for political action drawn from the two positions were profound, as the contradictions of capitalism were understood to be suspended under state capitalism while they were intensified under monopoly capitalism. Because of his acceptance of Pollock's state capitalist model, Horkheimer affirmed what had always been a tenet of Critical Theory: the absurdity of believing in historical necessity when discussing social revolution. If anything, he argued, the working class's faith in such a necessity had both rendered it passive and contributed to the flowering of authoritarianism. Freedom was not the mechanical consequence of the centralization and planning of the economy or the simple assumption of political power. In fact, he wrote, "dialectics is not identical with development. Two antagonistic moments, the takeover of state control and the liberation from it, are contained together in the concept of social revolution. It [this concept] brings about what will happen without spontaneity: the socialization of the means of production, the planned direction of production, and the domination of nature in general. And it brings about what without active resistance and constantly renewed struggle for freedom never appears: the end of exploitation. Such a goal is no longer the acceleration of progress, but rather the jumping out of progress."[11]

Here Horkheimer, like Benjamin with his exhortation to explode the continuum of history,[12] argued for a rupture in historical evolution far more drastic than that envisaged by the orthodox Marxists who saw socialism as a working out of the immanent dialectic of capitalism. Although the difficulties in effecting such a dramatic change in 1940 were not to be minimized, the potential, so Horkheimer still felt, was there. "The material conditions are fulfilled," he wrote. "With all the necessity of transition, dictatorship, terrorism, work, and sacrifice, the Other [*das Andere,* the Frankfurt School's shorthand for the alternative society whose description they could not give] is dependent solely on the wills of men."[13] "The possibility," he continued later in the article, "is no less than the hope."[14]

And yet, who was to be the historical agent of change if the structural contradictions of capitalism were not themselves sufficient to bring about the "jumping out of progress"? To this question, Horkheimer and his colleagues could give no answer. In "Autoritärer Staat," Horkheimer began to turn his attention to the individual as a repository of critical forces. Although at present impotent, the single person "is a power because everybody is atomized. . . . They have no other weapon than the word. . . . Thought itself is already a sign of resistance." [15] How this mental resistance was to be embodied in concrete social forms, however, Horkheimer could not say. By 1947, in his *Eclipse of Reason,* he was writing: "Is activism, then, especially political activism, the sole means of fulfillment? . . . I hesitate to say so. The age needs no added stimulus to action. Philosophy must not be turned into propaganda, even for the best possible purposes." [16]

Thus, by the 1940s, the *Institut*'s last decade in America, the unity of theory and *praxis,* which had been one of its most insistent themes in earlier years, had been split asunder. Although the Frankfurt School would never withdraw to a defense of speculative thought for its own sake, in later years it would seem to be arguing that theory, if genuinely critical, was itself a kind of *praxis.* Needless to say, this was a position calculated to win few adherents among the more activist followers of Critical Theory who referred back to the more militant texts of the *Institut*'s earlier years. By the 1960s, the internal tensions which the Frankfurt School experienced in its years of American isolation were played out again on a more public stage in Germany as Adorno and Jürgen Habermas were subjected to student abuse for "betraying" the activist imperative of their work.

A similar internal strain destroyed the *Institut*'s hope for the unity of theory and empirical work in the 1940s. While never acknowledged in print, the theoretical analyses of Horkheimer and Adorno in *Dialektik der Aufklärung, Eclipse of Reason,* and *Minima Moralia* were very different in intent and conclusions from the empirical work carried out under *Institut* direction in the *Studies in Prejudice,* especially *The Authoritarian Personality.* Although the necessity of collaborating with American social scientists unfamiliar with Critical Theory contributed to the differences, they were also a reflection of unresolved tensions within the *Institut*'s own thinking.

Once again, these tensions represented less a radical break with the Frankfurt School's earlier thinking than a new emphasis within it. From the beginning the Frankfurt School saw empirical studies such as its massive analysis of the family and authority published in 1936 [17] as aids in enriching and modifying its theory, but never in verifying it. Still, in the 1930s the general conclusions of the empirical work, primitive as it admittedly was, were in accord with those of the theoretical speculation. This, however, was no longer the case in the following decade.

On one level, the change was symbolized by the departure

of Erich Fromm from *Institut* affairs in 1939, one year after Theodor
Adorno became a full-time member. Fromm had been an enthusiastic
advocate of the coordination of theory and empirical work; in fact, one
of the reasons he decided to leave the Institut was to gain time to do
the clinical work he considered a necessary prerequisite to his theoretical writings. Well before *Escape from Freedom* [18] or even his long essay
in the *Studien über Autorität und Familie,* [19] he had attempted to measure authoritarian elements in the character structures of German workers. His survey, which was based on open-ended questions whose answers were interpreted psychoanalytically, was conducted before the
Institut had to flee Germany. Never completed to Horkheimer's satisfaction, however, it remained unpublished, much to Fromm's regret. [20]

By the 1940s, Fromm's former colleagues began to express
serious reservations about the integration of Marxism and psychoanalysis which underlay his attempt to merge theory and empirical verification. Fromm's efforts to establish a unified social psychology, which they
had applauded in the days when Critical Theory's synthetic impulse was
stronger, were now attacked for diluting Marx and Freud as well as for
serving an ideological purpose under present social circumstances. In
1946, Adorno, anticipating Marcuse's later critique of the neo-orthodox
revisionists in *Eros and Civilization,* [21] castigated Fromm for psychologizing sociology and sociologizing psychology as a premature reconciliation of contradictions. [22] In an antagonistic society, he argued, the
individual was nonidentical with himself, both social and psychological
at the same time, and therefore misunderstood if portrayed as a unified
"social character." "The stress on totality," he wrote, "as against the
unique, fragmentary impulses, always implies the harmonistic belief in
what might be called the unity of the personality and what is never realized in our society." [23] Freud, by stressing the instincts beneath the
social forces, had preserved the recognition of this tension, which the
neo-orthodox revisionists had mistakenly smoothed over.

Accordingly, the Frankfurt School felt justified in isolating the
sociological and psychological dimensions of the problems they studied
in a manner which seemed to contradict the synoptic goals posited in
earlier years. In one of the memoranda he composed for the *Institut's*
unpublished study of anti-Semitism in labor in 1944, Adorno explained
what this new direction meant:

This means methodologically that our psychological analyses lead us the deeper
into a social sense the more they abstain from any reference to obvious and
rational socio-economic factors. We will rediscover the social element at the very
bottom of the psychological categories, though not by prematurely bringing into
play economic and sociological surface causations where we have to deal with

the unconscious, which is related to society in a much more indirect and complicated way.[24]

The goal, therefore, was not to sever psychology from sociology, but rather to recognize that their *methodological* integration was dependent on the *social* integration, in a future society without contradictions, of the two dimensions of what was now a nonidentical personality. This shift in the Frankfurt School's perspective helps account for the apparent abandonment of its neo-Marxist, sociological approach in *The Authoritarian Personality,* which led one set of critics to charge that "the authors take the irrationality out of the social order and impute it to the respondent, and by means of this substitution, it is decided that prejudiced respondents derive their judgments in an irrational way."[25] *The Authoritarian Personality* was criticized for being psychologically reductionist and overly concerned with subjective rather than objective phenomena because the methodological dichotomy expressed in the Adorno memorandum cited above was never made fully clear in the *Institut*'s published work. The complementary sociological analysis of the same problems dealing with the "objective" trends of the society was contained in *Dialektik der Aufklärung* and *Eclipse of Reason,* which rarely reached the same audience as the empirical work in the *Studies on Prejudice.* If these theoretical works had been as widely read as their empirical counterparts, the Frankfurt School's full explanation of the phenomena under scrutiny might have been better understood. As it was, the American public seized on the psychological notion of the authoritarian personality and ignored its relationship to the more sociological analysis in the other books.

And yet, if a close reading of the two types of work had in fact been made, it is doubtful that an entirely consistent picture would have resulted. As noted earlier, the Frankfurt School was increasingly reluctant to analyze the social totality as a coherent unity, stressing instead the complexity of mediations and inconsistencies in an effort to highlight those areas of negation still left in the "administered," "one-dimensional" society of the postwar world. If this meant on occasion a conflict between the conclusions of the empirical and theoretical work, Horkheimer and his colleagues seemed willing to risk such inconsistency in order to preserve the integrity of their approach.

One example of such a conflict can be found by comparing the discussions of anti-Semitism in *Dialektik der Aufklärung* and *The Authoritarian Personality.* The former, which had echoes of Marx's controversial treatment of the Jewish question, situated anti-Semitism in the larger context of the modernization process. Its conclusions were pessimistic about ending prejudice without a radical rupture in the course of rationalization as it had proceeded until then. The latter, in sharp contrast, treated anti-Semitism primarily as a subjective problem which could be solved by education within the present order. With its emphasis on toleration as an end in itself, *The Authoritarian Personality* clearly placed itself in the moderate, liberal camp, a far cry from the Frankfurt School's usual resting place. Although in large measure attributable to the sponsorship of the project by the American Jewish Committee and to the *Institut*'s collaborators, this position anticipated Horkheimer's own development in later years, at least in some respects.

Another example of the inconsistency in the conclusions of the theoretical and empirical works can be found in their respective analyses of the ego in modern society. One of the purposes of the authoritarian personality project was the investigation of those familial conditions which contributed to the genesis of high-scorers on the "F-scale," i.e., individuals with authoritarian character structures. Among its conclusions was the discovery that homes in which discipline was strict but arbitrary, and parental values were conventional and rigid, were likely to produce authoritarian offspring. This was so, according to the accompanying analysis, because the values of the parents generally remained ego-alien to the child, thereby preventing the development of an integrated personality. Resentment at parental harshness was often displaced onto others, while the outward image of the father and mother proved to be highly idealized.

By contrast, the parents of the low scorers on the F-scale were remembered as less rigid and arbitrary and more emotionally demonstrative and ethically nondogmatic. Accordingly, their children idealized them less and were able to accept their moral norms without as much repressed hostility. The obvious conclusion of all this was that integrated personalities without considerable ego-alienation of moral norms were less likely to be authoritarian because the displacement and projection of unassimilated traits onto outgroups was minimized. The goal of programs for tolerance, therefore, was to stimulate the creation of well-adjusted, self-confident individuals with strong egos.

How this goal was to be implemented in a society in which integrated personalities had been declared impossible by Adorno in his earlier critique of Fromm was never made clear. In fact, *The Authoritarian Personality,* even in those sections written by Adorno, represented a withdrawal from that critique of Fromm, a change justified on the grounds that reified "personalities" did exist in the administered society of the present day.[26] This helped explain why a character typology could be used to delineate the various types of authoritarian personali-

ties, but it was useless in defending the proposition that healthy, tolerant, integrated alternatives could be fostered in a still antagonistic world.
This problem was passed over in silence by the *Institut* and their collaborators.

Moreover, in *Dialektik der Aufklärung* and *Eclipse of Reason*, the ego was treated from a very different perspective. In these works,
it appeared in the context of a broader, more ambitious critique of the
Enlightenment attitude toward nature, an attitude which implied the
subjugation and domination of nature by man. This relationship, it should
be noted in passing, was the key theoretical concern of the Frankfurt
School in the 1940s: "the Enlightenment" was shorthand for the basic
trend of western civilization which stressed instrumental, subjective,
formal rationalism. In *Eclipse of Reason*, Horkheimer connected the ego
to this tradition:

> As the general principle of self endeavoring to win in the fight against nature in
> general, against other people in particular, and against its own impulses, the ego
> is felt to be related to the function of domination, command, and organization.
> . . . The history of Western Civilization could be written in terms of the growth
> of the ego as the underling sublimates, that is internalizes, the command of his
> master who has preceded him in self-discipline. . . . At no time has the notion
> of the ego shed the blemishes of its origin in the system of social domination.[27]

Here the ego was meant partly in philosophical terms—the
ego cogito from Descartes to Husserl had been attacked by the Frankfurt School from the beginning—but it clearly had psychological significance as well. Marcuse's later concept of the "performance principle,"[28] which he equated with the reality principle of Western society,
was rooted in this earlier critique of the ego as the tool of domination.
The implications of the analysis were certainly very different from those
of *The Authoritarian Personality.* In the empirical work, strong ego development was praised as a bulwark against authoritarian intolerance. In
Eclipse of Reason, it was damned as a major organ of modern man's
antagonistic domination of nature. On a very basic level, the two perspectives might be reconciled, as Adorno said he hoped would be the
case in his memorandum, but in the *Institut*'s work during this period
no indication of how this might occur was suggested.

During its last decade in America, the Frankfurt School saw
its earlier hopes for the unification of social theorizing and both political practice and empirical social science fade away. The balance between the synthetic and dissonant impulses in Critical Theory shifted
perceptibly in the latter direction. Although a working out of tendencies immanent in their work from its beginnings, this development also

reflected a response to the Frankfurt School's experience in America, or at least to that experience as filtered through its theoretical prism. To Horkheimer and his colleagues, the progressive diminution of the family as a mediating force in society, the end of the market economy in favor of state capitalism, and the eclipse of bourgeois individualism meant a society in which contradictions had not really been harmonized but were somehow muted and obscured instead. The result was that dialectical thought, if it were to be truly in the service of emancipation, had to stress negation rather than positive reconciliation. In later years, those who maintained a more optimistic appraisal of revolutionary potential would accuse the Frankfurt School of having lost its integrity by turning its back on its work of the twenties and thirties. Although in fact such a development had occurred, it was by no means capricious or a function of the conservatism of old age. As Brecht had noted, emigration did sharpen the dialectical skills of at least this group of refugees. The 1940s were the real watershed in the Frankfurt School's history. Despite efforts to establish continuity with the *Institut* which had been chased out of Germany in 1933, the intervening years in America had left their indelible mark. Between the Bonn Institut and its Weimar predecessor were sixteen years of history whose effects were reflected in the changes discussed above. To ignore these changes in order to recapture the more radical and optimistic tone of the earlier period would be to violate the spirit of Critical Theory itself, which always recognized the historical relatedness of intellectual endeavor. To apply the thinking of the 1930s to the problems of our age uncritically would be to falsify the intent of that thought and use it in the instrumental way the Frankfurt School always heatedly opposed.

II

If the *Institut* can be said to have experienced internal strains in its work during its last decade in America, it is not surprising to see that the impact of that work in this country was highly uneven. There were, to be sure, a number of other factors which complicated the relationship between the Frankfurt School and its potential American audience. The most obvious of these was the great reluctance of its members to adopt the language of their new home. It was not until 1940, when the Nazi takeover of Paris forced the closing of their European publishing outlet, that the *Zeitschrift,* renamed *Studies in Philosophy and Social Science,* was compelled to use English as its primary language. Even during the forties, much of the Frankfurt School's theoretical work continued to be written in its members' native tongue.

The reasons for this reluctance are not difficult to discern. Because of their relative financial independence, the members of the *Institut* were never forced to earn their living from their writings or teachings as were other less fortunate refugees. In addition, they were keenly aware of the need to preserve the peculiarly German cultural tradition which Germany's current rulers were doing so much to debase. And finally, they considered their native language far more appropriate for the expression of dialectical thinking than English and therefore the more suitable medium for the articulation of Critical Theory. Of all the *Institut's* members, Adorno was the most sensitive to this last argument. Although he wrote prolifically before returning to Germany in 1953 for good, only a small fraction of his work appeared in English. In 1957, he admitted to Lowenthal that "I believe 90 percent of all that I've published in Germany was written in America."[29] As a result, his theoretical work stirred attention only in Europe, while in America, he remained known almost exclusively as the first author on the title page of *The Authoritarian Personality*.[30]

In addition to its linguistic isolation, the Frankfurt School's institutional framework served in certain ways to set it apart from its American environment. In a recent article in *Daedalus,* Edward Shils argued that the impact of Horkheimer's ideas was far greater than that of another, less successful refugee, Karl Mannheim, because of their contrasting institutional situations. The history of the Frankfurt School, Shils wrote,

is a testimonial to the skill of a shrewd academic administrator, who by good luck and foresight inherited a favorable institutional situation and developed its connections within the various universities in which it was located, maintained its internal structure *and* extended its connections outside the university. As a result it became the mechanism by which some of the most influential ideas of present-day social science developed. . . . In contrast to this, Karl Mannheim, having created no following, has found none since his death, despite the repeated calls for a sociology of knowledge.[31]

Although Shils may be right about Mannheim's isolation, his picture of the Frankfurt School's manipulation of its institutional solidarity as a springboard to success is highly oversimplified, if not basically incorrect.

First of all, the positive function of the institutional unity of its members has been called into question by no less a figure in its history than Erich Fromm, who has written:

Here was an institute which had as its members some excellent minds of left-wing radical though mostly noncommunist thinking. It got out of Germany before Hitler and was one of the few, if not the only institute which saved its funds. . . . Yet what were its achievements? The only real scientific achievement is the volume on *Autorität und Familie* and a number of valuable papers in the *Zeitschrift*. But that is all, and I do not think that was enough, given the great possibilities the *Institut* had. In fact, I think it was relatively little. This does not mean to imply that the individual work of its members . . . has not been of value, but these authors would have pursued their work without the *Institut* also.[32]

Fromm's estimation of the *Institut*'s productivity is, of course, colored by the aftereffects of his break. Yet, even if exaggerated, it warrants consideration as the opinion of a former member of the *Institut*'s inner circle. It is, in fact, probable that certain figures in the *Institut*'s history developed in ways which showed little real influence by Critical Theory. The careers of Franz Neumann and Otto Kirchheimer at Columbia after the war, for example, seem to have been only superficially affected by their exposure to the Frankfurt School philosophy.

Still, since it can never be known for sure whether or not "these authors would have pursued their work without the *Institut*" in quite the same way, it is more useful to focus on what the function of that institutional unity actually was in determining their influence in America. To Shils, its effects were clearly positive. Yet as late as 1946, twelve years after the *Institut* first came to Morningside Heights, members of the Columbia Sociology Department were still in the dark about much of its work. There is clear evidence of this in a letter Paul Lazarsfeld sent to Theodore Abel in an effort to persuade the Department to extend an invitation to the *Institut* to revive its activities after the war. Lazarsfeld, who had been marginally associated with the *Institut* despite his methodological differences, was anxious to assure Abel of its value:

I have a strong feeling that an injustice has been done, and that our committee is called upon to make amends. I understand, for example, that you are using Mirra's study [Mirra Komarovsky's *The Unemployed Man and His Family* (New York, 1940)] as one of the three major research contributions to your own book. . . . Everyone has now forgotten that the plan for the study was completely laid out by the Institute. . . . Take another example: Everyone speaks now of the authoritarian character in connection with the German problem. Who knows that this whole complex of ideas was developed fifteen years ago in the Institute, and spelled out completely in their book on "Authority and Family"? I still consider this book the outstanding effort to combine theory and empirical studies.

In assessing the reasons for their relative neglect, Lazarsfeld put the blame on Horkheimer and his colleagues rather than on Columbia:

Of course the whole mess is due to the idiocy of the Institute group. I told them for years that publishing in German will finally destroy them. But they had the fixed idea that their contribution to America will be greater if they preserve in this country the last island of German culture.[33]

The invitation, it might be added parenthetically, was extended, but Horkheimer declined partly out of the fear that too intimate a connection with Columbia or any other university would jeopardize the *Institut*'s independence. What is apparent in Lazarsfeld's letter is the extent to which the *Institut*'s relative autonomy served to isolate it from its American audience. Instead of acting as a mechanism of frictionless interaction, it provided a buffer behind which the *Institut* could pursue its own work undisturbed. The resulting disruption of communications worked, of course, in both directions. By encapsulating itself to the degree that it did, the Frankfurt School remained insensitive to certain nuances of American culture. Thus, for example, Adorno's critiques of jazz often suffered from an exaggerated hostility which reflected the inflexibility of his European sensibility.[34] Similarly, the Frankfurt School's tendency to categorize all American philosophical trends, especially pragmatism, as variants of positivism shows an unfamiliarity with the local terrain. These occasional crudities of perception were the calculated cost of the *Institut*'s deliberate aloofness from its new surroundings. By avoiding absorption into the American academic community, the Frankfurt School felt itself more capable of preserving the uncompromising quality of Critical Theory. By sacrificing immediate scholarly recognition, its members hoped to avoid the co-optation which they felt had been the fate of a number of other emigrés. Adorno was perhaps the most intransigent of those who refused to be "Americanized." The tone of his reminiscence in *The Intellectual Migration* may have been conciliatory and his expression of gratitude sincere,[35] but in an earlier article written during his stay in this country, he displayed a less mellow mood:

There has arisen a civilization [in America] which absorbs all of life in its system, without allowing those loopholes which European laxness left open into the epoch of the great business concerns. It is made unmistakably clear to the intellectual from abroad that he will have to eradicate himself as an employee of the supertrust into which life has condensed.[36]

This, of course, is what the *Institut* wished most to avoid. In fact, it was not until it suffered a financial reversal in the late 1930s, due in part to unsuccessful investments and in part to its utilization of capital to help other refugees, that this self-imposed encapsulation was bro-

ken. Only then did it reach out for external financial support which finally bore fruit in two sizeable grants from the Jewish Labor Committee
and the American Jewish Committee. The first of these led to a study of
anti-Semitism in labor which was conducted primarily in the *Institut's*
New York office in 1944–45. A.R.L. Gurland, Paul Massing, Felix Weil,
Friedrich Pollock, and Leo Lowenthal were primarily responsible for its
execution. For several reasons, including the difficulty of rendering the
results in readable form, the study was stillborn.

The other grant proved far more productive. In November
1944 Horkheimer assumed the reins of the A.J.C.'s scientific division with
the intention of initiating a long-range program of research on the problem of prejudice. The ultimate goal was not merely scholarly, but pedagogical as well. The few initial studies were designed to set off a chain
reaction in which other foundations and universities would support similar
research leading to the dissemination of their results to the general public. How well this succeeded can be seen from the impact of the five
volumes of the *Studies in Prejudice* produced by the research: *Prophets
of Deceit* by Leo Lowenthal and Norbert Guterman, *Dynamics of Prejudice* by Bruno Bettelheim and Morris Janowitz, *Rehearsal for Destruction* by Paul Massing, *Anti-Semitism and Emotional Disorder: A Psychoanalytic Interpretation* by Nathan W. Ackerman and Marie Jahoda,
and, most important, *The Authoritarian Personality.* Although many
methodological and substantive criticisms were made of the work, the
stimulus provided by *The Authoritarian Personality* alone was enough
to justify Horkheimer's expectations.[37]

The popular reception of the *Studies,* although more difficult to gauge accurately, also seems to have been substantial. One of
their indirect influences might well have been on the psychologizing of
politics that characterized the "end-of-ideology" fifties. The Frankfurt
School, to be sure, had always been interested in the psychological
component of political movements,[38] but in the *Studies,* the implications of the analysis shifted in a crucial way. Whereas in the earlier period the *Institut's* image of mental health implied a left-wing negation
of the status quo, now the "healthy liberal" who advocated piecemeal
reform became the model of sanity. In the *Studien über Autorität und
Familie* in 1936, the foil of the "authoritarian character" was the "revolutionary"; in *The Authoritarian Personality,* it had become the "democratic." Although the remnants of the *Institut's* earlier Marxism were
sufficiently preserved to arouse the wrath of such critics as Edward Shils,[39]
who complained that left-wing dogmatism was excluded from the study,
the door was open to the equation of left and right authoritarianism by
the study's assumption that the tolerant liberal was the most psycholog-

ically fit. There were no critiques of "repressive tolerance" in the *Studies* as there had been elsewhere in the Frankfurt School's work.[40]

As we have noted before, the *Institut*'s theoretical work and its empirical work during the forties were at odds in a number of ways. That Horkheimer realized this is evident in a letter he wrote to Lowenthal in February 1950:

> It is my opinion that through our solidarity and the theoretical endeavors up to 1943* we have not only given courage to us, but have been able to maintain our intellectual integrity and independence until today.[41]

> *[in the margin] Everything since was an interim even though it is meaningful and productive.

In fact, throughout this period and into the next few years when he was engaged in the reconstruction of the *Institut* in Frankfurt, Horkheimer's correspondence was filled with expressions of regret about the demands his other activities made on the time he hoped to devote to his theoretical work. To Horkheimer, Adorno, and Marcuse, theoretical speculation was still the most urgent task for radical intellectuals. In the midst of the final work on the *Studies in Prejudice,* Horkheimer could write to Lowenthal: "In view of our attitude . . . I am not frightened by the impotence into which we perhaps might fall; theoretical thinking, and it alone, is our most important task in the world as it is."[42] Although it may appear paradoxical that Horkheimer was worried about the Frankfurt School's impotence at a time when the *Studies* were almost completed, his appraisal was not without justification in judging the influence of Critical Theory. All of the Frankfurt School's earlier theoretical work remained buried in the *Zeitschrift.* The unique mixture of Hegelianized Marxism, psychoanalysis, and certain elements of *Lebensphilosophie* which comprised Critical Theory scarcely made a ripple in the American philosophical community, which remained wedded to more analytic and empiricist modes of thought. *Eclipse of Reason,* on which Horkheimer had labored so strenuously for a number of years, was disappointingly received. John R. Everett spoke for many in the American philosophical establishment when he wrote:

> That Professor Horkheimer appears ignorant of the most important work done by contemporary naturalistic philosophers is apparent. . . . His own rather thinly disguised left-wing Hegelianism allows him to lump all who disagree into categories called either positivism or neopositivism. . . . Such criticism is particularly inappropriate when directed against Dewey when one remembers his forthright social philosophy, based on an ethic of self-realization, and issuing in his concept of a new individualism.[43]

If the philosophers were unimpressed by Critical Theory, the sociologists were almost as unsympathetic, despite the excitement caused by *The Authoritarian Personality*. In 1954, C. Wright Mills urged the creation of an alternative sociology to that practiced by the "scientists" and "grand theorists" then dominating the profession. As an example of what he advocated, he pointed to the *Institut*:

I know of no better way to become acquainted with this endeavor, in a high form of modern expression, than to read in the periodical, *Studies in Philosophy and Social Science*, published by the Institute of Social Research. Unfortunately, it is available only in the morgue of university libraries, and to the great loss of American social studies, several of the Institut's leading members, among them Max Horkheimer and Theodore [sic] Adorno, have returned to Germany. That there is now *no* periodical that bears comparison with this one testifies to the ascendency of the Higher Statisticians and the Grand Theorists over the Sociologists. It is difficult to understand why some publisher does not get out a volume or two of selections from this great periodical.[44]

There is little evidence to show that Mills' suggestions were followed in the fifties, and even if they had been, the most important theoretical statements of the Frankfurt School were contained not in the *Studies in Philosophy and Social Science*, but in its German predecessor. Even Mills, it should be noted, had only a superficial contact with the *Institut*. In the early forties he exchanged some letters with Franz Neumann[45] and after 1946 he met frequently with Lowenthal in New York, but there is little evidence in his work that the writings of the Frankfurt School were very influential.[46]

If the Frankfurt School had little impact on the academic establishment, their following in the more general intellectual community of the forties and fifties was even smaller. This must have been a source of some chagrin in the light of the substantial audience that had grown from the writings of their former colleague, Erich Fromm, especially *Escape from Freedom* and *The Art of Loving*. The political implications of their earlier work, which began to arouse attention in Germany after their return, were totally unknown to the modest, domestic radical movements of the relatively quiet 1950s. Not until the meteoric rise of Herbert Marcuse in the middle of the next decade amid the stirrings of a nascent New Left did the theoretical work of the Frankfurt School begin to attract notice among a significant number of Americans.

There was, however, one area in which Critical Theory did have an influence in the fifties: the debate over mass culture, which reached its crescendo in the middle of the decade. As Leon Bramson has noted in *The Political Context of Sociology*,[47] America was slow to react to the dangers of the "massification" of society and culture until the Weimar emigration. Even when native American sociologists such as Robert Parks and Herbert Blumer of the Chicago School wrote about atomization and mob psychology, they did so with considerable ambiguity, often stressing positive as well as negative effects. Although earlier critics like H. L. Mencken had covered similar ground, prewar writers on the subject, such as Clement Greenberg, were generally isolated figures. By the forties and fifties, however, the influence of such emigrés as Hannah Arendt and Erich Fromm was beginning to be felt. The century-old European concern over the costs of cultural democratization whose most articulate early spokesman had been Tocqueville finally became common coin in the American intellectual marketplace. With the recent horrors of fascism fresh in mind (some critics would say obsessively so), the refugees often advanced an analysis relating mass culture to mass society and ultimately to totalitarianism. That there were some exceptions to this tendency—Paul Lazarsfeld's empirical work, for example, showed the continued vitality of the family as a mediating buffer between the allegedly atomized individual and the social totality—does not detract from the validity of the generalization.[48] The influence of the Frankfurt School does much to support it, as well as to give credence to the other frequently made observation that, for the first time, critics of mass culture came from left-wing rather than traditionalist, religious, or elitist backgrounds.

As early as the 1930s with Horkheimer's accession to the directorship, the *Institut* had become increasingly interested in the cultural superstructure which orthodox Marxists had tended to relegate to a derivative role in their analyses of society. Although still Marxist enough to appreciate the permeation of the cultural sphere by socio-economic factors,[49] they were convinced that the relationship between superstructure and base was far more problematical than the reflection theory of their orthodox opponents would allow. Although this is not the place to give a full exposition of the Frankfurt School's aesthetic theory,[50] a few of its elements must be grasped to understand its critique of mass culture.

First, the Frankfurt School never sought to isolate culture from its function in the social totality, even though they recognized that the function was often difficult to discern directly. Second, they were intent on analyzing all cultural artifacts in relation to the totality, not merely as reflections of specific class interests within it. Third, because the totality contained contradictions, they were insistent on the dialectical complexity of specific cultural phenomena; in other words, they believed that both negative and positive impulses, elements of opposition and affirmation, were expressed in genuine works of art. Fourth, in a society which saw the progressive absorption of other oppositional forces, the critical element in art became increasingly important as one of the last refuges of negation. As Horkheimer phrased it, "art, since it became autonomous, has preserved the utopia that evaporated from religion."[51] And finally, if the distinguishing characteristic of authentic art was such a negative impulse, the most telling sign of pseudo-art was its absence.

These and other aesthetic precepts were spelled out in a series of articles in the *Zeitschrift* by Horkheimer, Adorno, Lowenthal, Marcuse, and Benjamin. Although most of them were concerned with what might be called "high art," a certain number were devoted to popular culture. Lowenthal, for example, wrote on the faddish reception Dostoyevsky received in Germany before World War I.[52] Adorno, even before emigrating to America, analyzed its most characteristic musical mode, jazz.[53] And Benjamin, in one of his most important articles, investigated the revolutionary potential of the newest cultural medium, the film.[54] These articles appeared in German (in Benjamin's case, in French), but when the *Zeitschrift* began publishing in English, a number of similar articles appeared in the language which was accessible to a sizeable domestic audience. Although the *Studies in Philosophy and Social Science* was soon a casualty of the war and Horkheimer's departure for California, it did manage to devote one issue to mass communications before it ceased publication.[55] The product of a collaboration with Paul Lazarsfeld's Bureau of Applied Social Research at Columbia, it included essays by Adorno and George Simpson on popular music, Herta Herzog on daytime radio sketches, William Dieterle on Hollywood, and Horkheimer's "Art and Mass Culture," a more programmatic statement which started out as a review of Mortimer Adler's *Art and Prudence.* Another of Adorno's papers from his stormy days as Lazarsfeld's colleague at the Princeton Radio Research Project in the late thirties was published in *Radio Research, 1941,* followed by Lowenthal's analysis of "Biographies in Popular Magazines" in the next volume of the *Radio Research* series, 1942–43.

These articles were the first major contributions of the Frankfurt School to the still embryonic debate on mass culture. David Riesman, one of the central figures in the controversy in later years, has acknowledged the excitement he and others felt when reading these early forays into a yet unmapped territory.[56] In his own work, which had a widespread impact in the early and mid-fifties, Riesman often cited *Institut* members, especially Lowenthal, for their pioneering efforts.[57] Others, such as Dwight MacDonald in his well-known essay on "Masscult and Midcult," which first appeared in *Politics* in 1944 under the title "A Theory of Popular Culture," also voiced their indebtedness.[58]

While the ending of the *Studies in Philosophy and Social Science* closed off the Frankfurt School's forum for expanding on these initial efforts, its members' interest in mass culture continued to be keen throughout the remainder of their stay in America. In the "Kulturindustrie" chapter of *Dialektik der Aufklärung,* Horkheimer and Adorno, aided by Lowenthal, presented their most systematic statement of a theory of mass culture. Unfortunately, it was never translated into English and, like most of their theoretical work, had little impact on the American discussion.[59] In the following years, Lowenthal began adding studies of the history of popular culture to his content analyses of specific cultural phenomena, which were finally collected in 1961 as *Literature, Popular Culture and Society.*[60] During the fifties, after a stint at the Voice of America, he pursued earlier efforts to write on the sociology of literature. Before joining the Berkeley faculty in 1956, he enjoyed a year of leisure as a Fellow of the Center for Advanced Study in the Behavioral Sciences at Stanford. Here he put the finishing touches on the series of essays published in 1957 as *Literature and the Image of Man,* which included a number of articles that had originally appeared in German in the *Zeitschrift.*

Although Adorno's aesthetic concerns were generally with "high art"—he completed his *Philosophie der neuen Musik,* which in manuscript had a profound impact on Thomas Mann's *Doctor Faustus*— he did not entirely abandon his interest in more popular cultural phenomena. During his last year in America in 1953, he worked at the Hacker Foundation in Los Angeles on a content analysis of television and a critique of the *Los Angeles Times'* astrology column.[61] His continued dismay over the implications of American popular music produced a final article on jazz in the volume of essays he published soon after returning to Frankfurt as *Prismen.*[62]

Adorno's resettlement in Germany, however, removed him from the thick of the battle, which reached its height in the years after the McCarthy scare. An attempt in 1955 to get him to contribute to a book on David's Riesman's *The Lonely Crowd* produced a negative response because he considered Riesman a popularizer of his and Horkheimer's work.[63] Once back in Frankfurt as Assistant Director of the *Institut,* Adorno concentrated his energies on more esoteric philosophical and aesthetic questions, leaving mass culture behind with scarcely disguised relief. His abortive attempt to adapt cultural criticism to American social scientific techniques, which had made his first years on these shores so difficult, was never repeated. By the 1960s he had returned to a basically hostile attitude toward quantifying cultural phenomena, which he dismissed as "equivalent to squaring the circle."[64]

Adorno's recognition that his aesthetic analyses could not be translated into empirically verifiable categories was shared by the entire Frankfurt School. In a contribution to one of the central anthologies of the mass culture debate,[65] Lowenthal outlined the *Institut*'s position as the opposite of the market research practiced by most American social scientists. In doing so, he pointed out that subjective "taste" was a poor starting point for a cultural analysis because of the diminution of individual autonomy. Market research data, he contended, reflected reified, unmediated reactions rather than the underlying social or psychological function of the cultural phenomena under scrutiny. Only by understanding popular culture—here he specifically cited Dilthey's notion of *Verstehen*—rather than merely measuring its effects, while at the same time maintaining valid aesthetic standards, could the inadequacies of the empiricist approach be overcome.

If the Frankfurt School's work in the forties saw a split between its theoretical and empirical elements, their studies of mass culture were clearly on the theoretical side of the ledger. Although the conclusions were occasionally supported by the empirical findings of *The Authoritarian Personality*, the methods of analysis were very different. Moreover, the basic goal of the *Studies in Prejudice*, an increase in toleration, was implicitly opposed by the *Institut*'s critique of mass culture, which saw the indiscriminate "toleration" of kitsch as an unmitigated disaster. As noted before, the political implications of *The Authoritarian Personality* were liberal and pluralist. In the context of the mass culture debate, however, pluralism was the rallying cry of those who repudiated the *Institut*'s position.[66]

The failure on the part of a number of commentators to see that the Frankfurt School's critique of mass culture was ultimately unverifiable in empiricist terms, and was not intended to be, led them to dismiss it as unsuccessful. Thus J. P. Nettl wrote:

the very form of the discussion has itself tended to take place more and more within the context and according to the concepts of sociology, so that the intellectuals fought under the, for them, false colors of social science. Their battle was thus half lost from the start. Nothing shows more clearly the inherent contradiction in the position of the left-wing intellectuals fighting a losing battle *within the confines of an ideologically hostile sociology* than the way in which the proponents of left-wing democracy and humanism have dug themselves in along the last ditch of an elitist defense of high culture.[67]

In fact, as noted before, the Frankfurt School's notion of *"Sozialforschung"* had always been opposed to American sociology in a variety of basic ways, especially to its insistence on empirical verification. Their critique of mass culture was rooted in an alternative methodology,[68] despite occasional attempts—such as Adorno's collaboration with Lazarsfeld—to ground it in a more "scientific" framework.

Because the theoretical structure which underlay the methodology was largely hidden from view, hostile critics could score the easy point that here was a group of former Marxists who had ended up as snobbish elitists. The charge, to be sure, was given some weight by the fact that in the case of certain other critics of mass culture, this seemed to have been true. (Dwight MacDonald's essays on the subject display little of his former radicalism). It was also substantiated by the fact that criticizing mass culture brought them together with avowed conservatives like the psychologist Ernst van den Haag.[69] Edward Shils, ever the scourge of the *Institut*, was the first to level this attack,[70] which was most extensively developed in later years by Herbert J. Gans. To Gans, the critique of popular culture was no more than "a plea for the maintenance of restoration of an elitist order by the creators of high culture, the literary critics and essayists who support them, and a number of social critics—including some sociologists—who are unhappy with the social, economic, and political tendencies of modern society."[71]

Although applicable in the case of such unequivocally conservative critics as Ortega y Gasset or T. S. Eliot, and arguably so with others like Karl Mannheim and Dwight MacDonald, the charge of elitism was far more problematical when directed at Horkheimer and his colleagues. The argument that their denunciation of certain elements in popular culture constituted a betrayal of their Marxism rested on a shallow understanding of what dialectical materialism really meant. Marxism, after all, had never been equivalent to populism, which tended to glorify the "people" as they actually were. The concept of proletarian false consciousness, traditionally manifested in such ways as trade-union economism or religious other-worldliness, could also be extended to explain the narcotized acceptance of mass culture. Other twentieth-century Marxists like Lukács, with his notion of "imputed class consciousness," and Gramsci, with his concept of "hegemony," had been keenly aware of the difference between classes "in-themselves" and "for-themselves." The Frankfurt School, although far more pessimistic about arousing class consciousness, was not really betraying Marxism by refusing to romanticize the present state of the working class's consciousness. If they had accepted the idea of mass *society,* on the other hand, this would have been very different, for this concept denies the persistence of class antagonisms. The Frankfurt School, however, concentrated on mass culture, not mass society, which was the basis of the analysis of other refugees such as Hannah Arendt. As late as the 1960s,

Adorno could write: "Society remains class society, today as in the period when that concept originated."[72] The class struggle might be muted, but it had not been entirely swallowed up in an atomized, massified society.

By recognizing the gap between promise and reality and refusing to ascribe to the proletariat a nonexistent militancy, the Frankfurt School was forced to defend high culture as an alternative "negative" reality. But—and this was crucial—they never considered elitist culture as an end in itself. As early as 1937, Marcuse castigated the elevation of "culture" above material "civilization" as a status-quo-oriented ideology.[73] Such a notion of culture, he argued, lacked a critical quality and was "affirmative" instead. In its place, he advocated the social realization of the values inherent in aesthetic phenomena. Similarly, in the lead essay in *Prismen,* also regrettably untranslated until the 1960s, Adorno savagely attacked both the notion of high culture and those who were its self-proclaimed guardians:

The greatest fetish of cultural criticism is the notion of culture as such. For no authentic work of art and no true philosophy, according to their very meaning, has ever exhausted itself in itself alone, in its being-in-itself. They have always stood in relation to the actual life-process of society. . . . That the fatal fragmentation of society might some day end, is for the cultural critic a fatal destiny. He would rather that everything end than for mankind to put an end to reification. This fear harmonizes with the interests of those interested in the perpetuation of material denial. Whenever cultural criticism complains of "materialism," it furthers the belief that the sin lies in the man's desire for consumer goods, and not in the organization of the whole which withholds these goods from man: for the cultural critic, the sin is satiety, not hunger.[74]

To the Frankfurt School, the mass obsession with consumption was by no means the unqualified horror that more conservative observers imagined. Understood dialectically, it expressed a demand for the realization of that *"promesse de bonheur"* which genuine art always contained. As Horkheimer wrote to Lowenthal in 1942,

We cannot blame people that they are more interested in the sphere of privacy and consumption rather than production. This trait contains a Utopian element; in Utopia production does not play a decisive part. It is the land of milk and honey. I think it is of deep significance that art and poetry have always shown an affinity to consumption.[75]

In fact, far from criticizing mass culture out of a covert Puritanical asceticism, as Shils and others suggested, the Frankfurt School attacked it for precisely the opposite reason. Mass culture, they felt, was really more life-denying, despite its entertainment value, than even the most difficult Schoenberg quartet. One passage in a letter from Horkheimer to Lowenthal in 1955, at the height of the mass culture debate, is especially relevant:

> You are right in defending "popular culture" against the haters of the masses. On the other hand, it is horrible that it never comes to satisfaction. Connected with this is the fact that the masses show more interest in the real love affairs of Lollobrigida than in the films, because in reality, it comes to something. One must point out that in a poem of Hölderlin or Baudelaire or a painting by Picasso more is ultimately offered than by the poets of the day and, in specific ways, one must show what that means. Yes, I would go so far as to assert that art is differentiated from "popular culture" precisely in that it achieves unsublimated happiness again, while a moment of denial belongs to "popular culture."[76]

In arguing for a true happiness, to be sure, the Frankfurt School was opening itself to the charge of becoming philosopher-kings, dictating wants to people who empirically desired something else.

To mention the perennial problem of philosopher-kings is to focus attention on the Frankfurt School member who, at least in this country, has been most frequently accused of wanting to don that lofty mantle, Herbert Marcuse.[77] Here once again there has been vulgarization and misinterpretation. Despite their emphasis on the crucial task of critical thought, and by extension of critical thinkers, Marcuse and his *Institut* colleagues never ascribed a direct political role to intellectuals as such. Here a comparison with another group of Weimar left-wing intellectuals who have received much recent attention,[78] the so-called "Activists" around Kurt Hiller, may be instructive. For the Activists, intellectuals were the vanguard of a new society. *Geist* (spirit or mind in the ambiguous German meaning) was to rule in the form of a "logokratie," an intellectual elite which would transcend petty social differences. Significantly, Hiller and his circle were raised as neo-Kantians, stressing the ethical imperative of *Geist* as a force opposed to material concerns. The Frankfurt School, in contrast, began as Hegelian Marxists, aware of the importance of consciousness in the social totality, but never elevating it above the socio-economic substructure as the true determinant of history. As we have seen, Marcuse criticized the notion of cultural autonomy as an affirmative ideology; similarly, he and his colleagues were highly skeptical of the claims of intellectuals to play a leading political role. The *Institut,* from its inception, had no illusions or regrets about its political impotence, despite the frequent stress its members laid on connecting theory and practice. The Frankfurt School certainly wanted to be philosophers, but never kings. Marcuse, in clarifying the misinterpretation of his essay on repressive tolerance in its 1968 re-edition, was very much in the Frankfurt School tradition when he wrote, "The alternative to the established semidemocratic process is *not* a dictatorship or elite, no matter how intellectual and intelligent, but the struggle for real democracy."[79] Weimar certainly produced its share of politically ambitious intellectuals, but the Frankfurt School was not among them.

Marcuse, to be sure, has been far more politically involved in the last decade than any of his former colleagues. Personal considerations have prevented the widening split between his position and theirs from leading to public conflict, but close observers of the Frankfurt School's history could not help noting the growing tension. The precise relationship between Marcuse and the others in the Frankfurt School, however, has remained a somewhat clouded subject to his American audience. As one of his more sympathetic interpreters noted in 1968:

> *One-dimensional Man* and the *Repressive Tolerance* essay, let alone his earlier works, remain unread by large portions of the Left; only a very small percentage has, or cares to have, more than the vaguest comprehension of the philosophical tradition in which Marcuse stands.[80]

III

Since it was the sudden rise of Marcuse's popularity a decade and a half after the *Institut* left the United States which rearoused interest in its work on these shores, it seems fitting to end our discussion of the Frankfurt School's impact on America by concentrating on his transmission of their legacy. A full treatment of Marcuse's work would, of course, be beyond the scope of this essay, as would a summation of his influence. The former has already been attempted by a number of commentators,[81] while the latter must await the passage of much more time for the proper perspective. What can be done usefully here is to situate Marcuse in the Frankfurt School tradition, showing both his indebtedness and his departures.

It is not meant as a derogation from his originality to point out that most of the ideas in Marcuse's recent work, ideas which seemed so fresh to Americans in the 1960s, were worked out in the pages of the *Zeitschrift* three decades before; for despite Horkheimer's preeminence in the *Institut*, Marcuse was one of the most creative contributors to the genesis of Critical Theory. Of all the *Institut* members, he was most clearly committed to theoretical work. At no time in his career did he participate in the empirical investigations carried out by the

Institut in the thirties and forties. Accordingly, when the growing tension in the Frankfurt School's work came to a head, Marcuse was securely on the side of theory. The pessimistic arguments of the *Dialektik der Aufklärung*, which Marcuse considered Horkheimer and Adorno's best work,[82] echo throughout *One-dimensional Man.*[83] The conclusions of *The Authoritarian Personality*, on the other hand, were rarely reproduced in his later writing. The minor role of the Oedipus Complex in his *Eros and Civilization,*[84] to take one example, contrasts very sharply with its crucial place in the explanatory structure of the empirical study. To Marcuse, the Freudian notion of individuals socialized through Oedipal struggles with their fathers had been rendered obsolete by the withering away of the family as mediating agent in society.[85] This was a conclusion in agreement with the theoretical sections of the *Studien über Autorität und Familie*, but not with those of the later project. Similarly, his notorious critique of repressive tolerance referred back to arguments that were made by Horkheimer, Adorno, and even Fromm in previous years, but that were absent in *The Authoritarian Personality.*[86] And finally, by rejecting the pedagogical goals of the *Studies in Prejudice*, he placed himself squarely in the more uncompromising radical tradition of the *Dialektik der Aufkärung.*

Marcuse's closeness to the analysis in his former colleagues' theoretical writings was also demonstrated in his critique of technological society, which found its classic expression in his most popular book, *One-dimensional Man.* Its arguments had special appeal in the countercultural regions of the New Left, where the animus against bureaucratization and dehumanization was far greater than against economic exploitation. His more orthodox critics from the Old Left, on the other hand, attacked him for abandoning a class analysis based on the structural contradictions of capitalism.[87] In attempting to uncover the roots of his apostasy, several commentators focused their attention on his early training under Heidegger.[88] Although there may indeed have been some residues of his teacher's influence, it was not necessary to go so far back in his intellectual development in order to discern the origins of his ambivalence toward technological society.[89]

One of the major concerns of the Frankfurt School in the thirities and forties had been the tightening of what Weber had called the "iron cage" of rationalization. During the war, its members had heatedly debated the staying power of capitalism. Franz Neumann, A.R.L. Gurland, and Otto Kirchheimer had maintained that the contradictions of capitalism were still operating in an explosive direction. As noted earlier, Friedrich Pollock had constructed a model of state capitalism, initially applicable to Germany and the Soviet Union but potentially to the Western democracies as well, which was far more stable and durable. Horkheimer, Adorno, and Lowenthal clearly favored Pollock's more pessimistic analysis. Marcuse, although apparently personally closer to Neumann than to any of his other colleagues, seems also to have adopted Pollock's position. In his 1941 essay on "Some Implications of Modern Technology," he argued that technological rationality had contributed to the internalization of self-control in a way which caused the absorption of potential social opposition into the total apparatus.[90] In the same article he briefly included an anticipation of one of the major strains of his later thought when he noted how machines divert libido from other human beings to themselves, thereby increasing the power of the system.

The use of psychoanalytic arguments to explain the stabilization of technological society was one of the Frankfurt School's key concerns in the forties. When Marcuse developed his concept of the "performance principle" in *Eros and Civilization,* he was building on a conceptual framework worked out in such books as *Dialektik der Aufklärung.* Similarly, his lack of confidence in the existence of any genuinely negative force in advanced industrial society mirrored the bleak prognosis of his former colleagues in their last decade in America—his encouragement of student, black, and third-world protest in the 1960s was never more than cautious support for prerevolutionary catalysts. And finally, his advocacy of the "Great Refusal," a total rejection of one-dimensional society, rested on the same premises as Horkheimer's call for a "jumping out of progress" in his wartime essay, "Autoritärer Staat."

To stress the similarities between Marcuse's point of view and that of his former associate in the *Institut,* however, is not to deny the differences which emerged in the years after Horkheimer and Adorno returned to Germany. In some ways, it might be argued that Marcuse has remained faithful to the theoretical intentions of the Frankfurt School's earlier work in a way which the others did not. After 1950, the members of the Frankfurt School who returned to Germany were concerned primarily with the rebuilding of the *Institut* and the education of a new generation of German students. This meant the loss of the *Institut's* outsider status in a way that threatened to undercut the critical edge of its earlier work. One manifestation of this was the tactical trimming of the group's opposition to such elements of the "administered world" as empirical social scientific techniques, which at the beginning had been central to Critical Theory. This intransigent hostility had, of course, been relaxed when the *Institut* worked on the *Studies in Prejudice.* For the first few years after 1950 it was no longer a matter of easing a traditional opposition to empiricism. The Frankfurt branch of the *Institut* continued to concentrate on empirical work, which Horkheimer had always protested was only a temporary expedient. When Lowenthal, who remained in America, expressed his dismay over this turn of events, Horkheimer replied defensively:

We stand here for the good things: for individual independence, the idea of the Enlightenment, science freed from blinders. When Fred [Pollock] reports to me that you and other friends see the type of empirical social science we are conducting here as in many ways conventional, I am convinced that you would be of another opinion could you see the thing with your own eyes. . . . As much as I yearn for pure philosophical work again, as much as I am determined to take it up again under the right conditions and devote myself solely to it, so much do I also know that effectiveness here, either for the education of students or for ourselves, is not lost.[91]

Horkheimer's appeal to effectiveness was a new element in the Frankfurt School's program; previously, the integrity of the theory had been paramount. Clearly a choice had been made to abandon the *Institut*'s isolation in order to contribute to the reconstruction of post-Nazi Germany. This was by no means a dishonorable decision, but it did mean the sacrifice of the Frankfurt School's speculative energies. Although Adorno continued to write at his characteristically prodigious rate, Horkheimer's dream of returning to philosophical work never materialized. In the fifties and sixties, he produced a number of short essays, which were included with a translation of *Eclipse of Reason* as *Kritik der instrumentellen Vernunft,*[92] but few were as interesting as those he had published in the *Zeitschrift* during his American exile.

The *Institut*'s decision, to be sure, did contribute to the reinvigoration of the Federal Republic's social scientific profession. One of its earliest successes, which was of interest to an American audience, was the work of a visiting scholar from the United States who worked under Pollock's direction. Milton Mayer's *They Thought They Were Free*[93] was based on interviews with former Nazis using some of the techniques the *Institut* had perfected during its last decade in America. By 1956, Horkheimer still felt that the dissemination of social scientific methods was important enough to justify the creation of a separate *Institut* methodological section under the direction of Rudolph Gunzert. He also tacitly admitted the cost of the *Institut*'s concentration on teaching these techniques during its first few years back in Germany, when he outlined its advantages to Lowenthal:

First, empirical studies in these areas, despite our acknowledged opinion, still have an enlightening function here in Germany; second, it will relieve us of the trouble of caring for these techniques, which we truthfully did not suckle with

our mother's milk, and Teddie [Adorno], on whom alone the burden has increasingly fallen, can concern himself with theoretical matters; third, it will also make
my departure from the Institut's milieu better understood.[94]

In later years, Adorno was to take up the cudgels against the
overreliance on empirical techniques, thereby returning to the original
emphasis of Critical Theory. The effectiveness of the *Institut*'s educa-
tional program had in a sense been too great, and the balance once again
had to be redressed. By the 1960s, Critical Theory was to become engaged in a bitter polemic with the advocates of a more empirical social
science.[95] One result of this revived stress on the abuses of empiricism
was that the theoretical work of the Frankfurt School was grounded neither in the epistemology of empirical social science nor in the experience of a negative social class. Instead, it was forced to rely solely on
the insights of the theoreticians themselves, a base whose narrowness
the Frankfurt School's critics did not fail to notice.

Marcuse, however, never flirted with empirical techniques
at all, nor did he abandon the search for a revolutionary subject. As a
result, his work, for all its celebrated pessimism, was not as marked by
the paralyzing tensions which plagued Horkheimer's and Adorno's
thinking during the 1960s. In many ways, he remained more closely
wedded to the Critical Theory of the thirties with its radical tone and
stress on practice. While Horkheimer began to focus his attention on
the theological undercurrents in his earlier work,[96] Marcuse was careful
to keep his utopia purely secular. When the question was raised of re-
publishing his *Zeitschrift* essays, Marcuse willingly allowed their reis-
suance in both German and English; Horkheimer, in contrast, only re-
luctantly approved the republication of his *Zeitschrift* articles in *Kritische
Theorie*.[97] Although by no means immune to criticism from certain radical factions such as the Progressive Labor Party, Marcuse's political record was judged by most of those on the left as "an exemplary one."[98]
His former colleagues in Frankfurt, on the other hand, had to endure
considerable abuse on the part of overzealous students in Frankfurt who
read their work of the thirties in pirated editions and accused them of
betraying earlier ideals.

It seems likely that Marcuse's political impact, not only in
America but globally, climaxed in 1968, the year of the French uprising,
the Czech experiment, and the Yippee assault on the Chicago conven-
tion. For it was then that the New Left's countercultural impulse, to which
Marcuse's work most urgently spoke, was at its height. Marcuse's *Essay
on Liberation,* which appeared in the following year, summed up his

solidarity with the "new sensibility" which seemed to be challenging the one-dimensional mentality whose impenetrability he had declared only a few years before. Three years later much of the romance had ended. The New Left had begun to "re-Marxify"[99] itself in a way which excluded the cultural dimensions from "serious" politics. And for his part, Marcuse began to show signs of regretting his earlier enthusiasm about the revolutionary pretensions of the counterculture.[100]

If Marcuse's stock among some radical factions declined after 1968, the interest in his ideas in scholarly circles continues to be strong. Doctoral dissertations on his work have proliferated, as have the inevitable popularizations for beginners.[101] One of the indirect results of his celebrity, especially noteworthy for our purposes, has been a recent American interest in the entire Frankfurt School which promises to go well beyond the reception its members received during their actual stay in the United States. Consisting of Marcuse's former students at Brandeis University and in California and others who have come to Critical Theory solely through his writings, a loose network of young, usually politically radical, scholars has started from his more recent writings and worked its way back to his origins in the Frankfurt School. Angela Davis, who actually studied at the *Institut* in Frankfurt after being Marcuse's "best student" in this country,[102] is only the most celebrated of their number. Others include Jeremy J. Shapiro and Shierry Weber of the California Institute of the Arts, who have translated a number of key Frankfurt School texts; Paul Breines of Boston University, the editor of *Critical Interruptions,* the most imaginative collection of essays by young Marcuseans; Paul Piccone and his associates at the University of Buffalo, who publish a journal of left-wing phenomenology entitled *Telos;* Trent Shroyer of the New School for Social Research, whose interest has been focused primarily on the work of Jürgen Habermas, the most gifted member of the Frankfurt School's postwar generation; and William Leiss, Erica Sherover, and John David Ober, who contributed to the *Festschrift* in Marcuse's honor, *The Critical Spirit.*[103]

Another indication of the growing interest in the Frankfurt School is the recent spate of translations, many long overdue, sponsored by the Beacon Press and Herder and Herder. As a result, much of Adorno's work will be finally available to an American public which, as noted before, knew him as little more than the first name on the title page of *The Authoritarian Personality.* Other younger members of the Frankfurt School, such as Habermas, Alfred Schmidt, and Albrecht Wellmer, are also now reaching an English-speaking audience for the first time.[104] In short, Horkheimer's lament to Lowenthal of 1943, that "beyond the

three or four of us there are certainly other hearts and brains that feel
similarly to ours, but we cannot see them, and perhaps they are prevented from expressing themselves,"[105] is no longer the case.

The contrast between the current enthusiasm for the Frankfurt School's work and its relative isolation during the period of exile is
a result of more than intellectual faddism. It expresses something crucial about changes in the climate of ideas in this country. As I have argued elsewhere, a rough pattern of acceptance can be discerned in
America's treatment of the central European refugees who arrived in the
thirties.[106] Those who received the warmest welcome were the emigrés
most closely identified with the aesthetic style which thrived during the
mid-Weimar years known as the *Neue Sachlichkeit* (new objectivity).
Following the self-indulgent subjectivism which marked much of
Expressionist art, literature, and politics, the *Neue Sachlichkeit* soberly
emphasized the power of "facts" and the need for technological pragmatism. In the place of the utopian fervor of the Expressionists, which
had been tarnished by the failure of the German revolutions after the
war, the *Neue Sachlichkeit* offered an uncritical acceptance of the "realities" of Weimar life. Foremost among these were those trends of modernization which the Expressionists had greeted with ambivalence if not
outright hostility. Thus, to take one example, the Bauhaus's frequent
aesthetic manifestos made clear its allegiance to an architecture which

would be *sociologically* objective in its quest for an architecture consonant with
the metropolitan culture of the modern world. . . . It would be *psychically* and
symbolically objective in accepting the clarity, lucidity, tautness, and dynamism
assumed to be the qualities of the modern world.[107]

The striking success of the Bauhaus in America scarcely needs
documentation.[108] Nor does the favorable reception granted to other such
embodiments of the *Neue Sachlichkeit* spirit as the quantitative social
research practiced by Paul Lazarsfeld at Columbia's Bureau of Applied
Social Research or the Logical Positivism of the Vienna Circle. Although
counterexamples could doubtless be given, it can be asserted with some
confidence that America absorbed these emigrés with greater facility and
sympathy than any others.

To anyone familiar with the Weimar cultural scene, this should
come as no surprise, for the *Neue Sachlichkeit* was itself grounded in
an enthusiasm for American technology and pragmatism. As Helmut
Lethen has recently pointed out in what is perhaps the first extensive
study of the *Neue Sachlichkeit*,[109] the middle Weimar years were marked
by a retreat from political hysteria and an eager acceptance of the hope
that, as apparently in America, technological solutions might be found

for social conflict. *"Fordismus"* became the rallying cry of practical intellectuals after Henry Ford's autobiography was translated in 1923; the idea that mass production might provide the material sop to quiet the socially discontented was their implicit faith. Although the reception of *"Fordismus"* in Weimar was by no means unequivocal, a significant and articulate segment of the intellectual community was won over to its support. That their sober and "realistic" confidence in technology as an answer to conflict was as utopian in its own way as the chiliastic politics of certain of the Expressionists was not clear until the Nazis were to give it the lie a few years later.

During the heyday of the *Neue Sachlichkeit,* the Frankfurt School had been highly critical of its political and cultural implications. The clearest expression of this disdain appeared in the aphorisms Horkheimer published in his first year of exile as *Dämmerung* under the pseudonym Heinrich Regius.[110] As Marxists, they still derided the possibility that social conflict could be engineered away. As cultural critics, they saw the spread of *"Fordismus"* tied to the mass culture they found so ideological. As dialecticians, they were suspicious of any attempt to obliterate subjectivity in the name of objective reality. In short, as early as the twenties, the Frankfurt School had begun to criticize the cult of modernity in a way which anticipated their late theoretical work of the 1940s.[111]

As we have seen, in the thirties and forties, Horkheimer and his colleagues were still voices crying in the wilderness. This was due in part to their hostility to the *Neue Sachlichkeit* ethos, which prevented them from fitting in as smoothly in American society as other refugee intellectuals. By the 1960s, however, American opinion had itself shifted away from the cult of technology, instrumental rationality, and depoliticization which characterized the *Neue Sachlichkeit* and colored the selective acceptance of the emigrés. The re-awakened interest in the Frankfurt School, whose members were among the first to offer a sustained critique of those trends without at the same time descending into a sentimentalized, intellectual Luddism, thus suggests that America has reached an important turning point in its historical development. Perhaps the first phase of the intellectual migration's impact is over and a second has only just begun.

4.

The Frankfurt School's Critique of Karl Mannheim and the Sociology of Knowledge

I n its initial contract with the Education Ministry of the city of Frankfurt signed in 1923, the *Institut für Sozialforschung* agreed to provide office space for two university professors on the first floor of its soon-to-be-completed building on the Victoria-Allee. During the early thirties, in the period that began with Max Horkheimer's accession to the directorship and ended with the *Institut*'s forced departure from Germany, the tenants were two scholars of considerable distinction. The first was the political economist Adolph Löwe, recently of the Institute for World Economics in Kiel. Löwe had been a boyhood friend of Horkheimer and his codirector Friedrich Pollock and continued his close association with them during his years in Frankfurt. Together with Paul Tillich, Kurt Riezler, and Karl Mennicke, they met periodically in a small discussion group known as the *Kränzchen,* which retained its coherence for some time after its members regrouped in exile in New York. Although Löwe was a luminary of the New School for Social Research, a center of opposition to the *Institut für Sozialforschung* during its days at Columbia, he remained close friends with Horkheimer and his circle.

The second tenant in the *Institut*'s building was the sociologist of knowledge, Karl Mannheim, who had just moved from the University of Heidelberg to Frankfurt. Although he too was an occasional member of the *Kränzchen,* it appears from the testimony of his former pupil Kurt H. Wolff and others that Mannheim's relations with the *Institut,* unlike Löwe's, were never more than correct.[1] Although all the

First published in *Telos* (Summer 1974), vol. 20.

sources of his distance from the *Institut* cannot be known, it is likely that substantive disagreements were the most responsible. In fact, the first article that Horkheimer ever published was a slashing attack on Mannheim's *Ideology and Utopia,* which appeared in the *Archiv für die Geschichte des Sozialismus und der Arbeiterbewegung* in 1930.[2] That Horkheimer chose Mannheim as the first object of his critical scrutiny is itself significant. More significant still is that in years hence other members of what became known as the Frankfurt School returned again and again to Mannheim and the sociology of knowledge.[3] Max Scheler, the other chief exponent of that nascent discipline during Weimar, was also a frequent target of their attack.[4] Clearly, the sociology of knowledge and the related issues of ideology and true and false consciousness were deemed of great importance by Horkheimer and his colleagues. For with the collapse of both positivism and its historicist alternative, bourgeois and Marxist thinkers alike were faced with the need to establish the ground of their value systems to fend off relativism. The neo-Kantian revival of the prewar years had clearly failed in this task. Bourgeois neo-Kantians like Max Weber withdrew into a stoical resignation when confronted with the irrationality of value choices. Marxist neo-Kantians like Bernstein and Adler could offer little more to overcome the antinomy of facts and values. After the war, which generalized the crisis of meaning well beyond the intellectuals whose preserve it had been before 1914, several new bourgeois alternatives emerged. Existentialism, whose most political exponent was the jurist Carl Schmitt, argued for a decisionism in which men posited their values through irrational action. Another position, equally sinister in its implications, was the *völkish* or social conservative claim that values were "rooted" in a people or race, an answer that historians traditionally include in the pathology of proto-Nazism. Within religious circles, the so-called neo-orthodoxy of Karl Barth turned to unreasoning faith as an antidote to Ernst Troeltsch's failure to ground Christian values in the flux of history. But none of these satisfactorily dealt with the crisis in bourgeois values, a crisis whose origins could not be found in the sphere of culture alone.

A recognition that society rather than culture was the source of the confusion led other intellectuals, either in the Marxist movement or on its fringes, to consider the sociology of knowledge as a possible answer. Broadly speaking, this was the tack taken by the neo-Hegelian Marxists, Georg Lukács, Karl Korsch, and the Frankfurt School. It was also taken, however, by the non-Marxist Karl Mannheim, whose challenge to the Marxist position was all the more important because of a shared stress on the connection between culture and society. In fact, Mannheim's *Ideology and Utopia* has been called by some the bourgeois response to Lukács' *History and Class Consciousness,* at least by those who challenge that attribution to Heidegger's *Being and Time.*[5] Consequently, before one can understand the Frankfurt School's critique of Mannheim, his relationship to Lukács must be clarified, a task made much easier by the research of David Kettler.[6]

From 1916 through 1919, Mannheim and Lukács were members of a circle in their native Budapest known as "The Sprites" *(Szellemkek),* a name derived from the German word *Geist.* Among their associates were Béla Fogarasi, Arnold Hauser, Béla Balázs, and Béla Bartók. Mannheim's essay of 1919, entitled "Soul and Culture," was the leading manifesto of the group, which advocated what Kettler has called "revolutionary culturalism." Although to the left politically, the Sprites were strongly opposed to the mechanical materialism they associated with the Orthodox Marxism of the Second International. Instead, they supported a moral-cultural revolution that derived in part from Ervin Szabó, the leading Hungarian disciple of Georges Sorel. Lukács' sudden conversion to Marxism in December 1918, during the revolutionary turmoil following World War I, thus came as an enormous shock to his colleagues. Although a number of the Sprites were to follow his lead and join the newly created Communist Party, Mannheim did not. He was apparently unaffected by Lukács' political metamorphosis. But on a crucial intellectual level, if Kettler is right, Lukács' transformation did have a profound effect on Mannheim's subsequent thinking, especially after the publication of *History and Class Consciousness.*

The change was most important, at least for our purposes, in his work on the relation between culture and society. In his first study of that relation, "On the Peculiarity of Cultural-sociological Knowledge,"[7] written in 1921 but left unpublished, Mannheim had explicitly rejected the genetic fallacy he saw lurking behind attempts to relate the validity of values to their social origins. He took pains instead to maintain the neutrality of a sociological analysis in judging values. But in a second essay on the same theme written three years later, after Lukács' *History and Class Consciousness,* an essay entitled "A Sociological Theory of Culture and its Knowability,"[8] Mannheim's position had altered drastically. Now the barrier between social function and intrinsic value was broken, at least for a certain type of knowledge he called "conjunctive." By this term, Mannheim meant the moral-cultural-practical knowledge that was the special preserve of the so-called *Geisteswissenschaften.* A more recent student of the sociology of knowledge, Werner Stark, has chosen the term axiological to denote the same area of human concern.[9] Its antithesis, to remain with Mannheim's vocabulary, is "communicative" knowledge, by which he meant the natural sciences with their goal of mastering nature.

This distinction, of course, was a familiar one in central Europe during the first decades of this century. Lukács, however, has been the first to employ it in a Marxist framework in his polemic against Engels' and Kautsky's scientistic rendering of dialectical materialism. What Lukács had done by this integration was to *socialize* the vantage point from which true moral-cultural-practical knowledge, Mannheim's "conjunctive" knowledge, was possible. The prewar theoreticians of the *Geisteswissenschaften* had assumed that this type of knowledge could be obtained independently of the social position of the knower. But for Lukács, only the proletariat could possess the *total* vantage point such knowledge required, because only the proletariat was both the subject and the object of history, a role guaranteed by its pivotal position in the labor process. Behind this epistemological argument, as Lukács acknowledged, was the assumption Giambattista Vico had articulated in the eighteenth century: man can understand the historical world better than the natural world, because only what one makes can one fully comprehend.

In his essay of 1924, Mannheim accepted this critical link between social function and the validity of "conjunctive" knowledge. He also endorsed Lukács' stress on the sociocultural totality, itself a frequently emphasized concept in the 1920s at a time when cultural fragmentation seemed particularly threatening. He went beyond Lukács, however, in also accepting Troeltsch's irrationalist *Gestaltist* notion of totality, which he saw as applicable in certain areas of history where rationalism was not significant, e.g., art history.[10] Finally, he embraced Lukács' argument, which was doubtless current among the Sprites before Lukács's conversion to Marxism, that the rise of bourgeois society meant an unfortunate domination of "communicative" over "conjunctive" knowledge. But where he stopped short of Lukács was in refusing to identify the proletariat with the new bearers of a totalistic moral-cultural-practical orientation. Instead, he turned to the intellectual, whose insight into the totality was understood to be a product of the *Bildung* (self-cultivation) presumably attending the work of cultural sociology, a position also close to Troeltsch's. This was, however, only a way station to his more celebrated treatment of the intellectuals as a collectivity in *Ideology and Utopia.* Here the integration of individual perspectives was the new means through which totalistic knowledge was possible. The partial validity of these perspectives was rooted in each intellectual's social situation, but as a collective they were the least beholden of any social group to a partial vantage point. What Mannheim was later to call "relationism" meant that the relativism suggested by his concept of "total ideology," a relativism implicit in the breakdown of German historicism's essentially religious faith in the inherent meaningfulness of the world,[11] could be overcome through a dynamic synthesis of partial truths. The totality Lukács had sought in the special universal nature of the proletariat, Mannheim claimed to find in the harmonious integration of all the viewpoints represented by the collectivity of "free-floating intellectuals." What made such an integrated viewpoint "true" was its appropriateness as a reflection of the social reality of the period under question. Traditional notions of truth as immutable for all time he rejected as outmoded; truth was historical, but this was not a problem for those who denied the eternal component in the definition of truth.

In his search for a total truth that would be grounded in the social situation of the here and now, Mannheim was clearly accepting Lukács' problematic, if somewhat modified by his continuing adherence to Troeltsch's alternative use of totality as an irrationalist *Gestalt.* But the essay in which Lukács' influence was specifically acknowledged remained unpublished. By 1929 and *Ideology and Utopia,* Mannheim was content to refer to what he called Lukács' "profoundly important work" only in passing, although he did footnote him in his chapter on "The Prospects of Scientific Politics." In the 1931 essay "Wissenssoziologie," appended to later versions of the book, an essay written when Mannheim, according to Kettler, was making every "effort to appear more Weberian than the Weberians,"[12] the tone of his remarks turned more hostile. He singled Lukács out for failing "to distinguish between the problem of unmasking ideologies on the one hand and the sociology of knowledge on the other,"[13] by which he meant the failure to see Marxism as merely one ideology among others and not the standard of truth by which other theories could be measured and found wanting as false consciousness. Because of his unmasking of Marxism in this way, Mannheim has been called a relativist in opposition to Lukács, despite his desperate efforts to salvage truth through relationism. Mannheim has been seen by such commentators as Fritz Ringer and Maurice Mandelbaum as one of the last to grapple with the relativistic implications of historicism and ultimately, like so many others, to have failed.[14]

There is, however, another perspective from which Mannheim's work can be seen. Here the importance of *History and Class Consciousness* is crucial, for although Mannheim repudiated the role assigned by Lukács to the proletariat, he was considerably more faithful in other ways. The first of these was his acceptance, which we have already noted, of the necessary relationship between a social situation and the truth value of the cultural products created in any specific context. Here a link between theory and some version of practice was suggested, although without the connection between practice and the labor process which Marxism demanded. In fact a number of later observers were to stress the element of commitment and action in Mannheim's analysis of the means by which valid "conjunctive" knowledge was to be obtained.[15] His "free-floating intellectuals" were not to be understood as floating amidst the parapets of an ivory tower. On the contrary, their participation in the world they hoped to understand was a precondition for a real contribution to that understanding.

Mannheim was essentially faithful to Lukács in another way as well: in his adherence to the concept of totality, to which he had been committed as early as his 1922 study of the "Structural Analysis of Epistemology."[16] In *Ideology and Utopia,* Mannheim was to write: "The study of intellectual history can and must be pursued in a manner which will see in the sequence and coexistence of phenomena more than mere accidental relationships, and will seek to discover in the totality of the historical complex, the role, significance, and meaning of each component element. It is with this type of sociological approach to history that we identify ourselves."[17] Although Mannheim was careful to disengage himself from what he called the "ontological-metaphysical" reading of the idea of totality in Lukács and seems to have identified more closely with the hypothetical usage of the concept in the work of Ernst Troeltsch,[18] it is clear that a synthetic, holistic impulse was at the root of his attempt to overcome the cultural crisis of his time. His belief that the solution might well be at hand was expressed in his 1924 essay on "Historicism," where he wrote: "the present trend toward synthesis, toward the investigation of totalities may be regarded as the emergence, at the level of reflection, of a force which is pushing a social reality into more collectivist channels."[19] What the force was Mannheim did not specify. Clearly, there was an element of wishful thinking here, as there was in Lukács' identification of the proletariat as the universal class, both subject and object of history. His yearning for synthesis was of such intensity that Karl Popper, for all his other faults, was probably correct in singling out Mannheim as a leading advocate of holism in *The Poverty of Historicism.*[20] In Werner Stark's use of the term, both Lukács and Mannheim were "functionalist" sociologists of knowledge; that is, they assumed that culture and society form a totality with analogous interrelationships among its various constituent elements. Both rejected the "causalist" alternative that posited a centrally determining factor, such as the economic substructure of Orthodox Marxism.

With the relationship between Mannheim and Lukács pre-

sumably a bit clearer, we can now turn to the Frankfurt School's critique of Mannheim and the larger issue of the concept of ideology. When
Lukács finally confronted Mannheim's arguments in an article in *Aufbau*
in 1946, eight years before his diatribe against him in *Die Zerstörung
der Vernunft*, he based his arguments on relatively Orthodox Marxist
grounds.[21] As a result, the task of defending and refining the arguments
of *History and Class Consciousness* from within the Marxist tradition
was left to others outside the orbit of the Communist Party, where such
issues as totality, *praxis*, reification, and the distinction between history
and nature were rarely treated with sophistication, if discussed at all.
Among the first to respond to Mannheim's challenge to Marxism were
the members of the still inchoate Frankfurt School.

In addition to Horkheimer's article in the *Grünberg Archiv*,
to which we will return shortly, *Ideology and Utopia* was subject to
almost immediate scrutiny by Herbert Marcuse in an article in Rudolf
Hilferding's *Die Gesellschaft* in 1929.[22] At that time, Marcuse was not
yet a member of the *Institut für Sozialforschung*, which he joined only
shortly before its departure from Germany. In fact, he was still very much
a student of Martin Heidegger, whose philosophy he attempted to reconcile with Marxism in a number of essays written before his entrance
into the *Institut*'s circle in 1932.[23] But despite what can be seen as its
impure status as a Frankfurt School response to Mannheim, Marcuse's
article should be examined for its anticipation of later points made by
his future colleagues, as well as for its positing of other arguments that
they, and later Marcuse himself, would reject.

What immediately strikes the reader of the piece is Marcuse's surprisingly favorable attitude towards *Ideology and Utopia*. The
central problem of the contemporary period, he argued, was discussed
in Mannheim's book, that problem being the universal historicity of human existence and the correspondingly questionable nature of the traditional separation of real and ideal being. Mannheim, Marcuse noted
with approval, recognized the inevitably temporal dimension of all cultural phenomena, as well as their situational relatedness. In fact, even
when applied to Marxism itself, which Mannheim reduced to the particular ideology of the working class, these arguments served a useful
function in Marcuse's eyes. For what Mannheim did was to free Marxism from the transcendental, ahistorical status accorded it by the Revisionists and Neo-Kantians such as Max Adler and thereby reveal it as the
concrete theory of proletarian *praxis*. In so doing, he restored the relationship between theory and practice which the Revisionist and Orthodox theoreticians of the Second International alike had denied. Still
another virtue of Mannheim's analysis, as Marcuse interpreted it, was his

undermining of the assumption that truth is timeless. Like Marx, he recognized that the historical conditioning of a theory does not necessarily call its validity into question. As a result, the old antithesis of relativism and absolutism could no longer be grounded in the notion that truth and immutability were synonymous.

Having thus praised Mannheim, however, Marcuse was quick to point to a number of inadequacies in his version of the sociology of knowledge. Mannheim was perhaps at his worst on the question of true and false consciousness, a distinction that Marcuse as a Marxist was anxious to retain. To call consciousness "true" when it corresponded to the given social reality of the group which spawned it and "false" when it was incompatible with that reality failed for several reasons. First was the problem of the means by which an appropriate correspondence of thought to social being might be ascertained. Nowhere did Mannheim really provide a mechanism by which such a decision might be made. Second was the inadequacy of Mannheim's treatment of the "social being" to which ideologies were to correspond. To Marcuse, Mannheim's understanding of society was undialectical, lacking an appreciation of what he called the "intentional" character of social being. That is, Mannheim reified society as a given and missed the constitutive role consciousness itself played in the creation of social reality. To posit a fixed social being which unreciprocally conditions thought was to fall back to a pre-Lukácsian, indeed pre-Marxist materialism. Third, Mannheim's hope for a dynamic synthesis of partial viewpoints into a total truth valid for a specific period in history could not be realized because the concrete preconditions for such a reconciliation were left unexplored in Mannheim's theory of the free-floating intelligentsia. The necessity of mediations between or among different, even contradictory viewpoints was lost in Mannheim's harmonistic belief in the possibility of a grand synthesis of partial views. What was to happen, Marcuse implied, if Mannheim's relationist symphony played out of tune? Fourth, Marcuse argued that Mannheim's attempt to judge a theory's worth by its relation to a specific social situation was only partially successful, for there is—and here Marcuse the Heideggerian was speaking—a transcendent dimension to truth. Historical facticity was part of a deeper structural reality which had to serve as the final court of appeal for the validity of a theory, and then only in the long run.

This last argument, the appeal to long-run historical processes as the court of last resort, was later to become a major element in the Frankfurt School's critique of pragmatism.[24] That Mannheim himself was something more than a pragmatist can be grasped from his expression of concern over the decline of utopian thought in *Ideology and Utopia*,[25] a fear the Frankfurt School itself was frequently to voice. But Marcuse, like Horkheimer after him, paid little attention to this common sentiment and focused instead on Mannheim's failure to integrate the utopian into his epistemology, which he saw as essentially pragmatist in inclination.

Marcuse finished his review on a positive note, the last time such a note would be sounded by a Frankfurt School member in discussing Mannheim. According to Marcuse, Mannheim's historicization of knowledge, with its reopening of the question of theory and practice, had helped recapture the "ground of genuine decision without which existence in the world *(Dasein)* cannot exist in the long run."[26] This conclusion is striking not only because it links Marcuse to the existential decisionism which he was to criticize in the work of Carl Schmitt only a few years later,[27] but also because it was directly opposed to Horkheimer's appraisal of Mannheim in "A New Concept of Ideology?" published in the following year.

To Horkheimer, there was no real connection between theory and practice in Mannheim's thinking. Whereas Marx had wanted the transformation of society, Mannheim was only interested in the salvation of a totalistic view of cognition. In the language of an article Horkheimer was not to write until seven years later, the sociology of knowledge was thus a "traditional" rather than "critical" theory.[28] Mannheim was still in the historicist tradition of *Geistesgeschichte* with its unwarranted belief in the meaningfulness of the world. The very goal of total knowledge, Horkheimer argued, betrayed an underlying acceptance of the classical German Idealist notion of a transcendent subject capable of a harmonious, all-embracing view of the whole. Such a hypostatized subject did not, indeed could not, exist in a contradictory world. As long as men did not rationally plan their history, social contradictions could not end. Thus, even though Mannheim had a relativistic moment in his belief in "total ideology," a metaphysical, absolutist residue remained in his quest for the means to overcome partiality. Indeed, to speak of *partial* ideologies was only possible if the absolutist notion of total truth was lurking in the shadows. In fact, Horkheimer argued, Mannheim's desire for totality suggested the undialectical holism of the *Gestalt* psychologists and harkened back to Hegel's hypostatized *Volksgeist* with its attendant suppression of concrete subjectivity. Mannheim also fell back behind Marx to Hegel in minimizing the social contradictions which refused to be harmoniously reconciled at the present time.

In so arguing, Horkheimer expressed that abhorrence of identity theory which was to surface in more obvious ways during the later years of the Frankfurt School, especially after the entrance of Theodor W. Adorno into *Institut* affairs on a full-time basis in 1938. In attacking Mannheim's holism, Horkheimer was also criticizing Lukács' version of the same theme, at least implicitly. This article was the first example of the Frankfurt School's growing distance from Marxist Humanism as it has traditionally been understood, a distance I have attempted to trace elsewhere.[29] Neither the proletariat in its imputed role as the subject and object of history, nor the free-floating intelligentsia with their symphony of partial viewpoints could really attain a total view of truth, for truth did not reside in the totality, at least not yet.

On most other points, Horkheimer and Marcuse were very much at one in their criticism of Mannheim. Like his future colleague, Horkheimer dismissed the notion of judging truth or falsehood by the timeliness of the theory in relation to the social reality it purported to reflect. Like Marcuse, he attacked the notion of "social relatedness" as undialectical without a critique of social existence itself. Lacking this analysis, Mannheim had regressed back to Hegel's metaphysical notion of Being in his *Logic.* Even Mannheim's celebrated study of "Conservative Thought," so Horkheimer claimed, failed to provide a concrete analysis of social reality, remaining instead on the levels of a "phenomenological-logical analysis of style," an "immanent analysis of *Weltanschauungen,*" or other essentially intellectual historical categories.

Clearly Horkheimer was far more hostile to the sociology of knowledge than Marcuse, seeing it as a perversion of the critical idea of ideology in the Marxist tradition with ultimately conformist implications. Significantly, he did not repeat Marcuse's claim that Mannheim was useful in pointing out that Marxism was the theoretical expression of the *praxis* of the working class. Even though he fervently argued for the necessity of transforming rather than merely understanding the world, he refrained from naming the agency assigned by history to accomplish that task. As a consequence, Lukács' solution to the question of how one might acquire a valid understanding of the world, a solution rooted in the belief that one could understand what one made, could not be embraced by the Frankfurt School. On the positive side of the ledger, this meant that they did not delude themselves, as Lukács did, and believe that the Party spoke for the masses on the basis of an "imputed class consciousness." But on the negative side, it meant that the door was open for what might be described as a neo-Mannheimian solution to the problem of true and false consciousness. For in later years, the Frankfurt School would come to believe that true consciousness rested in the minds of certain critical theorists who were able, for reasons they did not wholly explore, to avoid the gravitational pull of the prevailing universe of discourse.[30] To be sure, these theorists and their unwitting allies in the art

world did not achieve a total, synthetic perspective, as Mannheim had
hoped; they had to be satisfied instead with fragmentary negations of
the status quo in the name of a superior possibility whose outlines they
could only dimly perceive. In this they were less affirmative and harmonistic than Mannheim's free-floating intelligentsia. But in terms of their
social rootedness, they began to approach the very status more traditional Marxists have always scorned as characteristic of petit-bourgeois
intellectuals who consider themselves above class. Only Walter Benjamin, himself a relatively peripheral figure in the *Institut*'s circle, would
try to argue against this tendency in their thinking, and without much
success because of his closeness to the distrusted Bertolt Brecht.[31]

Unfortunately, no real sensitivity to this problem was evident in the next major Frankfurt School statement on Mannheim, Adorno's 1953 essay on *Man and Society in the Age of Reconstruction*, which
Mannheim had published during his exile in England in 1940.[32] In many
ways, Adorno's arguments duplicated those made in the earlier critiques
of his colleagues. "Like its existentialist counterpart," Adorno wrote, "[the
sociology of knowledge] calls everything into question and criticizes
nothing."[33] Mannheim erroneously took social phenomena at face value,
his notion of totality glorified "the social process itself as an evening-
out of the contradictions in the whole,"[34] his reliance on the intelligentsia was a justification for elitism, and so on. Where Adorno struck a
new note was in charging Mannheim with being at once positivistic and
idealistic. Mannheim's English experience, reinforcing his growing
movement to the right, had driven him away from the Troeltsch-Lukác-
sian source of many of his earlier ideas. In fact, the English translation
of *Ideology and Utopia* in 1936 had moved it in a far more pragmatist
direction than the German original. As Adorno noted, the positivist side
was expressed in his naive reliance on "facts" which could be generalized into causal laws. The very search for alleged examples of general
laws was highly undialectical in that general laws themselves are hypo-
statizations of a more fluid reality. The latent idealism resulted from a
similar source: the research for abstract laws which rule history, a search
which mirrored Mannheim's new fetish of planning with its potentially
authoritarian implications.

Having leveled these and other charges, including an attack
on what he saw as Mannheim's crude psychologism, Adorno failed to
come to grips with the central challenge of the sociology of knowledge
as we have noted it above: what is the Archimedean point in which a
true consciousness can be said to be grounded? Having long since abandoned Lukács' faith in the proletariat, having nothing but scorn for
Mannheim's intellectual class with its implied role of advising the polit-

ically powerful, Adorno offered no real alternative which transcended idealism. The closest he came was in the following sentence: "The answer to Mannheim's reverence for the intelligentsia as 'free-floating' is to be found not in the reactionary postulate of its 'rootedness in Being' [presumably the Heideggerean position], but rather in the reminder that the very intelligentsia that pretends to float freely is fundamentally rooted in the very being that must be changed and which it merely pretends to criticize."[35] What is lacking in this sentence is the confidence that true knowledge comes through the very process of changing society. The intellectual, either as an individual or as a group, could not serve as the agent of change. How then certain of their number possessed access to truth, albeit in its negative, fragmentary form, the Frankfurt School could not really say.

After Adorno's attack on *Man and Society in an Age of Reconstruction,* only three years went by until the Frankfurt School's next serious encounter with the issues raised by the sociology of knowledge. In 1956, an article on "Ideology" jointly written by members of the *Institut,* by then once again in Frankfurt, appeared in a volume entitled *Soziologische Exkurse,* recently translated as *Aspects of Sociology.*[36] In the article, the problem of the grounding of knowledge was put aside for a more urgent question: the potential obsolesence of the concept of ideology itself. This fear reflected the Frankfurt School's growing pessimism about the closing off of negation in what Marcuse was to call "one-dimensional society." As usual, Adorno had been the first to sound the tocsin. In the early 1940s, he wrote an article entitled "Cultural Criticism and Society," later reprinted in *Prisms,* in which he warned, "There are no more ideologies in the authentic sense of false consciousness, only advertisements for the world through its duplication and the provocative lie which does not seek belief but commands silence."[37] This argument, which might ironically be called the Frankfurt School's version of the end-of-ideology, grew out of their belief that liberal society was being replaced by an almost totally "administered world" in which ideological justifications were no longer necessary. The full ramifications of this development were spelled out in the 1956 collective essay.

The very existence of ideology, its authors contended, was historical in nature. Only at the beginning of the bourgeois world, when Francis Bacon had developed his theory of the Idols, or collective prejudices, did the concept first appear. Although Bacon had universalized the Idols to apply to all men at all times, by the Enlightenment and Helvétius and Holbach, the social origins of ideology were beginning to be understood. Bourgeois society needed ideological justification because of its antagonistic character, at once universal and particular. The universal tenets of liberalism were needed to hide the contradictions of class society. Moreover, the possibility of a universal ideology rested on the bourgeois supposition of rational men with an equal access to discursive logic. This egalitarian premise, although only formal in character, was crucial in creating the dialectical potential of ideology in the bourgeois world. That is, substantive ideologies could be confronted with their own truth, which rested in the rational, egalitarian kernel inherent in their attempt at universal justification.

By the mid-twentieth century, however, these conditions had ceased to exist. The change was most apparent when looking at Nazism, where naked power relations no longer really needed universalist ideologies to justify them. The buffering mediations of bourgeois society— the free market place, civil liberties, the *Rechtstaat*— were all suspended by the Nazis, who ruled through psychological and political mechanisms that approached a pure form of Hegel's master-slave relationship. The Nazis did not have an ideology in the classical bourgeois sense; their propaganda was a "manipulative contrivance, a mere instrument of power."[38]

Accordingly, the critique of ideology as false consciousness was itself increasingly problematical, for the rational kernel in universal justifications was absent. This change was reflected in the theoretical sphere most clearly in Pareto's cynical reduction of all ideas to derivations of irrational residues, but it had echoes as well in Mannheim's concept of "total ideology," which was incapable of dealing with false consciousness as a reality. In fact, although he did not acknowledge it, Mannheim had returned to the days of Francis Bacon with his ahistorical Idols applicable to all men. Besides the loss engendered by the jettisoning of liberal universalism, even in its formal guise, another critical aspect of the traditional notion of ideology had been lost in Mannheim's work: the truth value latent in the assumption that ideology transcended social roots. The so-called "culture industry" had destroyed the independent moment in ideologies, which had existed in a less administered time. The very idea of "total ideology," the Frankfurt School argued, expressed a rage against the possibility of a superior future. "With the crisis of bourgeois society," they wrote, "the traditional concept of ideology itself appears to lose its subject matter. Spirit is split into critical truth, divesting itself of illusion, but esoteric and alienated from the direct social connections of effective action, on the one hand, and the planned administrative control of that which once was ideology, on the other."[39]

Needless to say, this pessimistic conclusion was a far cry from Marcuse's 1929 review of *Ideology and Utopia* with its praise for

Mannheim's understanding of the relations between theory and practice, and an even further one from Lukács' insistence that only the proletariat, and its spokesmen, could achieve an undistorted view of reality through their creation of the social world. The article, like much of the Frankfurt School's postwar work, expressed a gloom that can itself perhaps be called one-dimensional. The model of unmediated power relations so blatant that they needed no justification, a model extrapolated from Nazism, soon, in fact, proved inadequate, although it had provided a powerful insight into the potential direction of all late capitalist societies. By the time of *One-dimensional Man* in 1964 and the more recent work of Jürgen Habermas, especially his essay, "Technology and Science as 'Ideology,' "[40] the Frankfurt School was once again using the concept of ideology to denote false consciousness. But in these works, the ideology singled out for debunking was no longer the classical bourgeois notions of civil liberties, free enterprise, and the *Rechtstaat;* instead, they focused on the new ideology of technology and instrumental rationalism as an answer to social conflict, an illusory belief reflected in the then fashionable assumption that ideology had itself ended.

Even Adorno, the most insistent advocate of the total oppressiveness of our "administered world," began to accept the reality of this new ideology. In addition, he pointed to an even greater ideological threat in his *Negative Dialectics:* the philosophical search for first principles or an underlying identity of elements amidst the contradictions of social reality. "Identity is the primal form of ideology," he argued. "Identity becomes the authority for a doctrine of adjustment, in which the object—which the subject is supposed to go by—repays the subject for what the subject has done to it. . . . The critique of ideology is thus not something peripheral and intrascientific, not something limited to the objective mind and to the products of the subjective mind. Philosophically, it is central: it is a critique of the constitutive consciousness itself."[41]

In so arguing, Adorno was seemingly rejecting the notion of Archimedean points as such. In his polemic against Heidegger, Adorno sought to undermine the primacy of such concepts, or better put, preconceptual realities, as Being. Anything smacking of ontology was itself ideological in that reality was inherently contradictory and thus irreducible to any one of its elements. A moment of false consciousness necessarily adhered to the belief that philosophy could adequately conceptualize reality. As the title of his book implied, the correct position was that of a negative dialectics that defied reconciliation.

And yet it can be argued that the Frankfurt School—if such a term can still be applied to such increasingly disparate thinkers as

Adorno, Habermas, and Marcuse—had not fully freed itself of the need to establish the ground of a "true" consciousness. Habermas was the most candid in acknowledging the need. In *Knowledge and Human Interests* he sought the answer not in history, as Lukács and the early Frankfurt School had done, but in a brand of philosophical anthropology instead. The three cognition-directing interests he posited were understood to be grounded in the necessary conditions for the production and repro- duction of human life itself; a technical interest in the mastery of na- ture, a hermeneutic interest in widened intersubjective communication, and an emancipatory interest in the liberation from illegitimate author- ity and distorted communications. The concept of ideology was useful in unmasking an attempt by any one of these—in the modern world, the technical interest in mastering nature—to assert its absolute hegemony over the others.[42]

Although Habermas' typology was his own, his attempt to dehistoricize the ground of truth was anticipated in the later work of his elders in the Frankfrut School. As the early faith in the world-histor- ical role of the proletariat was shattered, the Frankfurt School moved further and further away from a Lukácsian insistence on the relation be- tween truth and action, which, as we have seen, was dimly echoed in Mannheim's stress on the commitment of his free-floating intellectuals. In the postwar era, Marcuse's decisionist tone of 1929 was completely muted. The appeal to philosophical truth in a manner uncomfortably close to that condemned by Horkheimer in his seminal essay, "Traditional and Critical Theory," began to creep into their writings. In fact, as early as 1937, Marcuse had written: "When Critical Theory comes to terms with philosophy, it is interested in the truth content of philosophical con- cepts and problems. It presupposes that they really contain truth. The enterprise of the sociology of knowledge, to the contrary, is occupied only with the untruths, not the truths of previous philosophies."[43] These same sentiments were repeated in Adorno's *Negative Dialectics,* almost three decades later:

A sociology of knowledge fails before philosophy: for the truth content of philos- ophy it substitutes its social function and its conditioning by interests while re- fraining from a critique of that content itself. . . . . In the realm of objective truth, materialist dialectics necessarily turns philosophical—despite, and because of, all its criticisms of philosophy. A sociology of knowledge, on the other hand, denies not only the objective structure of society but the idea of truth and its cognition.[44]

In the light of earlier Frankfurt School pronouncements on the sociology of knowledge, these statements suggest an important shift, one which was a response to changed social conditions as the Frankfurt

School understood them. First, they are noteworthy because they attribute to Mannheim a relativism that is the exact opposite of the absolutism for which Horkheimer had chastised him in his 1930 essay, "A New Concept of Ideology?" And in so doing, it seems to me, they are far less accurate in their description of Mannheim's intentions than Horkheimer had been. Second, they are striking because of the extent to which they suggest the departure of the Frankfurt School from a "functionalist" sociology of knowledge in Werner Stark's sense, which was present in both Lukács and Mannheim. That is, the Frankfurt School no longer accepted the existence of a totality in which thought and institutions, superstructure and substructure have essentially analogical relations. Instead, they approached the position Stark identifies as that of "elective affinity," which he sees operating in the work of Max Weber and Max Scheler. Here the argument is that ideas and social reality may intersect at times in history and reinforce one another, but there is no simple analogical parallel between them and certainly no causal connection. Such an attitude may, in fact, be said to have always been latent in the Frankfurt School's distrust of identity theory, most clearly articulated in Adorno's idea of a negative dialectic without positive reconciliation. For truth must always refer to something transcending the present social reality. At a time when the one-dimensionality of society meant that no social agency was on the horizon to actualize the Marxist dream, it would be impossible to find a social parallel to a truly negative philosophy.

But what saves the Frankfurt School from a complete identification with the Weber-Scheler position is the muted hope, strongest in Marcuse and weakest in Adorno, that such a reconciled totality might be a future reality. For even amidst the incessant admonitions against identity in *Negative Dialectics,* the following admission is made: "Dialectical reason's own essence has come to be and will pass, like antagonistic society." [45]

Thus, there is an Archimedean point in the Frankfurt School's thinking that is employed as a standard against which false consciousness can be measured. It is not the production of the world by a proletariat which is inherently a universal class, both the subject and object of history, nor the collective perspective of a class of free-floating intellectuals whose integrated views illuminate a harmonious totality in the here and now. The Archimedean point of Critical Theory is the reconciled totality that will accompany the end of the story, similar to the type of synoptic view one gets at the very end of Proust's *Remembrance of Things Past.* Although it is impossible to flesh out this fulfilled condition and give it concrete substance—an impossibility Horkheimer would come to explain by a reference to the Jewish taboo on naming or picturing God—it functions nonetheless as the ultimate ground of cognition.

It is in this spirit, I would argue in conclusion, that one might loosely interpret Walter Benjamin's fascination for Paul Klee's painting, "Angelus Novus." The picture as Benjamin describes it in his *Theses on the Philosophy of History* "shows an angel looking as though he is about to move away from something he is fixedly contemplating. His eyes are staring, his mouth is open, his wings are spread. This is how one pictures the angel of history," Benjamin explains. "His face is turned toward the past. Where we perceive a chain of events, he sees one single catastrophe which keeps piling wreckage upon wreckage and hurls it in front of his feet. The angel would like to stay, awaken the dead, and make whole what has been smashed. But a storm is blowing from Paradise; it has got caught in its wings with such violence that the angel can no longer close them. This storm irresistibly propels him into the future to which his back is turned, while the pile of debris before him grows skyward. This storm is what we call progress."[46]

Fragments of the truth, so the Frankfurt School believed, can be found among the debris, but the whole truth is only visible to the angel as he retreats into the future. An almost Kantian agnosticism about the limits of reason began to reemerge in their writings. Without a faith in angels or the usefulness of final reconciliations as the ground of truth, however, the rest of us may well be left with the feeling that, as in other instances, the Frankfurt School has punctured the claims of rival theoretical positions without, alas, offering a truly satisfactory alternative. For from the point of view of Horkheimer's "Traditional and Critical Theory"—that is, from an immanent vantage point within the Frankfurt School's own tradition—the challenge of the sociology of knowledge to the doctrine of true and false consciousness has not yet been convincingly refuted.

5.

Anti-Semitism
and the Weimar Left

On page 121 of *Behemoth,* Franz Neumann's classic study of Nazism, there appears a curious and arresting sentence. It reads as follows: "The writer's personal conviction, paradoxical as it may seem, is that the German people are the least anti-Semitic of all."[1] The sentence was written in 1942, before the full extent of Nazi policy was known, but was retained in the revised edition two years later, by which time the outlines of the Holocaust were clearly visible. In the second edition, Neumann did add a short appendix on the implications of the worsening situation, but only to reaffirm his belief that anti-Semitism was imposed from above and lacked widespread popular support. "The extermination of the Jews," he wrote, "is only the means to the attainment of the ultimate objective, namely the destruction of free institutions, beliefs, and groups. This may be called the spearhead theory of anti-Semitism."[2]

Neumann's denial of the popular basis of German hatred for the Jews is striking for two reasons. The first is the challenge it presents to the conventional wisdom that Nazism had a fertile ground in German culture and history, an assumption that has been given scholarly credence through the work of George Mosse, Peter Pulzer, Paul Massing, Peter Viereck, and many others.[3] No such effort has been expended in the examination of other nations' anti-Semitic traditions, so that the comparative claim in Neumann's statement would be hard to test, but the extent of the German evidence is such that the implied exoneration in his argument is still startling.

But if Neumann's remarks serve to upset one element of the conventional wisdom, they tend to buttress another, which is the second reason why they warrant our attention. For Neumann was a Marx-

First published in *Midstream* (January 1974), 20(1).

ist, and as has often been observed, Marxists, beginning with the founder himself and his controversial reply to Bruno Bauer on the Jewish question in 1843, have tended to deny the uniqueness of anti-Semitic oppression. That is, they have tended to subsume it under the more general rubric of the exploitation of the working class and as a result have relegated it to a secondary role. Or worse, at times they have even condoned Judeophobia, implicitly or explicitly, as an expression of anticapitalistic resentments. Here too scholarly research, most notably that of Edmund Silberner and George Lichtheim, has helped to confirm the image of left-wing myopia regarding anti-Semitism.[4]

The irony of this situation has not been lost on those who have been hostile to the libertarian pretensions of socialism, especially when, as in the case of Neumann and of course Marx himself, the socialists in question were from Jewish backgrounds, however assimilated. To many aroused by the bitter fruits of ethnic self-denial in the name of a more universal identification, Marxism has therefore seemed seriously deficient in understanding the multiple wellsprings of human misery, some of which defy reduction to a common denominator. As one example of the forms this disillusionment can take, Isaiah Berlin has argued that Moses Hess surpassed Marx in prescience because he was shrewd enough to move from socialism to a combination of Zionism and socialism.[5] Arguments of this type have become more frequent in recent years with the intensified furor over Soviet treatment of Russian Jews and the rising leftist identification with the Palestinian cause.

At no time in modern history, however, has the relationship between anti-Semitism and Marxism been as heatedly discussed as during the interwar years in Germany. Despite the melancholy fact that the issue is no longer really relevant on German soil itself, the questions it raised are perennial enough to warrant opening up old wounds in order to set the historical record straight. What in fact was the response of the Weimar left to Judeophobia? How serious was the threat itself? How representative was Neumann's denial of the popular basis of the phenomenon? Although definitive answers to these and similar questions are still to be ascertained, recent research has allowed us to refine some of the vaguer generalizations usually made on this topic. In what follows, I will try to suggest some of the directions taken by this research, including my own investigations of the Frankfurt *Institut für Sozialforschung.*

The peculiar dilemma of the Weimar left, as those who have defended themselves against the charge of self-hatred have been quick to point out, arose from the fact that the right often accused socialism of being itself a Jewish invention. Many even went so far as to charge that the newly founded republic was also inspired and controlled by Jewish politicians. That the reality was clearly otherwise, especially after the first few years of the new order,[6] did little to undercut the charge. The dilemma was experienced with particular keenness by leftists of Jewish origin, however broadly defined, who found themselves in a painful double bind. If they acknowledged their ethnic roots, they gave ammunition to the right; if they denied them, they were open to accusations of self-hatred and cowardice. All of this was severely complicated by the highly uncertain character of Jewish identity itself, a problem whose difficulties need not be belabored here. The Nuremberg Laws, whatever else they did, at least helped to end the confusion over the definition of Jewishness, a confusion which runs throughout the Weimar left's attempt to grapple with anti-Semitism.

In the light of these considerations, it is not surprising to find certain Socialists of Jewish origin retreating into the comforting illusion that anti-Semitism had no other major source than the manipulation of the masses from above by various ruling circles. To many apparently assimilated German Jews, socialist or otherwise, the Jewish question thus appeared all but already solved, despite efforts by rightwing groups to keep it artificially alive. That Neumann was by no means atypical in holding this view became clear to me during the course of my recent research on the *Institut für Sozialforschung,* which Neumann himself joined in 1936, two years after its transfer from Europe to New York. A sizable majority of the *Institut*'s membership, and even more overwhelmingly of its inner circle later to be known as the Frankfurt School, came from a Jewish background. Yet all the living ex-members with whom I spoke expressed views similar to their former colleague's. In fact, when I circulated drafts of the first chapter of my study in which I discussed the possible impact of their ethnic origins on their theoretical positions, the response was swift and almost unanimous disapproval.

In the words of Friedrich Pollock, the *Institut*'s associate director for many years, "All of us, up to the last years before Hitler, had no feeling of insecurity originating from our ethnic descent. Unless we were ready to undergo baptism, certain positions in public service and business were closed to us, but that never bothered us. And under the Weimar Republic many of these barriers had been moved away."[7] Even more emphatic were the disclaimers of Felix J. Weil, the financial sponsor of the *Institut* and other leftwing ventures such as the Malik Verlag and the Piscator Stage. "Discrimination against Jews," he wrote me, "had retreated completely to the 'social club level.' "[8] Thus, the *Institut*'s indifference to the importance of anti-Semitism was justified by the objective situation in Weimar. In more than a score of letters, Weil exhorted me to ignore the Jewish questions entirely in my treatment of the *Institut*; to bring it up once again, he contended, would play into the hands of earlier detractors who had "explained" the *Institut*'s radicalism by pointing to the cosmopolitan roots of its personnel.

Although this was advice I was ultimately to reject as no longer apposite in a time when passions had cooled, I was troubled by the cumulative testimony of a number of participants in the period itself, testimony which supported Neumann's paradoxical assertion. Perhaps, I speculated, historians had been misled by extrapolating Nazi anti-Semitism back too far into the German past. Although Mosse, Pulzer, and others had found numerous examples of "protofascism" in German history, might it not be argued that explorations of similar thoroughness into other national histories would produce equally damaging evidence? Thus, for example, France with its Dreyfus case, its Action Française, and its advocates of a "Better Hitler than Blum" policy might in fact support Neumann's generalization that Germany was the least anti-Semitic European country. Other obvious competitors would include Russia, Poland, Rumania, and the Austria which had spawned Hitler himself. The *Ostjuden*, after all, had reasons for flooding into Germany from the east. Seen in proper perspective, then, the German socialists' indifference to anti-Semitism, so often seen as ideological blindness or, in the case of Jewish socialists, as self-hatred, might be claimed to have had a certain objective justification.

Further support for this suspicion appeared in Geoffrey Barraclough's articles on German historiography in 1972 in *The New York Review of Books*.[9] According to Barraclough, Donald L. Niewyk's monograph, *Socialist, Anti-Semite, and Jew*,[10] argues against the exaggeration of anti-Semitism during Weimar. In his words, "as Donald Niewyk has pointed out, it was an 'irritant' rather than a major problem, and no one took Nazi anti-Semitism 'very seriously' until long after 1933."[11] If this were in fact true, then the testimony of Neumann, Pollock, Weil, and others I had spoken with on the issue had been given scholarly confirmation for the first time.

But happily for the conventional wisdom and my own sense of the realities of the Weimar situation, it turns out that Barraclough had distorted Niewyk as he had a number of other historians treated in his survey (a salient example being his transformation of Fritz Stern from an exponent of liberal historiography into its leading critic). For instead of minimizing the importance of anti-Semitism in Weimar, Niewyk argues that the years immediately after 1918 produced "anti-Semitism of greater violence than any experienced in Germany since the middle ages."[12] The sentence from which Barraclough had extracted the word "irritant" in order to diminish the importance of the phenomenon reads as follows: "Although the early postwar agitation reached its greatest intensity from the revolution through the Kapp putsch and again during the inflationary crisis of 1923, it remained a serious irritant throughout the period 1918–1928."[13] Moreover, as Niewyk later points out, the years after 1928 were even more extensively rife with anti-Jewish agitation.

As for Barraclough's assertion that no one took the problem very seriously until long after 1933, the sentence in Niewyk's book directly after the one just quoted states, albeit with some hyperbole: "The SPD was forced to realize that occasional denunciations of discrimination against Jews would no longer suffice at a time when pogroms after the Russian model threatened to add to Germany's postwar chaos."[14] In fact, if one had to characterize Niewyk's central thesis, it would be that the SPD, although failing to realize the full seriousness of the threat, did respond to rightwing anti-Semitism frequently and with considerable vigor. This included, among other things, swallowing class consciousness and working at times with the essentially bourgeois Central Association of German Citizens of the Jewish Faith, the most outspoken defense organization of German Jewry.[15] It also included, at least for a few SPD theoreticians, going beyond the simple rationalistic model of political behavior that usually informed socialist thinking—a model whose weaknesses have drawn the criticism of later historians like Erich Matthias.[16] As Niewyk shows, certain SPD spokesmen, to be sure still a minority, developed sophisticated psychological explanations of the power of Judeophobia, some of which anticipated in detail the "reaction to modernization" analysis fashionable among many historians in our own day. Thus, to Niewyk, the SPD provided the "most important source of organized support"[17] for the beleaguered Jewish community in Weimar.

This is not to say, of course, that he finds no fault with the SPD record, especially with its reluctance to abandon a conspiracy theory to account for anti-Semitism, a late variant of which we have seen in Neumann's "spearhead theory." He also levels the curious charge that however extensive the SPD's campaign against anti-Semitism, it never matched the proportionate amount of time devoted by the Nazis themselves to Jew-baiting. This is answerable on the grounds that the SPD's strength, such as it was, lay in whatever positive programs it could offer rather than in defensive counter-Nazi propaganda. Spending even more time refuting the right, as Niewyk suggests it should have been doing, would have decreased still further the SPD's chances of building a positive program to deal with the crises of the republic.

These, however, are only marginal criticisms of a book which goes a long way towards redeeming the left's record in dealing with the anti-Semitism in Weimar, whose virulence Niewyk, supporting the conventional wisdom, ratifies. Or, more precisely put, the book helps redeem the record of one faction on the left, having as it does little to say about other leftist groups besides the SPD. One of the most confusing elements in the whole discussion about the left and anti-Semitism has of course been a lack of discrimination over which segment of the left is meant when a generalization is made. This murkiness has also affected arguments about the related question of the Jewish composition, defined in whatever manner, of the factions themselves. For example, a few years ago in *Commentary*,[18] Lewis Wurgaft reviewed George Mosse's *Germans and Jews* and endorsed Mosse's contention that Weimar's "leftwing intellectuals" had been predominantly Jewish. This assertion had been confirmed through his own research into the circle of so-called Activists around Kurt Hiller as well as by Istvan Deak's earlier study of the writers for the leftwing journal, *Die Weltbühne*.[19]

Shortly after Wurgaft's review was printed, an angry rebuttal appeared in *Commentary*'s letter columns by Henry Pachter, himself a distinguished Jewish socialist emigré.[20] According to Pachter, Wurgaft and Mosse had fallen prey to rightwing propaganda about the predominatly Jewish nature of the Weimar left. In the manner of Felix Weil in his private correspondence with me, he berated Wurgaft for repeating unsubstantiated generalizations without empirical support. Thus, for example, of the 81 Communist Party deputies to the Reichstag in 1932, not one, he pointed out, was Jewish. Nor were there ever more than a "few" SPD leaders who were themselves Jewish; even the nonparty leftwing opposition consisted of gentiles like Kurt Schumacher, a Christian Socialist, Carl von Ossietzky, the editor of *Die Weltbühne*, and Erwin Piscator, the director whose theater often staged the works of another non-Jewish Marxist, Bertolt Brecht.

Pachter's examples were sound and of course many others could have been given; but what he failed to do, as Wurgaft pointed out in his reply, was to distinguish among the various factions of the left. That there were no Jewish deputies in the Communist delegation to the Reichstag in 1932 was no surprise, the party having lost whatever Jewish leadership it once had had in the days of Ruth Fischer and Paul Levi during the process of Bolshevization in the early and mid-twenties. But the KPD was by no means representative of the left as a whole. In the SPD, according to Niewyk's figures, approximately 10 percent of the party leadership was Jewish, a significantly larger representation of Jews than in the population as a whole (564,000 out of 62,400,000 in 1925—less than 1 percent). Although this might correspond to Pachter's claim that "few" leaders were Jewish and although it clearly does not mean Jewish domination of the party, it certainly suggests a disproportionately high Jewish presence in the inner councils of the SPD.

But it is not until one looks at the so-called "homeless left," the party socialists meant by Mosse, Deak, and Wurgaft when they talk about the "leftwing intellectuals," that the really significant correspondence occurs. Of the sixty-eight writers for the *Weltbühne* whose ethnic backgrounds Deak was able to ascertain, some forty-two were of Jewish descent, two were half Jewish, and twenty-four were gentile.[21] Thus, although it is incorrect to talk about the predominantly Jewish nature of the Weimar left as a whole, it is valid to point to certain of its segments and admit that Jews were proportionately more active than their numbers in the general population would warrant.

This is not, however, to give credence to the potential corollary that their actions and beliefs necessarily reflected a sectarian point of view. In fact, as Werner Angress has recently shown,[22] the Jews who were so active during the republic's early years of revolutionary upheaval consistently espoused a universalist program without any specifically Jewish overtones. Insofar, of course, as the Jews benefited from the Enlightenment and its liberal legacy, there was a logic to this position. But to view all universalistic aspirations, whether in liberal or socialist form, as *specifically* Jewish programs would be utterly perverse, not to mention totally unfair to gentiles with similar views. This was, of course, an argument the anti-universalist right often advanced. Its obvious absurdity, however, ought not to blind us to the validity of the accompanying observation we have already discussed: the disproportionate Jewish participation in certain segments of the left. Although the right was wrong in making this into a blanket statement about the left as a whole, we need not reject out of hand the grain of truth in the charge.

That socialists who were also Jews followed a nonsectarian path is confirmed by an examination of that question which originally concerned us, the response of the Weimar left to anti-Semitism. For the correlations between the frequency of Jewish members and the vigor of the response is imperfect at best. It does, to be sure, seem to hold for the two established parties. The KPD, as a recent study has shown,[23] rarely took anti-Semitism with any real seriousness. This neglect was due in part to the KPD's adherence to a more rigidly orthodox line, but also, it seems clear, to the effects of Stalinist control of the party after the early twenties. As in the Soviet Union, "cosmopolitan" party members were somehow less trustworthy than those who could more easily adapt to the notion of socialism in one country. These considerations on the theoretical level were doubtless strengthened by the undercurrent of hostility towards "Jewish intellectuals" within the party's rank and file. Even some Jewish intellectuals who continued to ally themselves with the party were indifferent to the anti-Semitic issue, at least if Georg Lukács' influential article on Moses Hess in 1925 is any indication.[24] (Lukács, to be sure, was a member of the Hungarian party, which still had a sizable Jewish contingent, but the article was published in German and probably played a role in the KPD's theoretical discussions.)

Not only was the KPD largely unconcerned about anti-Semitism; on certain occasions, the Communists were even capable of exploiting a veiled form of Jew-baiting for their own purposes. The most notable example of this took place during the Ruhr crisis of 1923 when, in its search for a "new course," the KPD followed Karl Radek's lead and appealed to the lower class for a national Bolshevik alliance.[25] This "Schlageter Line," as it was called in honor of a Freikorps member who had been "martyred" by the French, was only a short-lived tactical move without success. But it did manage to spawn, among other things, an ugly speech by Ruth Fischer on July 25, 1923, in which the masses were exhorted to "trample the Jewish capitalists down, hang them from the lampposts."[26] In 1930, when national Bolshevism was once again on the KPD agenda, comparable appeals to anti-Semitism were also sounded. Although these incidents ought not be overemphasized, they certainly suggest that the KPD was far from vigorous in its response to anti-Semitism.

The SPD, whose leadership throughout the period was more extensively Jewish (although it must not be forgotten, still only about 10 percent), was far more active, as we have already established on the basis of Niewyk's study. Here the higher incidence of Jewish members might have been a contributing factor, for according to his figures, approximately one third of the Socialist Party's attacks on Jew-baiting came from the pens of Jewish writers. In these cases, the accusation of self-denial seems to be unwarranted and the generalization about Marxist indifference to anti-Semitism underminded. Certain Socialists, especially around the revisionist *Sozialistische Monatshefte,* even had a good word for Zionism, if not as a program for themselves, at least as a solution to the problem of the *Ostjuden* who were flocking into Germany at the time.

A possible link between the number of Jewish members in a faction and its response to anti-Semitism, which the examples of the two established parties might support, is undercut, however, when one looks at the nonparty left. Here the attitude expressed in the letters from members of the *Institut für Sozialforschung* quoted earlier seems to have prevailed. Deak's study of the *Weltbühne* rarely mentions a serious response to anti-Semitism on the part of his subjects, most of whom appear to have considered their Jewish descent as little more than a stigma and the problem of anti-Semitism a minor "irritant." The attitude of Brecht's play, *Die Rundköpfe und die Spitzköpfe* (1931), in which Nazis and rich Jews are seen as united in the end, was shared by many of the "left-wing intellectuals."

Several possible interpretations can be offered for this curious attitude. First, the very fact that the SPD was concerned with anti-Semitism was taken as a sign of its nonrevolutionary Revisionism. The Revisionists, after all, had been the only socialists to take seriously the continued survival of the *Mittelstand,* the class composed of artisans, clerical workers, civil servants, and technicians, which the more orthodox left insisted on seeing as inevitably disappearing in the process of class polarization.[27] As early as the turn of the century, Eduard Bernstein had been castigated for acknowledging the continued existence of the *Mittelstand,* which he hoped socialism might win over by speaking to its special concerns. Although this was to prove a vain hope, the Revisionists' sensitivity to the troubled condition of this crucial stratum of society meant that they were more keenly aware of the reality of anti-Semitism. For it was to anti-Semitism that the *Mittelstand* often turned when the strains of modernization became too much to bear. The more militant and uncompromising "homeless left," wishing to dissassociate itself from the betrayal of Marxism by the Revisionist Socialists, tended to neglect the special plight of the lower middle classes and with it the threat of Judeophobia.

Minimizing this threat also meant a refusal to explore the positive ways in which a Jewish posture of self-assertion might be reconciled with socialism. What all factions sorely lacked was the concept of a "national liberation struggle," which has been introduced into Marxist thought only in recent decades with the breakdown of colonialism. Such a concept might have tied the Jewish and socialist causes together, at least as a compromise until the transcending of national differences could become a reality. Trapped by their theoretical insistence on universalism, which they rigidly embraced—if a Hegelian term may be permitted—as an abstract immediacy, the Weimar Socialists of Jewish origin failed to see the positive potential in communal cohesion based on ethnic identity. Although many of the "homeless left" were attracted to a fraternal, *"bündische"* solution to alienation, they rarely saw the Jewish question in this light. Or if they did, they turned to Zionism and left a Europe-oriented socialism behind. (One significant Jewish leftist who did try to avoid the extremes of assimilation and Zionism was the anarchist

Gustav Landauer, but he had been killed in 1919). Nor could they rest content with a pluralist solution which recognized the right of the Jews to remain a nonassimilated subgroup within the German society—the type of program supported by the Central Association. The negative connection with SPD Revisionism was too strong to allow either of these answers to suffice. It might, in fact, be argued that the essential tragedy of the Weimar left, at least concerning anti-Semitism, was the unfortunate linkage in the minds of many of the more radical Socialists between the disliked revisionism of the SPD and its efforts toward a serious response to the dilemma of the Jews.

A second reason that might possibly account for the indifference of the "homeless left" was the clear relationship between attacking the Jews and attacking the republic itself. Because the SPD supported the Weimar status quo, its members were extremely sensitive to the covert way in which anti-Semitism was a threat to their own position—in fact, Niewyk takes them to task for thinking at times that anti-Semitism was no more than displaced antirepublicanism. The nonparty leftists, on the other hand, were like the Communists in having no use for the Weimar system, at least after the mid-twenties. As a result, they were not as instinctively alarmed by attacks on the republic, even if these took the obnoxious form of Jew-baiting.

A third and final explanation arises out of the special nature of the nonparty left itself. As their refusal to align themselves with any organized faction suggests, many of the left-wing intellectuals were alienated men incapable of forming any lasting group identifications beyond the sectarian level. As Hannah Arendt has argued in her study of Walter Benjamin,[28] they often engaged in fierce generational struggles with their parents which precluded a sense of ethnic solidarity. Some of their peers, to be sure, turned to Zionism out of disgust with the watered-down Reform Judaism of their forebears, but these were rarely the men who also joined the nonparty left. As many of their less sympathetic critics have pointed out, this almost constitutional nay-saying prevented the nonparty left from dealing constructively with the concrete issues of the day, anti-Semitism among them. With the brutal slaying of Rosa Luxemburg in 1919, herself a Jewish Socialist indifferent to the irreducible reality of anti-Semitism,[29] many of the "homeless left" lost the political figure around whom they might have rallied. As in the case of the inner circle of the Frankfurt *Institut,* this meant a turn toward a theoretical purity that tended to ignore the less central issue of Judeophobia. On the positive side of the ledger, of course, such a stance provided a constant prod to the left-wing parties to realize the goals of socialism, which each was betraying in its own way. But negatively, it prevented them from seeing that anti-Semitism was more than a passing epiphenomenon in the terminal crisis of late capitalism. The German people may or may not have been "the least anti-Semitic of all," but enough of them were sufficiently anti-Semitic to warrant more attention than the nonparty left was willing to pay.

In conclusion, then, it might be said that the record of the Weimar left toward anti-Semitism was spotty, with the SPD showing the most serious concern. But before the left is too heavily castigated for its sins, its position must be compared with bourgeois organizations and parties during the same period. Although such a comparison cannot be attempted here, I suspect it would do little credit to the nonsocialists. As the polemical storm aroused a decade ago by Hannah Arendt's *Eichmann in Jerusalem* demonstrates, the center as well as the left can be faulted for its inadequate response to the threat posed to Jewish existence. There is still much to be learned about, and learned from, the multiple ways in which Weimar's Jews of all political persuasions reacted to their increasingly precarious situation in the "least anti-Semitic country of all."

6.

The Jews and the Frankfurt School: Critical Theory's Analysis of Anti-Semitism

The posthumous appearance of Max Horkheimer's *Notizen* of 1950 to 1969 in the same volume as a new edition of *Dämmerung,* his aphorisms of 1926 to 1931,[1] amply documents many of the transformations of the theoretical and political positions of the Frankfurt School's leading figure. None is perhaps as striking as that of his attitude toward anti-Semitism and what was once known as "the Jewish question." In the later collection, at least a dozen entries discuss these and related issues, often from the very personal vantage point of a survivor of the Holocaust. In contrast, *Dämmerung* virtually ignores anti-Semitism as a problem in its own right and has little to say about the plight of the Jews in Weimar Germany. The one major exception is an aphorism entitled "Belief and Profit," which contains a debunking reduction of Jewish identity to class interests:

As the material base of ghetto life was left behind, the willingness to sacrifice life and property to one's religious belief also became a thing of the past. Among bourgeois Jews, the hierarchy of goods is neither Jewish nor Christian but bourgeois. The Jewish capitalist brings sacrifices to power, just like his Aryan class colleague. He first sacrifices his own superstition, then the lives of others, and finally his capital. The Jewish revolutionary in Germany is not different from his "Aryan" comrade. He commits his life to the liberation of man.[2]

The young Horkheimer's facile dismissal of specifically Jewish problems was shared, at least in their written work, by all of his colleagues at the

First published in *Geschichte und Gesellschaft* (1979), 5(4) and *New German Critique* (Winter 1980), vol. 19.

Frankfurt *Institut für Sozialforschung,* whose director he became in 1930. Indeed, their tendency to subsume anti-Semitism under the larger rubric of class conflict persisted throughout the 1930's even after the Nazi seizure of power and their forced emigration to America in 1934. In their collective project of 1935, *Studies on Authority and the Family,* no specific discussion of anti-Semitism was attempted in either the theoretical or empirical sections of the work.[3] Nor were the Jews mentioned in such *Institut* treatments of Nazi or *völkisch* ideology as Herbert Marcuse's "The Struggle against Liberalism in the Totalitarian Concept of the State" of 1934 or Leo Lowenthal's "Knut Hamsun: On the Prehistory of Authoritarian Ideology" of 1937.[4] And although anti-Semitism was introduced into Theodor W. Adorno's analysis of Wagner, where it was related to the sadomasochistic dynamics of the composer's world view, only fragments of that work appeared in the *Institut*'s journal, its full publication coming not until 1952.[5]

When Horkheimer did finally compose an essay entitled "The Jews and Europe" in 1939,[6] he continued to subsume anti-Semitism under the more general rubric of the crisis of capitalism. The predicament of the Jews, he claimed, reflected the liquidation of the sphere of economic circulation in which they had been particularly active. Moreover, he went on, Nazi anti-Semitic propaganda was directed more at external audiences than internal ones; the German people were themselves not its major target. Not surprisingly, other German Jews more sensitive to the complexities and dangers of the situation, such as Gershom Scholem,[7] were outraged at the essay, which seemed little more than an echo of Marx's controversial remarks in his treatise on the Jewish question of a century before.

In their faithfulness to Marx's own attitude toward anti-Semitism, Horkheimer and his colleagues conformed to a pattern that many observers have noted: the more radical the Marxist, the less interested in the specificity of the Jewish question.[8] Of all the members of the German socialist movement in both the Wilhelmian and Weimar eras, the Revisionists were the most attentive to anti-Semitism as a problem in its own right. And, of course, the *Institut* had no use for revisionism in any form. Its members tended as well to hold to another pattern that often accompanied this inverse relationship between radicalism and sensitivity to anti-Semitism: those among them with Jewish backgrounds rarely, if ever, found their ethnic identities significant for their work. Not until the 1950s, when Horkheimer in particular attempted to compensate for his earlier neglect,[9] was this latter pattern reversed. In addition to the *Notizen* published only after his death, which are mentioned above, he published several essays affirming his commitment to the Jewish community and even alleging that certain aspects of his Critical Theory could be traced to Jewish influences.[10] None of his former colleagues went this far, but it is more than likely that they all shared an awareness of the insufficiency of their prewar attitudes on these issues.

It was, in fact, during the war that their position began to change. Plans were laid for a major project devoted to anti-Semitism,[11] and works written under the *Institut*'s auspices such as Franz Neumann's *Behemoth* began to pay more attention to the problem.[12] A brief glance at the latter will show, however, how hesitant the shift was at first. Although *Behemoth* was in some ways, particularly in its critical attitude toward the concept of state capitalism,[13] at odds with mainstream *Institut* thinking, its treatment of anti-Semitism seems to have been fairly representative of the general attitude. In the work's first edition, published in 1942, Neumann devoted a chapter to "Racism and Anti-Semitism." He distinguished between totalitarian and nontotalitarian variants of the phenomenon, the former based on "magic and beyond discussion,"[14] the latter preserving "remnants of rationality"[15] and thus open to analysis. The rationality in question was above all that of economics: the distribution of the spoils among strata of the population necessary for the regime's support, the distorted satisfaction of "the anti-capitalist longings of the German people,"[16] the displacement of the aggressive energies of class struggle, and the justification of eastern expansion. Although Neumann recognized religious sources of anti-Semitism as well as purely social ones, his main emphasis was on its economic rationality. Because of this stress and the concomitant belief that anti-Semitism was manipulated from above rather than spontaneously generated from below, Neumann could reveal that "the writer's personal conviction, paradoxical as it may seem, is that the German people are the least anti-Semitic of all."[17] In this belief, he was at one with his Institute colleagues.[18]

In the second edition of *Behemoth*, which appeared in 1944, Neumann appended a section on anti-Semitism in which he acknowledged the new ruthlessness of Nazi policy towards the Jews but still saw it as "only the means to the attainment of the ultimate objective, namely the destruction of free institutions, beliefs, and groups."[19] This view he dubbed "the spearhead theory of anti-Semitism" because of his conviction that the economic goals of the system were still paramount. Many years later, in the last work he was to complete before his untimely death in 1954, Neumann reaffirmed his belief that spontaneous German anti-Semitism was relatively minor.[20]

That reaffirmation, however, appeared in an essay significantly entitled "Anxiety and Politics," which marked a milestone in

Neumann's intellectual development because of its belated acknowledgment of the power of the irrational in political life. Neumann's former colleagues in the *Institut* had come to the same understanding much earlier. In fact, the increased integration of psychoanalysis into Critical Theory coincided very closely with the growing attention they began paying to anti-Semitism during the war. For all their agreement with Neumann's stress on the manipulative nature of Jew-hatred, they did not hold to his distinction between totalitarian and nontotalitarian anti-Semitisms, only the latter being amenable to critical analysis because of its rational foundation. Although Horkheimer and the inner circle of the *Institut* never abandoned the economic dimension of their theory, they came increasingly to stress the psychological aspects of the problems they studied, anti-Semitism in particular.

Anticipations of this shift were apparent as early as the fragments of Adorno's Wagner study published in 1939, where the category of sadomasochism, developed in Erich Fromm's contributions to the *Institut*'s work,[21] was extensively employed. The first systematic efforts to probe anti-Semitism took place in 1943, when the *Institut* began a massive investigation of American labor's attitude towards the Jews, conducted under the auspices of the Jewish Labor Committee.[22]Although a great deal of raw data was accumulated, much of it damaging to the liberal image of American labor, and several drafts were completed, no results were published because of a number of organizational and theoretical difficulties. The experience of using empirical techniques proved invaluable, however, when the *Institut*'s next investigation of anti-Semitism began shortly thereafter, this time under the sponsorship of the American Jewish Committee. In 1944, Horkheimer became the Committee's Director of Scientific Research and launched an ambitious program which culminated in the five-part *Studies in Prejudice*, finally published in 1949 and 1950. One of the volumes, Paul Massing's *Rehearsal for Destruction*,[23] was a traditional historical account of Germany's anti-Semitic movements before World War I, which stressed the importance of the economic depression of the 1873–96 era in stimulating resentment against the Jews. The other four volumes, however, were predominantly psychological in methodology. Two were by non-*Institut* authors and thus merit no comment here.[24] The others were *Prophets of Deceit* by Leo Lowenthal and Norbert Guterman and *The Authoritarian Personality* by Adorno and three members of the Berkeley Public Opinion Study Group, Else Frenkel-Brunswik, Daniel J. Levinson, and R. Nevitt Sanford.[25]

In his introduction to *Prophets of Deceit*, Horkheimer, who oversaw the entire project, argued that because men at present were

denied significant political choices, the people themselves did not suffice as an object of study. Instead, those who manipulate them from above
must also be scrutinized. Lowenthal and Guterman thus focused on the
techniques of demagogic agitators, whose appeals they subjected to a
qualitative content analysis using what they called a "psychological Morse
code."[26] The specific context was American society, where the potential for mass anti-Semitism seemed sufficiently threatening to justify this
careful investigation. Arguing against the assumption that the exposure
of deliberate deception was enough to discredit the demagogue, they
sought to unmask the arsenal of unconscious devices that accounted for
his appeal. Among those discussed was that of the projected enemy, who
was conceived of as both strong and weak. The most frequent embodiment of this projection, they claimed, was the Jew, who appeared as
both persecutor and quarry in the fantasy world of the agitator. Equated
with the "other," the Jew was the victim of a paranoid projection. His
gestures and mannerisms were mimicked by the agitator, who made the
vulnerable Jew a "symbol on which he centers the projection of his own
impotent rage against the restraints of civilization."[27] As we shall see
momentarily, these findings perfectly complemented the more theoretical analysis offered by Horkheimer and Adorno (and partly coauthored
by Lowenthal himself) a few years before the publication of *Prophets of
Deceit.*

In *The Authoritarian Personality,* Adorno and his colleagues turned to the character types who would be most receptive to
the appeal of these demagogic devices. Although the most ambitious interest of the study was the generation and testing of a quantitative scale
to measure the "authoritarian" potential of individuals (the celebrated
"F" scale"), the authors also developed a specific "A-S scale" to uncover
latent anti-Semitic tendencies as well. In fact, the study began with a
specific focus on this problem. And although Adorno wrote that "we came
to regard it as our main task not to analyze anti-Semitism or any other
antiminority prejudice as a sociopsychological phenomenon *per se,* but
rather to examine the relation of anti-minority prejudice to broader ideological and characterological patterns,"[28] *The Authoritarian Personality* still contained a significant discussion of the phenomenon in its
own terms. In addition to a long presentation of the procedures of the
A-S scale by Daniel Levinson, Adorno himself contributed a chapter devoted to the qualitative analysis of the indirect or "screened" interviews
conducted on a sample population by the project's staff. Among his conclusions were that anti-Semitism was subjective and irrational in nature,
generally grounded in stereotypically distorted experience, rationalized
in moralistic, superegoistic terms, inclined to the "mythological" con-

fusion of mental dispositions and physical categories, and often linked to "antidemocratic feeling."[29]

This last formulation, with its uncritical acceptance of the norm of bourgeois democracy combined with the generally psychologistic orientation of the work as a whole, led some observers to believe that the Frankfurt School had abandoned its Marxist past entirely. Moreover, nowhere in the work was an attempt made to see anti-Semitism in essentially class terms, although the motivations behind it were acknowledged to differ according to social background.[30] The study of American labor had convinced Adorno and his colleagues that the problem was no longer confined to one stratum of the social whole. "Sociologically," Adorno wrote, "this syndrome [the authoritarian personality of high scorers on the F-scale] used to be, in Europe, highly characteristic of the lower middle class. In this country, we may expect it among people whose actual status differs from that to which they aspire."[31]

There were, however, frequent suggestions in the work of the Frankfurt School's continued desire to situate the psychological dimension of prejudice in a wider social setting. For example, in discussing the sources of stereotyping and personalization, Adorno wrote: "Ever more anonymous and opaque social processes make it increasingly difficult to integrate the limited sphere of one's personal life experience with objective social dynamics. Social alienation is hidden by a surface phenomenon in which the very opposite is being stressed: personalization of political attitudes and habits offers compensation for the dehumanization of the social sphere which is at the bottom of today's grievances."[32] These instances tended, however, to be lost in the work's more subjective approach. Indeed, as Adorno himself recognized, a satisfactory theory of anti-Semitism "could be approached only by recourse to a theory which is beyond the scope of this study. Such a theory would neither enumerate a diversity of 'factors' nor single out a specific one as 'the' cause but rather develop a unified framework within which all the 'elements' are linked together consistently. This would amount to nothing less than a theory of modern society as a whole."[33]

Although such a general theory was absent from all the volumes of the *Studies in Prejudice*, Horkheimer and Adorno had attempted in 1944 to isolate the "Elements of Anti-Semitism" in a chapter of their joint work, *Dialectic of Enlightenment*.[34] Published in 1947, this crucial statement of Critical Theory was generally ignored in America because it was written in German. As a result, the objective complement to the subjective approach of the *Studies* was lost to view until the book was rediscovered in the 1960s by young German New Left followers of the Frankfurt Schoool, a rediscovery which ultimately brought it to the attention of an English-speaking audience as well. Horkheimer and Adorno had perhaps counted on its immediate neglect because it was in "Elements of Anti-Semitism" that they voiced sentiments clearly at odds with the liberal orientation of their American sponsors and co-workers. Whereas, for example, *The Authoritarian Personality* refused to investigate the role of the object of anti-Semitism, which had "little to do with the qualities of those against whom it is directed,"[35] the theoretical essay entered the dangerous territory in which the contribution of the Jews was also open for discussion. And instead of making vaguely complimentary remarks about liberal democracy, Horkheimer and Adorno reverted to the more traditional Frankfurt School position that liberalism was itself implicated in the rise of fascism.

The overarching theory they presented was, however, far more than an echo of the reductive Marxist approach that had characterized their work through Horkheimer's "The Jews and Europe." In addition to the residues of that position, the Freudian categories they were than applying to their empirical investigations were also in evidence. But beyond both was an analysis grounded in the general argument of the book, which stressed the ambiguous implications of the age-old domination of nature in Western culture and the concomitant apotheosis of instrumental reason. To outline the intracacies of that argument is beyond the scope of this essay,[36] but certain of its implications for the issue of anti-Semitism must be discussed.

One problem in doing so, however, derives from Horkheimer's and Adorno's refusal to organize the arguments they presented in a hierarchical fashion. No attempt was made to weigh the relative significance of each "element" in the compound that was anti-Semitism, nor were the causal links among them fully delineated. Instead, Horkheimer and Adorno offered what might be called a decentered constellation of factors juxtaposed in unmediated fashion. Although brilliant and original in many places, the resulting whole was less than fully satisfying.[37] It is nonetheless useful to extract those elements that Horkheimer and Adorno especially stressed, even if a totally coherent and integrated summary of their entire argument cannot be constructed.

Among the most obvious elements in their analysis, and the one perhaps most absent from the *Studies in Prejudice,* derived from the Frankfurt School's early indebtedness to Marx. "Bourgeois anti-Semitism," Horkheimer and Adorno wrote, "has a specific economic reason: the concealment of domination in production."[38] Like Neumann in *Behemoth,* they recognized the function of the Jews as scapegoats for anticapitalist sentiments: "They were the representatives—in harmony with their patriarchal religion—of municipal, bourgeois, and finally, industrial conditions. They carried capitalist ways of life to various countries and drew upon themselves the hatred of all who had to suffer under capitalism."[39] Although they were sensitive to the fact that "commerce was not [the Jews'] vocation but their fate."[40] an acknowledgment that Marx had callously omitted from his earlier diatribe against the Jews, they nonetheless implicated the Jews in—or perhaps, better put, did not exonerate them from—the responsibility for capitalism's triumph and the reaction it engendered. "They are now experiencing to their own cost the exclusive, particularist character of capitalism."[41]

But beyond this more traditional Marxist approach, with its echo of Bebel's celebrated characterization of anti-Semitism as "the socialism of fools," Horkheimer and Adorno provided an analysis of the postbourgeois anti-Semitism that characterized fascism per se. Based on earlier Frankfurt School work on the nature of modern authoritarianism,[42] they argued that fascism represented a more naked form of repression than classical capitalism with its reliance on the mediation of the market place: "Whereas there is no longer any need for economic domination, the Jews are marked out as the absolute object of domination pure and simple."[43] Fascism is an order of undiluted force led by rulers who "long for total possession and unlimited power, at any price."[44] These megalomaniacal yearnings produce a certain measure of guilt, however, which is alleviated by claiming that it is the Jews who in fact crave total control.

The long-range tendency toward this type of domination, which went through the classical capitalist stage before reaching its apotheosis in fascism, had to be understood in more fundamental terms than the scapegoat theory would allow. For "anti-Semitism is a deeply imprinted schema, a ritual of civilization."[45] It is thus to the fundamental dialectic of civilization (or the Enlightenment, as they alternately call it) that Horkheimer and Adorno turned for a deeper explanation.

The essence of that explanation was the equation of civilization with the domination of nature, a domination whose sinister implications were only then becoming fully manifest. "Those who spasmodically dominate nature," they wrote, "see in a tormented nature a provocative image of powerless happiness. The thought of happiness without power is unbearable because it would then be true happiness."[46] The Jews are singled out for special attack because they are confused with nature itself, and thus seen as having "happiness without power, wages without work, a home without frontiers, religion without myth."[47] But ironically, the Jews are not merely identified with the nature that is dominated and envied; they are also closely associated with the process of civilization itself. As was the case with their being scapegoated for the sins of capitalism, here, too, there was a grain of truth, for the Jews were the "colonizers for progress."[48] From Roman times on, they had promoted civilization and its concomitant domination of nature with "enlightenment as with cynicism."[49] When nature rebelled against its age-old domination, as Horkheimer and Adorno claimed it did with the rise of irrationalist politics, the Jews were inevitably singled out for revenge. But the revolt of repressed nature was itself turned into yet another manifestation of domination; fascism, in fact, "seeks to make the rebellion of suppressed nature against domination directly useful to domination."[50] The ultimate significance of this reversal is that the Jews, who were implicated in the original domination of nature, are sacrificed to the demands of a new type of domination which assumes the guise of a rebellion against its traditional form.

In developing the intricacies of this argument, Horkheimer and Adorno introduced a complicated discussion of the role of mimetic behavior in civilization and its distortion in the fascist mimicry of its Jewish victims. They also analyzed the Christian contribution to the process, which they stressed could not be ignored despite the moribund status of the church in the modern world. But their most interesting argument drew upon the psychoanalytic theory they were then applying to the subjective side of anti-Semitism in their more empirical work: "Anti-Semitism is based on a false projection. It is the counterpart of true mimesis, and fundamentally related to the repressed form; in fact, it is probably the morbid expression of repressed mimesis. Mimesis imitates the environment, but false projection makes the environment like itself."[51] This type of false projection was equivalent to paranoia, but instead of being a personal problem, paranoia had been politicized in the modern world. To many who succumbed to its appeal, fascism provided a mass delusional system that was mistaken for reality.

However, Horkheimer and Adorno went beyond the purely psychoanalytic reading of paranoid false projections by adding an epistemological dimension to their analysis. Projection, they argued, is not in and of itself at fault, for as Kant in particular had shown, all perception contains a projective moment. But a healthy projection preserves the tension between subject and object, neither reducing the former to the latter, as in the case of positivism, nor vice versa, as in idealism. Reflection on the mediated nonidentity of subject and object was, they contended, the key to a healthy, nondominating enlightenment; accordingly, "the morbid aspect of anti-Semitism is not projective behavior as such, but the absence from it of reflection."[52] The domination of nature entailed by a less benign form of enlightenment was thus closely tied to the psychological condition of paranoia and the philosophical tendency of idealism.

Objectifying (like sick) thought contains the despotism of the subjective purpose which is hostile to the thing and forgets the thing itself, thus committing the mental act of violence which is later put into practice. The unconditional realism of civilized humanity, which culminates in fascism, is a special case of paranoic delusion which dehumanizes nature and finally the nations themselves.[53]

This argument, which Adorno was later to develop in much greater detail in *Negative Dialectics*,[54] thus situated anti-Semitism at the culmination of a process at once social, psychological, and philosophical, a process which was the dialectic of the Enlightenment itself. The somber implication of this fact was that it would take nothing short of the reversal of that process to end persecution of the Jews, a conclusion far bleaker than that of the *Studies of Prejudice* with its call for increased education for tolerance.

If thought is liberated from domination and if violence is abolished, the long absent idea is liable to develop that Jews too are human beings. This development would represent the step out of an anti-Semitic society which drives Jews and others to madness, and into the human society. This step would also fulfill the Fascist lie, but in contradicting it: the Jewish question would prove in fact to be the turning point of history.[55]

In short, once utopia were achieved, anti-Semitism would take care of itself. The inverse of this proposition, however, did not necessarily hold, as Horkheimer and Adorno acknowledged in a final section of "Elements of Anti-Semitism" added after the war's end in 1947. That is, the end of Jew-hatred did not entail the liberation of thought from domination and the abolition of violence. For although "there are no more anti-Semites"[56] now that Hitler has been defeated, the conditions which made fascism possible have not really been changed. The stereotyped "ticket-mentality" that spawned anti-Semitism has survived its decline. Indeed, "the Jewish masses themselves are as prone to ticket-thinking as the hostile youth organizations."[57] The content of fascist propaganda, indeed of fascist action itself, is less important than its source in the paranoid false projection that characterizes the domination of nature. "The ticket mentality as such is as anti-Semitic as the anti-Semitic ticket. The anger against all that is different is teleologically inherent in the mentality, and, as the dominated subjects' resentment of natural domination, is ready to attack the natural minority—even when the social minority is threatened first."[58]

For Horkheimer and Adorno, then, perhaps the ultimate source of anti-Semitism and its functional equivalents is the rage against the nonidentical that characterizes the totalistic dominating impulse of western civilization. The Jews, in other words, by their very refusal to be assimilated, represent an obstacle to the total integration of the "ad-

ministered world" or "one-dimensional society," as Marcuse was to call
it. In fact, at least Horkheimer came to see the "negative" relation of the
Jews to the rest of mankind as a healthy state of affairs. Not surprisingly,
this made his reaction to Zionism and the creation of Israel ambivalent,
for now the Jews were merely one nation among others:

Jewry was not a powerful state but the hope for justice at the end of the world.
They were a people and its opposite, a rebuke to all peoples. Now, a state claims
to be speaking for Jewry, to be Jewry. The Jewish people in whom the injustice
of all peoples has become an accusation, the individuals in whose words and
gestures the negative of what is reflected itself, have now become positive themselves. A nation among nations, soldiers, leaders, money-raisers for themselves.[59]

Whether or not this lament, with its echoes of Franz Rosenzweig's much
earlier celebration of the Jews as a nonhistorical people,[60] was shared
by all of his former colleagues, it is clear that Horkheimer was expressing a cardinal tenet of Critical Theory: the prohibition of premature
positivity. In his mind, and perhaps in that of certain of his collaborators, the Jews became the metaphoric equivalent of that remnant of society preserving negation and the nonidentical. Indeed, Horkheimer came
to argue that underlying the Frankfurt School's refusal to describe the
utopian alternative to the present society was the traditional Jewish taboo on naming God or picturing paradise.[61]

The striking disparity between the references to the Jews and
anti-Semitism in the two collections of Horkheimer's aphorisms thus
mirrored a fundamental shift in the Frankfurt School's attitude. As it moved
further away from the traditional Marxist belief in the proletariat as the
agent of positive totalization and more toward the conclusion that the
best to be hoped for in the present world was the preservation of en-
claves of negation, the attention its members paid to the Jewish question increased. Although assertions of a causal relationship between their
own status as Jewish survivors and their vision of a negative dialectics
"after Auschwitz" can only be speculative,[62] it is nonetheless clear that,
as least in Horkheimer's case, the Critical Theorist was understood as
"the Jew" of the administered society. And conversely, anti-Semitism
became a model of the totalistic liquidation of nonidentity in the one-
dimensional world.[63] In "Elements of Anti-Semitism," Horkheimer and
Adorno had written that "the fact that anti-Semitism tends to occur only
as part of an interchangeable program is sure hope that it will die out
one day,"[64] but, when that day would dawn, Critical Theory chose not
to say. In fact, for the later Frankfurt School, no hopes could be called
sure, although the need to hope was no less urgent.

7.

Introduction to a *Festschrift* for Leo Lowenthal on his Eightieth Birthday

To the extent that the core members of the *Institut für Sozialforschung* have been perceived as constituting a coherent school of thought, recognition of their individual achievements has tended to be obscured. No one has perhaps been more the victim of this process than Leo Lowenthal, one of the *Institut's* earliest members and a central figure in its intellectual life on two continents for nearly a quarter century. In most treatments of the Frankfurt School, Lowenthal is faithfully listed as its expert on literary issues, while the actual content of his work is ignored. Zoltán Tar, for example, pauses only long enough to misstate the date of Lowenthal's entry into the *Institut* before passing on to other matters.[1] Little more of a really substantive nature appears in most other general studies of Critical Theory, such as those by Slater, Connerton, Söllner, or Apergi.[2] And although the editors of *The Essential Frankfurt School Reader* are insightful enough to include Lowenthal's masterful critique of Knut Hamsun, they turn his birthdate into a mystery and wrongly credit Adorno with his epigram that mass culture is "psychoanalysis in reverse."[3]

Part of the reason for Lowenthal's relative neglect must be attributed to the seriousness with which he took the *Institut's* collective identity. Of all his colleagues, only Friedrich Pollock matched Lowenthal's dedication to the communal project envisaged by the *Institut's* founders. In a variety of roles—managing editor of the *Zeitschrift für Sozialforschung* and director of its extensive review section, editor of the third part of the *Studien über Authorität und Familie* devoted to

First published in *Telos* (Fall 1980), vol. 45.

individual studies, codirector of the *Institut*'s New York branch after Horkheimer and Adorno left for California, informal American archivist of many of its documents following its return to Frankfurt—Lowenthal was at the center of its institutional existence. He was no less active in the communal stimulation of its intellectual work, that dialectical interaction of *Darstellung* and *Forschung* recently analyzed by Helmut Dubiel.[4] His regular participation in the discussions surrounding the work published under his colleagues' names is attested to by the abundant appearance of his own in their acknowledgments. Horkheimer and Adorno, for example, credit him with co-authoring the first three sections of the "Elements of Anti-Semitism" chapter of *Dialectic of Enlightenment*. Adorno thanks him for contributing to the chapters in *The Authoritarian Personality* written under Adorno's name. And as late as *The Aesthetic Dimension*, Marcuse praises him for once again proving "his reputation as a fierce reader and critic."[5]

In general, throughout his career, Lowenthal seems to have been comfortable with the kind of collaborative scholarship practiced by the *Institut*. His own volume in the series of *Studies in Prejudice, Prophets of Deceit*, was co-authored with Norbert Guterman. In later years, he worked collectively with Marjorie Fiske, Seymour Martin Lipset, and Joseph Klapper.[6] And he was an active member of the committee led by Charles Muscatine that produced the widely discussed report, *Education in Berkeley*, dealing with the university crisis of the 1960s. In short, Lowenthal was clearly skilled in the type of cooperative, often interdisciplinary work that is more frequently urged as a goal than celebrated as a reality. And perhaps as a result, his own intellectual profile has remained less distinct than it might have otherwise been.

There is, to be sure, a substantial body of work that appeared solely under his name. Indeed, if the Frankfurt School's main contribution to Western Marxism is identified with its investigations of cultural and aesthetic issues, as it sometimes is, Lowenthal's studies in these areas must be considered central to that endeavor. As pure examples of Critical Theory applied to literature, they are arguably more typical than the work of Benjamin and Adorno, for they were more directly composed under the theoretical guidance of Horkheimer's seminal *Zeitschrift* essays. As such, they are powerful statements of the Frankfurt School's ideology critique at a time when its members still held to relatively traditional Marxist expectations about the probable course of history. If they have perhaps received less attention than those of Adorno and Benjamin, it is likely because of their more direct and straightforward approach to the relationship between society and culture. Despite Lowenthal's early religious interests and his abiding philosophical concerns, there is far less of a mixture of profane theology, antimetaphysical metaphysics and critical sociology in his writings than in those of his two *Institut* colleagues. If, as a result, Lowenthal's work seems at times less startlingly and provocatively unique than theirs, his also suffers from none of the occasional perversity and arbitrariness that mar their texts. Here, too, paradoxically, may be a source of their respective reputations, for Lowenthal's writings do not lend themselves to the wildly divergent, often antithetical readings that have characterized the reception of Benjamin and Adorno.

The recognition of their work has also, of course, gone through cycles of intensity. And so to many familiar with the history of the Frankfurt School, it has only seemed a matter of time before Lowenthal would also find a wider audience. Happily, the moment has come while Lowenthal himself, the last surviving member of the *Institut*'s inner circle, is still among us to enjoy it (and, one suspects, to be somewhat embarrassed by it, for Lowenthal has always been made uncomfortable by the monumentalization of Critical Theory and the concomitant cultish reception of its spokesmen). The Suhrkamp Verlag has just announced the imminent publication of his collected works in Germany. A lengthy biographical interview with him was conducted by W. Martin Lüdke in the *Frankfurter Rundschau* on May 17, 1980. Helmut Dubiel turned a much more extensive series of interviews into a lively autobiographical volume—characteristically teased out of Lowenthal by collaboration—entitled *Mitmachen Wollte Ich Nie.*[7] And now a heterogeneous group of Lowenthal's admirers has accepted *Telos'* offer to present him with a series of essays on the occasion of his 80th birthday, which falls on November 3 of this year.

Jürgen Habermas, the most notable inheritor of the tradition that Lowenthal helped found, has contributed his preface to the new paperback edition of the *Zeitschrift,* which the Deutsche Taschenbuch Verlag will publish shortly. In it, he details the importance of the journal's massive review section, which Lowenthal directed. Ferenc Fehér and Agnes Heller, like Lowenthal deeply but not uncritically indebted to Lukács' forays into materialist culture criticism, have written an essay on "Comedy and Rationality." Lüdke, who co-edited a recent anthology of essays on Adorno's aesthetic theory,[8] has used Lowenthal's discussion of early Romanticism as a stimulus to reflections of his own on that subject. Robert Sayre has compared the work of the other major Marxist sociologist of literature, Lucien Goldmann, with that of Lowenthal. And David Gross has contrasted him with Adorno and Roland Barthes, concentrating on the issue of mass or popular culture. Prefacing these essays is the chapter entitled "Scientific Biography" from *Mitmachen Wollte*

Ich Nie, which was selected over another dealing in greater detail with the *Institut,* because it gives a greater sense of the sweep of Lowenthal's entire career.

In addition, an essay by Lowenthal himself, written for the *Zeitschrift* in 1932, is translated into English here for the first time.[9] The earliest substantive application of Critical Theory to literature, appearing shortly after Lowenthal's programmatic statement in the journal's inaugural issue, "Conrad Ferdinand Meyer's Heroic View of History," has been chosen for its exemplary qualities. With a confidence in the relatively direct relationship between society and literature that in later years he would come to qualify, Lowenthal skillfully explored the ideological implications of Meyer's novellas. Employing content analysis buttressed by reference to Meyer's nonfiction writings, he detailed the ways in which this seemingly historical Swiss author expressed the defensive world view of the upper-bourgeois-Junker alliance of the Germany of his day. Interestingly, many of the traits he detected in Meyer's novellas were to reappear in the twentieth-century forerunners of fascism, those purveyors of "heroic-folkish realism" examined by Marcuse two years later in the *Zeitschrift* in his seminal essay on "The Struggle Against Liberalism in the Totalitarian View of the State."[10]

Lowenthal's analysis not only anticipated Marcuse's essay, but also contained many of the same arguments that were to appear in Lukács's treatment of Meyer in *The Historical Novel,* written in Moscow in the winter of 1936–37.[11] Whether or not Lukács read Lowenthal can't be verified, although it is likely he did. What is certain is that he shared Lowenthal's insight into the essentially pseudohistorical, antipopulist hero-worshipping impulse behind Meyer's work. Two important differences, however, can be discerned in their analyses. Whereas Lowenthal, true to the Frankfurt School's generally positive attitude toward psychology, contends that Meyer's ineffable characters are presented in a psychologically opaque way, Lukács, as ever hostile to psychology, argues that Meyer's concentration on the inner life of his protagonists is "no less psychologistic than the writings of those of his contemporaries who were open adherents of psychological analysis."[12] For Lowenthal, there is a crucial difference between true psychological characterization and the attribution of ineffability to individuals, a difference that seems to have escaped the more insistently sociologistic Lukács.

Secondly, Lukács compares Meyer to Flaubert as a forerunner of the modernist destruction of realism, whereas Lowenthal, lacking Lukács's unqualified hostility to modernism, traces no such lineage. Here, ironically, Lukács is closer to contemporary non-Marxist criticism, which tends, to be sure, to honor Meyer for those ambiguities and equivocations that Lukács reads as signs of decadence.[13] Although Lowenthal seems to have shared Lukács' distaste for naturalism,[14] he never extended his critique of its inadequacies to include later forms of modernism. In fact, for reasons he defends in his interview with Dubiel, Lowenthal never applied his sociology of literature to works of the avant-garde. This neglect may in some ways be regrettable, but in the case of his critique of Meyer, it had a salutary effect. For as a consequence, the ideological function of Meyer's work is more concretely situated in the specific historical conjuncture of Wilhelmian Germany and not made into yet another example of that secular decline of the bourgeoisie after 1848 into decadence, so tiresomely rehearsed in Lukács' work. Although as any reader of *Literature and the Image of Man* or *Erzählkunst und Gesellschaft* can attest, Lowenthal had no objection to situating specific authors in the context of long-term developmental tendencies; but he was far more modest than Lukács, or most other Marxist critics for that matter, in abstaining from doing so for the literature of the present or recent past.

This prudence, it might be noted in conclusion, can also be detected in Lowenthal's general political attitudes during his long career. Without ever fully abandoning the utopian yearnings of his youth, he consistently expressed the characteristic Frankfurt School aversion to concrete political movements. *"Mitmachen"* of any kind has never attracted him. Yet, Lowenthal refused to allow his practical abstinence to degenerate into an unintended apologia for the status quo. It was more than just personal ties of friendship that bound him far closer to Marcuse than to Horkheimer during the 1960s and early 1970s. There is perhaps some symbolic value in the fact that in 1969, Lowenthal gave refuge to Marcuse in his Carmel Valley home when death threats in southern California grew particularly virulent.

During the heyday of the student movement in Berkeley in the 1960s, Lowenthal was active in the faculty struggle to effect academic reform as a leader of what he describes as the "left-wing of the Muscatine committee."[15] Unlike many who attempted to mediate in a difficult time, he emerged with the respect and affection of most combatants in both camps.[16] In the years since the Free Speech Movement, his stature has, if anything, increased. Continuing to teach on a part-time basis long after his official retirement, offering among other courses a private seminar that attracts applicants well beyond the confines of the sociology department, Lowenthal remains a potent intellectual force for new generations of students who would otherwise know Critical Theory only through the printed word. Although generalizations of this nature are often hazardous, it is really taking only a small risk to say that there are few figures on the Berkeley campus today who are as widely admired and deeply loved as Leo Lowenthal. Most of those who know his extraordinary physical and mental vigor would be astonished to learn he has reached the age of 80. But none would want to be excluded from the very genuine expression of affectionate tribute that informs the essays presented to him on the following pages.

8.

Positive and Negative Totalities: Implicit Tensions in Critical Theory's Vision of Interdisciplinary Research

Virtually all treatments of the early stages of Critical Theory have drawn attention to the remarkable fit between the organizational framework of the *Institut für Sozialforschung* and its intellectual program. With greatest acuity in the studies of Helmut Dubiel and Alfons Söllner,[1] it has been shown how an interdisciplinary model of materialist social research guided the interpersonal structure of the *Institut* in the years immediately after Max Horkheimer became its director. The collegial hierarchy headed by Horkheimer, who imaginatively used the "dictatorial" powers invested in the director by the *Institut*'s charter,[2] mirrored the methodological hierarchy of task allocation in its research program, thus creating what Söllner has dubbed "a kind of constitutional monarchy in social science."[3] Implicitly drawing on what Marx had called the dialectic of *Darstellung* (presentation) and *Forschung* (research), Horkheimer choreographed the *Institut*'s collective efforts in ways that sought to reveal the totality of social relations in all their contradictory, but still coherent, wholeness. To this end, he argued for the fruitful interaction of critical philosophy and empirical research. As he put it in his inaugural address as *Institut* director in January 1931:

The problems of empirical research and theoretical synthesis can only be solved by a philosophy which, concerned with the general, the "essential," provides the

First published in *Sozialforschung als Kritik: Zum Sozialwissenschftlichen Potential der Kritischen Theorie,* ed. Wolfgang Bonss and Axel Honneth (Frankfurt, 1982), and *Thesis Eleven* (1981), vol. 3.

respective research areas with stimulating impulses, while itself remaining open enough to be impressed and modified by the progress of concrete studies.[4]

More than merely a programmatic statement, these sentiments actively informed the *Institut*'s work during Horkheimer's years as its leader. The initial issue of its new journal, the *Zeitschrift für Sozialforschung,* contained a cross-section of articles on different aspects of the social and cultural totality, as did the massive project on authority and the family completed in the years immediately after the *Institut*'s forced departure from Frankfurt.[5] Even the *Zeitschrift*'s massive review section, edited by Leo Lowenthal, bore witness to the *Institut*'s interdisciplinary ambitions. "Never again," as Jürgen Habermas has recently written of it, "have both disciplinary and national distances been bridged so strikingly in the social sciences; never again has the unity of the social sciences been so convincingly portrayed as here."[6]

In the literature on the Frankfurt School, it has also, however, been recognized that this highly optimistic interdisciplinary program soon proved, at least in part, unworkable. Unmistakable signs of this realization can be seen in the 1940s in the widening gap between the *Institut*'s philosophy of history, most notably expressed in *Dialectic of Enlightenment,* and its empirical work in the *Studies in Prejudice.*[7] A quick glance, for example, at the discrepancies between the "Elements of Anti-Semitism" chapter in *Dialectic of Enlightenment* and the treatment of anti-Semitism in *The Authoritarian Personality* will make the extent of the gap obvious.[8] Evidence of it can, however, be discerned even earlier; Söllner, for example, contends that Horkheimer's seminal essay "Traditional and Critical Theory" along with its companion piece, Marcuse's "Philosophy and Critical Theory," both written in 1937, already demonstrate the *Institut*'s shift from a balance between theory and empirical research to an emphasis on theory, or even more significantly, on "philosophy" alone.[9] And one might also interpret Erich Fromm's departure from the *Institut* a short time later as further proof of the waning power of Horkheimer's original interdisciplinary ambitions, at least in their original form.

And yet, it is clear that the Frankfurt School never fully abandoned its holistic impulses or lost its desire to overcome the specialization of isolated disciplines. What then was the alternative model of interdisciplinary social research motivating its work, a model existing alongside of or perhaps even supplanting the dialectical methodology of *Darstellung* and *Forschung?* In order to answer this question, we must first turn briefly to Critical Theory's complicated relation to Lukács, whose concept of totality was so vital a stimulus to its early articulation. And then we will have to examine what might be called Adorno's essentially Benjaminian reformulation of that concept, which came to have increasing importance in the Frankfurt School's later history.

It was, of course, in *History and Class Consciousness* that Lukács made the celebrated claim, so often repeated in the course of Western Marxism, that *"the primacy of the category of totality is the bearer of the principle of revolution in science."*[10] In many ways, Horkheimer's initial program for the *Institut* derives from this assertion, but in two crucial respects it did not. First, Horkheimer refrained from rigidly opposing dialectical to scientific thinking in the way that Lukács, still fighting the battle of the *Geistes-* and *Naturwissenschaften,* felt compelled to do. Contrary to the later attempts by critics of the Frankfurt School such as Lucio Colletti and Göran Therborn to subsume both Critical Theory and the early Lukács under the rubric of "romantic, antiscientific, anticapitalism,"[11] Horkheimer acknowledged a legitimate, if subordinate, place for traditional scientific techniques in dialectical social research. His greater tolerance on this issue was clearly manifested in his promotion of psychology as a necessary tool in the examination of the social totality. Lukács, following Husserl and before him a long idealist tradition of transcendental subjectivity, had damned psychology as a natural science that had no place in philosophy or, by extension, in a philosophically grounded Marxism. The *Institut's* major psychological theorist, Erich Fromm, did his best to exorcise the biological dimension of psychoanalysis in his social psychology, but the mere acceptance of psychology of any kind as a component in a dialectical social analysis signaled a subtle departure from Lukács' more purely philosophical concept of totality. Even when Horkheimer began to stress the importance of philosophy in itself, he never regressed to the assumption that psychology was inherently incompatible with it.

The *Institut's* interest in psychology also, of course, reflected the change in the situation of the working class in the decade after *History and Class Consciousness.* For psychology was introduced primarily to explain why the Western proletariat had failed to fulfill its historical role. The *Institut's* growing recognition of this failure was also registered in the second major departure of Horkheimer's interdisciplinary social research from Lukács' concept of totality. For Lukács, as also for those other founding fathers of Western Marxism, Korsch and Gramsci, the epistemological claim to know the whole was gounded in the belief that the proletariat was the universal class that totalized social reality through the objectification of its collective subjectivity. Lukács, to be sure, distinguished between empirical and imputed class consciousness, thus allowing Marxist theory to express the objective possibility of the proletariat's class consciousness rather than its immediate manifestation. But the basic epistemological premise of his argument was still the same. Based on a Hegelian transformation of Vico's *verum-factum* principle,[12] it assumed that knowing and making were reciprocal and symmetrical processes: totalistic cognition was the privilege only of those who created the social totality or of their intellectual spokesman in the vanguard party. All others were condemned to partial and therefore ideological knowledge. Only the identity of collective metasubject and the objective social world could overcome the antinomies of bourgeois thought.

Although Horkheimer may have shared this assumption during the 1920s, by the time of his elevation to *Institut* director he clearly no longer did. The proletariat for Horkheimer, as Dubiel has pointed out,[13] ceased functioning as the equivalent of a metaphysical subject-object, the ultimate ground of valid cognition, to become instead the object of a sober, even disillusioned social-psychological analysis. It certainly remained the expected addressee of Critical Theory, its hoped-for audience, at least for a little while longer. But it ceased to be its epistemological touchstone. Theory was still linked to practice, but more as a stimulus to it than both as its expression and stimulus. Horkheimer's sharply worded critique of Mannheim's sociology of knowledge in his 1930 review of *Ideology and Utopia*[14] should also be read as an indirect attack on the genetic dimension of Lukács' theory of knowledge, to which of course Mannheim had been originally indebted. For Horkheimer, any theory of truth that rooted it too closely in the existing social reality diminished its critical and negative force, its ability to transcend that reality. Although Horkheimer at times still held to the classical Marxist belief that there remained immanent tendencies in the present that foreshadowed the future, it was really only a short distance to his notorious admission in 1937 that "under the conditions of later capitalism and the impotence of the workers before the authoritarian state's apparatus of oppression, truth has sought refuge among small groups of admirable men."[15]

Whether or not Horkheimer included the *Institut's* members in this category, he nonetheless continued to feel that totalistic knowledge of society could still be gained through the interdisciplinary methods promoted in the 1931 inaugural address. The essential incoherence of this position, based as it was on an unacknowledged rupture in the *verum-factum* principle, soon, however, became manifest and Critical Theory began to withdraw more and more into philosophy alone as the repository of negation.

The philosophy to which they were drawn was not, however, merely a reprise of the essentially idealist humanism informing the theory of Lukács and other founders of Western Marxism. For as Adorno grew in importance in the *Institut*'s inner circle, he infused Critical Theory with the more complicated amalgam of Lukács and Benjamin that ultimately became known as his special brand of "negative dialectics." What precisely this change meant for the *Institut*'s interdisciplinary project can best be understood by examining another inaugural address of 1931, this one in May by Adorno on the occasion of his joining the philosophy faculty of the University of Frankfurt. "The Actuality of Philosophy," [16] as Adorno called the talk, did not, to be sure, have the same immediate impact as Horkheimer's own inaugural address of January. In fact, it was never published during Adorno's lifetime, possibly because of the hostile reception it seems to have received when first delivered. In two letters to his friend Siegfried Kracauer, [17] Adorno in fact complained about the incomprehension of his listeners, offering Mannheim's conjecture that he, Adorno, had gone over to the Vienna Circle as the worst of many stupid responses. In retrospect, however, as Susan Buck-Morss has demonstrated, [18] "The Actuality of Philosophy" adumbrated many of the themes of Adorno's later work, most notably those developed in *Negative Dialectics*. It also offered, if in inchoate form, an alternative approach to interdisciplinary research to that proposed by Horkheimer, an approach that was later to supplement and in certain ways displace that Hegelian-Marxist dialectic of *Darstellung* and *Forschung* on which the *Institut* had based its earlier work.

Drawing on Benjamin's argument in the recently published *Ursprung des deutschen Trauerspiels*, Adorno began his talk with a bold denial:

Whoever chooses philosophy as a profession today must first reject the illusion that earlier philosophical enterprises began with: that the power of thought is sufficient to grasp the totality of the real. No justifying reason could rediscover itself in a reality whose order and form suppress every claim to reason; only polemically does reason present itself to the knower as total reality, while only in traces and ruins is it prepared to hope that it will ever come across correct and just reality. [19]

Tracing the recent history of holistic thinking in philosophy, Adorno located its breakdown in the terminal crisis of idealism. He then discussed efforts to reconstitute totality in existentialist and phenomenological circles, which culminated in the work of Scheler and Heidegger, efforts that were all in vain. Turning to the argument that science would somehow replace philosophy as the method of totalization, an assumption often held by vulgar Marxists, he contended that the two were fundamentally incompatible modes of cognition:

The separate sciences accept their findings, at least their final and deepest findings, as indestructible and static, whereas philosophy perceives the first finding which it lights upon as a sign that needs unriddling. Plainly put: the idea of science *(Wissenschaft)* is research; that of philosophy is interpretation.[20]

In so arguing, Adorno was implicitly criticizing the contention made by Horkheimer in his own inaugural address a few months before that social philosophy and scientific research could combine to give knowledge of the social whole.

The alternative he was presenting, philosophy as interpretation, did not, however, mean embracing traditional hermeneutics of the Schleiermacherian or Diltheyan kind. Instead, following Benjamin, Adorno denied that interpretation meant the recovery or recollection of an original intended meaning. There was no "real world" behind the veil of appearance, no fixed meaning to be exposed. Truth could only be discovered through permitting constellations of existing elements to become illuminations, sudden and momentary revelations of a nontotalized reality. Through such constructions, and here Adorno went beyond the preMarxist Benjamin, philosophy would become materialist:

Here one can discover what appears as such an astounding and strange affinity existing between interpretive philosophy and that type of thinking which most strongly rejects the concept of the intentional, the meaningful: the thinking of materialism. Interpretation of the unintentional through a juxtaposition of the analytically isolated elements and illumination of the real by the power of such interpretation is the program of every authentically materialist knowledge, a program to which the materialist procedure does all the more justice, the more it distances itself from every "meaning" of its objects and the less it relates to an implicit, quasireligious meaning.[21]

Materialist interpretation also meant rejecting the symbolizing mode of thought characteristic of idealism, which Benjamin had demonstrated was less appropriate than allegory to times of fragmentation:

If philosophy must learn to renounce the question of totality, then it implies that it must learn to do without the symbolic function, in which for a long time, at least in idealism, the particular appeared to represent the general.[22]

By calling for such a renunciation, Adorno was implicitly criticizing the premises of Hegelian Marxism, in particular those articulated in *History and Class Consciousness*. This challenge was made explicit in a thought experiment he proposed which was aimed at Lukács' solution of the antinomies of bourgeois thought:

Suppose it were possible to group the elements of a social analysis in such a manner that the way they came together made a figure which certainly does not lie before us organically, but which must first be posited: the commodity structure. This would hardly solve the thing-in-itself problem, not even in the sense that somehow the social conditions might be revealed under which the thing-in-itself problem came into existence, as Lukács even thought the solution to be; for the truth content of a problem is in principle different from the historical and psychological conditions out of which it grows.[23]

In other words, the reliance on Vico's *verum-factum* principle to collapse truth into class origin was ultimately untenable, as genesis and truth value are unrelated. Similarly, Mannheim's attempt to salvage truth by grounding it entirely in the social being of the contemporary totality misfired, for truth is a function more of the content of thought than the social status of its thinkers.

In severing truth from its social origins, Adorno did not, however, turn the search for it entirely into a contemplative enterprise. With an optimism that would be absent from his later work, he called for a certain unity of theory and practice:

The interpretation of given reality and its abolition are connected to each other, not, of course, in the sense that reality is negated in the concept, but that out of the construction of a configuration of reality the demand for its [reality's] real change always follows promptly. The change-causing gesture of the riddle process—not its mere resolution as such—provides the image of resolutions to which materialist praxis alone has access. Materialism has named this relationship with a name that is philosophically certified: dialectic. Only dialectically, it seems to me, is philosophic interpretation possible.[24]

The precise nature of the link between his anti-intentionalist hermeneutics and concrete praxis Adorno did not, however, specify. Instead, he intimated that philosophic interpretation, presiding as it did over the liquidation of traditional philosophy, would be a form of praxis itself. To achieve this goal, interpretation would have to derive certain of its insights from sociology, without, however, capitulating to what Adorno called its nominalist inclinations. Here he came close to endorsing Horkheimer's program for the *Institut,* which his earlier insistence on the incompatibility of philosophy and research had implicitly questioned. Interpretation would have to manipulate the findings of sociology into constellations whose truth value would be "legitimated in the last analysis alone by the fact that reality crystallizes about them in striking conclusiveness."[25] This rather empty and tautological principle of verification—who was to say what constituted "striking conclusiveness"?—showed that for all his insistence that the demand for "real change always follows promptly" the construction of an idea, he had little confidence in the practical validation of that idea. The complicated dialectic of verification and practice defended by Horkheimer in the 1930s against both contemplative scientism and pragmatism was absent from

Adorno's epistemology. The uncoupling of theory from practice that marked his later work was thus here in embryo.

So too was the type of interdisciplinary work he would come himself to pursue, and which at least in part the *Institut* would also collectively adopt. Its premises, as suggested by "The Actuality of Philosophy" were as follows:

1. No philosophy, no theory, however global in intention or linked with whatever social class, could legitimately claim to grasp the whole. For the object of knowledge, society, was too fragmented, contradictory, and incoherent to permit anything but an equally detotalized vision of it. Only in traces and ruins, those allegorical images Benjamin had detected throughout Baroque tragedies, could a premonition of a future whole be apprehended. There was, in other words, no purely methodological remedy to the fragmentation of knowledge expressed in the chaos of competing disciplines. The goal of a fully integrated interdisciplinary project was thus unattainable at present. Philosophy must be content, therefore, with the essay form and eschew the temptation to become systematic. To assume the possibility of totalistic knowledge would be to regress to the myth of transcendental subjectivity underlying idealism.

2. Philosophy and science are deeply opposed cognitive modes. Whereas science seeks knowledge *sub specie aeternitatis,* philosophy understands its task as an endless process of interpretation, of unriddling without a final answer. "Nothing more is given to it," Adorno wrote of philosophy, "than fleeting, disappearing traces within the riddle figures of that which exists and their astonishing entwinings. The history of philosophy is nothing other than the history of such entwinings. Thus it reaches so few 'results.' "[26] Although philosophy may relfect on material taken from the more scientific methods of sociology, it should never confuse its method with that of social science or fail to acknowledge the gap between them.

3. The true method of philosophy was thus hermeneutic rather than explanatory, but not in the traditional sense of privileging authorial intention. For there is no primal meaning that philosophy can recapture, no initial state of unalienated presence that can be restored. "The task of philosophy," Adorno argued, "is not to search for concealed and manifest intentions of reality, but to interpret unintentional reality."[27] The process of interpretation was thus more constructive than recuperative, drawing on what Adorno called "exact fantasy":

fantasy which abides strictly within the material which the sciences present to it, and reaches beyond them only in the smallest aspects of their arrangement: aspects, granted, which fantasy itself must originally generate.[28]

The desired end-product of these arrangements were those constellations of elements Benjamin had called "profane illuminations." 4. Such illuminations, Adorno argued, were achieved "through a juxtaposition of the analytically isolated elements."[29] The term juxtaposition was critical here, for although Adorno insisted that this method was truly dialectical, he chose not to invoke the Hegelian category of mediation so vital for Lukács and Horkheimer. This decision was manifest in his rejection of the symbolic function of traditional philosophy, which, as we have noted, he defined as the particular purporting to be the representation of the general. The implication for interdisciplinary research was obvious: the dissonant juxtaposition of disciplines rather than their smoothly integrated harmonization was more genuinely critical in this time of social and cultural detotalization.

5. Finally, despite the impossibility of resolving the tensions between disciplines through the mediation of an overarching philosophy, the stark alternative between either a globalizing philosophy or a nominalist and empiricist sociology must be avoided. "The point of interpretive philosophy," he argued with a striking metaphor,

is to construct keys, before which reality springs open. As to the size of the key categories, they are specially made to order. The old idealism chose categories too large; so they did not even come close to fitting the keyhole. Pure philosophic sociologism chooses them too small; the key indeed goes in, but the door doesn't open. A great number of sociologists carry nominalism so far that the concepts become too small to align the others with themselves, to enter with them into a constellation. What remains is a vast, inconsistent connection of simple this-here determinations, which scoffs at every cognitive ordering and in no way provides a critical criterion.[30]

To provide this criterion, such general concepts as class and ideology must be retained, but they cannot be substituted entirely for that micrological analysis of particular details whose arrangement into constellations provides illuminations of the truth.

Such then were the lessons of Adorno's essentially Benjaminian reflections on "The Actuality of Philosophy." In certain respects, they can been seen as presenting a covert challenge to the totalizing, Hegelian Marxist model of interdisciplinary research presented in Horkheimer's inaugural address. How significant, we must now ask, were these lessons for the subsequent development of Critical Theory, in particular for its interdisciplinary program? Can we sharply contrast a neo-Benjaminian model with that of Horkheimer and say it served as its ultimate replacement? The short answer, it seems to me, is that drawn this starkly, the contrast is misleading. For both impulses were potent in the Frankfurt School's later work, including that of Adorno himself.

To take an initial example, in the opening issue of the last volume of the *Zeitschrift*, then renamed *Studies in Philosophy and Social Sciences*, Horkheimer argued for a type of inductive reasoning that can be seen as echoing Benjamin's stress on nongeneralizable particulars as the foundation of critical social science:

Categories have to be formed through a process of induction that is the reverse of the traditional inductive method which verified its hypotheses by collecting individual experiences until they attained the weight of universal laws. Induction in social theory, *per contra*, should seek the universal within the particular, not above or beyond it, and instead of moving from one particular to another and then to the heights of abstraction, should delve deeper and deeper into the particular and discover the universal law therein.[31]

The Benjaminian emphasis on particulars was obvious here, but Horkheimer's method was still indifferent to the distinction between allegory and symbol, as his last phrase indicates. Horkheimer, moreover, then added that the concepts thus generated were nonetheless integrative in intention, aimed at grasping the entire social and historical totality.

Horkheimer's still powerful faith in the possibility of totalized knowledge, mixed as it now was with a Benjaminian stress on the micrological analysis of the particular, seems to have influenced Adorno away from the more extreme Benjaminianism, if I may coin a term, of "The Actuality of Philosophy." As his controversial and much-remarked epistolary critique of Benjamin's *Passagenarbeit* drafts show, he now felt some of the force of Mannheim's obtuse remark about the Vienna Circle; Benjamin's method, he came to understand, was too hostile to a general theory, too indifferent to mediating particulars:

I regard it as methodologically unfortunate to give conspicuous individual features from the realm of the superstructure a "materialistic" turn by relating them immediately and perhaps even causally to corresponding features of the infrastructure. Materialist determination of cultural traits is only possible if it is mediated through the *total social process*. . . . The "mediation" which I miss and find obscured by materialistic-historiographic invocation, is nothing other than the theory which your study omits. . . . If one wished to put it very drastically, one could say that your study is located at the crossroads of magic and positivism. That spot is bewitched. Only theory could break the spell—your own resolute, salutarily speculative theory.[32]

Adorno clearly referred back to Benjamin's *Ursprung des deutschen Trauerspiels*, the book that had been so decisive for his own inaugural essay, as the locus of that theory. But certain tendencies in that work were now, in perhaps exaggerated form, at the root of his discontent.

Thus, for example, he came to acknowledge the unfortunate similarity between Benjamin's constellations of juxtaposed elements and the montage techniques of the Surrealists. Benjamin had, as early as 1926, been drawn to these techniques, but Adorno was convinced that in their indifference to concrete subjectivity and mediation, the Surrealists were only pseudorevolutionary.[33] Similarly, he came to see that Benjamin's insistence on only unintended meanings could be turned too easily into acquiescence in reification. Benjamin's "dialectics at a standstill" thus had its dangers:

His target is not an allegedly overinflated subjectivism but rather the notion of a subjective dimension itself. Between myth and reconciliation, the poles of his philosophy, the subject evaporates. Before his Medusan gaze, man turns into the stage on which an objective process unfolds. For this reason Benjamin's philosophy is no less a source of terror than a promise of happiness.[34]

And yet, despite these very serious reservations, Adorno remained deeply indebted to many of Benjamin's ideas, especially when it came to defining an interdisciplinary methodology. Thus, for example, when considering the relations between sociology and psychology, he rejected the attempt to harmonize them in a systematic way, exemplified in the work of Fromm and, later, of Talcott Parsons. Disciplines cannot be merged by methodological fiat, for "the only totality the student of society can presume to know is the antagonistic whole, and if he is to attain the totality at all, then only in and through contradictions."[35] Within psychology itself, theories that recognize the conflict between ego and id are thus more faithful and ultimately critical of reality than those, such as Heinz Hartmann's ego psychology, that attempt to synthesize them. And *a fortiori* the conflicts between psychology and sociology should be both challenged and preserved:

The separation of sociology and psychology is both correct and false. False because it encourages the specialists to relinquish the attempt to know the totality which even the separation of the two demand; and correct insofar as it registers more intransigently the split that has actually taken place in reality than does the premature unification at the level of theory.[36]

Even more specifically Benjaminian was Adorno's method in *The Authoritarian Personality.* As Susan Buck-Morss has observed,

The idea that a cluster of elements which on the surface appeared to be unrelated and irrational (in this case, responses to an opinion questionnaire) could be rearranged in various trial combinations (the final F Scale was the product of many such arrangements) until they fell into a configuration with an inner logic which could be read as meaningful (here the structure of the authoritarian personality) fully paralleled the method of constructing constellations which Adorno had outlined in his 1931 inaugural address and hence his and Benjamin's Koenigstein position.[37]

Adorno, as Buck-Morss quickly admits, did temper his fidelity to this common position with a Horkheimerian stress on the necessity of mediating the elements of the constellation through a totalizing theory, in this case that of anti-Semitism developed in *Dialectic of Enlightenment.* But, as we noted earlier, the precise relationship between this theory and the findings of the empirical study were never made very clear, nor perhaps could they be. For the distinct methods of interdisciplinary research propounded by Benjamin and Horkheimer were never fully compatible.

Indeed, it might be argued that much of the creative ambivalence of Adorno's negative dialectics can be traced to the unreconciled tensions between these two impulses in his work. His own variant of Critical Theory can be seen as a nonidentical "force-field" between Benjaminian and Horkheimerian poles. As he once acknowledged, "since the individual phenomenon conceals in itself the whole of society, micrology and mediation through totality act as a counterpoint to one another."[38] It was, however, more of a dissonant counterpoint than a harmonious one. A truly liberating interdisciplinary method would therefore not try to force integration through methodological fiat, just as it would resist the utter fragmentation of intellectual life into hermetically sealed compartments. As he put it in the positivist dispute,

Science wishes to rid the world of the tension between the general and the particular by means of its consistent system, but the world gains its unity from inconsistency. . . . This inconsistency is the reason why the object of sociology—society and its phenomenon—does not possess the type of homogeneity which so-called classical natural science was able to count on.[39]

But conversely,

Insight into the heterogeneity of sociology as a scientific construct, that is, insight into the heterogeneity of the categorial, and not merely graded and easily bridgeable, divergence between disciplines such as social theory, the analysis of objective social conditions and institutions, and subjectively oriented social research in the narrower sense, does not imply that one should simply accept the sterile division between the disciplines. The formal demand for the unity of a science is certainly not to be respected when the science itself bears the marks of an arbitrary division of labor and cannot set itself up as if it could discern without difficulty the much-favored totalities, whose social existence is, in any case, questionable. But the critical amalgamation of divergent sociological methods is required for concrete reasons, for the cognitive goal.[40]

In calling for such a critical amalgamation of disciplines, Adorno, however, was only partially returning to that Lukácsian holistic impulse that we have seen initially motivating Horkheimer's project. For in the interim, his attitude toward totality had changed or, more precisely, his awareness of its objectionable features had deepened. Whereas the normative ideal of a perfectly harmonious, noncontradictory community to be realized through socialism had been the telos of both Lukács' Hegelian Marxism and the *Institut*'s early materialist social science, Adorno became wary of its potential dangers. "Totality," he came to insist, "is not an affirmative but rather a critical category. Dialectical critique seeks to salvage or help to establish what does not obey totality, what opposes it or what first forms itself as the potential of a not yet existent individuation. . . . A liberated mankind would by no means be a totality."[41]

What this assertion paradoxically implies, I would suggest in conclusion, is that the very incompatibilities and tensions that Horkheimer's initial *Institut* program sought to overcome through its interdisciplinary method of *Darstellung* and *Forschung* were not merely inevitable because of the incoherence of even the current one-dimensional totality. Even more importantly, they should be understood to represent, if in perverted and distorted form, the nonidentical liberation of the possible future. Rather than bemoaned as obstacles to a totalistic, philosophically directed social science, they might therefore also be seen as manifestations of resistance to the oppressive totalization of the present. Indeed, one might say that the reproach of eclecticism sometimes made by more orthodox Marxist critics of Critical Theory—here I am thinking in particular of Göran Therborn's attack on Habermas[42]—can be refuted precisely by reference to the justification of a nonidentical interdisciplinary method present in that unreconciled amalgamation of Benjaminian and Horkheimerian models in Adorno's work. Here the apparent failure of the *Institut*'s initial ambitions can, paradoxically, be seen as a source of its ultimate strength.[43]

9.
Adorno in America

The exemplary anecdotes are known to us all. Adorno arrives in America in 1938 to work on Paul Lazarsfeld's Princeton Radio Research Project. Lazarsfeld writes of his new acquaintance: "He looks as you would image a very absent-minded German professor, and he behaves so foreign that I feel like a member of the Mayflower society."[1] Adorno travels to the Project's offices in an abandoned brewery in Newark, New Jersey, through a tunnel under the Hudson River and admits "I felt a little as if I were in Kafka's Nature Theater of Oklahoma."[2] The attempt to adapt his ideas to the needs of the Project soon proves, not surprisingly, a failure, as Adorno's concept of fetishization resists all efforts to operationalize it. Lazarsfeld's hope to achieve what he later called "a convergence of European theory and American empiricism"[3] is quickly abandoned with no small amount of embarrassment and bitter feelings on both sides.

A decade later, the *Institut für Sozialforschung* is invited back to Frankfurt, and Adorno, with no hesitation, joins Max Horkheimer and Friedrich Pollock in its reconstruction. Having noted in *Minima Moralia* that "every intellectual in emigration is, without exception, mutilated," in particular because "his language has been expropriated, and the historical dimension that nourished his knowledge, sapped,"[4] he leaves his exile home for good in 1953 and never looks back. Twelve years later, he tells his German audience in a radio talk entitled "Auf die Frage: Was ist Deutsch?"[5] that both subjective and objective reasons determined his return. The former include the slight to his self-esteem dealt him by an American publisher who criticized *Philosophie der neuen Musik* for being "badly organized."[6] The latter, which he claims are more substantial, center around his desire to write in his native tongue, whose

First published in *Adorno-Konferenz 1983,* ed. Ludwig von Friedeburg and Jürgen Habermas (Frankfurt, 1983) and *New German Critique* (Winter 1984), vol. 31.

"elective affinity" for philosophy, in particular its speculative and dialectical moment, he claims is superior to that of English.

When Adorno dies in 1969, *The New York Times* carries a short obituary, which soon gains modest notoriety for its remarkable garbling of Adorno's life and work.[7] Focusing for mysterious reasons on an obscure piece he once wrote on jitterbugging, it fails to record any of the important theoretical dimensions of his thought. At the time of his death, Adorno is known in America almost entirely as the first name on the title page of *The Authoritarian Personality*, a study whose uneasy mixture of empirical methods and Critical Theory was very atypical of his work as a whole. The only translation of his writings on cultural themes then available is *Prisms*, which a small British publisher had brought out in 1967 and failed to distribute in America. Not a single philosophical work is accessible to readers unable to take on the challenge of Adorno's formidable German.

The image of Adorno's relation to America conveyed by these anecdotes is not difficult to discern. The sensitive European mandarin is shocked and bewildered by the commercialism, vulgarity, and theoretical backwardness of his temporary home. Belittling the assimilationist tendencies of other emigrés as a form of craven accommodation to economic necessity, he hustles back to Germany as soon as the opportunity avails itself. America in return finds him arrogant, snobbish, and incomprehensible. His departure is little noted and even less mourned.

That this image is more than just impressionistically anecdotal is confirmed by a sample of the critical literature on Adorno's relation to America. The linguistic barrier, for example, is widely remarked even after translations are attempted. The musicologist and Stravinsky confidante Robert Craft speaks for many when he complains that "a more convoluted, abstruse, and floridly unintelligible style is scarcely conceivable. It can have been designed for one purpose only, that of maintaining the highest standards of obfuscation throughout."[8] No less disconcerting to many is Adorno's merciless critique of mass culture, which offends the populist pieties of progressive American thought. Edward Shils, Leon Bramson, and Herbert Gans lead a phalanx of critics who point to the apparent paradox of a self-proclaimed leftist so contemptuous of democratic tastes and values.[9] Adorno is called a covert Puritan and ascetic for his hostility to the simple pleasures of the common man.[10] Behind the facade of a modernist, one critic spies "a yearning for European liberal-bourgeois society and the life-style of its cultured upper-middle-class members."[11] According to another, Adorno's debts to figures like Spengler and Nietzsche make it "far more useful and evocative to regard" him and his colleagues in the Frankfurt School "as men of the Right than of the Left."[12] To still a third, Adorno can "be described, not *altogether* unfairly, as a materialist *dandy* . . . a stranded spiritual aristocrat doomed to extinction by the 'rising tide of democracy.'"[13]

These examples are all taken from American responses to Adorno, but the image they convey has not been confined to our shores. In 1976, a very hostile essay entitled "'Beute der Pragmatisierung': Adorno und Amerika" was published in a collection on *Die USA und Deutschland* edited by Wolfgang Paulsen.[14] Its author, Dagmar Barnouw, compared Adorno with the French aristocrats who emigrated during the French Revolution. Criticizing his "autocratic snobbism" and paranoiac *ressentiment,* she concluded that works like *Dialectic of Enlightenment* were little more than "poetic performances in total reaction against a social reality"[15] that Adorno neither understood nor appreciated.

The grain of truth in these contentions, however exaggerated and one-sided they may be, must be acknowledged. The Adorno who could complain that "it is made unmistakably clear to the intellectual from abroad that he will have to eradicate himself as an autonomous being if he hopes to achieve anything"[16] was clearly not an eager convert to the "American way of life." There can be no question that the linguistic uprootedness that Adorno felt with a keenness more typical of literary than scholarly emigrés[17] was a genuine trauma, as his frequent quarrels with Siegfried Kracauer over the use of English abundantly demonstrate.[18] Nor is it disputable, as Adorno's notoriously unsympathetic treatment of jazz illustrates, that he tended to flatten out the dynamic contradictions of the popular culture he knew only from afar. It is equally clear that many of the analyses he made of his emigré home were colored by the aftereffects of his forced departure from Europe. As one commentator has recently noted, the major works he completed in exile all "contained many passages which assimilated American society to that of Nazi Germany"[19] with an insensitivity obvious in hindsight. And it would be no less difficult to detail the ways in which the American reception of Adorno mirrors this image of hostility and incomprehension.

But it would nonetheless be a travesty of the truth to remain content with so one-dimensional an account of the impact of America on Adorno and the impact of Adorno on us. To make better sense of this dual relationship, it would be useful to borrow the celebrated image of a constellation which Adorno himself borrowed from Benjamin. It is, in fact, helpful to conceptualize Adorno's general place in the intellectual life of the twentieth century by understanding the multiple impulses contained in his work as forming a figure of juxtaposed elements irreducible to any one dominant star. For rather than turning Adorno into essentially an elitist mandarin merely pretending to be a Marxist or an aesthetic modernist with only residual nostalgia for the world he left behind, it is better to acknowledge the countervailing energies of each of these forces in his field. If we add to them several others, most notably his ambiguous identification with the Jews, which appears in his dark ruminations on the meaning of the Holocaust, and what might be called his proto-deconstructionist impulse, to which I will return later, a more fully nuanced understanding of the irreconcilable tensions in Adorno's formation can be grasped. Rather than reduce Adorno to any one star in his constellation, be it Western Marxist, elitist mandarin, aesthetic modernist, or whatever, we must credit all of them with the often contradictory power they had in shaping his idiosyncratic variant of Critical Theory. For what made Adorno so remarkable a figure was the fact that the negative dialectics he so steadfastly defended, with its valorization of nonidentity and heterogeneity, was concretely exemplified in his own intellectual composition, which never produced any harmoniously totalized world view.

The same approach, I want to argue, will allow us to make sense as well of his uneasy relationship to America, which was far more complicated than the conventional image expressed in the anecdotes and scholarship mentioned a few moments ago. For although there can be little doubt that the European star in Adorno's constellation shone brighter than the American, the gravitational pull of the latter was by no means negligible. If the aphorisms of *Minima Moralia* were reflections on an emigré's damaged life, it is, after all, important to recognize that the original source of the damage was not the culture industry in America, but rather the crisis of European culture and society that forced him into exile in the first place. Although it would be foolish to claim that the damage was somehow healed during his stay, it is also not entirely correct to see his experience as merely deepening his pessimism about the universality and irreversibility of the crisis. For when Adorno returned to Frankfurt, he was a changed man. "It is scarcely an exaggeration to say," Adorno would ultimately acknowledge, "that any contemporary consciousness that has not appropriated the American experience, even if in opposition, has something reactionary about it."[20] Although Adorno's appropriation was largely in opposition, it nonetheless did include two positive elements.

First, the doubts he had already entertained about the redemptive power of high culture, doubts instilled in him in part by his Marxist and aesthetic modernist inclinations, were immeasurably strengthened by his contact with a society in which no such faith could be found. "In America," he later wrote, "I was liberated from a certain naive belief in culture and attained the capacity to see culture from the outside. To clarify the point: in spite of all social criticism and all consciousness of the primacy of economic factors, the fundamental importance of the mind—'Geist'—was quasi a dogma self-evident to me from the very beginning. The fact that this was not a foregone conclusion, I learned in America."[21] Adorno put this knowledge to good use in the essay he wrote in 1949 entitled "Cultural Criticism and Society," which was first published two years later in a *Festschrift* for Leopold von Wiese and then served as the opening essay of *Prisms.*[22] His American-induced critique of the fetishism of high culture, which expanded on the earlier analysis of "affirmative culture"[23] made by Horkheimer and Marcuse in the years shortly after their own arrivals in New York, might, in fact, be seen as evidence of the radicalizing effect of Adorno's emigration. One commentator has gone so far as to claim that this change shows that "in certain ways Adorno now moved closer toward a Marxian analytical framework."[24]

In more directly political terms, however, the emigration seems to have had the opposite effect. For the second lesson Adorno appropriated from his years in the United States was derived from what he called his "more fundamental, and more gratifying . . . experience of the substance of democratic forms: that in America they have penetrated the whole of life, whereas in Germany at least they were never more than formal rules of the game."[25] Here Adorno seems to exemplify the deradicalization familiar in the histories of many leftist intellectuals who came to America, much to the chagrin of some later observers like Joachim Radkau.[26] But interpreted more generously, these remarks can be seen as indicating a cautiously realistic optimism about the value of trying to contribute "something toward political enlightenment"[27] in his native land, as he was to put it many years hence. For by his actions after his return, it is clear that Adorno, like the other members of the repatriated *Institut* staff, had hopes that the substance of democratic forms might also be introduced to a Germany which had never known them in the past. Rather than bemoaning the penetration of American commercialism and vulgarity, which to be sure he did in other contexts, Adorno came back to Europe with the belief that something of genuine political value might be brought with him across the Atlantic.

It was in this spirit that Adorno, obviously fighting his earlier inclinations, cautiously defended the usefulness of public opinion research in Germany in the 1951 conference on empirical social research in Frankfurt.[28] Pointing to the disparagement of such techniques during the era that had just ended, he noted that the Nazis had understood all too well the democratic potential of a method that treats every voice as having equal weight. With belated recognition of the original aim of Lazarsfeld's Radio Research Project, he contended that the unmediated opposition posited by some between "administrative" and "critical" social research was a fallacious oversimplification. His positive experience working on *The Authoritarian Personality* project clearly left its mark on Adorno, as it did other members of the *Institut.*[29] Although in later years he would reconsider some of his enthusiasm for empirical techniques, because of their threat to replace Critical Theory entirely, he never lost his respect for their potential as tools of enlightenment.

In a country where most of the basic "facts" of social and political life had been systematically distorted for a dozen years, it is not difficult to see why Adorno would have modified his earlier hostility to empiricism or even have begun talking positively about the possibility of enlightenment. It was, of course, with the hope of reeducating his countrymen about those facts that Adorno would later contribute to the debate about Germany's "unmastered past" in such essays as "Was bedeutet: Aufarbeitung der Vergangenheit" in 1959 and "Erziehung nach Auschwitz" in 1966.[30] That Adorno could speak positively about pedagogy rather than revolution shows how deeply impressed by his American experience he was. So too does his emphasis on the importance of psychoanalysis in the process of reeducation, for it was one of the cardinal lessons of *The Authoritarian Personality* that the traditional progressive faith in reason alone was inadequate. As the concluding sentences of the study assert, "we need not suppose that appeal to emotion belongs to those who strive in the direction of fascism, while democratic propaganda must limit itself to reason and restraint. If fear and destructiveness are the major emotional sources of fascism, *eros* belongs mainly to democracy."[31] It was in the hope of harnessing the insights of psychoanalysis for emancipatory purposes that Adorno and his *Institut* colleagues organized the influential conference on "Freud in die Gegenwart" in Frankfurt in 1956[32] and were supportive of the work of Alexander Mitscherlich and the Sigmund Freud Institute.

In his essay on "Aufarbeitung der Vergangenheit," Adorno explicitly tied the absence of a lively psychoanalytic culture in Germany to the effects of anti-semitism, whose central importance seems only to have become gradually apparent to Adorno and his colleagues during their American exile. When they returned to Germany, the glib Marxist formulas that had characterized their work at least as late as Horkheimer's "Die Juden und Europe" of 1939 were now things of the past.[33] In the "Elements of Anti-Semitism" section of *Dialectic of Enlightenment* in particular, Adorno had come to understand the intimate relationship between hatred of the Jews and the extirpation of non-identity that was the dominant bugbear of his negative dialectics. It was not merely the supposed guilt of the survivor that made him sensitive to the implications of Auschwitz for Western culture, but also the experience he had in America of a nonreductive reaction to anti-Semitism that avoided the trivializations of the European left.

In summary, although it might be said that while in America Adorno tended to interpret his new surroundings through the lens of his earlier experience, once back home he saw Germany with the eyes of someone who had been deeply affected by his years in exile. Negatively, this meant an increased watchfulness for the signs of an American-style culture industry in Europe.[34] Positively, it meant a wariness of elitist defenses of high culture for its own sake, a new respect for the value of democratic politics, a grudging recognition of the emancipatory potential in certain empirical techniques, and a keen appreciation of the need for a psychological dimension in pedagogy. To put it in capsule form, only an Adorno who had spent time in the United States could have written a sentence like the following from his *Introduction to the Sociology of Music:* "In general, outrage at the alleged mass era has become an article for mass consumption, fit for inciting the masses against politically democratic forms" (p. 132).

If it is misleading, then, to discount the effects of Adorno's American experience as a subtle counterweight to his European origins and thus miss the dynamic tensions in his intellectual force-field, it would be no less so to characterize the American response to his work as entirely uncomprehending and hostile. For here too the relation between Adorno and America is far more complex and ambivalent than the anecdotal impressions mentioned earlier would suggest. As early as 1954 and C. Wright Mills' acknowledgment in *The Saturday Review* that the return of Horkheimer and Adorno to Germany was "to the great loss of American social studies,"[35] a positive awareness of his work has been evident among growing circles of American intellectuals. Benefiting from the popularity of their former colleague Herbert Marcuse in the 1960s, the Frankfurt School as a whole gained widespread attention in the United States only a few years after its explosive rise to prominence in West Germany. Critical Theory seemed the most appropriate form of heterodox Marxism for a society without a large-scale militant working-class movement and with a growing counterculture distrustful of technological rationality. Unlike in Britain, where Althusser's brand of scientistic scholasticism and political orthodoxy attracted extensive admiration, in America, the New Left found Marcuse's version of the Frankfurt School's ideas especially congenial. Some of its members, like Donald Kuspit,[36]

Samuel and Shierry Weber, Jeremy Shapiro, and Angela Davis, were stimulated enough to go to the source and study in Frankfurt.

Adorno, of course, was initially far less well known back in America and was thus spared the type of controversy over the practical implications of his ideas that swirled around him in Germany shortly before his death. Although I can recall a heated conversation in 1968 with the leader of the Columbia University SDS and later member of the Weatherman underground, Mark Rudd, who dismissed Adorno as a betrayer of the revolution, this attitude rarely surfaced in the American New Left's reception of his work, such as it was. Far more typical was the joint dedication of a book edited by Paul Breines called *Critical Interruptions: New Left Perspectives on Herbert Marcuse*, published in 1970,[37] which, with no apparent irony, was addressed to Adorno and another recently deceased hero of the movement, Ho Chi Minh. Although by the mid-1970s, some of the same complaints against Adorno's politics that had appeared in Germany were repeated in America, it was in the less volatile context of the postpolitical academization of Marxism.[38]

If the moment when Adorno's work became more than merely an enticing rumor for the American New Left could be dated, it would probably be 1967 with the publication of an essay entitled "Adorno: or, Historical Tropes" by the Marxist literary critic Fredric Jameson in the journal *Salmagundi*.[39] Four years later, it served as the opening chapter in his widely influential *Marxism and Form*, which presented the first substantive survey of Western Marxism to an English-speaking audience. Although concluding that *Negative Dialectics* was "in the long run a massive failure," Jameson nonetheless praised Adorno's concrete studies as "incomparable models of the dialectical process, essays at once both systematic and occasional, in which pretext and consciousness meet to form the most luminous, if transitory, of figures or tropes of historical intelligibility."[40] In the same year as Jameson's essay first appeared, George Steiner's highly lauded collection *Language and Silence* introduced Adorno's lament about the impossibility of writing poetry after Auschwitz to American readers.[41] Scattered remarks throughout the rest of the book indicated that Steiner saw Adorno and other continental Marxists like Benjamin and Lukács as major cultural critics, whose absence from the Anglo-American scene was a scandalous indication of its sterility. No less powerful an endorsement came from the other leading guide to recent European theory of those years, George Lichtheim, whose interest lay more in political and philosophical matters than aesthetic or cultural ones. Although many of his best pieces appeared in British journals like the *Times Literary Supplement*, in 1968 Northwestern University's *Triquarterly* published his sympathetic overview of Western Marxism entitled "From Marx to Hegel," which treated Adorno as the "spiritual antipode"[42] to Lukács in that tradition. Three years later, Lichtheim republished the piece in a collection with the same name that included an admiring essay solely on Adorno, which had first appeared anonymously in the *TLS* in 1967, as well as several other essays on Critical Theory. Although somewhat journalistic in tone, Lichtheim's sympathetic appreciations of the Frankfurt School, with whose general position he explicitly identified,[43] played a constructive role in the early years of Adorno's American reception.

Although Adorno's death in 1969 was, as we have seen, an event of little importance in the popular media, it was followed by a more serious appraisal of his significance in academic circles. In December 1969, the Jewish review *Midstream* published my essay on "The Permanent Exile of Theodor W. Adorno,"[44] which tried to provide a broad overview of his career, including its last, unhappy episodes. In the following year, the newly founded radical philosophy journal *Telos* brought out the first of its many considerations of Adorno's work, Russell Jacoby's ecstatically favorable review of *Aufsätze zur Gesellschaftstheorie.*[45] Jacoby, whose admiration for Adorno went so far that he emulated many of his stylistic mannerisms, soon became his major American defender against all attacks from the right or left. Intransigently insisting that negative dialectics was completely compatible with Marxism at its most radical, he quickly became notorious for his sharply worded critiques of all attempts to make sense of the Frankfurt School's work in less glowing terms.[46]

Telos was also the journal where other very positive assessments of Adorno's work by Dick Howard and Susan Buck-Morss first appeared.[47] Although far from the center of American intellectual life during these years—in its Spring 1970 issue it proudly described itself as "a philosophical journal *definitely outside* the mainstream of American philosophical thought"[48]—it soon established itself as the major interpreter of Western Marxist ideas for the English-speaking world. Its only rival was the *New Left Review* in England, which was much more favorably inclined towards Althusserian and other allegedly scientific Marxisms than towards Critical Theory.[49] Other journals like *Social Research, New German Critique, Theory and Society,* and *Cultural Hermeneutics* also opened their pages to articles about Adorno and his colleagues, but none was as tenacious as *Telos* in promoting his work in America, not only through articles about him, but also by translating many of his more important essays.

The difficult task of rendering Adorno's longer works into

English began in earnest in the early 1970s: *Dialectic of Enlightenment* and *Aspects of Sociology* in 1972, *Philosophy of Modern Music, Negative Dialectics,* and *Jargon of Authenticity* in 1973, *Minima Moralia* in 1974, *Introduction to the Sociology of Music* and *The Positivist Dispute in German Sociology* in 1976, *In Search of Wagner* in 1981, and *Against Epistemology* and the republication of *Prisms* in 1982. Further translations of the *Notes on Literature* and the *Aesthetic Theory* have been announced. Although of very mixed quality—Edmund Jephcott's rendition of *Minima Moralia* is often said to be the most successful, while several others vie for the honor of being the least—the English translations of Adorno's major works in the past decade did make it possible for a much wider audience to confront his work. Against the backdrop of several accounts of the Frankfurt School as a whole, which began with my *The Dialectical Imagination* in 1973 and continued with the surveys and collections of Slater, Tar, O'Neill, Held, Friedman, Connerton, and Arato and Gebhardt,[50] they provided the basis for an increasingly sophisticated American reception of his work, which is by no means at its end.

One of the clearest indications of that sophistication is the progressive refinement of the American perception of Adorno's unique place in the Western Marxist tradition, which is now no longer understood in the simplified terms of a return "from Marx to Hegel." In 1977, Susan Buck-Morss published her penetrating study of *The Origin of Negative Dialectics,*[51] which used previously untapped primary sources to demonstrate Adorno's indebtedness to Benjamin and subtle differences with Horkheimer. Moving beyond my emphasis on the relative coherence of a unified Frankfurt School in *The Dialectical Imagination,* she persuasively showed the ways in which Adorno was always an idiosyncratic member of the *Institut*'s inner circle. Other scholars have scrutinized the complexities of Adorno's relationships with his friends Siegfried Kracauer and Leo Lowenthal, as well as exploring the implications of Lichtheim's remark that he was the "spiritual antipode" of Lukács within Western Marxism.[52] More recently still, the full ramifications of his complicated interaction with Benjamin have been reexamined, most probingly in excellent new books by Richard Wolin and Eugene Lunn.[53] Lunn, in fact, has succeeded in modifying still further Buck-Morss's modification of my argument about the collective coherence of the Frankfurt School by demonstrating the differences between Adorno and Benjamin even in the 1920s, before their celebrated dispute over mass culture, technology, and political engagement. Stressing Adorno's roots in an Expressionism that was moving beyond its subjective phase toward the objectification of its anguish, he contrasted Adorno's version of aesthetic modernism with Benjamin's, which was more deeply indebted to Surrealism and Symbolism with their relative indifference to the fate of subjectivity.

Adorno's differences with Habermas, most extensively spelled out in an article by Axel Honneth translated in *Telos* in 1979,[54] have also attracted widespread comment in recent years. Those like the ecologically minded anarchist Murray Bookchin use Adorno's analysis of the domination of nature against Habermas, whom they accuse of complicity with the instrumental rationality the older Frankfurt School found so oppressive.[55] Others like Joel Whitebook invoke the ambiguities of the dialectic of enlightenment against what they see as Habermas' "compulsively modernistic"[56] project. Still others, like the English sociologist Gillian Rose, the author of a major study of Adorno entitled *The Melancholy Science,* chastise Habermas for violating Adorno's injunction against identity theory through his positing of an ideal speech situation.[57] Those, on the other hand, who find Habermas' position more politically promising, often contrast his stress on intersubjectivity with Adorno's retreat into the wreckage of the bourgeois subject.[58] Admiring Habermas' attempt to break the logjam of classical Critical Theory and develop new ways of conceptualizing the still unresolved contradictions of contemporary society, they also applaud his search for a more viable normative ground than the immanent critique whose power Adorno himself often came to question.

Although these debates cannot be pursued in greater detail now, I hope the general point has been made. The American reception of Adorno's work has been immeasurably improved by the increasing precision of our understanding of his place in the general context of Western Marxism. Not only are we increasingly aware of the differences as well as similarities between Adorno and the other members of the Frankfurt School, we are also far more sensitive than we were to the unexpected convergences between his position and that of other Western Marxists in the anti-Hegelian camp, like Althusser and Colletti.[59] Although there are still some defenders of the absolute distinction between critical and scientific Marxisms,[60] the second thoughts many American leftists have had about the virtues of neo-Hegelianism have led them to seek new ways to conceptualize the legacy of Western Marxism and Adorno's place in it.

If we turn now to the ways that specific dimensions of Adorno's work have been treated in America, the implications of this shift will become apparent. As might be expected, certain aspects of Adorno's work have been more readily accepted than others. In large measure because of the absence of translations, his writings on literature and aesthetics have been less widely discussed than his cultural criticism and philosophy. Aside from still unpublished dissertations by Michael Jones on the literary essays and Lambert Zuidervaart on the *Aesthetic Theory*,[61] there have been no full-length treatments of these themes. Although scholars who teach European literatures, like Jameson, Russell Berman, and Peter Uwe Hohendahl,[62] have incorporated and debated Adorno's ideas, those who concentrate on English and American literature have not. As Frank Lentricchia concedes in his magisterial survey, *After the New Criticism,* Adorno and other Western Marxist aestheticians "have a great deal to say to American critics, but . . . they have not been shaping influences."[63]

Adorno's musical writings, which are somewhat more readily available in English, have fared marginally better. But scattered essays by Ronald Weitzmann (who is English), Donald Kuspit, Wesley Blomster, Rose Rosengard Subotnik, and James L. Marsh cannot really compare with the very extensive reception of Adorno's musicological works in Germany.[64] In Charles Rosen's widely admired book on Schoenberg, for example, there is no mention of Adorno, nor is he widely cited in the American literature on Wagner.[65] And if Adorno has had little impact on musicological circles, it is even less likely, although I cannot be absolutely certain, that he has influenced actual American composers, as Carl Dalhaus claims was the case in Germany during the 1950s and 1960s.[66] Perhaps Robert Craft's remark in his critical review of the translation of *Philosophy of Modern Music* suggests the reason: it "comes twenty-five years too late to exert any active influence. Not that Adorno's interpretation has been proved or disproved. It simply has been passed by, relegated to academe when the music finally escaped the custody of theoretical critiques and entered the live performing repertory."[67]

Adorno's thoughts on culture in general, however, have been far more influential in the still lively debate over the implications of mass culture. The model of the "culture industry" was, after all, first developed with America in mind and several of Adorno's former colleagues who remained in the United States, especially Lowenthal and Marcuse, were notable contributors to the discussion which followed. In the 1950s, many respected American intellectuals, including Dwight MacDonald and David Riesman, drew on Adorno's work, even if indirectly. By the 1960s and 1970s, many younger commentators, such as Diane Waldman, Andreas Huyssen, Stanley Aronowitz, Douglas Kellner, Philip Rosen, Miriam Hansen, Mattei Calinescu, John Brenkman, and Thomas Andrae, found Adorno a source of even greater inspiration.[68] Interestingly, one of the keenest areas of interest has been Adorno's scattered remarks on film, which have attracted attention in part because of the increased American awareness of the new German cinema. The impact of Adorno's criticisms of traditional Hollywood films on directors like Alexander Kluge has not gone unnoticed by American critics. The translations of Adorno's essays "Culture Industry Reconsidered" and "Transparencies on Film"[69] have also led to an appreciation of the ways in which he came to nuance the remittingly bleak prognosis of the original analysis in *Dialectic of Enlightenment*. His reconsiderations in this area have allowed his critique of film to be taken more sympathetically than his less forgiving attack on jazz, which is probably the least successful aspect of his work in America.

Adorno's powerful critique of mass culture has been especially influential because of its roots in his social psychology. Although the dust raised by the controversy over *The Authoritarian Personality* settled long ago in the 1950s, other aspects of Adorno's appropriation of Freud have continued to attract attention. In works like Bruce Brown's *Marx, Freud, and the Critique of Everyday Life* and Russell Jacoby's *Social Amnesia*,[70] Adorno's defense of the radical potential of Freud's early work and his critique of the premature harmony of sociology and psychology, a critique elaborated by Marcuse in his attack on Fromm in *Eros and Civilization*, have been endorsed with enthusiasm. In the even more influential studies of Christopher Lasch, *Haven in a Heartless World* and *The Culture of Narcissism*,[71] many of the Frankfurt School's arguments about the decline of the family and its invasion by the professional bureaucracies of the administered world have been given still greater currency. Joel Kovel's probing dissections of contemporary analytic practice, *A Complete Guide to Therapy* and *The Age of Desire: Reflections of a Radical Psychoanalyst*,[72] are also indebted to Critical Theory's earlier considerations of this issue. Thus, although the general Frankfurt School use of Freud has not been spared criticism from a variety of perspectives,[73] it has nonetheless been and continues to be an enormous stimulus to the American attempt to harness Freudianism for emancipatory ends.

If, however, we really want to understand the implications of the shift I mentioned a few moments ago in the perception of Adorno's place in the Western Marxist tradition, it is to the reception of his philosophy that we must turn. For it is here that the most movement has occurred in the past ten years in the American understanding of Adorno's work. In fact, just as Adorno's differences from more mainstream Western Marxists like Lukács were becoming increasingly appreciated, so too were his similarities with non-Marxist continental philosophers. Adorno's complicated relationship with phenomenology, for example, has been the source of considerable interest, in part because of the translations of his critiques of Heidegger and Husserl and in part because of a prior awareness of Marcuse's debt to these same thinkers. In the early 1970s, *Telos,* in particular its editor Paul Piccone, was hopeful of finding a common ground between Critical Theory and phenomenology. Bemoaning the overt hostility of Adorno toward Husserl and Heidegger, Piccone and the Italians he translated in *Telos* like Pier Aldo Rovatti,[74] refused to take their apparent incompatability as the final word on this issue. To reach the opposite conclusion, their strategy was to emphasize the importance of Husserl's late work, in particular *The Crisis of European Sciences,* which appeared after the Frankfurt School's position against Husserl had hardened. Finding common ground in their critical attitudes towards technology and hoping to integrate the phenomenological investigation of the *Lebenswelt* with negative dialectics, Piccone and his allies contended that the results would offer a better basis for a more genuinely materialist Marxism than that provided by Lukács' neo-Hegelianism. By the end of the decade, however, Piccone's faith in Marxism of any kind had waned so far that any thoughts of a creative synthesis had vanished, although he continued to rely on the traditional Critical Theory idea of an administered world in his notion of "artificial negativity."[75]

At about the same time, a parallel effort was being made by Fred Dallmayr to find fruitful links between Adorno and Heidegger. Once again the strategy was to claim that Adorno's hostility was directed more against his target's early than late works. In an essay he published in 1976 and a book entitled *Twilight of Subjectivity: Contributions to a Post-Individualist Theory of Politics* that appeared five years later,[76] Dallmayr argued that despite the outward signs of animosity, a close kinship existed between the two thinkers:

Adorno's strictures against individualism and the philosophy of consciousness correspond closely to Heidegger's critique of "subjectivism" and of the tradition of Western "metaphysics" with its accent on subjective reflection. Likewise, Adorno's comments on the ambivalence of Enlightenment thought and modern rationalism find a parallel in the existentialist posture toward logical calculation and the conception of man as "rational animal"; in particular, the argument that the growing sway of "instrumental" rationality reflects ultimately man's "will to power"—the desire to subjugate and control nature—is reminiscent of Heidegger's treatment of modern technology as an anthropocentric stratagem. A further affinity . . . can be found in the common stress of the two thinkers on historical exegesis and on the importance of "pre-understanding" or tradition in human cognition.[77]

Thus, like Hermann Mörchen,[78] Dallmayr called into question Adorno's own self-understanding in order to find convergences where previously only antagonism had been recognized. What made Dallmayr's rapprochement plausible was his emphasis on Heidegger's late works with their critique of identity and defense of difference. Insisting as well on the parallels between both of their positions and Merleau-Ponty's philosophy of ambiguity, Dallmayr sought to forge a postsubjectivist and posthumanist philosophy that would avoid the domination of nature and "egological" individualism present in so many traditional Western philosophies.

To establish his point, Dallmayr also drew on the work of a fourth figure, whose surprising resemblance to Adorno has received increasing notice in America, Jacques Derrida. Indeed, as I mentioned earlier, it is arguable that one of the stars in Adorno's intellectual constellation can be identified with the poststructuralism of Heidegger's heterodox French disciples. This is not to say, however, that Adorno should be construed as a deconstructionist *avant la lettre* or that we can ignore the very important differences between his position, with its still Hegelian and Marxist dimensions, and theirs. Indeed, as one of the poststructuralists, Jean-François Lyotard, has recognized,[79] a very nondeconstructionist nostalgia for a lost totality still permeates even a negative dialectics. And yet, it makes even less sense to build impermeable walls between two of the most significant theoretical movements of our time.

The most compelling historical reason for the similarity is, of course, the common respect for Nietzsche found in both Adorno and the poststructuralists. Virtually all of the literature on Adorno in English recognizes his remarkable debt to a philosopher for whom most other Marxists, Western or otherwise, had only contempt.[80] It is partly for this reason that writers like the English critic Terry Eagleton have contended that

the parallels between deconstruction and Adorno are particularly striking. Long before the current fashion, Adorno was insisting on the power of those heterogeneous fragments that slip through the conceptual net, rejecting all philosophy of identity, refusing class consciousness as objectionably "positive," and denying the intentionality of signification. Indeed there is hardly a theme in contemporary deconstruction that is not richly elaborated in his work—a pointer, perhaps, to the mutual insularity of French and German culture, which now, ironically, converge more and more only in the Anglo-Saxon world.[81]

An even more extensive attempt to defend the comparison has been made by Michael Ryan in his 1982 *Marxism and Deconstruction*.[82] Although acknowledging that Adorno's emphasis is on society and Derrida's on language, he nonetheless argues that both share a hatred of logocentric hierarchies, both attack "the idealist privilege of identity over nonidentity, universality over particularity, subject over object, spontaneous presence over secondary rhetoric, timeless transcendence over empirical history, content over mode of expression, self-reassuring proximity over threatening alterity, ontology over the ontic, and so on."[83] In fact, in his zeal to assimilate Adorno and Derrida, Ryan goes so far as to make them common enemies of the domination of reason, without acknowledging that Adorno's more discriminating wrath was directed against only certain forms of rationality rather than rationality *tout court.*

If the parallels between Adorno and Derrida have been noted in America, so too have those between Adorno and Foucault.[84] In particular, the striking similarity between the arguments of *Dialectic of Enlightenment* and *Discipline and Punish* about the pervasiveness of disciplinary power in our administered world has been remarked.[85] Although it would be misleading to ignore their different evaluations of psychoanalysis, both Adorno and Foucault share a common skepticism about the sexual utopianism of certain Freudo-Marxists, including Marcuse. And both are at one in their sensitivity to what in *Dialectic of Enlightenment* he and Horkheimer called the "underground history"[86] of the European body, which Foucault's investigations of "bio-power" have helped bring to the surface. One final parallel might be mentioned, which concerns Adorno's regretful insistence in "The Actuality of Philosophy" that it was no longer possible for thought "to grasp the totality of the real" and Foucault's contention in *Power/Knowledge* that "the role for theory today seems to me to be just this: not to formulate global systematic theory which holds everything in place, but to analyze the specificity of mechanisms of power, to locate the connections and extensions, to build little by little a strategic knowledge."[87] In both cases, a micrological analysis takes the place of the grand syntheses that were so much a trademark of Hegelian Marxism at its most ambitious. Or more precisely, for both Adorno and Foucault, totality is retained only as a term of opprobrium to indicate the pervasive domination of power relations that can only be challenged on the local and particular level.

One way, to be sure, in which Adorno and the poststructuralists part company is in their differing attitudes towards aesthetic modernism. Whereas Adorno seems to have had little faith in an art that would follow the classical modernism of Schoenberg and Beckett, many poststructuralists such as Lyotard eagerly defend the postmodernism that apparently has. Interestingly, leftist American students of Critical Theory who have struggled with the elitism inherent in Adorno's position have found this alternative a promising one. Thus, for example, the same Fredric Jameson who did so much to introduce Adorno to American audiences now complains that his later work in particular fails to register

the inevitable historicity of modernism.[88] Rather than eternally contrasting avant-garde modernism and the culture industry, postmodernism, so Jameson suggests, calls into question the very dichotomy. Against
Adorno, Jameson now argues for "some sense of the ineradicable drive
towards collectivity that can be detected, no matter how faintly and fee-
bly, in the most degraded works of mass culture just as surely as in the
classics of modernism."[89]

Whether or not postmodernism can be harnessed for radical
purposes is, of course, not yet clear, as Habermas has frequently warned.[90]
It may therefore be healthy to contrast Adorno in some respects with
those recent philosophical currents that support it, rather than assimilate him too quickly to them. Moreover, as Habermas has also recently
cautioned,[91] there are important distinctions that ought not to be forgotten in their different appropriations of the Nietzschean critique of
the Enlightenment, which prevented Adorno, contrary to the hasty reading
of Ryan, from attacking all forms of rationality as oppressive.

And yet, despite the dangers of turning Adorno into a deconstructionist with a German accent, it would be equally misguided to
ignore the undeniable parallels that allow us with hindsight to see the
implication of Adorno's thought as more complicated than would have
been foreseen during his own lifetime. And if Eagleton is correct in
claiming that this recognition has happened primarily in the Anglo-Saxon
world because of the "mutual insularity of French and German culture,"
then we must take seriously the impact of his American reception. For
if Adorno had to leave home to learn the lessons about democratic politics and the fetishization of high culture described earlier, the emigration of his thought may also have been necessary to bring out all of its
potential implications. It has sometimes been argued that the first de-
tached and analytical overviews of the Frankfurt School's history could
only have been written by outsiders with no stake in the polemical wars
within Germany that surrounded Critical Theory.[92] No less perhaps might
be said of the reception of Adorno's work, some of whose implications
may be more apparent on foreign shores than at home. Although, as I
mentioned earlier, Adorno never returned to America after 1953, it is
thus perhaps symbolically just that when his heart gave out in Switzerland sixteen years later, he was in fact preparing to do so in order to
give the Christian Gauss lectures at Princeton University. The lectures
were never delivered, but Adorno's thought did return nonetheless.[93]

We might therefore in conclusion adopt the trope of chiasmus, so frequently used by Adorno himself, to describe his complicated
relationship to America.[94] As in such sentences as "history is nature; nature is history," Adorno employed chiasmus to indicate the unrecon-

ciled and unsublated relationship between two elements that nonetheless are inextricably intertwined. It is appropriate to call his peculiar
status as a thinker tensely suspended between his native land and his
emigré home a form of chiasmus. For as an American, he was obviously
a displaced European, while as a European, he was deeply affected by
his years in America. As a result he was able to remain in permanent
exile from both contexts, and still does after his death. Although surely
a source of pain, this condition, as Adorno doubtless knew, was also a
stimulus to his creativity and originality. It also paradoxically made him
into something of an exemplary figure for contemporary man. For as he
argued in his essay in *Noten zur Literatur* entitled "Die Wunde Heine,"
"today, the fate Heine suffered has literally become the common fate:
homelessness has been inflicted on everyone. All, in language and being,
have been damaged as the exile himself was."[95]

It is perhaps especially fitting that I borrow this citation from
the opening remarks made by the American literary critic Harvey Gross
at the earlier symposium honoring Adorno that was held in Los Angeles
on the tenth anniversary of his death.[96] For not the least of Adorno's
gifts to his emigré asylum, a country known for receiving rather than
generating refugees, was the knowledge that in some sense we too are
still suffering from Heine's wound, we too are still leading the damaged
lives of men unable to find their way home.

Part II
Other Emigrés

10.

The Loss
of George Lichtheim

Among the many emotions aroused by
the news of a suicide, anger at the
perpetrator is the most difficult to confront. It seems most inappropriate alongside sorrow, pity, and anguish, the more socially expected
responses. Yet, as psychoanalysts tell us, hostility toward even those who
have died a natural death is a normal part of mourning. And when the
survivors have been willfully abandoned, the suppressed anger tends to
be keener still. This is especially true of family situations, but in certain
cases it holds for public figures as well. It is the measure of George
Lichtheim's stature that the news of his self-inflicted death in April of
this year could provoke such a response from many who, like myself,
knew him only slightly, or not at all.

Lichtheim was, as Norman Birnbaum pointed out a few years
ago in *Commentary,* very much a "modern master." This was true in
two senses of the word. He was the master of a vast and complex body
of thought, which he skillfully interwove with a profound knowledge of
the history of the modern age, at least in the West. His basic talent lay
in synthesizing the research of others rather than in performing the spade
work himself, but in this endeavor he had few if any peers in the postwar world. Whether evaluating the historical role of a Churchill, debating the fine points of Hegelian metaphysics, or dissecting the intricacies
of contemporary French politics, he combined a global perspective with
a mastery of detail that was extraordinary. Although there will be no
specific thesis of major proportions associated with his name, Lichtheim
will be remembered for his uncanny ability to nose out the critical issues of any problem he explored. To take but one example, his essay

First published in *Midstream* (October 1973), 19(8).

on "The Concept of Ideology" provides a brilliant summary of the several metamorphoses that often loosely used word has undergone in the time since its coinage in the early nineteenth century. His argument is especially useful in exposing the intricate connections between the notion of ideology and the tradition of rationalism, and in demonstrating the costs of severing those connections.

The other sense in which Lichtheim was a master lay in his having been a teacher who initiated an entire generation of readers in England and America into the mysteries of Central European thought. Although his books were not for beginners, as anyone who has tried to use them in an undergraduate course can attest, they offered to the more sophisticated a range of synoptic insights available nowhere else. Part of the anger of those of us who have been his students from afar stems from the fact that so authoritative a mentor has prematurely closed the lesson.

The special quality of Lichtheim's perspective came from a number of sources. Not the least of these was his having combined the sensibility of a citizen of a lost world with an acute interest in the workings of its contemporary successor. His sympathies, as he wrote in the *Collected Essays* published shortly before his death, may have been with the "representative thinkers of the age that ended in 1914," but his work expressed little of the soft-headed nostalgia of those bemoaning the horrors of modernity. In fact, Lichtheim can be called as much a journalist as a scholar, if that calling so often maligned by academics is understood in the sense of someone whose talents and learning are applied to the most pressing questions of the day. Without any university affiliation, except for a short, unhappy period at Columbia and Stanford in the mid-sixties, he lived off his writings in the tradition of the Weimar *Literat*. Although easily comparable in learning to many of his academic competitors, Lichtheim never took an advanced degree. Friends like the historian George Mosse have testified to his ability as a teacher, but Lichtheim preferred the hazards of free-lance writing to the security of an academic post. To this choice we owe the enormous productivity of his last dozen years, which opened with the publication in 1961 of his magisterial *Marxism: An Historical and Critical Study* and closed with the *Collected Essays* and his tour de force, *Europe in the Twentieth Century.*

If Lichtheim can be seen as journalist, the manner in which he played that role was highly unorthodox. For he did not enter into the life of the outside world with great relish. His last decade was spent predominantly in the flat he occupied alone on the top floor of the London home of Francis Carsten, the distinguished historian of fascism and modern Germany. He had been foreign editor of the *Jerusalem Post* during the war and, in 1957–58, an associate editor of *Commentary*, but in his last years he preferred putting his own ideas on paper to editing the work of others. His personal library was lavishly stocked and, once again according to George Mosse, he rarely found reason to spend long afternoons in the British Museum or other public libraries. Although constantly offered speaking engagements in England and abroad, he turned almost all of them down.

Perhaps his major source of personal contact was the stream of visitors he received in his London rooms. In the winter of 1969, I made a pilgrimage there to talk about my research on the Frankfurt School. Before we got to that subject, Lichtheim plied me with questions about recent happenings in America. As I recall, he showed greatest interest in the rise of the Black Panthers and the potential dangers of Black anti-Semitism. When we finally arrived at the reason for my visit, he spoke at great length of his respect for the Frankfurt School's work, but expressed considerable reservations about the recent "anarchistic" turn in Marcuse's thought. He was a compelling conversationalist and I listened with fascination for the better part of a long and increasingly crepuscular English afternoon. The last half hour of our talk was spent in total darkness because Lichtheim, utterly absorbed in his train of thought, had neglected to turn on the lights.

His ability to carry on extended, associative soliloquies will be familiar to anyone acquainted with some of his book-length works, especially *A Short History of Socialism* and *Imperialism*, where sections of the narrative read like internal monologues. At these times the richness of his mind led him into obscure tangents and arcane allusions that many of his readers found exasperating to follow. Lichtheim could be forgiven these moments, however, because of the extraordinary mastery of English prose he demonstrated throughout his writings. What is all the more remarkable is that English was not his native tongue, although he did speak it before his final settlement in London in 1946, his family having lived in that city for several years in the early twenties when he was a child. The wit, pungency, and suppleness of his prose was especially evident in the countless short essays and reviews he wrote over the years, first under the pseudonym G. L. Arnold and then under his own name. Although at times his tone could be supercilious and condescending, especially when demolishing a position he disliked, he also possessed a gift for finding fresh words to praise one he admired. He had a talent as well for compressing the maximum number of ideas into the minimum amount of space. On occasion this could be taxing for his readers, and unraveling overly packed segments of his narrative could evoke the dizzying sensation of trying to absorb the plot of an opera in those few harried moments before the curtain goes up.

But our chagrin at his death is not only at the loss of one of the most skilled practitioners of rhetorical vivisection; for Lichtheim was a gifted member of that now dwindling band of Central European Jewish emigrés who have done so much to enrich the intellectual life of the Anglo-Saxon world. He was born in 1912 in Berlin, the son of Richard Lichtheim, the influential Zionist leader, and Irene Hefter, the daughter of a former fighter for Garibaldi who later became a merchant in Constantinople. The elder Lichtheim was editor of the Zionist journal *Die Welt* from 1911 to 1913, the Zionist representative in Constantinopole during World War I, a member of Chaim Weizmann's Zionist Executive Board in London in the early twenties, which he left to join Jabotinsky's Revisionists in 1925, and finally a member of the Jewish State Party in Palestine, to which he moved in 1933. Except for a period during World War II when he was in Geneva, he continued to live in Jerusalem until his death in 1963.

Although his son George grew up in a Zionist atmosphere and emigrated with his family to Palestine in 1933, he seems to have retained little of the father's commitment. Jewish questions, especially the problem of anti-Semitism, remained, to be sure, a major concern, as witnessed by his trenchant essay on "Socialism and the Jews" in the *Collected Essays.* As he showed in his critique of Arthur Hertzberg's *The French Enlightenment and the Jews,* he was careful to distinguish between attacks on religion, which he could support, and attacks on the Jewish people, which he could not. But despite his continued emotional ties to Israel, he did not consider Zionism to be a satisfactory solution to anti-Semitism. In a positive review of Georges Friedmann's *The End of the Jewish People,* he remarked, "Like communism in Russia, Zionism in Israel has become a hollow shell, the ideological remnant of a buried European past." With Friedmann, he held that the Jewish people as traditionally understood was by no means coterminous with the Israeli nation, nor was it likely to become so. Lichtheim's Jewish allegiance was clearly to the Central European diaspora community of a Central Europe that no longer existed.

Moreover, while recognizing the crucial role of nationalism in the modern world, Lichtheim remained too loyal to another tradition to accept particularist solutions to social problems. That other tradition of course was Marxism. George Mosse recalls that Lichtheim thought of himself as "the last Marxist." It was in the presentation and interpretation of this legacy in such books as *Marxism: An Historical and Critical Study, Marxism in Modern France, A Short History of Socialism, The Origins of Socialism, From Marx to Hegel, George Lukács,* and in sections of his other works, that Lichtheim achieved his greatest influence in England and America during the last decade.

It would be impossible to investigate his complex understanding of Marxism with any rigor at this time, but certain of its basic themes can be extracted. Although Lichtheim was well-versed in the economic and social intricacies of Marxist theory, his central concern was for its philosophical and political dimensions. Philosophically, he took pains to stress the Hegelian underpinnings of Marx's thought from beginning to end. He did have an "early Marx–late Marx" categorization, but it was very different from the humanist-scientist distinction drawn by Louis Althusser and his followers with their belief in an epistemological break in 1845. Although Lichtheim admitted that the dialectical materialism of the Second International was a departure from the critical, *praxis*-oriented Marxism of the classical texts, a departure in a scientific and nonrevolutionary direction, he absolved Marx himself of any blame. Instead, following the lead of Lukács and Karl Korsch, he turned Engels into the villain of the piece. Part of his sustained antipathy toward Bolshevism grew out of his conviction that theoretically it perpetuated the undialectical and crude materialism of the Second International. His prime piece of evidence in this regard was Lenin's *Materialism and Empirio-Criticism* and he rejected the contentions of commentators like Raya Dunayevskaya that Lenin's discovery of Hegel's *Logic* in his last years produced a serious refinement of his earlier position. His sympathy for the Hegelian roots of Marxism, which entailed *inter alia* an appreciation of the constitutive role of consciousness in the historical process, led him to praise the work of twentieth-century Marxist Humanists like Gramsci, Korsch, and the early Lukács. He was somewhat less enthusiastic about Sartre's attempts to marry Marxism to Existentialism after the war, which he saw as mired in the irretrievably Cartesian workings of Sartre's mind. His greatest encomiums, however, were reserved for the work of Horkheimer, Adorno, and Habermas, although his own thought lacked the utopian dimension present in all but the most pessimistic of their writings. His was a safer, more domesticated Marxism, without the practical intentions of at least the Frankfurt School's earlier work. In addition, he remained wary about their integration of psychoanalysis into what became known as "Critical Theory" (the one essay he wrote on the subject, which appeared in Jonathan Miller's *Freud: The*

Man, His World, His Influence, was relatively skeptical about their efforts in this direction, though it gave cautious praise to the more recent work of Habermas and Alexander Mitscherlich).

Lichtheim's lukewarm approval of psychoanalysis reflected the strongly rationalist cast of his mind. Perhaps the choicest epithets in his writings were reserved for the irrationalist opposition to the Hegelian tradition. Unlike the Frankfurt School, he belittled Nietzsche's "so-called critique of traditional thought." In contrast to the tender Nietzscheanism so successfully promulgated in recent years by Walter Kaufmann, he contended that it was only a short step from the "essential coarseness of Nietzsche's mind" to "the biological vitalism of the Third Reich." Similarly, Lichtheim found nothing of value in Heidegger's existentialism and saw an integral connection between *Being and Time* and his notorious pro-Nazi rectoral address in 1933. Georges Sorel was no less a culprit, being "in a fundamental sense one of those writers who were responsible for the temporary triumph of Fascism in Italy and for its virulence in France during the 1930s and 1940s." As for our own counterculture's fascination with Eastern mysticism and the occult, his statement that "the mental rubbish of Calcutta and Benares flows into the gutters of Europe and America" suffices to express his attitude.

Lichtheim's adherence to an essentially Hegelian notion of Reason—an adherence he regrettably never really defended in systematic terms—was such that he could charge Max Weber and his followers with softening up the German intelligentsia in the pre-Nazi era. The liberal, positivist, instrumentalist version of reason in Weber's thought, he contended, was "too formal to constitute an effective barrier against irrationality." Although the concept of rationality he defended was a product of German philosophy, he nonetheless insisted that Germany's problems were due in large measure to her imperviousness to the rationalism of the West. In a sentence he repeated in similar form a number of times, he argued that "the basic fact about German history since the eighteenth century has been the failure of the Enlightenment to strike root." Where he remained a Central European was in his insistence that reason must be understood in an historical sense; the lack of such a sense was a charge he leveled time and again at figures as disparate as Bertrand Russell and Seymour Martin Lipset. *How* reason was to be realized in history he never really explained, and, as we shall see shortly, at one point in his writing he even faltered in his faith that it could be.

If Lichtheim was a Hegelian-Marxist in his philosophy, he was a social democrat in his politics. The only serious discontinuity he per-

ceived in Marx's own development was between an early Jacobin phase
and a later democratic one. Leninism, he argued, had revived the Jacobin Marx—admittedly for objective reasons in a Russia lacking an advanced labor movement—and was thus as much of a revisionism as the
more celebrated variety associated with the name of Eduard Bernstein.
On the implications of this revision, he was somewhat ambivalent. Mar-
tov's attempt to translate the German model of social democracy into
Russian terms he justifiably dismissed as historically premature. Yet, the
consequences of Lenin's more successful reading of the Russian situation he saw as execrable: "The manner in which Lenin turned a perfectly reasonable and unexceptionable statement of fact, i.e., the fact that
the labor movement normally acquires its socialist consciousness from
outside its ranks, into a justification of practices running counter to the
whole Socialist tradition establishes him as the true progenitor of Stalinism." For Lichtheim, it seems as if there were no alternatives to the failed
revolution of the Mensheviks and the betrayed revolution of the Bolsheviks.

A major reason for this pessimism was his appreciation of
the consequences of Russia's immature and badly organized labor
movement. Similarly, his disdain for Chinese Communism, which Ross
Terrill in *The New York Times* saw as smacking of "blinkered ignorance," derived in large measure from his observation that Maoism was
rooted in a populist rather than working-class movement. To Lichtheim,
a glorification of the "people" was suggestive of proto-Nazi *völkisch*
demagoguery more than of true proletarian socialism. The Maoist transformation of Marxism from a *theory* of working-class emancipation in
advanced industrial societies into an *ideology* of modernization in a
backward country completed a distortion begun in Lenin's Russia. That
Maoism might lead to something besides "modernization" in the Western sense was a possibility he neglected to explore with any rigor. Nor
did he venture to say how a true socialism more faithful to the spirit of
Marx's thought was possible, if at all, in backward countries. The revolution had to happen in Western Europe or America, as Marx had
prophesied, or not at all.

Yet despite his insistence on the importance of a democratic
labor movement, Lichtheim also stressed the crucial role of the intelligentsia in making and leading revolutions. "The simple truth," he wrote
in a review of Eric Hobsbawm's *Laboring Men,* "is that a Marxist movement (or any other) can establish its hold over society only if it begins
by winning the intellectual elite. . . . Laboring men by themselves cannot make a revolution. Lenin knew this; so did the Fabians." In so arguing, it might be contended that Lichtheim subtly moved away from

his allegiance to classical Marxism. To use his own words in another context against him: "In the Marxian perspective, the emancipation of the working class is the business of that class itself, and not of a revolutionary elite of intellectuals."

In other ways as well, his position diverged from Marx's own thought. His study of imperialism, for example, downgraded the economic element in favor of more political and precapitalist motivations. Elsewhere he expressed skepticism about the continued relevance of class struggle in the modern world, arguing instead for the growing importance in our postbourgeois (but not post-capitalist) society of "a hierarchy of planners, managers, bureaucrats, and technicians." The intellectuals were the beneficiaries of these developments not only in a political and economic sense, but in a cultural one as well. "For the present and immediate future," he wrote in 1960, "it remains true that standards will either be set by the intellectual elite or by those interested in reducing the general level to the lowest common denominator." With these sentiments, it is no wonder that Lichtheim was drawn to the cultural elitism of the Frankfurt School.

But his attitude toward the role of the intellectuals, as Steven Lukes and others have pointed out, was highly ambivalent. In the same article that contained the lines quoted above, he wrote:

It is at any rate possible to think that we are in for a new era of rationalism. For reasons which should now have become a little clearer, a new rationalist ethos, if it should prevail, is likely to run parallel with a considerable growth in the sociopolitical weight of the intellectual stratum. Alternatively, if one prefers the simplified version of historical materialism popular in some quarters, one may invert this statement and say that the growing importance of the technical and scientific intelligentsia is going to reduce the area of mischief still open to political movements of a more primitive type.

With little change, this statement could have been composed by the end-of-ideology ideologists of the fifties with their naive belief that political problems can be solved by technical means. In the intervening decade or so since this prophecy was made, events have shown their confidence to be premature at best.

Lichtheim, to his credit, was able to modify his position on the role of the technical intelligentsia. The change was manifested in a number of ways. One obvious instance was his frequent denunciation of the Fabians, whose authoritarian, pro-imperialist elitism he saw as of a piece with their desire to introduce a kind of pseudosocialism from above through the "permeation" of the existing ruling classes. The passive welfare state mentality which resulted, so Lichtheim charged, was the greatest barrier to socialism in England today. Another manifestation of his eroding optimism about the technocrats' capacity for leadership was his reaction to the recent popularity of Louis Althusser, whom he disparagingly dubbed "the Talcott Parsons of Marxism." Althusser's structuralist reading of Marx, he argued, was the ideological correlate of the technocratic and bureaucratic mentality of the French Communist Party. "In the end," he wrote in 1969, "the technocrats themselves may discover to their surprise that they cannot function unless someone tells them what the whole expenditure of energy is supposed to be *for*. And that someone won't be another technocrat." A growing sensitivity to the differences between technical, instrumental rationality and what might be called emancipatory rationality is also what drew Lichtheim towards an appreciation of the work of Jürgen Habermas, which he characterized as "the most impressive body of philosophy and sociology to come out of Central Europe during the 1960s."

Perhaps the most sustained, if problematical, expression of his increasing ambivalence about the role of the intellectual elite was his critique of Georg Lukács in the Modern Masters Series. To many Lukács devotees further to the left, this seemed Lichtheim's least successful effort. Paul Breines in the journal *Telos* called it "crisply written false consciousness" and Andrew Arato impugned its authority by denouncing Lichtheim's "inadequate scholarship" in the pages of *The Journal of Modern History*. Lichtheim's animus toward his subject seemed far in excess of the objective stimulus. Lukács, to be sure, deserved many of his critic's negative strictures. His silence in the face of Stalinist horrors, his idealist reading of Marx (especially obvious in his most celebrated work, *History and Class Consciousness*), and his insensitivity to modern art all warrant the type of criticism leveled by Lichtheim. But the overall tone of the book betrayed a stronger hostility than that justified by these and other weaknesses in Lukács's record.

Part of the overkill may have resulted from Lichtheim's personal distaste for an activist Marxist intellectual whose dedication to *praxis* persuaded him to remain in the Communist Party for almost his entire mature life. "Lichtheim was a loner, he sought no followers and was not supported by any group. . . He represented independent opinions without opportunistic reservation. Equipped by nature with great self-confidence, he carried himself with a certain aristocratic lack of concern." These words were written by Pinchus F. Rosen in the introduction to Richard Lichtheim's autobiography, *Rückkehr*. They refer to the father, but there can be little doubt that they were applicable to the son as well. Except for his years in Jerusalem, when he was part of the circle around Gershom Scholem, George Lichtheim seems to have rarely broken his isolation. Lukács, the loyal party stalwart, and Lichtheim, the unattached outsider, were temperamental opposites.

But more than this personal distance was at the root of Lichtheim's animosity. What was also operative, it seems fair to conjecture, was the projection of facets of Lichtheim's own ambivalences onto Lukács. As already noted, Lichtheim was at once an anti-Jacobin social democrat and a believer in the special role of the intellectual elite. In confronting Lukács, he found the perfect outlet for his anxiety about the incompatibility of those two impulses. Lichtheim so disliked Lukács' elitist attitude toward the masses because for all his cynicism, he had difficulties in overcoming a bad conscience about a similar bias in his own thinking. Equally suspect is his attack on the idealistic, even Platonic elements in Lukács's thought, not because it is wrong, but rather because the same charge can easily be made against Lichtheim himself. And finally, in his discussion of Lukács' treatment of German intellectual history, his remark that Lukács' "invariably operates with a simple distinction between reason and unreason" could be applied to much of Lichtheim's own writings as well. In fact, when he came to criticize Lukács' *Die Zerstörung der Vernunft,* Lichtheim allowed the distinction between reason and unreason and attacked Lukács only for his ahistorical attempt to ground irrationalism in the breakdown of bourgeois society as a whole instead of in the pecular national experience of the German people, where Lichtheim felt it more accurately belonged.

In short, Lichtheim left us with a series of unreconciled and contradictory observations about the modern world and the role of Marxism in its transformation. A social democrat with a strong belief in the labor movement, he also argued for the necessity of intellectual leadership in directing revolutionary change. When such an elite did exercise this function, however, he was among the first to chastise it for betraying the revolution. A man of the Enlightenment with nothing positive to say about the irrationalist opposition, he was still able to castigate Bertrand Russell for his naive, ahistorical version of the Philosophes' creed and then add pessimistically that "the attempt to reconcile the rationalist myth with historical reality must surely by now be reckoned a failure." A fervent critic of European imperialism, including attempts to transfer Marxist models nurtured on European soil, he was nevertheless totally unsympathetic to the efforts of Third World countries to fashion their own brand of socialism. With these and other unreconciled positions, it is not surprising that in the end Lichtheim could embrace the passive detachment of the later Frankfurt School and write in 1971 that "the central problem now before us is not so much to change the world (that is being done independently), but to understand it."

The anger provoked by his suicide thus has another reason besides those mentioned earlier. For the self-assurance of Lichtheim's tone could not mask his failure to go beyond a mode of thought that can no longer provide an adequate understanding of our independently changing world, or more critically, help us master that change. As a result, he has bequeathed to us a score of unanswered questions and a heightened awareness of seemingly irreconcilable antinomies. In most cases, the questions are the right ones and the antinomies actually rooted in the social reality of our time. It would of course have been too much to expect Lichtheim to have solved dilemmas which are more social than conceptual. And yet, for those of us with a residue of faith in the rationalism Lichtheim so fervently espoused, his suicide strikes a sobering blow at the assumption that social dilemmas can ever be solved by the efforts of reasonable men. For whatever the private agonies that dictated his act, the self-destruction of the "last Marxist" has an inevitably public dimension, which touches all who profited from his work. Our anger is thus in part resentment at his leaving us with the gnawing doubt that the best of a lost world cannot be successfully salvaged and applied to the problems of our own. For if a man of the intelligence and learning of George Lichtheim could despair of the task, who among us can perform it?

11.

The Extraterritorial Life of Siegfried Kracauer

On February 8, 1889, Siegfried Kracauer was born in Frankfurt am Main, the son of a businessman, Adolf K. Kracauer, and his wife, the former Rosette Oppenheim; he died seventy-seven years later in New York City on November 26, 1966. For any normal biography, this bracketing of a life between two chronological points is a natural and unexamined beginning. For a biography of Kracauer, however, it constitutes a betrayal of the strongest taboo of his later life, a taboo he expressed in a series of letters deliberately set aside in his well-organized *Nachlass*[1] to give any future biographer pause. These letters, written in the 1960s when Kracauer was consumed by his final project on the philosophy of history, were filed under the heading of "extraterritoriality." In all of them, Kracauer vehemently opposed any effort to disclose his correct age, a campaign, as he surely must have known, which could only meet with temporary success.[2] His reason for waging it, despite the certainty of ultimate failure, transcended the petty vanity of those who refuse to age gracefully. As he wrote to his friend Theodor W. Adorno in 1963: "It is not as if there is something for me in appearing young or younger; it is simply the horror of losing chronological anonymity through the fixating of a date and the unavoidable connotations of such a fixation."[3]

The "chronological anonymity" he so insistently guarded had two functions. First, it helped discourage efforts to place Kracauer in the context of any one period, such as those that would define him as a "Weimar intellectual" with all the resonances that label has acquired over the years. By avoiding such a placement, he hoped to thwart the compartmentalization of his own work that he had sought to resist in the work of those he studied. But secondly, and perhaps more signifi-

First published in *Salmagundi* (Fall 1975–Winter 1976), vol. 31–32.

cantly on a psychological level, it served to ward off thoughts of the approaching death that would signify the closure of his work and give his life whatever final meaning it might have. When he finally did die, Adorno wrote in his obituary that Kracauer's utter refusal to confront death or aging had a heroic dimension to it, consonant with his long-standing concern for the redemption of the living.[4] To Kracauer, final meanings were anathema, whether in cultural phenomena or the record of a man's life. Wholeness and death were inextricably intertwined in his thinking, an association that energized much of his thought and set him apart from the Weimar intellectuals who, in Peter Gay's phrase, "hungered for wholeness."[5]

Kracauer's concern for "chronological anonymity" grew out of a more general fascination with the condition he chose to call "extraterritoriality." Marginality, alienation, outsiderness have been among the stock obsessions of intellectuals ever since the time of Rousseau. Few, however, focused as consistently on the manifestations of the malaise throughout their entire careers as did Kracauer. Fewer still found ways to fashion their own marginality into a positive good in quite the manner he did. As we shall see, Kracauer's life's work can be read as a series of seemingly disparate projects almost all with the common goal of redeeming contingency from oblivion. In important if not fully transparent ways, this effort paralleled Kracauer's personal struggle with the extraterritorial nature of his own life.

Kracauer's sense of marginality must have begun almost at birth. Physically, he was set apart from his peers by two characteristics. The first was a speech defect, a stammer which would preclude, among other things, a teaching career at any time in his life. The second was his physiognomy, whose peculiarity struck all who knew him. To Adorno, who actually used the word "extraterritorial" in describing his face, he looked as if he were from the Far East.[6] Asja Lacis, the Latvian Marxist director who met him in the late 1920s, said he looked like an "African."[7] To Hans Mayer, the Marxist literary critic, he was a "Japanese painted by an Expressionist."[8] And Rudolf Arnheim, the aesthetic theoretician, remembers him as having a squashed nose that made his face, "almost grotesque, but somehow beautiful."[9]

Added to whatever stress may have been caused by these physical peculiarities was the trauma of his father's death, when Kracauer was still a young child. He moved shortly thereafter to the house of his uncle, Isidor K. Kracauer, a distinguished historian of Frankfurt's Jewish community.[10] The atmosphere of the home was apparently religious, but the young Kracauer, like so many of his generation, sought assimilation rather than ethnic identification. Later, in the 1920s, he be-

came friendly with the circle around the powerfully attractive Rabbi
Nehemiah Nobel, which included Ernst Simon, Martin Buber, and Franz
Rosenzweig. He even contributed a piece to the Rabbi's *Festschrift* in
1921,[11] and played a small role in the creation of the Frankfurt *Lehrhaus* which emerged from Nobel's circle. By 1926, however, what interest he may have had in the Jewish revival stimulated by the *Lehrhaus*
group was clearly dead. In that year, he published a stinging criticism
of the Buber-Rosenzweig translation of the Bible, which he damned as
neo-*völkisch* in inspiration.[12] Thereafter, Jewish issues played no overt
role in any of his writings, although certain residues can perhaps be said
to have remained if the religious element in his interest in redemption
is stressed. Still, what his upbringing in a religious household whose tenets
he rejected meant was a strengthening of that marginality which characterized his life. After 1933, the myth of assimilation was exploded in
a way that could only have reinforced his sense of outsiderness. Although Kracauer never dealt directly with the consequences of his Jewish background, there can be little doubt that it played a serious role in
the development of his sensibility and intellectual concerns.

Kracauer's career pattern shows equal signs of deviation from
the norm of intellectual maturation, if indeed such a norm can be said
to exist. Before World War I, he studied at the Klinger-Oberrealschule
in Frankfurt and then at universities and technical colleges in Darm-
stadt, Berlin, and Munich. Although preparing fields in philosophy and
sociology, his main interest was in architecture, which he hoped to make
his career. In 1915, he earned a doctorate in engineering at the technical college of Berlin-Charlottenburg with a dissertation on the development of wrought iron decorations in Prussia from the seventeenth to
the nineteenth centuries.[13] During the war, he seems to have avoided
serious military service, if his semi-autobiographical novel, *Ginster,*[14] is
any indication. Instead, he served as an apprentice architect in Han-
nover, Osnabruck, Frankfurt, and Munich.

Although architecture was only to be a temporary career, it
left its mark on Kracauer's subsequent development. His heightened visual sensitivity, "the primacy of the optical" in Adorno's phrase,[15] led to
a series of articles on urban space, both interior and exterior, in the
1920s.[16] It also, of course, underlay Kracauer's life-long fascination with
film, for which he is best known in the English-speaking world. In addition, the constructive impulse nurtured by his architectural experience reappeared in the technique Kracauer called "construction in the
material," which he developed in the Weimar period, as well as in the
highly structured way he organized his books and articles.

But for reasons that are not entirely clear, architecture failed to engage his total personality and he gave it up in 1920. Encouraged by the eminent philosophers Georg Simmel and Max Scheler, with whom he was personally acquainted, Kracauer turned to philosophical and sociological analysis as a new career. The first fruits of his shift were studies of the recently deceased Simmel, published only in part in 1920, and of sociology as a science, which appeared in 1922.[17] In both, the marks of Kracauer's interest in phenomenology as an antidote to neo-Kantianism were evident, but a phenomenology closer to Scheler's "material eidetics" than to Husserl's intuitionist search for essences beneath the flux of history. Central to Kracauer's vision of sociology was an antipsychological, antisubjectivist perspective. That is, he claimed that the attempt by the phenomenologists to counter psychologism in philosophy was appropriate to sociology as well. The reason for this parallel, Kracauer argued, could be found in the nature of his age. In characterizing it, Kracauer explicitly borrowed from Georg Lukács' recently published *Theory of the Novel,*[18] specifically his distinction between meaningful, fulfilled periods of history and empty, barren ones. Like Lukács, Kracauer put his own era in the second category. A phenomenological sociology without psychological subjectivity was appropriate because the age was one in which meaning, community, and purpose were absent. The reality of the social world, he wrote, is a "bad infinity"[19] without a material totality. The integrated personality so valued by generations of German philosophers was also an ideological illusion. Idealism, with its implicit assumption of an immanently meaningful world, was thus a misleading metaphysics. The only alternative was a scientific sociology that would investigate the structural regularities of the de-individualized social realm without worrying about the need to integrate subject and object in a larger whole. Sociology, however, should not be expected to provide answers to the present cultural crisis, when the source is in society itself. Although Kracauer was soon to lose his enthusiasm for Scheler's materialist phenomenology, especially when Scheler began searching for eternal verities,[20] his underlying premise about the meaninglessness of the present period was a life-long conviction. Unlike Lukács, however, he never came to see a solution to the dilemma it presented.

Although Kracauer was now seriously devoted to intellectual work, his speech defect and lack of advanced training in academic areas meant the impossibility of a university career. Following phenomenology's injunction to return to the *Lebenswelt* from the heights of philosophical speculation, and taking advantage of the increased pres-

tige of journalism in the Weimar period, Kracauer took a position with
the *Frankfurter Zeitung* in 1920. The *FZ*, founded in 1856 by Leopold
Sonnemann, was one of the most prestigious of Germany's newspapers
and a pillar of the democratic left wing of bourgeois liberalism. Although its circulation after the war never exceeded 70,000, it retained
a large measure of political and cultural influence among the middle
classes, especially the educated Jewish bourgeoisie from which Kracauer himself had come. It was, of course, not without its detractors. As
a recent student of its history has written,

In *Mein Kampf* Hitler devoted more space and invective to the *FZ* than to any
other newspaper, considering it the Gorgon of the *Judenpresse,* the sophisticated
and highly effective organ of the Jewish world conspiracy, and an important con-
tributor to Germany's defeat in the war.[21]

Although its liberal fervor began to slip by the late twenties, when its
ownership changed hands, it continued to be a leading voice of middle-
class opinion until the end of the Republic. Kracauer remained in its
employ until 1933, when the Nazis decapitated "the Gorgon of the *Judenpresse"* with scarcely any resistance. He survived the purge of left-
leaning staff after the change of owners because he was not directly
concerned with political reporting. Kracauer was assigned instead to its
feuilleton section, where the emphasis was on cultural affairs.

Throughout the Weimar period, Kracauer and his colleague
Benno Reifenberg[22] made the *feuilleton* page of the *FZ* the most brilliant in the German-speaking world. Here he carried out an extensive
and penetrating critique of everyday life, reminiscent of Simmel's, with
the goal of stimulating his readers' critical faculties rather than merely
diverting them. Among his more important substantive contributions was
the systematic investigation of the cinema in social terms, which culminated in his widely read series "The Small Shopgirls Go to the Movies,"[23] written in 1927. Except for an isolated article by the Expressionist Kurt Pinthus in 1913,[24] Kracauer's pieces were the first in Germany
to analyze the film from a social perspective. From a stylistic point of
view, Kracauer's innovation was equally significant, reversing as it did
one of the central weaknesses of the *feuilleton* as a genre. The *feuilleton* had its origins in the July Monarchy in Paris when advertising had
expanded the market for newspapers by lowering prices.[25] It served as
a lure for new subscribers by printing gossip, intrigues, and serialized
novels. By the turn of the century, especially in Vienna where it reached
its greatest popularity under Theodor Herzl in the *Neue Freie Presse,*
the *feuilleton* had become an occasion for the self-indulgence of personal impressions. As a recent historian has observed,

the subjective response of the reporter or critic to an experience, his feeling-tone, acquired clear primacy over the matter of his discourse. To render a state of feeling became the mode of formulating a judgment. Accordingly, in the *feuil-leton* writer's style, the adjectives engulfed the nouns, the personal tint virtually obliterated the contours of the object of discourse.[26]

This was the style, it might be noted in passing, that had aroused the ire of that scourge of Viennese decadence Karl Kraus, who denounced its narcissism and duplicity.

Although there is no evidence of Kraus's scorn having had a direct effect on him, Kracauer filled the *feuilleton* page with pieces of a very different kind. Instead of drawing attention to his own quivering sensibility, he assumed a tone of ironic naiveté that allowed the material to speak for itself. Somewhat in the manner of the *Neue Sachlickeit* (New Objectivity) style, which grew to prominence in Weimar's postexpres-sionist middle period, he maintained a cool, if clearly ironic, detach-ment towards his subject matter. From Simmel and the phenomenolo-gists, he gained an attentiveness to the things themselves, which reinforced his architect's sensitivity to the visual world. But underlying his distance from the material he described was a subterranean fury at the irrationalities of Weimar life, which he saw embodied in such diverse phenomena as the waiting room of an employment office or the recep-tion given to the Tiller girls, those "ornaments of the masses" whose precision dancing reflected the disenchantment of the modern world.[27] Kracauer's attitude towards this trend was ambivalent; although he ap-plauded its progressive, demythologizing side, he recognized the costs of social standardization and atomization. Moreover, as we shall see shortly, he identified many of its worst aspects with capitalism.

Throughout the twenties, Kracauer's reputation and influ-ence steadily increased. For example, his advocacy in 1929 of the Soviet documentaries of Djiga Vertov and Esther Schub led to their popularity in Germany and ultimately in the USSR as well.[28] In retrospect, 1930 appears as the year of his greatest success. The *FZ* offered him the di-rectorship of the cultural section of its Berlin office and, anxious to be at the center of Weimar life, he accepted. In the same year, his study of the harried lower middle classes, which had been serialized in the *FZ* the year before, was published in book form to generally favorable re-views.[29] *Die Angestellten: Aus dem neuesten Deutschland* dealt with the more than 3.5 million members of the recently enlarged white-collar sector of the working population, the group whose vulnerabilities the Nazis were to exploit with such moment. Caught between the inexor-able rationalization of industrial production, which rendered their po-

sitions precarious, and the fear of lowering their status through an identification with blue-collar proletarians, the *Angestellten* were fair game
for political manipulation. Kracauer's most trenchant passages dealt with
the weaknesses of the *Angestelltenkultur*, which made this manipulation possible. Here an earlier diatribe against the *Tat* circle's *völkisch*
ideology gained new urgency because of the clear evidence of its widespread success. Protesting against the vulgar Marxist assumption that the
unemployed *Angestellten* would soon join their working-class brethren,
Kracauer pointed out that, lacking an ideological faith, they were spiri-
tually as well as often materially homeless. The condition he had described in general terms in *Soziologie als Wissenschaft*, that Lukácsian
"transcendental homelessness"[30] expressed in the modern novel, was
now understood to be especially apparent in the lower middle class, or
new *Mittelstand*.

    Apart from its substantive value, which helped inspire a widely
read novel dealing with the same theme, Hans Fallada's *What Now, Little Man*,[31] *Die Angestellten* broke new methodological ground. Based
on the qualitative evaluation and reconstruction of a number of interviews with Berlin white-collar workers, the book pioneered a technique
the Lynds were developing in America at approximately the same time
in their study of *Middletown*,[32] a technique known as participant observation. Kracauer made no pretense of polling the average mentality
of the people whose values he was investigating. "Reality," he argued
"is a construction,"[33] consisting of a mosaic of different observations. In
a letter to Adorno, he spelled out the significance of his approach.

I consider the work methodologically very important insofar as it constitutes a
new form of presentation, one which does not juggle between general theory
and special practice, but presents its own special way of observation. It is, if you
will, an example of materialist dialectics. Analogous cases are the analyses of
situations by Marx and Lenin, which are excluded by Marxism as we know it
today.[34]

Although difficult to emulate, Kracauer's method did produce a striking
evocation of the *Angestellten* dilemma, which repays reading today, despite the large amount of subsequent work on the same subject.[35]

    If 1930 saw Kracauer at the height of his public fame, it was
also the year of perhaps his most important personal decision. On March
5th, at the age of 41, he ended his long bachelorhood and married Anna
Elisabeth (Lili) Ehrenreich, then a librarian at the *Institut für Sozialforschung* in Frankfurt. Before his marriage, Kracauer's strongest personal
attachment seems to have been a platonically erotic bond with Adorno,
fourteen years his junior.[36] Lili Kracauer, almost 37 at the time of her

marriage, was born a Catholic in Strasbourg when it was part of the Second German Reich. She studied art history and philology in Strasbourg and Leipzig before the war and was beginning to study music at the Leipzig conservatory when the postwar inflation forced her to take the *Institut* job. From all indications it was an extraordinarily successful match with Lili Kracauer sharing her husband's intellectual interests and helping his work until her death in 1971. To Kracauer, she was "the greatest happiness of my existence."[37] They remained inseparable for thirty-six years, except for the short period when Kracauer was interned in France in 1940.

And yet, despite the personal and professional success Kracauer enjoyed in 1930, he still remained very much the "extraterritorial" intellectual. As already noted, spiritual homelessness was a theme which ran throughout his writings in the Weimar period, mocking the myth of the "Golden Twenties." When attempts were made to transcend the meaninglessness of modern life, whether religious in the case of Buber or Scheler, or political in the case of the *völkisch Tat* circle[38] or Lukács, Kracauer treated them with scorn. Similarly, the then current *Wissenschaftskrise,* that collapse of historicism into relativism which Troeltsch and Weber had confronted but not resolved, was impervious to correction through solely methodological means. Kracauer reasoned:

Not from science itself or with the help of philosophical speculation may the . . . crisis of science be resolved; its overcoming demands instead a real departure from the entire spiritual situation . . . Annihilation of relativistic thinking, blocking of vision against the infinite without bounds: that is all tied to a *complete change in the entire essence of reality*—and perhaps not only in it alone.[39]

In fact, what gave Kracauer much of his success in the Weimar period was his willingness to face the dilemmas besetting Germany without illusions. Success did not signify an end to his "extraterritoriality" so much as his ability to speak for others in similar situations.

No better expression of Kracauer's continuing personal estrangement can be found than *Ginster,* the semi-autobiographical novel he published without affixing his name in 1928. Although it would be hazardous to draw overly precise parallels between Kracauer and his main character, it is clear that he exploited many of his own experiences and attitudes in writing the novel. Set in the vacuous world of the petit-bourgeoisie, *Ginster* traces the attempts of one of its inhabitants to confront the idiocy of World War I. Its hero, if the name is really applicable, is known simply by his nickname, Ginster, which means a type of shrub that grows by the side of railroad tracks. He is shown as a somewhat naive and passive victim of forces he cannot understand, although he musters the cunning to survive them. Trained, like his creator, as an architect, his uneventful and aimless life is interrupted by the war and the threat of conscription. He avoids the army for two years, but is finally drafted only to be released a few weeks later after starving himself into collapse. After he returns to civilian life, his existence resumes its meaningless ramble without Ginster having learned a great deal from his experience. His opposition to the war had been more visceral than ideological at the start and remains so at the end. No *Bildungsroman, Ginster* is written in a restrained, bittersweet, laconic style that would place it as a product of the *Neue Sachlichkeit*, if not for the frequent flashes of surrealistic energy that indicate Kracauer's impatience with pure objectivity. Ginster reacts, but when he does so it is without any real introspective growth. Unlike Kracauer himself, he fails to transcend the world of the architect to become a writer with the power to give his life at least aesthetic order. An aura of melancholy pervades the novel, although its final chapter, which was unaccountably dropped from the 1963 re-edition, can be read in a somewhat optimistic way.[40]

Kracauer manages, however, to maintain a consistently critical tension in the work by juxtaposing Ginster's obviously underplayed reactions and the horrors of bourgeois life and the war which demand a more vigorous response. Included among his targets is his uncle, who had died in 1924. Kracauer gently although pointedly satirizes him as an archivist incapable of connecting his fascination with the past to the problems of the present. In contrast to Ginster, his attitude toward the war is that of a superpatriot who would "give up his entire Middle Ages for the occupied piece of land and become the Fatherland in person."[41]

Although never achieving the notoriety of Erich Maria Remarque's *All Quiet on the Western Front, Ginster* ranks as one of Weimar's most effective fictional exposés of the insanity of the war and the society that spawned it. That Kracauer chose to publish it anonymously reveals much about the status of antiwar writing in the last years of the republic. Publicly lauded by Thomas Mann, Joseph Roth, Hermann Kesten, and Hermann Hesse, Kracauer was proudest of the private praise he received from Alban Berg, whose letter of December 12, 1928, he cherished throughout his life. To Berg, *Ginster* was "not only a literary masterpiece, but also, in the truest sense of the word, a human document. . . . Something appears that always seems to me as the ideal condition of a work of art, which I have found only in the most infrequent cases." Many years later, Adorno would concur with this judgment, calling the book Kracauer's "most meaningful achievement."[42]

With all of the critical energies underlying Kracauer's work in the last half-decade of the Weimar period, it is not surprising that he was drawn into the orbit of the leftist opposition to the Republic. But here too he remained an extraterritorial man, isolated from the dominant currents of radicalism. Judging from a biting satire of the postwar revolution in Osnabruck near the end of *Ginster*, Kracauer had not been caught up in the utopian climate of the early 1920s. And he consistently avoided any flirtation with the various parties of the left that survived those years. Nor did he regularly contribute to leftist publications, choosing instead to remain with the staunchly bourgeois *FZ*, even during its swing to the right. His attitude toward the Soviet experiment seems to have turned sour at an early point in its history. In short, he remained very much on the margins of Weimar left-wing life. As an intellectual, he had no illusions about his qualifications as a potential proletarian. In the introduction to *Die Angestellten*, he wrote: "The intellectuals are either themselves employees or they are free, and then the employees are uninteresting to them because of their routineness *(Alltäglichkeit)*. The radical intellectuals also do not easily come behind the exotica of the everyday."[43] Kracauer's hope in that work was to awaken the consciousness of intellectuals to the condition of the white-collar workers. His target was the glib assumption of certain vulgar Marxists that this potentially dangerous stratum of society would join the working class. Just as he warned against the subsumption of the *Angestellten* under a simplified bipolar class rubric, Kracauer resisted the integration of the critical intellectual into any one movement or party.

This general stance was shared by the men who formed his closest friendships during the Weimar period: Theodor W. Adorno, Walter Benjamin, Ernst Bloch, and Leo Lowenthal. Like Kracauer they were all unaffiliated and experimental leftists who could have merited Benjamin's description of Kracauer's "consistent outsiderness."[44] All were fascinated by cultural questions more than economic ones and had little patience with the mechanistic economism of the Second International orthodoxy. Kracauer was less interested in high art than Adorno or Lowenthal, less drawn to religious questions than Benjamin or Bloch, but he shared with them a common vocabulary and general outlook. As friends, they avidly read each other's works, often reviewing them with an appreciative, if not always uncritical eye.[45] On certain occasions, one would complain about the appearance of his ideas in the writings of another,[46] and in fact it is difficult to establish whose claim to originality is correct in many cases. Stylistically, they were also relatively similar, although Bloch's Expressionist prose was all his own. The similarity rested in their frequent reliance on short, aphoristic evocations to make a philosophically laden point. Benjamin's *Einbahnstrasse,* Bloch's *Spuren,* and Adorno's *Minima Moralia,* all bear comparison with Kracauer's *feuilleton* pieces in the *FZ*.

Where they perhaps most strikingly differed was in their attitude toward the revolution in Marxist theory signaled by the appearance of Lukács's *History and Class Consciousness* and Karl Korsch's *Marxism and Philosophy* in 1923. Bloch and Adorno, although not entirely in agreement with the Hegelianized Marxism posited by those works, were far more favorable than Benjamin, Lowenthal, or Kracauer. Kracauer's interest in Simmel and Scheler had reinforced his strong distrust of the idealism so prevalent in the neo-Kantian prewar period. In fact, his general attitude towards metaphysical speculation was such that Benjamin could call him an "enemy of philosophy"[47] in 1923. If he did have a philosophical interest in the early 1920s, it was in the work of the master anti-Hegelian, Søren Kierkegaard, whose impact is clear on Kracauer's ambitious investigation of the detective novel, which has only recently been published.[48]

Although Kracauer had endorsed Lukács's diagnosis of the meaninglessness of the modern world in *Theory of the Novel,* he was far less willing to accept the solution implicit in Lukács's conversion to Communism. An unpublished manuscript on "The Concept of Man in Marx," directed against Lukács, was lost during the emigration, but his argument has largely survived in a series of letters to Bloch during the mid-twenties. On May 27, 1926, he wrote:

It seems to me that [Lukács] has attacked empty and worn out idealism, but instead of transcending it, has fallen into it again. His concept of totality, if despairing of its own formality, has more similarity to Lask than Marx. Instead of penetrating Marx with realities, he returns to the Spirit *(Geist)* and metaphysics of exhausted idealism and allows the materialist categories to fall on the way. . . . Rudas and Deborin [the Soviet philosophers who attacked Lukács], however disgustingly shallow they may be, unconsciously are correct against Lukács in many things. . . . He is philosophically—a reactionary; please think of his concept of personality.

After a return letter from Bloch, in which Lukács's materialist credentials were defended and the characterization of him as a reactionary was found wanting,[49] Kracauer replied on June 29th that

I spoke with [Korsch] in the Reichstag in January [1926] about Lukács. He approved of my arguments in general and explained that only out of very weighty tactical reasons did he intend to remain silent. . . . Through his reception of Hegel, Lukács covers the actual source of Marx's fundamental concepts in a fateful way. Marx comes, more decisively than Lukács presents and perhaps knows, from the French Enlightenment and, to be sure, from one branch of the Enlightenment that goes back to Locke and is represented by the names Helvétius and Holbach; that is, decisive categories of Marxism, such as the concept of "Man" or "Morality" can be understood only if one builds a tunnel under the massive mountain of Hegel from Marx to Helvétius. . . . Had Lukács seen clearer, it would not have been possible in the final chapter of his book, which dealt with organization, to introduce a bad concept of personality. . . . I would really like to know where, according to your conviction, Lukács's materialist intention can be placed. There is no room in the progress of this formal dialectic, which so smoothly leads to an empty totality. I can name many sentences in Marx which judge this dialectic. It means a regression behind Marx.

Although finishing with a positive appraisal of the brilliance of some of Lukács's passages on reification, Kracauer clearly rejected the basic burden of Lukács's argument. His distrust of totality, concern for the integrity of the individual personality, and adherence to the Enlightenment view of materialism informed all of his later work as well. In *Die Angestellten,* for example, he was to write of a "hunger for immediacy that without a doubt is the consequence of the undernourishment produced by German idealism."[50] Politically, his critique of *History and Class Consciousness,* especially of its advocacy of personal realization through submission to the will of the party, led in one direction: "I am in the last analysis," he wrote Bloch, "an anarchist, to be sure skeptical enough to consider anarchism as it exists as a distorter of its intentions."[51] As Lili Kracauer would acknowledge after her husband's death, all forms of conformity, including solidarity with the working-class movement and its parties, were anathema to him.[52]

What is, however, also significant in this correspondence is Kracauer's appeal to Marx, as he interpreted him, against Lukács. His self-image as a defender of Marxism during the late Weimar period is apparent in an exchange he had with Bloch in 1932 after he published a critical review of Brecht's film *Kuhle Wampe.*[53] Bloch was outraged by the review and its placement in the bourgeois *FZ;* he claimed Kracauer had a personal bias against Brecht (which was true, as several of his letters reveal)[54] and argued that he had abandoned his militancy of only a short time before. There were no classless intellectuals, Bloch warned. Kracauer responded with equal indignation, arguing that whatever his personal feelings toward Brecht, he had never allowed them to interfere with his critical judgment. As for writing for the *FZ,* he remarked that his reputation as an "enemy of the bourgeoisie" was known to all and that writing in a non-Marxist paper gave his words greater public impact. The accusation that he had repudiated his militancy was also nonsense: "I have advocated Marxism visibly enough and more than others and will continue to advocate it in a way that corresponds to my talents and energies and with growing influence on the general development."

This view of Kracauer as militant was also expressed in Benjamin's review of *Die Angestellten,*[55] which Kracauer always praised. The book, Benjamin argued, was a "signpost on the road to the politicization of the intellectuals. . . . This indirect influence is the only one that a revolutionary writer from the bourgeoisie can have today. Direct effectiveness can only come from praxis." Kracauer was a "rag-picker" in the "dawn of a revolutionary day." The characterization of rag-picker was one Kracauer always liked,[56] but unlike Benjamin, his faith in the dawning of a revolutionary day soon wavered. In more recent years, the nature of his radicalism has been debated by Adorno and Hans G. Helms, the former concerned about a growing conformity in his work, the latter anxious to maintain its radical impetus as long as possible.[57] Although Adorno's perception has been borne out by Kracauer's most recent work, Helms has successfully drawn attention to the extent of Kracauer's radicalism during the Weimar period. The correspondence with Bloch quoted above, which could not be examined when Helms wrote, confirms his case. So too does a remark Kracauer's friend and colleague on the *FZ,* the Austrian novelist Joseph Roth, made to Stefan Zweig in 1930. Kracauer, he wrote, "is one of those Jehovah-Jews, Marxism is his bible; the eastern Jews have a name for these people: God's policemen."[58]

For all his Marxist rhetoric and intentions, however, it is clear that Kracauer was more a member of Weimar's celebrated "homeless left" than any established Marxist movement. *Die Angestellten* candidly admits that "the work is a diagnosis and as such consciously refuses to make suggestions for improvements."[59] Although Kracauer ends the text with the ringing words: "It does not depend on the institutions being changed, it depends on men changing the institutions,"[60] how this is to be accomplished is never determined. Thus, one might say that despite his increasing celebrity during the waning Weimar years, he remained very much an extraterritorial figure in political terms.

In yet another way Kracauer remained an insecure and marginal intellectual. During the twenties, the lion's share of Kracauer's energies were spent in preparing his *feuilleton* columns, which were usually thrown out with the next day's trash. To a man of his philosophical and cultural ambitions, the ephemeral nature of his writings was a source of considerable chagrin, which he expressed in a letter to Adorno in 1930.[61] Other journalists such as Tucholsky and Ossietzky of the *Weltbühne* praised his work and tried to entice him into their circle, but he refused.[62] In later years, he would reject comparison with them, just as he would bristle at the label of journalist.[63] But without a proper academic connection, Kracauer was never really accepted in the scholarly world either. In the twenties, several manuscripts, including his highly speculative study of the detective novel, went unpublished because they fell between two stools. Philosophers were uninterested in his subject matter and readers of detective novels had no patience with his method.

Ultimately, however, Kracauer's fears were to prove unfounded as collections of his early work appeared in German.[64] And now thanks to the efforts of Siegfried Unseld of the Suhrkamp Verlag and Karsten Witte, who is preparing a major biography of Kracauer, his collected works are in the process of being published. Included in the seven-volume series is Kracauer's second novel, *Georg,* written in 1934 but prevented from publication because of Kracauer's emigration from Germany. A social critique of the waning years of the Republic centering around a newspaper editor, *Georg* was warmly praised by no less a figure than Thomas Mann while still in manuscript,[65] but attempts to place it with a Dutch publishing house were unsuccessful. Unlike some of his other manuscripts, however, it survived his sudden departure from Germany in March of 1933, after the burning of the Reichstag and shortly before some of Kracauer's own books were burned in the famous conflagration of May 10th.

Kracauer was already in Paris when a letter came from the Frankfurter-Societäts-Druckerei on August 25th informing him that his tenure with the *FZ* was at an end. The pretext was an article he had written for the left-wing *Das Neue Tagebuch,*[66] but it is clear that Kracauer had no place in the *FZ*'s future, which reached its nadir in 1939, when Max Amann presented it to Hitler as a birthday present. Still, Kracauer did not relish the exile that awaited him; in September, Benjamin reported to Brecht that he was still very depressed by the change.[67] From a position of power and prestige, he was reduced to free-lance writing in a hostile environment. In his last work on history, when much of the pain had passed, Kracauer remarked on the condition of the emigré, who was like a palimpsest composed of different cultural superimpositions. Here the ambivalence of his attitude toward extraterritoriality was clear:

As he settled elsewhere, all those loyalties, expectations, and aspirations that comprise so large a part of his being are automatically cut off from their roots. His life history is disrupted, his "natural" self relegated to the background of his mind . . . since the self he was continues to smolder beneath the person he is about to become, his identity is bound to be in a state of flux; and the odds are that he will never fully belong to the community to which he now in a way belongs. . . . Where then does he live? In the near-vacuum of extraterritoriality. . . . The exile's true mode of existence is that of a stranger.[68]

In Paris, Kracauer supported himself by writing film criticism and book reviews for Swiss newspapers such as the *Basler National-Zeitung* and the *Neue Züricher Zeitung* and for French journals like the *Revue du Cinéma, Mercure de France, La Vie Intellectuelle,* and *Figaro.* Ginster was translated into French by Clara Malraux, at that time the wife of the novelist. Although gaining him a reputation in Parisien intellectual circles, the translation brought in very little income. Most of his efforts were directed toward the publication of a book that would help him stay above water. His subject was a German Jew of an earlier era who had also lived in exile, albeit voluntary, in Paris, Jacques Offenbach.

In 1937, *Jacques Offenbach and His Time* was published in German, French, and English editions.[69] Rather than the conventional life and works study, Kracauer attempted a "Social Biography" that paid as much attention to Second Empire Paris as to Offenbach himself. Continuing his interest in marginal cultural phenomena, he probed the world of the operetta and the related milieus of boulevard and journalistic society, where the deracinated modern man ruled supreme. The operetta, he argued, had "originated in an epoch in which social reality had been banished by the Emperor's orders";[70] its phantasmagorical quality mirrored the illusory nature of Napoleon's reign, where class conflict was only apparently overcome. But for all its escapist tendencies, it fulfilled a critical function during the Empire's most repressive period: "At a time when the bourgeoisie were politically stagnant and the Left was impotent, Offenbach's operettas had been the most definite form of revolutionary protest."[71]

Although a massively researched and fluidly written study, which successfully conveys the flavor of the period it examined, *Offenbach* was a less penetrating work than Walter Benjamin's *Passagenarbeit,* the unfinished project that dealt with much the same subject matter.[72] It lacked Benjamin's conceptual daring and breadth of vision and broke no new ground in probing the commodity form in bourgeois society, as had the *Passagenarbeit.* Although clearly indebted to Marx's *Eighteenth Brumaire, Offenbach* was no real landmark in Marxist cultural criticism, as Benjamin's work has come to be seen. Perhaps its greatest weakness, as Adorno predictably pointed out in a mixed review,[73] was its failure to deal directly with Offenbach's music, focusing instead on the libretti of Halévy and the general atmosphere surrounding the operetta world.

Although the appearance of *Offenbach* lessened his financial burden somewhat, it was clear by 1938 that continued life in Paris was intolerable. With the growing threat of war and the lack of real opportunities to get a foothold in French society, emigration to America seemed the only solution. Although certain friends, such as Benjamin and Joseph Roth, remained in Paris, others, including Bloch, Adorno, and Lowenthal, were already in America or about to depart. The next three years were spent in a grim and frantic struggle to obtain the proper papers for the emigration. Reading his correspondence of those years is a painful experience, revealing as it does the desperation that Kracauer and doubtless many others felt in their desire to leave. In the light of his later disdain for filming historical dramas, it is a mark of his plight that on April 5, 1939, he wrote to the Hollywood producer Max Laemmle to ask about the possibility of filming his *Offenbach*.

In 1939, some aid was given by the American Guild for German Cultural Freedom, but only for three months. Kracauer's best hope at that time was the *Institut für Sozialforschung*, which had resettled in New York in 1934. In 1937–38, he had worked on a commissioned study of "Totalitarian Propaganda: A Political Treatise" for the *Institut*'s *Zeitschrift für Sozialforschung*, but Adorno's editorial emendations were of such magnitude that he withdrew it in disgust. Nonetheless, Kracauer continued to hope that his friendships with Lowenthal and Adorno would lead to *Institut* support, even though he had never had very cordial relations with Max Horkheimer, the *Institut*'s director. In the late thirties, however, the *Institut* suffered serious financial reversals that severely curtailed its ability to help other refugees. Still, Kracauer maintained his hopes even as he sailed for America and his disappointment was proportionately keen.[74]

Institut members, in particular Leo Lowenthal, were instrumental, however, in obtaining the necessary affidavits which allowed Kracauer to emigrate. Also helpful in this regard were Meyer Shapiro, the distinguished art historian, Iris Barry of the Museum of Modern Art's Film Library, and Varian Fry, who helped secure his release from the Centre de Rassemblement, into which he had been put at the war's outbreak. In March of 1941, he left Paris for Lisbon and then on April 15th he and his wife set sail for New York on the Niassa; they arrived ten days later. His state of mind at this time can be seen in the letters he continued to send to *Institut* figures for help. To Adorno, he wrote that his time in Paris had been "eight years of an existence that doesn't deserve that name. I have grown older, also inside me. Now is the last station, the last chance that I don't dare misplay or else everything is lost."[75] To Friedrich Pollock, the *Institut*'s Associate Director, he wrote of his anxiety, "anxiety at beginning with nothing that I can call my own and perhaps without a chance at the start."[76] Kracauer's situation was certainly not enviable, but at least, unlike Walter Benjamin and many others, he was alive to try to make a new start in America. At the age of 52, Kracauer still had his most influential work ahead of him.

Although disappointed by the *Institut*, Kracauer was fortunate to have found a sponsor with the Museum of Modern Art, where Alfred Barr and Iris Barry were making the serious study of film respectable. In subsequent years, grants from the Rockefeller, Guggenheim, Bollingen, and Mellon Foundations made his financial survival possible. Lili Kracauer continued to do research for her husband, but also worked for the Central Location Index, which helped in the search for displaced persons in Europe. Their combined income, in addition to a compensatory stipend paid by the German government in the 1950s, prevented a repetition of the last years in Paris.

Kracauer's first project with the Museum was a study of Nazi war propaganda. Bernard Karpel, the Museum's Film Librarian, remembers him camped in the projection room watching films over and over again, smoking foul cigars, and bemoaning his diminished status.[77] The result was "Propaganda and the Nazi War Film," published in 1942.[78] Analysing both the form and content of the Nazi films, with a long and penetrating look at Leni Riefenstahl's *Triumph of the Will*, Kracauer came to a conclusion about the contrived nature of pseudodocumentaries that anticipated his later argument in *Theory of Film:* "Most films of fact affect audiences not so much through the organizations of their material as through the material itself. . . . The two Nazi campaign films differ from them in that they not only excel in solid composition of their elements, but also exploit all propagandistic effects which may be produced by the very structure."[79] Kracauer was especially interested in the Nazis' perverse use of the montage technique developed by the Russian directors of the 1920s to a fine art. Another argument foreshadowing his later position concerned the relative absence of anti-Jewish activities in the films he viewed, which suggested the Nazis feared a reaction produced by the direct presentation of their atrocities. "The image," he wrote, "seems to be the last refuge of violated human dignity."[80]

For the next five years, Kracauer was occupied with the first book that brought his name to prominence in the American film world, *From Caligari to Hitler: A Psychological History of the German Film.* In 1932, Kracauer had defined the task of the film critic in politically charged terms:

The film in the capitalist economy is a commodity like other commodities. Apart from a few outsiders, they are produced not in the interest of art or the en-

lightenment of the masses, but for the sake of the profits they promise to yield.
. . . They exercise extraordinarily important social functions that no film critic,
who earns the name, can leave unobserved.[81]

"The film," he wrote six years earlier, "is the mirror of the existing society."[82] These presuppositions still underlay *From Caligari to Hitler,*
despite its subtitle's stress on psychology; for Kracauer, the psychic states
worth probing were "those deep layers of collective mentality which
extend more or less below the dimensions of consciousness."[83]

To uncover this subconscious dimension of the collective
psyche, Kracauer qualitatively analyzed hundreds of German films, whose
immanent development he tried to link to the changing fortunes of the
Weimar Republic. Qualitative analysis of German cultural phenomena
was in fact a popular occupation in the America of the 1940s, and Kracauer was in the company of other emigré scholars like Ernst Kris.[84]
While paying some attention to technical developments, such as the increasing use of studio interiors and new lighting techniques, Kracauer
focused primarily on plots and significant motifs. His basic conclusion
was that the cinema mirrored the shifts in the Republic's history with
extraordinary fidelity. Among his most notable discussions was a critique of the Expressionist classic, *The Cabinet of Dr. Caligari,* which
revealed for the first time the reversal of its originally radical script by
the director, Robert Wiene. No less significant was his devastating attack on Fritz Lang, then in Hollywood, in whose films Kracauer saw many
of the marks of protofascism. Even *The Testament of Mr. Marbuse,* which
Goebbels banned in 1933, "betrays the power of Nazi spirit over minds
insufficiently equipped to counter its peculiar fascination."[85] The result,
so a later defender of Lang claimed, was unfortunate: "No one has done
more damage to Lang's reputation. . . . Kracauer gives the impression
of carrying on a personal feud."[86]

In general, Kracauer's verdict on the German cinema was
strongly negative. As in his *Offenbach* study, he found a parallel between a mystifying cultural phenomenon and the general prevalence of
false consciousness. Even the films of the middle years of the Republic,
the "stabilized era" dominated by the *Neue Sachlickeit,* came under fire.
Following a critical reference to the *Neue Sachlichkeit* in *Die Angestellten,*[87] which demonstrated a certain uneasiness about his own "hunger for immediacy," Kracauer argued that "New Objectivity marks a state
of paralysis. Cynicism, resignation, disillusionment; these tendencies point
to a mentality disinclined to commit itself in any direction."[88] Even
G. W. Pabst, whose fidelity to the photographic essence of film Kracauer
found laudable, undercut the critical implications of his film through a

weakness for melodrama and desire to remain a neutral observer. Here, in other words, was a realistic cinema with problematic political implications, implications which Kracauer was to minimize when he wrote his next major film book. *From Caligari to Hitler* bitterly condemned the German people as a whole with little effort spent on determining which film appealed to which audience: "Irretrievably sunk into retrogression, the bulk of the German people could not help submitting to Hitler. Since Germany thus carried out what had been anticipated by her cinema from its very beginning, conspicuous screen characters now came true in life itself."[89]

As might be expected, the book stirred an enormous critical storm.[90] Its obvious leftist political slant was denounced in a vicious anticommunist review by Seymour Stern, which appeared in several places. Kracauer's method, especially his reliance on "collective soul" was attacked by Franklin Fearing, Hans Sahl, and Eric Bentley, who called the book a "refugee's revenge" in *The New York Times Book Review.* Arthur Schlesinger, Jr. approved of Kracauer's conclusions, but argued "that the main trouble, of course, is that Dr. Kracauer knows in advance which dreams panned out." Others worried about the possibility of tracing a similar protofascist lineage in non-German cinema, a thought that continued to trouble Adorno as late as the 1960s, when he wrote that *King Kong* could be taken as an allegory of comparable regression in America.[91]

Kracauer was not, however, without his defenders. David T. Bazelon praised his method in *Commentary;* Iris Barry did the same from a not totally disinterested point of view in *The New Republic,* and Richard Griffith called it "the best book on the movies I have ever read" in *New Movies.* Robert Warshow was moved to answer Stern's Red-baiting attack in the *New Leader's* letter columns and Herman Weinberg did the same in *Sight and Sound,* where he called it "perhaps the greatest book on the film ever written." The controversy has yet to be stilled as the different appreciations of the book in recent works by Peter Gay, I. C. Jarvie, Dieter Prokop, David Stewart Hull, and Michael Schröter illustrate.[92] And devotees of a non-social interpretation of the Weimar cinema still continue to draw sustenance from Lotte H. Eisner's *The Haunted Screen,*[93] originally written in French five years after *From Caligari to Hitler.*

With some distance between us and the book's publication, it seems safe to say that Kracauer's method, as flawed as it surely was, did uncover some remarkable tendencies in the cultural life of the Weimar years that make the collapse of the Republic more plausible. If disputable on certain films and occasionally doctrinaire in tone, *From Cal-*

igari to Hitler nevertheless represents a milestone in the application of a sociological-psychological approach to a mass medium that can scarcely resist it. Although Kracauer's own later work contained certain implicit criticisms of the book, which will be examined shortly, it still deservedly commands the attention of students of both film and fascism.

Thirteen years passed before Kracauer's next major analysis of the film. In that period, he continued to write film criticism and book reviews, now for American journals like *Harpers, Theater Arts,* and *Partisan Review.* He also helped support the efforts of others connected to the film in his new capacity as consultant to the Guggenheim Foundation. Project proposals by Arthur Knight, Robert Warshow, Shirley Clarke, Parker Tyler, Hans Richter, Gregory Markopoulos, and others all received Kracauer's endorsement.

But financial considerations compelled Kracauer to direct his energies in less interesting areas. In 1950, Leo Lowenthal, then director of research at the Voice of America, offered his old friend a post as research analyst. Two years later, Kracauer began an association with Columbia University's Bureau of Applied Social Research, founded by Paul Lazarsfeld and headed at the time by Charles Y. Glock. The fruit of these two connections was an empirical study of the thinking of recent refugees from eastern Europe, prepared in collaboration with Paul L. Berkman. Based on more than 300 interviews conducted in 1951–52 with exiles from Hungary, Poland, and Czechoslovakia, *Satellite Mentality* was published in 1956 under the auspices of the Bureau.[94] When first entering the Bureau, a stronghold of quantitative methods, Kracauer had published a paper defending the virtues of qualitative techniques.[95] *Satellite Mentality* was based on such a methodology, but it lacked the imaginative "construction in the material" that gave *Die Angestellten* its unique power. The conclusions reached by the authors, occasionally couched in Cold War rhetoric, were not very startling, and in later years, Kracauer would regard the book somewhat as an embarrassment.[96]

During the 1950s, the Kracauers had the opportunity to make several trips to Europe for the first time since their departure in 1941. Old friends like Adorno and Bloch had already returned; others like Benno Reifenberg, who helped found and edit the postwar periodical *Die Gegenwart,* were involved in reestablishing the continuities of German culture severed by the Nazis. Although Kracauer was encouraged to join them, like the majority of emigrés to America, he chose to remain in his adopted land where life, however "extraterritorial," was preferable to starting anew in Germany. Unlike Adorno, whose disparagement of the

undialectical qualities of English is well known, Kracauer took to his new
language with total acceptance. His repudiation of Adorno's position was
in fact a sore point between them.[97] In the early forties, he insisted on
writing only in English and engaged friends like Bernard Karpel of the
Museum of Modern Art to help him. When the editorial corrections of
his works in the new language were minor, he was overjoyed, but he
must have been equally chagrined when Pauline Kael belittled his English in a long critique of *Theory of Film* in 1962.[98]

   If the Kracauers ever considered returning to Germany, their
trips quickly disabused them of the notion. The Europeans, he wrote
Lowenthal after a three-month stay in 1956, "have lost the power of as-
similating the new. Somehow it is suffocating over there."[99] "We would
die if we had to live in Germany for good," he wrote two years later; it
is a country "frightening in its prosperity, politeness, sham depth, and
complete formlessness."[100] And again in 1960: Germany "is no country
but a place lying somewhere in a vacuum."[101] Kracauer enjoyed seeing
old friends like the publisher Peter Suhrkamp, the Blochs, the Adornos,
and the Malraux's and welcomed meeting new ones like the philosopher Karl Heinz Haag; but now over sixty, he was clearly loath to break
once again with a relatively comfortable environment.

   The environment became more comfortable still when the
Bollingen and Chapelbrook Foundations and later the American Philosophical Society awarded him the grants to work on his long-planned
second book on the cinema. Once again the Museum of Modern Art put
its film library and viewing room at his disposal; additional assistance
came from Henri Langlois' Cinémathèque Française in Paris and the British
Film Institute in London. In 1960, *Theory of Film; The Redemption of
Physical Reality* was published by Oxford University Press.

   The book represented the culmination of Kracauer's lifelong
fascination with film, which began, so he recalled in his preface, as a
child when he devoted his first critical effort to "Film as the Discoverer
of the Marvels of Everyday Life." Issues treated in the book—the primacy of photography, the nonfilmic nature of historical or artistic subject matter, the virtues of the documentary, to mention a few—had all
been treated in earlier essays.[102] His stress on the "redemptive" power
of film, which meant its ability to make us attend to realities that were
usually ignored, echoed his earlier concern for the neglected regions of
cultural life: detective novels, the operetta, urban landscapes, troops of
dancing girls, popular biographies, and the like. His reliance on what he
called a "material" rather than formal aesthetic continued his quasi-
phenomenological concern for the *Lebenswelt,* which had informed his
work as early as *Soziologie als Wissenschraft.* And the motif of extra-

territoriality strongly underlay his interpretation of the filmmaker's vision.

But what had disappeared in the years between *Caligari* and *Theory of Film* was Kracauer's earlier stress on the specifically social content of the reality film redeemed. In his 1927 essay on photography, Kracauer had discussed *inter alia* the function of illustrated newspapers as enemies of true consciousness through their meaningless juxtaposition of unrelated phenomena. In the same article, he developed the relationships between photography, the domination of nature, and capitalism that would be taken up by Benjamin and Adorno in later years. In his series on "The Small Shopgirls Go to the Movies," he probed the function of the film in the cultural desert of petit-bourgeois life. In his 1928 discussion of abstract films, he chastised Expressionism in the cinema for becoming *"Kunstgewerbe"*[103] (art commodities), not for being nonfilmic. "The film," as we have already noted he said, "is the mirror of the existing society," not of physical reality *per se*. In fact, his entire critique of formalism, whether in sociological theory or daily life, was tied to a nuanced attack on capitalist rationalization.[104] All of this was absent from *Theory of Film*. As Adorno and other radical critics were to complain,[105] redemption seemed to imply affirmation as well. Kracauer protested vehemently against this charge, but it was clear that the critical impetus of his previous work had been blunted. Although it would be mistaken to say it had disappeared entirely, the crucial absence of any analysis of capitalism meant an undeniable shift had occurred.

Within the world of film criticism as such, however, the issues *Theory of Film* provoked were very different.[106] The major impulse behind most serious film theory during the early years of the medium had been a desire to elevate movies into films, that is, to lift them from entertainment into an art form. Theoreticians like Rudolf Arnheim, who drew upon Gestaltist psychology for his arguments, Paul Rotha, Vachel Lindsay, and even the Marxist Béla Balázs were all anxious to stress the disparity between the event photographed and the artistic end-product that was the film.[107] Directors like Georges Méliès and Abel Gance in France and Pudovkin and Eisenstein in the Soviet Union were equally interested in exploiting the artistic potential of film, although of course the Russians had an ultimately political purpose. Techniques, especially the creative use of editing known as montage and the expressive employment of camera angles to produce dramatic images, were given primary attention by these critics and directors. When sound was introduced, Arnheim and some of the others bemoaned its injurious effect on the artfulness of film; true cinematic language was visual, not verbal.

In opposition to this position, which gained sufficient prominence to be called the "orthodoxy" by one recent observer,[108] two voices were raised: those of André Bazin,[109] the major theoretician of the *Cahiers du Cinema* in the 1940s and 1950s, and Siegfried Kracauer. Although neither ever acknowledged the existence of the other, it is clear with hindsight that they were fighting a common battle. Whereas the artistic theorists had chosen Méliès as their model, Bazin and Kracauer picked the Lumières brothers, whose documentary realism and rejection of illusory effects prefigured a very different cinematic tradition. What the Lumières had called, in a frequently quoted phrase, "the ripple of the leaves," only the film could capture and preserve. Both Bazin and Kracauer agreed on the priority of *what* was photographed over *how* it was photographed and spliced together. "Photography and the camera," Bazin wrote in a phrase that Kracauer could have seconded, "are discoveries that satisfy, once and for all and in its very essence, our obsession with realism."[110] The artistic theoreticians' stress on montage and the expressive image were no more than misplaced fetishes. The great film comedians like Chaplin and Keaton, whose unimaginative use of the camera had earned them bad marks from the "orthodox" establishment, were now admitted to the company of successful film-makers. Conversely, previous heroes like Eisenstein suffered, rightly or wrongly,[111] a fall from grace because of their excessive formalism.

Although Bazin was not as extreme in his insistence on non-artistic realism as Kracauer—compare, for example, their attitudes toward mixed cinema—[112] together they helped reorient the critical discussion about cinema in a radical way. The wave of Italian neorealist films in the forties and fifties seemed a confirmation of their position. In more recent years, the rise of *cinema verité* provided yet another blow to the artistic orthodoxy of the medium's infancy. What perhaps served most to aid their cause was the very success of the orthodox campaign; by the time of the realistic counterreformation, movies had indeed become films, and it was no longer necessary to defend their artistic credentials.

Kracauer's version of the anti-orthodox position is, of course, what concerns us here. Most commentators have found it to be more vulnerable than Bazin's, partly because Kracauer lacked the Frenchman's remarkable feel for individual films, partly because *Theory of Film* was far more doctrinaire than anything that Bazin wrote. According to Rudolf Arnheim,[113] Kracauer was a dogged conversationalist, who would worry an idea until all of its implications had been exposed; the argument in *Theory of Film* shows the effects of this character trait. Its basic premise is that there exists in film, as in all media, an essential characteristic that sets it apart from all others. This characteristic, which is derived from a phenomenological probe into its nature, is more than a descriptive term; it has normative value as well and can be used to separate "cinematic" from "noncinematic" films. According to Kracauer, what makes a film conform to this norm is its fidelity to the photograph, which captures its subject matter, its "raw material," in a realistic way. The opposite genre is painting, where a "formative" tendency holds sway and the artist's subjective intervention is paramount. Without banishing the filmmaker's creative side entirely, Kracauer clearly believed that in the mix between realistic and formative tendencies, the former must be dominant. On a continuum between documentaries and cartoons, the truly "cinematic" is at the documentary end. But to be fair to his position, a balance must be struck which admits both impulses, even if one is more heavily weighted than the other.

In using the term "realism," however, Kracauer was anxious to avoid sounding like a positivist with a belief in the pristinely mimetic character of the photographic image. The photograph, he acknowledged at one point in his argument, is not a mirror.

Photographs do not just copy nature but metamorphose it by transferring three-dimensional phenomena to the plane, severing their ties with the surroundings, and substituting black, gray, and white for the given color schemes. Yet if anything defies the idea of a mirror, it is not so much these unavoidable transformations—which may be discounted because in spite of them photographs still preserve the character of compulsory reproductions—as the way in which we take cognizance of visible reality.[114]

What is striking in this paragraph is the ease with which he dismisses the "unavoidable transformations" that had been at the heart of the artistic theoreticians' argument. The fact that photographs are "compulsory reproductions" is enough to justify his insistence that the objects of perception are preserved, indeed "redeemed" by the camera. Later in his argument, Kracauer goes so far as to forget his admission that photographs are not mimetic reproductions of the physical world: "Now of all the existing media the cinema alone holds up a mirror to nature. Hence our dependence on it for the reflection of happenings which would petrify us were we to encounter them in real life."[115] Unfortunately, he failed to draw the obvious distinction between realism and naturalism, which might have helped him out of this dilemma.

But what is equally important in this paragraph is Kracauer's shift at its end away from the object of perception to the subject, to "the way in which we take cognizance of visible reality." To Kracauer, the subjective vision necessarily entailed by photography is an alienated one. The selectivity exercised by the photographer is relatively passive

in comparison with that of the painter; it is more emphatic than spontaneous. Significantly, Kracauer identifies this vision with a melancholic,
elegiac reaction to the world:

Now melancholy as an inner disposition not only makes elegiac objects seem
attractive but carries still another, more important implication: it favors self-es-
trangement, which on its part entails identification with all kinds of objects. The
dejected individual is likely to lose himself in the incidental configurations of his
environment, absorbing them with a disinterested intensity no longer determined
by his previous preferences. His is a kind of receptivity which resembles Proust's
photographer cast in the role of a stranger.

Here we have all the elements of the *Neue Sachlichkeit,* disillusioned
estrangement and unflinching objectivity, reproduced in an aesthetic of
film. But whereas in his earlier comments on the *Neue Sachlichkeit,*
Kracauer had shown some critical distance from its implications, here
he succumbs to them entirely. The motif of extraterritoriality, which we
have seen so evident in his life and much of his work, is transformed
into a prescriptive norm by which the "cinematic" nature of films are
to be judged.

Having postulated this normative realism, Kracauer then
proceeded to spell out the "affinities" photography has for certain types
of reality, which also draw upon his earlier attitudes. These affinities are
for "unstaged reality," "the fortuitous," "endlessness," "the indeterminate" and "the flow of life."[117] All of these are clearly related to his life-
long concern for the flux of the *Lebenswelt,* which resists formalized
categorization. The film "redeems" these aspects of reality, which it alone
can capture and preserve. In the present age, this power of redemption
is extremely important. In his epilogue, Kracauer stressed two characteristics of the age as crucial: "the declining hold of common beliefs on
the mind and the steadily increasing prestige of science."[118] The former
confronts us with a normative void; ideology (understood in the non-
Marxist sense of a unifying belief system) is on the wane. The latter in-
terferes with our capacity to experience the physical world directly
without the filter of formal abstractions.

Films cannot help us by restoring the lost sense of community and meaning, for "the cooling process is irreversible."[119] This is in
fact the major reason, so Kracauer argued, that prevents films from being
seen as works of art: "Art in film is reactionary because it symbolizes
wholeness and thus pretends to the continued existence of beliefs which
'cover' physical reality in both senses of the word."[120] Tragedy is especially inappropriate to the cinema because it presupposes an ordered
cosmos, which the film relentlessly denies.[121]

If film is worthless in helping us recapture our sense of a meaningful universe, it is nonetheless useful in overcoming the other tendency of the modern world, scientific over-abstractness. Films help reawaken our openness to the concrete by making us confront unpleasant realities. As a "materialistically" minded medium, it proceeds from "below" to "above."[122] (Here one hears a dim echo of his argument in the letter to Bloch in 1926 that Lukács had badly underestimated the influence of the Enlightenment materialists on Marx.) But anything beyond this "redemption of physical reality" was beyond the power of the film:

> Belá Balázs's thesis that the cinema comes into its own only if it serves revolutionary ends is an untenable one as are the kindred views of those schools of thought, neorealistic and otherwise, which postulate an intimate relationship between the medium and socialism or collectivism.[123]

Implicitly, this debunking of Balázs also contains a criticism of Walter Benjamin's celebrated essay "The Work of Art in the Era of Mechanical Reproduction,"[124] which followed Brecht in seeing a revolutionary potential in the mass distraction of the cinema. Although it may appear as if Kracauer was attributing to the film something akin to Brecht's celebrated *Verfremdungseffect*, it is clear that he had no confidence in the cognitive and ultimately political benefits of this estrangement. Kracauer may have still been a "rag-picker," but the "revolutionary day" had clearly failed to dawn.

Theory of Film created even more of a critical furor than *From Caligari to Hitler.* Positive voices were not absent, among them Herbert Read's, and surprisingly, Rudolf Arnheim's.[125] A friend of Kracauer's since the 1940s who had helped him choose the subtitle of the book,[126] Arnheim generously acknowledged the place of both his and Kracauer's approaches in understanding the cinema. *Theory of Film,* he wrote, "is probably the most intelligent book ever written on film";[127] although needing "correction and clarification," "the core of his thesis is surely valid and important."[128] Arnheim endorsed Kracauer's stress on the realistic tendency in the cinema, a remarkable reversal of his own *Film as Art,* but unlike Kracauer, he connected it to a cultural decline rather than a return to our senses: "a concern with unshaped matter is a melancholy surrender rather than the recovery of man's grip on reality. Perhaps, then, we are witnessing the last twitches of an exhausted civilization, whose rarefied concepts no longer reach the world of the senses."[129]

Most of the critical reception of *Theory of Film* was, however, essentially hostile. The least charitable of his accusers was Pauline

Kael, who wrote a lengthy and vitriolic attack in *Sight and Sound* in 1962.[130] Miss Kael's ire was aroused by the very attempt to theorize about film in the grand manner:

What do movies [N.B. not "films"] have to do with the "redemption" of "physical reality"? Our physical reality—what we experience around us—is what we can't redeem: if its good, marvelous, if it isn't we can weep or booze, or try to change it. Redemption, like sublimation, is a dear sweet thought. And Kracauer's theory of film is a theory imposed on motion pictures.[131]

In elaborating her attack, she scored her most telling points in demonstrating the lengths to which Kracauer went to include cinematic phenomena he liked, such as Fred Astaire's dance routines, under the rubric of realism. She was somewhat less persuasive when hearing a German accent and noting a speculative mind, she compared Kracauer to Hegel, the philosopher he spent much of his adult life opposing.[132] Equally questionable was her call for movies to be "judged by the same kind of standards that are used in other arts,"[133] as if there were such a thing as "art" with one set of standards for all its subdivisions.

Other critical appraisals by Tyler, Linden, Engels, Jarvie, Perkins, and Tudor,[134] to mention the most prominent, were less bilious than Miss Kael's, but scarcely less disparaging. As a whole, the points they made, embellished by some of my own, are as follows:

(1) The search for the essence of a medium (which Miss Kael called "the great lunatic tradition")[135] is itself a highly questionable endeavor. There is no "nature" of film with prescriptive value by which good films can be separated from bad. Nor are there immanent laws of the cinema that can be abstracted from the social context in which films are made.

(2) Film is particularly difficult to see in essentialist terms because the assumption that photography is its primary source is erroneous. One might equally stress the opposition between the static photograph and the dynamic motion picture. In a technical sense, such nineteenth-century phenomena as the magic lantern and other optical toys simulating motion are equally important. In a substantive sense, the traditions of the theater and the novel cannot be discounted. In short, Méliès as well as the Lumière brothers must be given his due.

(3) The distinction Kracauer makes between reality and "camera reality," the latter taking into account the distortions that cannot be overcome, is poorly developed and inconsistently used. Although anxious to avoid a positivist copy-theory of reality, he frequently sounds as if he believes films "mirrored" the material world. At times, Kracauer calls films cinematic solely because of the techniques

used, a stress on movement, for example, rather than because of their content. He sometimes justifies illusions that are convincing to the audience because of their fidelity to "camera reality," but in what way do they then redeem the physical world? Once technique is admitted as a criterion of realism, then the emphasis is once again shifted away from the object photographed to the subjective photographer and Kracauer is back on "orthodox" grounds.

(4) In establishing his prescriptive aesthetic, Kracauer has posited norms that are far too exclusive. Not only do they rule out cartoons, fantasies (such as those of Cocteau, one of Kracauer's *bêtes noires*), filmed operas and plays, almost all avant-garde films including expressionist classics like *Caligari,* history films, and movies made from novels, but they also deny a priori the significance of the most widely admired directors of the postneorealist 1960s: Fellini, Antonioni, Resnais, Buñuel, Godard, and Bergman.[136] Any theory of film that lacks the room for these types of movies is intrinsically inadequate.

(5) Finally, the more general cultural tasks Kracauer sets the cinema are grounded in questionable assumptions. Is it true that all normative systems have been shipwrecked, or is Kracauer merely succumbing to the myth of the 1950s: the end of ideology? Moreover, even if one were to grant Kracauer's assumption about the impoverishment of our perceptual apparatus caused by scientific abstraction, can one then say that films really return us to the sensuous, nonreified flow of "life?"[137] In fact, doesn't the very mediation of the film suggest an experience that is still passive and estranged? That melancholic alienation Kracauer sees as the essence of the camera eye is a poor candidate for the means to bring us back to our senses. Is there, in fact, any evidence that film-watching really leads to renewed participation in "life," rather than compensating for its absence? Indeed, the very notion of "life," which Kracauer once criticized in Simmel,[138] but now accepted wholeheartedly, is highly suspect. To identify the real solely with process and flux is itself a Romantic assumption of dubious merit, as even Arnheim in his favorable review noted.[139] Finally, the desire to redeem physical reality suggests a kind of indiscriminate yea-saying that fails to separate what needs to be saved from what doesn't. The implications of this are apparent in Kracauer's reaction to films that force us to see the monstrosities of the world:

The mirror reflections of horror are an end in themselves. As such they beckon the spectator to take them in and thus incorporate into his memory the real face of things too dreadful to be held in reality. In experiencing the rows of calves' heads or the litter of tortured human bodies in the films made of the Nazi concentration camps we redeem horror from its invisibility behind the veils of panic and imagination. And this experience is liberating in as much as it removes a most powerful taboo.[140]

What Kracauer fails to consider here is the extent to which films numb us to horror through overexposure. The increasing tolerance for and even delight in graphic horror has been one of the most unsettling tendencies of the last decade. Removing taboos, especially if it entails the loss of our capacity for panic (or at least disgust) and imagination, may not always be liberating after all.

With the rough treatment it received at the hands of most commentators, *Theory of Film* marked the end rather than the beginning of an era in film criticism. It helped lay to rest the old debate over the artfulness of film, but in turn, its failures made the extreme realist position clearly untenable. Attempts to judge films as "cinematic" or not according to a prescriptive aesthetic soon seemed highly dubious. Instead, film criticism turned to the so-called "auteur theory," which emerged from the pages of the *Cahiers du Cinéma* and was propagated in America by Andrew Sarris,[141] or it focused on the more modest task of investigating the nature of specific genres within the larger corpus of films. Most recently, a structuralist method has been applied to the language of film by Christian Metz in France and Peter Wollen in Britain.[142] *Theory of Film* remains a monument in the history of thinking about movies, but it also serves as a warning against building other monuments of its kind.

In the 1960s, Kracauer's career took a relatively new turn. These last several years before his death appear to be among the happiest of his life. Within the academic world, he finally received a measure of the recognition that had eluded him previously; he became an associate member of the Seminar on Interpretation at Columbia University and was invited on several occasions to Germany for colloquia on poetry and hermeneutics at Cologne and Lindau. His early *FZ* writings were rediscovered by an appreciative German audience, which began to see his relationship to the more celebrated trio of Bloch, Benjamin, and Adorno. *Ginster* was republished in 1963 with its author's name affixed; the critical acclaim was almost universal. There was talk of a Kracauer renaissance,[143] as some of his English works were translated into German for the first time. In Frankfurt, a student of Adorno's named Erika Lorenz prepared a *Diplomarbeit* on his career, which would have been expanded into a doctoral dissertation if not for her return to East Germany for personal reasons.[144] Although Kracauer was not completely won over by her interpretation—he objected to her attempt to assimilate him to the Frankfurt School's Critical Theory and to her calling him a journalist—he glowed in the recognition that such a project signified.

In 1964, Adorno himself wrote a piece on Kracauer for his 75th birthday, entitled "The Whimsical Realist."[145] Although initially flattered, Kracauer's opinion changed drastically when he read between the lines to see a number of implied criticisms. In a series of heated letters he defended himself and struck back at Adorno. Although it would be impossible here to detail the issues between them, which I hope to do elsewhere at a later date, suffice it to say that their friendship of over forty years was severely strained by Adorno's "tribute."

Kracauer's increased concern for his place in history was matched by a new fascination with the philosophy of history itself. After a long period of wandering, he returned, at least intellectually, to his boyhood home with his uncle Isidor. From the completion of *Theory of Film* until his death, he worked with almost total absorption in an area he had never really explored with any rigor before. Although losing valuable time in preparing the German translation of the film book, Kracauer completed the lion's share of his manuscript by the time of his relatively sudden death from pneumonia in November 1966. His architect's habit of constructing the manuscript in meticulous fashion before writing the final draft made its posthumous publication possible. In 1969, *History: The Last Things Before the Last* was brought out by Oxford University Press, but not without serious difficulties in the interim.

Sheldon Meyer of OUP had wanted Lili Kracauer to edit and organize her husband's manuscript, but lacking the self-confidence, she refused. Instead, a former acquaintance of Kracauer's, a German living in New York named Reinhard Koehne, was hired to put the book in order. The decision proved an unhappy one as Koehne and Lili Kracauer quickly developed a mutual distrust; her fidelity to the letter of Kracauer's drafts was not shared by Koehne, who finally withdrew in anger. A law suit followed but was ultimately dropped, and the book was eventually published without any mention of Koehne's name. A very generous foreword was provided by Paul Oskar Kristeller, the distinguished historian of Renaissance philosophy with whom Kracauer had become close during his final years.

If *History* was ill-starred in its preparation, its fate after publication was scarcely more fortunate. The prepublication review by the Virginia Kirkus Service was unsympathetic, and despite a very positive reaction by Georg Iggers in the *American Historical Review,* the book sank with scarcely a ripple.[146] By the early 1970s, it was remaindered and taken out of circulation. Kracauer was widely known in the film world, but he was neither a professional philosopher nor a historian and thus lacked a real constituency in those fields. The private expressions of enthusiasm by such celebrated historians as J. H. Hexter and Werner Kaegi were of little help.[147] Kracauer had had extraordinarily high expectations for what he considered his master work, but these were to be disappointed, at least in the short run.

And yet, in many ways, *History* is one of Kracauer's most compelling and original works, which deserves to be "redeemed," if one may borrow his own word, from an unmerited oblivion. In concluding this appreciation of Kracauer's career, it would be useful to linger a while with his final book, not merely because it has been denied the critical examination it deserves, but also because it ties together many of the themes of his previous work. Without an understanding of the perspective expressed in *History,* Kracauer's varied interests and conflicting approaches make little coherent sense. With that understanding, they begin to knit together.

In the book itself, he makes some astute observations about Proust's *Remembrance of Things Past,* which raise crucial questions about Kracauer himself. Discussing Proust's attempt to reconcile the antinomy between objective, chronological time and subjective, recapturable, time, he remarks:

the story of his (or Marcel's) fragmentized life must have reached its terminus before it can reveal itself to him as a unified process. And the reconciliation he effects between the antithetic propositions at stake—his denial of the flow of time and his (belated) endorsement of it—hinge on his retreat into a dimension of art. But nothing of the sort applies to history. Neither has history an end nor is it amenable to aesthetic redemption.[148]

Before Proust, Dilthey had also argued that meaning was only perceivable at the end of a life, when its constituent moments could be seen as parts in a completed whole:

One would have to wait for the end of a life and, in the hour of death, survey the whole to ascertain the relation between the whole and its parts. One would have to wait for the end of history to have all the material necessary to determine its meaning.[149]

But unlike Proust, Dilthey did not believe that an artificial, premature end could be achieved through an aesthetic recapitulation of a life still in progress, even though one might withdraw into a cork-lined room to prevent the future from having any meaning. Kracauer clearly shared Dilthey's qualms about this solution, as he did his argument about full meaning coming at the end of history, an end that would never come.

Where it seems to me he was somewhat ambivalent was in his attitude toward the closure of an individual life signified by death. That desperate insistence on chronological anonymity we have noted before can be read not merely in a psychological sense; it also suggests a desire to thwart the attribution of final meaning to his life which would follow its end. Kracauer was both driven by the need to order his life retrospectively, which was perhaps responsible for his early semi-autobiographical novels, and repelled by the thought that this meant the exhaustion of its open-ended potential. This ambivalence clearly paralleled his attitude toward extraterritoriality, which we have noted earlier.

The question then that must be asked is whether or not his death does give us an insight into the whole meaning of his life. In other words, do we now have a vantage point like the spire of Proust's Combray Church from which the landscape before us (or more correctly, behind us) becomes coherent? Failing this, can we say that *History: The Last Things Before the Last* provides a substitute reconciliation, very much like Marcel's "retreat into the dimensions of art," which was the only redemption Kracauer himself could achieve?

To answer the first part of the question, there is little in Kracauer's biography to suggest that the extraterritoriality that marked it from an early age was ever really overcome. Although Adorno worried that his friend had decided to seek "happiness"[150] after emigrating to America, thus becoming a conformist of sorts, Lili Kracauer's word that her husband had resisted conformity to the end must be given at least equal weight.[151] Despite his continuing marginality, however, there is little to indicate that Kracauer fashioned his life in such a way that made nonconformity itself a positive life-style. There is no hint of a Rimbaud or Jarry here, seeking to make his life into an artistic whole through the acting out of an alternative vision. Nor is there any suggestion of a Lukács or T. S. Eliot, finding wholeness in obedience to an external authority. Kracauer remained an outsider to the end, skeptical of all belief systems, false reconciliations, and communitarian solutions to alienation. As the economist Adolph Löwe, who spoke at his funeral, remarked: "I remember him wearing the mask he liked best: as Sancho Panza trotting on his ass behind the frantic visionaries in his 'bunte Nuchternheit' [gay, many-colored sobriety], as his friend Ernst Bloch so well defined him."[152] In short, aside from whatever personal vision may have been granted him "in the hour of death," it is impossible for the historian to say that Kracauer's life achieved any really unified meaning at its end. Indeed, as Kracauer himself recognized in his discussion of Proust, personal histories cannot be set apart from the larger context of historical change, which admits of no real redemption.

What, then of *History: The Last Things Before the Last?* Does it function the way Marcel's novel did to render his life a whole through a surrogate aesthetic (or in this case, intellectual) reconciliation? Does it succeed where earlier fictional attempts like *Ginster* and *Georg* were only partially successful largely because of their prematurity? The answer, it seems to me, is a guarded yes, even though Kracauer's substantive argument throughout is directed against reconciliation. At first glance, the book seems an improbable candidate for this task. Less than a month before his death, in his last letter to Leo Lowenthal, he wrote: "I am not yet out of the tunnel, but in the distance there is already something like a dim light."[153] His final illness prevented him from reaching the light in its full brightness, but even if he had lived to complete the book, its final form would not have suggested wholeness. As he planned it *History* was to appear as a series of relatively autonomous meditations on aspects of history and historical craftsmanship.[154] It is not a sustained and rigorously developed argument and indeed many of its conclusions are directed against reconciliation. And yet, paradoxically, it does have certain unifying themes and, more importantly from our point of view, it resurrects all of the major concerns of his previous work, casting them in a new and revealing light.

Shortly after starting the work, Kracauer wrote to Lowenthal that he had suddenly realized that the new book "is a direct continuation of my theory of film: the historian has traits of the photographer, and historical reality resembles camera-reality. The similarities are really startling; I had gone on this route complete unconsciously."[155] He then asked Erika Lorenz to compile a list of his early essays in which history played a role. She wrote back that she had found six: "Die Wissenschaftskrise," "Der verbotene Blick," "Die Reise und die Tanz," "Das Ornament der Masse," "Zu den Schriften Walter Benjamins," and perhaps most importantly, "Die Photograpie," the first time in which Kracauer explored the link between history and photography.[156] In his introduction to *History,* which he completed in February 1962, he spelled out the connections revealed when he saw the link between the film book and his current interest: *Theory of Film*

now appears to me in its true light: as another attempt of mine to bring out the significance of areas whose claim to be acknowledged in their own right has not yet been recognized. I say "another attempt" because this was what I had tried to do throughout my life—in *Die Angestellten,* perhaps in *Ginster,* and certainly in the *Offenbach.* So at long last all my main efforts, so incoherent on the surface, fall into line—they have all been served, and continue to serve, a single purpose: the rehabilitation of objectives and modes of being which still lack a name and hence are overlooked or misjudged. Perhaps this is less true of history than photography; yet history too marks a bent of the mind and defines a region of reality which despite all that has been written about them are still largely *terra incognita*.[157]

The analogy between history and photography turned out to be a central prop of his argument, and not merely because of their shared redemptive role, to which I will return shortly. They resemble each other in a number of ways. Both are "a means of alienation,"[158] which for reasons he never fully developed is a healthy condition to foster in the modern world. Both investigate and reveal the realities of the *Lebenswelt* in all its contingent, indeterminate open-endedness. Both are produced by a balance between "realistic" and "formative" tendencies, with an emphasis on the former. Both underwent a period when simple mimesis was assumed to be its special genius (the positivist historicism associated with Ranke's *wie es eigentlich gewesen* and the early years of nineteenth-century daguerrotypy.) Although this period was marked by naiveté, both are still more heavily weighted on the realistic side, which separates history from historical fiction as it does film from painting. Both use close-ups and establishing shots, which in the historians' vocabulary are known as microhistory and macrohistory. Finally, both are "anteroom areas," which elude oversystematization, ultimate answers, and the holistic shaping of art.

In drawing these parallels, Kracauer exhibited a far lighter touch than in *Theory of Film*. Whereas in the earlier book, overly artistic films were banished as "uncinematic," historical writing that fell on the formative side of the scale was now admitted as legitimate. In dealing with the structure of the historical universe, Kracauer arrived at a conclusion that had eluded him in his analysis of the film universe: that its structure was "nonhomogeneous." Although suspicious of overly ambitious attempts to discern secular or cyclical patterns in history, he granted validity to macrohistorical efforts on the scale of Burckhardt's study of the Renaissance, where the interpretive genius of the historian was allowed almost free reign. Arguing against advocates of what has been called "historical pointillism" such as Sir Lewis Namier and Tolstoy, he rejected the notion that the ultimate subject matter of history is the smallest possible detail, everything else being an inductive generalization from these fundamental "facts." Instead, he invoked two "laws" that govern historical understanding: the "law of perspective," which posits that

in the micro dimension a more or less dense fabric of given data canalizes the historian's imagination, his interpretive designs. As the distance from the data increases, they become scattered, thin out. The evidence thus loses its binding power, inviting less committed subjectivity to take over[159]

and the "law of levels," which parallels the cinematic distinction between close-ups and establishing shots, and means that

contexts established at each level are valid for that level but do not apply to
findings at other levels; which is to say that there is no way of deriving the
regularities of macrohistory, as Toynbee does, from the facts and interpretations
provided by microhistory.[160]

   In stressing the nonhomogeneous structure of the historical
universe, Kracauer was reinterpreting in historical terms what sociologists as far back as Comte and Durkheim had been advocating: social
facts were in some sense generic and thus irreducible to psychological
facts. Although not denying the traffic between the various levels, he
was stern in warning against the belief in an effortless passage from one
to another. In holding that no one level was primary, he contested the
views of both psychohistorians and social historians who claim their level
is the bedrock of historical analysis. Yet, still very much a champion of
the realistic rather than formative tendency, he was anxious to warn
against the dangers of an overly abstract and general history. An opponent of unrestrained methodological individualism, he nonetheless warned
against the dangers of holism as well. The broadened intelligibility of
macrohistory did not, in fact, mean greater significance for its findings.
In history, abstraction ought not to be equated with superior insight.
Indeed, "one of the underlying assumptions of the present study" was
that "the traditional identification of the extreme abstractions—say, the
idea of the 'good' or that of 'justice'—as the most inclusive and essential
statements about the nature of things does not apply to history."[161] Yet,
it is equally mistaken to expect the accumulated data of microhistorical
research eventually to translate into a full and adequate understanding
of the past as a whole. Indeed, "the belief in the progress of historiography is largely in the nature of an illusion."[162]
   Why then continue to do the monographic research that
Carlyle, Nietzsche, Huizinga, Marc Bloch, and so many others have condemned as "dry-as-dust" pedantry? The answer Kracauer gave was taken
almost directly from Benjamin:

There is only one single argument in its support which I believe to be conclusive.
It is a theological argument, though. According to it the "complete assemblage of
the smallest facts" is required for the reason that nothing shall go lost. It is as if
the fact-oriented accounts breathed pity with the dead. This vindicates the figure
of the collector.[163]

Here the redemption Kracauer sought in so many secular ways was finally allowed an explicitly religious moment.

The nonhomogeneity of the historical universe had still further implications, which Kracauer explored in other chapters in the book. In his discussion of the relationship between history and nature and their corresponding methodologies, he admitted the Marxian point that "society is a second nature,"[164] which implies that scientific methods may well be applicable to history. But he also argued that there is an irreducibly contingent element in history which defies schematization. Thus narrative description is equally as valid as social history with its stress on morphological regularities. Similarly, Dilthey's celebrated notion of *Verstehen* still had a place in the historian's methodological arsenal, but it was only one of several approaches that depended on the historical level that was being investigated.

The argument for the present-mindedness of the historian's vision, most notably advanced by Croce and Collingwood, also foundered in the face of the nonhomogeneity of the historical universe. Kracauer contended that the historian cannot himself be understood as so embedded in his own period that all of his perceptions of the past are filtered through his current situation. The reason is simply that there is no present "period" to determine the historian's vantage point:

If the historian's "historical and social environment' is not a fairly self-contained whole but a fragile compound of frequently inconsistent endeavors in flux, the assumption that it moulds his mind makes little sense. It does make sense only in the context of a philosophy which, like Croce's, hypostatizes a period spirit, claims our dependence on it, and thus determines the mind's place in the historical process from above and without. Seen from within, the relations between the mind and its environment are indeterminate.[165]

The best counterexample is the maverick historian who defies his *Zeitgeist*; Kracauer defines him in now familiar terms:

Vico is an outstanding instance of chronological extraterritoriality; and it would be extremely difficult to derive Burckhardt's complex and ambivalent physiognomy as a historian from the conditions under which he lived and worked. Like great artists or thinkers, great historians are biological freaks: they father the time that has fathered them.[166]

Instead of present-mindedness, Kracauer called for an effort of self-transcendence not unlike Proust's ability to succumb to involuntary memory. The historian must "bracket" himself—note the phenomenological term—and prepare his mind through a kind of surrender, an "active passivity,"[167] which allows the material to reveal itself to him. Although the morphological patterns of history have to be more aggressively pursued, narrative accounts must arise from an expectant openness to the material.

Yet another implication of the heterogeneity of the historical universe was the inadequacy of induction as the sole method of historical inquiry. Following Benjamin's discussion in his *Ursprung des deutschen Trauerspiels,*[168] Kracauer distinguished between generalizations and what he called "ideas." The latter are "genuine universals" arising out of a leap from the cumulative data of empirical research. They transcend the simple distinction between right and wrong because of their extraordinary power to illuminate the historical landscape:

They are nodal points—points at which the concrete and abstract really meet and become one. Whenever this happens, the flow of indeterminate historical events is suddenly arrested and all that is then exposed to view is seen in the light of an image or conception which takes it out of the transient flow to relate it to one or other of the momentous problems and questions that are forever staring at us.[169]

Burckhardt's image of the Renaissance, Marx's distinction between substructure and superstructure, Weber's Protestant Ethic are examples of "ideas," which later historians have been able to refute in particular cases, but not really lay to rest. Beyond these "ideas" there is a realm—that "last" region referred to in Kracauer's title—that historians dare not enter. Here Kracauer conflated the truths of metaphysics (last in an ontological sense) with the end of history (last in a chronological sense). Because the end of history was unthinkable, it was wrong to expect the historian to possess the vantage point from which metaphysical truth was attainable. Not even universal history, if it can be said to exist, could encompass that ultimate region.

As in film, an overly harmonious rendering of the material is an aesthetic distortion of the open-ended nature of history. Robert Merton's reading of Sterne's *Tristram Shandy*[170] captured the impossibility of the task; like Tristram Shandy, the historian has too much to relate before he can get to the end of his tale. If he tries to short-circuit the process by arbitrarily calling a halt, he makes the mistake Proust made by withdrawing into his cork-lined room. The result may be artistically successful, but it does inevitable violence to the past as it opens into the future.

Of all the implications of the nonhomogeneity of the historical universe, one stands out as central: the nature of historical time. Kracauer, the architect trained more in spatial than temporal terms, had become increasingly preoccupied by the mysteries of time, as we have seen with his insistence on his own chronological anonymity. The first section of *History* to be published, appearing in German, Italian, and English while Kracauer was still alive,[171] was entitled "Time and History."

With minor emendations, it appeared in the book as "Ahaseurus, or the Riddle of Time."

Although he did not work out all the implications of his title, Kracauer did devote one very interesting paragraph to Ahaseurus, the Wandering Jew. After remarking that only this legendary figure might know at first hand of the continuity of history, he described the cost of his knowledge:

> How unspeakably terrible he must look! To be sure, his face cannot have suffered from aging, but I imagine it to be many faces, each reflecting one of the periods which he traversed and all of them combining into new patterns, as he restlessly, and vainly, tries on his wanderings to reconstruct out of the times that shaped him the one time he is doomed to incarnate.[172]

The pain distorting the Wandering Jew's face is thus a result of his trying to integrate the different experiences of his life into one coherent pattern. What is also implicit in the story, although Kracauer neglected to develop it, is the fact that Ahaseurus is condemned to eternal life because of his rejection of Jesus. In other words, he is denied the redemption that only death can make possible. He cannot step out of history to touch the eternal. His life will never have any meaning because it will lack an end. To Kracauer, he is thus an ambivalent figure, eternally extraterritorial, and yet possessed of an immortality that most men would envy.

Whatever the implications of his title, which might also be developed in an autobiographical direction, the content of the chapter is crucial for an understanding of Kracauer's position. Among other things, it demonstrates how far Kracauer himself had wandered from the assumptions of German historicism, which were still dominant during his youth. Historicism, either in its Rankean or Hegelian guises, had posited a continuous developmental flow of chronological time in only one irreversible direction. Homogeneous chronicity was the solvent in which all historical events were immersed. This notion of time was similar to the spatialized, quantitatively ordered temporality of the natural sciences, at least to the extent that both jettisoned the transcendental intervention into time preserved in the Judeao-Christian tradition. Even the dialectical process of Hegelian time presupposed a homogeneous, unidirectional medium in which the Absolute manifested itself, although dialectics meant that progress came through contradictions rather than the smooth working out of an evolutionary scheme.

In Germany, this view of time (or rather, the several views which shared a common belief in the homogeneity of the temporal process) had a strong hold on historical thinking well into the twentieth century, despite the crisis in values which befell historicism. Elsewhere, however, especially in modernist aesthetic circles, simultaneity and mythic recurrence were resurrected as legitimate alternatives. Nietzsche and Bergson were, of course, the prophets of the new sense of time, although they were not in perfect agreement on its characteristics. Within the artistic realm, the most sustained exploration of nonhistoricist time was carried out by Proust in his *Remembrance of Things Past,* although other writers like Thomas Mann, Virginia Woolf, and James Joyce were also concerned with similar questions. Aesthetic realism, best exemplified by the nineteenth-century novel, was on the defensive, but historical writing, which retained many of the characteristics of the novel (narrative form, omniscient narrator, stress on the public world, etc.) continued to rely on traditional notions of time.

Kracauer saw three implications following from this state of affairs. First, dates within a chronological sequence were value-laden; that is, simultaneous occurrences were implicitly assumed to relate to each other in certain ways, usually parallel, whereas successive events were more often understood as relating to each other in casual ways. Second, large-scale units were often traced over a period of time as if they constituted discrete entities with lives of their own (the classic example being the historicist belief in the state as the true "individual" of history, which implied the neglect of internal social contradictions). And third, the formal property of an inexorable flow was often invested with substantive characteristics, as in Hegel's construction of the world process as the realization of rationality, or the less ambitious but equally questionable notion of history as progress. All of these assumptions were undermined by a different, more subtle understanding of historical time.

Significantly, in making his case for this alternative view of temporality, Kracauer drew upon the work of art historians like Erwin Panofsky, George Kubler, and Henri Focillon,[173] with the figure of Burckhardt, the isolated antihistoricist in nineteenth-century German historiography, looming in the background. Of perhaps equal importance was his reading of Proust, which benefited from Hans Robert Jauss' interpretation of the *Remembrance.*[174] Even more interesting in the context of recent intellectual debates, he found another ally among the anthropologists in the person of Claude Lévi-Strauss. In December 1963, Kracauer sent him a copy of "Time and History," adding the comment that he had just read *La Pensée Sauvage*

and to my most pleasant surprise discovered that in the wonderful section against Sartre you tackle the issue of historical time in terms similar to mine. To the best of my knowledge, no philosopher or historian has ever discussed the antinomy at the core of chronological time this way. . . . I have well taken note of your hints regarding the problem of the relationships between histories at different levels of generality; I shall discuss this problem in my forthcoming book. One more remark: it will take people a long time to understand your thought in all its consequences.[175]

Lévi-Strauss read the article and wrote back that he "was of course impressed with the many points of contact between your thinking and my own.[176]

What Kracauer liked in Lévi-Strauss' attack on Sartre was his insistence that chronology was itself an arbitrary code that men imposed on the world, rather than an intrinsic part of its essential nature. But in the final version of his chapter on this problem, he moved slightly away from the complete denigration of unilinear flow in the structuralist attack on historicism. As he wrote to the French historian Henri I. Marrou in the spring of 1964:

my agreement with [Lévi-Strauss] and Kubler is only partial. Actually, I am going beyond them and coming closer to your own position with its emphasis on the uniform flow of time. As against Kubler-Focillon-Lévi-Strauss, I too affirm the validity of such a flow; but it is true, I also uphold the notion of [Kubler's] "shaped times," assigning to them the same reality character as to that continuous, linear flow, which results in my basic assumptions of the antinomy at the core of Time. Indeed, even as an individual I believe we live in a veritable cataract of times. . . . Since you also speak of the "polyphonic structure" of time, the difference, if any, between our approaches may lie only in the fact that you seem to emphasize more than I do the share of homogeneous chronological time in the historical process, whereas I also stress the significance of the various existing peculiar time sequences and therefore hesitate to identify history as a process.[177]

In the final version of the chapter, the phrases "antinomy at the core of time" and "cataract of times" reappear, as does Kracauer's criticism of the Kubler-Focillon-Lévi-Strauss dismissal of all homogeneous time. Walter Benjamin, who dealt with the same issue in his "Theses on the Philosophy of History,"[178] is upbraided for the same failing:

Benjamin on his part indulges in an undialectical approach; he drives home the nonentity of chronological time without manifesting the slightest concern over the other side of the picture. That there are two sides to it has rarely been recognized.[179]

Proust comes off a bit better, for even while blurring chronology, he was "at pains to keep it intact."[180] But, as we have already noted, Kracauer saw Proust's attempt to reconcile chronological and shaped, subjective time through an aesthetic, *a posteriori* synthesis as illegitimate. The antinomy between chronological flow and the multitude of shaped times which cut across it is insoluble, or if it can be solved, then only at the very last moment of Time itself. Short of this utopian apocalypse, the temporal visions of the historicists and the modernists are eternally at war.

In his final chapter, entitled "The Anteroom," Kracauer drew certain highly speculative conclusions from his investigations, many of which in fact were implicit in his earlier work.[181] As we have previously mentioned, he used the metaphor of the anteroom to characterize both photography and history, neither dealing with the "last things" of human concern. Just as there is an insoluble antinomy between chronological and shaped time, so one exists between the anteroom and what for want of a better term we may call the inner sanctum into which it may lead. The particular, contingent truths of history, which relate to the *Lebenswelt*, are different in kind from the universal truths sought by philosophy. Attempts to historicize philosophy in a radical way, whether in Hegelian, Diltheyan, or Heideggerian terms, fail to observe the boundary between the two spheres. Such immanentist absolutizations of the historical, which culminate in Hans-Georg Gadamer and the hermeneutics movement,[182] lead to a theodicy in which history becomes a success story. But the alternative of situating philosophical truths completely outside of history as transcendental and eternal verities is equally erroneous. Both the immanentists and the transcendentalists fail to meet the challenge of relativism raised by historical consciousness because of their outmoded views of time. Because of the antinomous character of time,

there are "pockets" and voids amidst these temporal currents, vaguely reminiscent of interference phenomena. This leads me to speak, in a provisional way, of the "limited" relativity of certain ideas emerging from such pockets. . . . Philosophical truths have a double aspect. Neither can the timeless be stripped of the vestiges of temporality, nor does the temporal wholly engulf the timeless. Rather, we are forced to assume that the two aspects of truths exist side by side, relating to each other in ways which I believe to be theoretically undefinable. Something like an analogy may be found in the "complementarity principle" of the quantum physicists.[183]

This insight, Kracauer believed, was best exemplified in the work of Burckhardt, who sought absolutes, but was sensitive to their ambiguities amidst the flux of historical change.

In getting us past the anteroom, however, Kracauer was no real help. The "side" he was concerned with in his "side-by-side" principle was clearly that of the *Lebenswelt*, for it was the anteroom "in which we breathe, move and live."[184] In trying to redeem this contingent and ephemeral world, the historian approaches the state Kafka attributed to

Sancho Panza as that of a "free man" who swells in a "utopia of the in-
between—a terra incognita in the hollows between the lands we
know."[185] To Kracauer, the best model for this type of intellectual stance
was Erasmus, who followed the "middle way" as the "direct road to
Utopia—the way of the humane."[186]

As an epilogue to *History,* Kracauer's editors appended a
quotation from Kierkegaard that Kafka had cited and Kracauer had especially liked. In essence, it praises the simple man who defies the con-
ventions of the world to remain true to his personal vision. The quotation is prefaced by an injunction that Kracauer himself had followed
throughout his long and uneven career.

Focus on the "genuine" hidden in the interstices between dogmatized beliefs of
the world, thus establishing a tradition of lost causes; giving names to the hitherto
unnamed.[187]

The book's epilogue is a just epilogue to Kracauer's own life's work.
History, despite its stress on nonhomogeneity and fragmentation, or more
correctly through its justification for that stress, gives a meaning to the
checkered corpus of Kracauer's writings. In Sartrean terms, it "totalizes"
the disparate elements of his work by revealing their inherent relatedness, without, however, reducing them to a single common denominator. It does this not merely by spelling out the implicit vision behind
them, but also by placing certain of his books in a juxtaposition that
turns their individual weaknesses into a composite strength. Thus *From
Caligari to Hitler* and *Jacques Offenbach and his Time,* if looked at solely
on their own terms, can be faulted for ignoring what Kracauer called
the nonhomogeneous structure of the historical universe. That is, both
of them assume a somewhat simplistic and unmediated correspondence
between social and cultural phenomena. The "shaped time" of the cinema and operetta are not differentiated to any real extent from the
"shaped time" of Weimar and Second Empire society. Within the works,
this is surely a shortcoming, as many critics were quick to notice. But
set side by side with *Theory of Film,* where the immanent development
of film is traced with scarcely any reference to social developments, *From
Caligari to Hitler* seems less one-dimensional. Although no comparable
book was written by Kracauer dealing with Offenbach's music in a solely
musical context, the argument of History suggests that he would have
recognized its validity alongside of his *"Gesellschaftsbiographie."* Similarly, *History* puts into greater balance his concern for flux and process
informing *inter alia Theory of Film* (criticized by commentators like
Parker Tyler for its overly Heraclitean bias)[188] with his somewhat more
muted desire for stable values and order, which is apparent in his con-

stant lament over the emptiness of modern life. It also allows us to view his earlier difficulties defining realism in *Theory of Film* with some understanding, for his several usages correspond to a reality which is itself multidimensional.

History also helps make sense of his strangely ambivalent attitude toward Marxism, which has continued to be a source of debate among his interpretors. Like so many of his contemporaries, Kracauer underwent a clear movement to the right during his exile in America. By the 1960s, so Kristeller remembers,[189] he was strongly hostile to the New Left and all it represented. In 1932, he could write that he was an advocate of Marxism and would continue to be one, but in *History,* Marxism came in for a large share of criticism. His basic complaint was that Marx, like Hegel before him, had succumbed to the magic of linear chronology. (Ironically, this charge was leveled at the same time that Louis Althusser in France was discovering a sensitivity to shaped times in the later Marx.)[190] To Kracauer, the humanist, even existentialist Marx championed by Sartre and others was far less important than the naturalist Marx who tried to apply scientific method to history and failed.

And yet, despite his clear shift to a kind of disillusioned liberalism, many of these same attitudes can be seen even during the Weimar period. In distrusting the idealistic Marxism of Lukács' *History and Class Consciousness,* Kracauer expressed his doubts about the Hegelian legacy in Marx's own writings, although he preferred to minimize it. In the 1960s, he still disapproved of Hegelianizing Marx, but now he admitted that both thinkers shared a fallacious view of time. What went along with this disapproval was a caution about the role of *praxis* in reshaping the world; the elegiac lethargy of *Ginster* went hand in hand with a view of Marx as a naturalist. It was not surprising that he would take Lévi-Strauss's side in his dispute with Sartre.

History is also illuminating in this regard because it helps us situate him more precisely in the context of his friendships with Benjamin, Bloch, and Adorno. As we have seen, Benjamin's distinction between "ideas" and generalities, his justification for the "collector," and his critique of unilinear time are all cited with approval by Kracauer although the last is criticized for ignoring the place of chronological time as one stream in the cataract. But what is absent is Benjamin's guarded optimism about achieving fulfilled, utopian time (what Benjamin called *Jetztzeit*).[191] The side of Benjamin that had responded positively to Brecht was completely closed to Kracauer, who endorsed Gershom Scholem's appraisal of the pathological character of that relationship.[192] In a letter to Rolf Tiedemann, who had just written a study of Benjamin, Kracauer wrote that he shared certain of Benjamin's ideas about history:

that nothing should be lost, that history must be shattered in order to find its actual content in details, and so forth. Other thoughts—such as his emphasis on surrealism—I considered bizarre. And I have always regretted that he hadn't seen the dialectic between the reality, in which we live, and the messianic end reality (which only plays a negative role for me).[193]

This negative attitude towards a utopian future also colored Kracauer's intellectual relationship to Bloch. Personally, the two men were on the best of terms in the years before Kracauer's death. The earlier friction over Kracauer's late Weimar politics had long since been forgotten. In fact, a still older dispute between them, which broke out in 1922, when Kracauer criticized Bloch's *Thomas Münzer als Theologe der Revolution* and Bloch answered in his *Durch die Wüste,* was also patched over, so much so that Bloch removed his rebuttal from the new edition of the book in 1964.[194] When Bloch's *Tübinger Einleitung in die Philosophie I* had appeared in the previous year, Kracauer had approvingly written: "You are to my knowledge the only one who presents the problem of time. And what you say about it strongly touches my own ideas on the antinomy at the center of the chronological concept of time."[195] Further evidence of their mutual affection appeared in Kracauer's contribution to a volume of tributes to Bloch in 1965.[196] In his essay, which took the form of a letter to Bloch, Kracauer stressed the side of Bloch's utopianism that was most amenable to him: its conservative, redemptive dimension. Bloch's love of narrative, which Benjamin had also shared, meant an awareness of continuities, even amidst the most radical changes. Bloch was thus superior to conceptual utopians who want to impose a rational form on the future, which severs it completely from the past. Bloch also possessed a laudable sensitivity to the concrete, material realities of the sensuous world; "you preserve something of the magic of things," Kracauer wrote, "which you disenchant."[197]

And yet behind the expression of solidarity was a clear acknowledgment of the distance between them. Kracauer identified himself with Sancho Panza, who was short of breath trying to keep up with Bloch's Quixotic race toward utopia. Significantly, he appended the section on Erasmus later published in his introduction to *History* as a "gift" to Bloch. Erasmus's utopia, that of the middle way, the way of the humane, was not, however, Bloch's, which called for a far more radical transformation of man and society. Without any actual filiation, Kracauer's reading of Erasmus came close to that of an old enemy, Stefan Zweig, whose *Triumph und Tragik des Erasmus von Rotterdam*

(1934)[198] also praised Erasmus's anti-extremism and moderation. In 1937, Georg Lukács had taken Zweig to task in *The Historical Novel* for advocating Erasmian nonrevolutionary, pseudohumanism.[199] Erasmus's position was suspect, Lukács argued, because it was grounded in an elitist condemnation of the masses as irrational. Although Bloch had his own quarrels with Lukács, it seems likely that the champion of Thomas Münzer would have shared some of his qualms about the adequacy of Erasmian utopianism.

   If Kracauer's disillusionment about Marxist utopianism distanced him from Benjamin and Bloch, the opposite complaint was partly responsible for his growing estrangement from Adorno in the last years of his life. Although I hope to give a detailed account of the complicated course of their friendship elsewhere, certain points can be derived from a reading of *History* alone, which should be made here. In his anteroom chapter, Kracauer devoted half a paragraph to Adorno's recently published *Negative Dialektik*,[200] which advocated a radically anti-ontological position without any first principles or fixed points of reference. To Kracauer, this was an "unfettered dialectics" with unfortunate consequences:

His rejection of any ontological stipulation in favor of an infinite dialectics which penetrates all concrete things and entities seems inseparable from a certain arbitrariness, an absence of content and direction in these series of material evaluations. The concept of Utopia is then necessarily used by him in a purely formal way, as a borderline concept which at the end invariably emerges like a *deus ex machina*. But Utopian thought makes sense only if it assumes the form of a vision or intuition with a definite content of a sort. Therefore the radical immanence of the dialectical process will not do; some ontological fixations are needed to imbue it with significance and direction.[201]

In other words, whereas Kracauer faulted Bloch and Benjamin for their hopes of realizing utopia in history, he attacked Adorno for eliminating ontology and utopia entirely. In his own thinking, history and ontology exist side by side, but still separately. Their coexistence, like that of the general and the particular, can only be defined by what he called "tact"[202] in each specific case.

   Although raising an interesting objection to Adorno's negative dialectics, which has left many readers suspended in a conceptual whirl, Kracauer's alternative failed to answer a number of questions. Although chastising Adorno for lacking a utopia "that assumes the form of a vision or intuition with a definite content of a sort," he never really offered one himself. Without any of that belief in dealienation or the reconciliation of man and nature that animated Marxist Humanism, Kra-

cauer fell back on a vague and general endorsement of Erasmian tolerance and flexibility. This may well be a posture worthy of emulation,
but it is scarcely a utopian vision. Similarly, his advocacy of "tact" as a
means to regulate the relationship between history and ontology, the
general and the particular, is not very instructive. Kracauer assumed
that speculations on the total nature of the universe are called for, or indeed
indispensible, as gambles in Kafka's sense. They meaningfully enter the scene on
(unpredictable) occasions and then presumably fulfill a vital function.[203]

But what the occasions were, which speculations are superior to others,
and what functions they fulfilled Kracauer could not say. There is, in
short, a phenomenon here which might be called "metaphysical fellow-
traveling": a belief in ontology and utopia without any specific content,
a recognition of the legitimacy of ultimate thoughts without the daring
to think them out loud, a belief that relativism can be overcome by the
"pockets" of the absolute that exist in the interstices of chronological
time, without speculating on the contents of the pockets.

Kracauer was surely right to point to the antinomies of time
and the nonhomogeneity of the historical universe. His efforts throughout his career to reawaken our sensitivity to the phenomenal *Lebenswelt* often lost amidst a welter of conceptual generalizations were equally
laudable. His sober defiance of ideological panaceas, although uncomfortably close to the end-of-ideology fantasy of the 1950s, also merits
respect. But despite these achievements, what leaves the observer of
Kracauer's career uneasy is his tendency to freeze the posture of extraterritoriality and chronological anonymity, which he had made a personal virtue, into a universal condition incapable of change. What Arnheim
called the "melancholy surrender"[204] in Kracauer's championing of cinematic realism was a leitmotif of his entire career, despite the utopian
intentions of *History*. Adorno certainly exaggerated when he wrote that
"in the treasure of motives in his thought one would have looked in
vain for outrage against reification,"[205] but there was a grain of truth in
the charge. Ginsterism may be a sensible reaction to certain circumstances, but it need not be made a model for all times. Nor is the mask
of Sancho Panza the only one men can use if they are to avoid the follies
of Don Quixote. In short, Kracauer's "side-by-side" principle may accurately represent the best hope in an era without integral meaning and
real human community, but who is to say that this era is the last we
shall experience in human history?

12.
Politics of Translation: Siegfried Kracauer and Walter Benjamin on the Buber-Rosenzweig Bible

German, perhaps more than any other European tongue, has been enriched by translations from other languages. Luther's Bible, Voss's *Iliad* and *Odyssey,* the Shakespeare of Wieland, Schlegel and Tieck, Hölderlin's Sophocles and Pindar have all had a profoundly formative effect on the German language and concomitantly on the sensibility of its speakers. In our own century, the major translation that once seemed most likely to follow in this distinguished line was that of the Old Testament begun by Martin Buber and Franz Rosenweig in 1926 and completed by Buber alone thirty-five years later.[1] For well-known reasons that need no rehearsing, the impact of this extraordinary achievement was blunted before its full force could be felt. There is little evidence that this parting gift of the Jewish to the German people, as Gershom Scholem once called it,[2] has had the effect of its predecessors.[3] Luther's Bible still holds the honored place among Gentiles, while the Jews for whom Buber and Rosenzweig labored, if they survive at all, are far more likely to turn to the original Hebrew.

As a monument of the translator's art, however, the Buber-Rosenzweig Bible still commands enormous respect from many observers. To the philosopher Walter Kaufmann, for example, it no less than "revolutionized the art of translation."[4] Although this revolution does not seem to have conquered the English-speaking world, where the Bible was translated only a few years ago on diametrically opposed principles, there is certainly some truth in Kaufmann's praise. His own ren-

First published in *Leo Baeck Yearbook* (London, 1976), vol. 21.

derings of Nietzsche into English support his point.[5] In addition to acting as a model for other translations, the Buber-Rosenzweig Bible has continued to be a source of interest because of its crucial role in the articulation of the translators' very similar religious philosophies, the most influential in modern Judaism with unquestioned impact on Christian theology as well. To understand Buber's prophetic faith and his celebrated philosophy of I-Thou as well as Rosenzweig's "New Thinking" is to enter into the spirit behind the translation. Finally, the Buber-Rosenzweig Bible and the considerable controversy that greeted its appearance are of continuing usefulness as vehicles of entry into the still incompletely mapped world of Weimar's Jewish intelligentsia.

It is primarily in this third context that I would like to place the discussion of the translation in this paper, partly because I lack the competence to discuss the other two and partly because the controversy itself is so excellent an illustration of important disputes within Weimar Jewry. Indeed, I would argue that it expresses many of the dilemmas faced by German intellectuals of all faiths when the prewar idealist and historicist orthodoxies underwent a serious decline in the 1920s.

More specifically, I will focus on the critique of the translation made by Siegfried Kracauer in the *Frankfurter Zeitung* and the reaction it evoked in several quarters. By so doing, I hope inter alia to illuminate the complex position of Kracauer's friend, Walter Benjamin, whose own thoughts on translation have been widely discussed, most recently in George Steiner's magisterial *After Babel.*[6] And finally, I will suggest some significant parallels with another Kracauer intimate, Theodor W. Adorno, who resumed the controversy in the 1960s with a different although clearly related target.

Before turning to the translation itself, however, certain points must be clarified about the context in which it arose, in particular the major sources of the so-called Jewish Renaissance in Germany whose most illustrious monument it is often acknowledged to be. As the Israeli scholar Uriel Tal has recently made clear,[7] the confidence German Jews once had in liberalism and political emancipation as an answer to their pariah status had been seriously eroded by the 1890s. The process of erosion was a complicated one, with many of the causes operating that led to the general decline of liberalism at the turn of the century. Beyond these, however, there was one factor that played a special role. Gentile liberals, even outspoken ones like Theodor Mommsen, had asked the Jews to pay a price in exchange for their acceptance into German society. That price was the complete abandonment of all remnants of their ethnic or religious heritage. Germany was to be a united national community with no place for cultural pluralism. Although many Jews refused to strike this bargain, an increasing number of them were less reluctant, as evidenced by the frequent number of conversions and intermarriages.

In the 1890s, however, new and significant outbreaks of antisemitism demonstrated the vulnerability of this course of action. For the first time, Jew-baiting was racial as well as religious in content, which demonstrated to many Jews that no matter how assimilated they became, German society was still closed to them. Clearly, the Gentile liberals had failed to keep their half of the bargain for reasons outside their control. One response to this failure was the rise of Jewish defense organizations, such as the *Centralverein deutscher Staatsbürger jüdischen Glaubens,* founded in 1893. As Ismar Schorsch and Arnold Paucker have recently demonstrated,[8] the *Centralverein* was not the weak, accommodating paper tiger that earlier commentators such as Hannah Arendt had claimed. Yet it still stressed its allegiance to the Second Reich, for which the majority of its members fought and many died after 1914, as did those of the much smaller German Zionist Federation.

After 1918, however, new eruptions of antisemitism ended any hopes renewed by the war that Jewish integration into German society through liberal means was a plausible goal. Increasingly, Jewish intellectuals turned to nonliberal solutions to their dilemma. Zionism, the idealist socialism discussed in recent years by Istvan Deak and George Mosse,[9] and various brands of Marxism were among the most hotly contested alternatives. Each grew out of a common sentiment: a severe disenchantment with liberalism and its intellectual underpinnings in universalist rationality. In this turn away from liberalism, many German Jews were at one with certain of their coreligionists in Austria, as Carl Schorske has demonstrated in his studies of Freud and Schnitzler.[10] And perhaps even more significantly, they were following the general trend away from liberalism that marked the Weimar period as a whole.

The Jewish Renaissance in Frankfurt to which Buber and Rosenzweig contributed clearly shared that "hunger for wholeness" which Peter Gay has identified as characteristic of much of Weimar cultural life.[11] There was little abstract univeralism in their attempt to revive Judaism as a living religion infused with mystical and irrationalist energy and set apart from and in some ways superior to Christianity. Although both Buber and Rosenzweig still continued to believe in a future for the Jews in Germany, which was apparent in the very act of translating from Hebrew into German, the future they envisaged was very different from that expected by many assimilated Jews in the generation of their fathers. Instead of hoping for an evolution toward full emancipation, they wished to escape from history itself and restore the unique place of the Jews as an eternal people in touch with higher truths. Like so many other negative reactions to modernization, the Jewish Renaissance sought to counter alienation by a fundamentalist return to values and life-styles of an earlier time. Most importantly, this meant showing that Judaism was not a legalistic, antispiritual religion of the intellect, as many critics, both Jewish and Gentile, had assumed in the nineteenth century, but rather an organic, *geistige* way of life that nourished the whole man. In this endeavor, the Old Testament itself had to be seen in a fresh way, which could best be accomplished through a new translation.

The story of how Buber and Rosenzweig came to translate the Old Testament has been told many times, preeminently by the authors themselves in a collection of essays published in 1936 as *Die Schrift und Ihre Verdeutschung*.[12] Before World War I, Buber had rendered a number of Hasidic tales into German[13] as part of his attempt to introduce the vital spirit of Hasidism into what he saw as the desiccated, overly rationalized theology of establishment Judaism. Overblown and romantic, his loose translations were done in the spirit of the then popular *Jugendstil,* the flowery and lush German version of Art nouveau, which Buber was soon to abandon. After the success of these first efforts, he was anxious to tackle the more ambitious task of a new German Bible and had acquired the cooperation of two collaborators, Moritz Heimann and Efraim Frisch, as well as a potential publisher. But the outbreak of the war put the project into abeyance, although Buber continued to talk about the need for a new biblical translation, which would be "nonparaphrasing."[14] Immediately after the war, Buber concentrated his intellectual energies on more expressly theoretical work, which culminated in his most celebrated book, *I and Thou,* in 1923. At the same time he was active during the early years of the *Freies Jüdisches Lehrhaus,* which had been founded in Frankfurt in 1919 by the circle around the charismatic Rabbi Nehemiah A. Nobel.[15] The *Lehrhaus,* which soon had imitators in several other German cities, brought a variety of Jewish intellectuals together to teach a broad selection of topics without any one dominating theoretical bias. In its zeal to go beyond a merely academic approach, however, it repudiated the dry, historicist *Wissenschaft des Judentums* that had dominated Jewish studies since the time of Zunz and Geiger.

Buber's invitation to join the *Lehrhaus* had come from Franz Rosenzweig, whom he had met in Berlin in 1914 when Rosenzweig, a student of Hermann Cohen,[16] had written a traditional doctoral dissertation on Hegel's political philosophy under the direction of Friedrich Meinecke before the war.[17] But in 1913, he underwent a severe spiritual crisis that caused him to reject the idealist and historicist assumptions of his mentor, and with them a teaching post in Berlin. Influenced by his cousins Hans and Rudolf Ehrenberg and a close friend, Eugen Rosenstock-Huessy, all converts from Judaism to Christianity, Rosenzweig briefly considered conversion himself as a way to satisfy his craving for certainty. The turning point towards conversion came during a feverish all-night conversation on July 7, 1913, with Rosenstock-Huessy;[18] the turning point away was reached three months later during a Yom Kippur service in Berlin. Although Rosenzweig rejected his friend's embrace of Christianity, he did retain Rosenstock-Huessy's stress on the centrality of speech in religious and philosophical discourse with consequences that will be apparent shortly. The momentous dialogue he had begun on July 7th, which led to a series of extraordinary letters between the two friends after his return to Judaism,[19] served as a model for the religious philosophy he was in the process of developing.

This philosophy, which he was later to call "The New Thinking,"[20] involved the rejection of a rational theology in favor of a more immediately experienced encounter with God through revelation. Among his reasons for turning against Christianity was his inability to accept the role of Jesus as mediator. In many ways similar to Buber's I-Thou philosophy,[21] "The New Thinking" stressed the whole man over the intellect and saw dialogue as the central religious experience. In 1921, Rosenzweig published his most important summation of his position, *The Star of Redemption*,[22] written during his wartime military service. It was immediately greeted by many as the manifesto of a new Jewish *Lebensphilosophie*, a challenge to reform as well as to orthodox modes of thought. Later it would be understood as the first major statement of Jewish existentialism. Focusing on the concrete individual's personal dilemma of death and its meaning, Rosenzweig demonstrated the distance he had traveled since his earlier interest in Hegel. History was no longer the realm in which coherence might be found, rational theodicies could offer no consolation for personal suffering, God was a transcendent rather than immanent reality. The source of hope, so Rosenzweig argued, was the possibility of communication between man and his distant God. Like Buber and Rosenstock-Huessy, he retained a confidence in the power of speech to express the divine, which set him apart from many of his contemporaries who stressed the limitations of language. Among them were thinkers as disparate as Fritz Mauthner, Hugo von Hofmannsthal, Henri Bergson and Bertrand Russell.

Rosenzweig's fascination with linguistic issues led him, as it did Buber, to an involvement with the theory and practice of translation. On his honeymoon in 1920, he translated the "Grace After Meals" from Hebrew into German.[23] And in 1924 he brought out a book of translated hymns and poems by the twelfth-century Spanish Jew Yehuda Halevi with a translator's epilogue explaining his method and its underlying assumptions.[24] Buber had been a consultant during the translation with apparently fruitful results.

Thus on May 6, when Buber received a letter from the young Gentile publisher Lambert Schneider asking him to revise the Lutheran version of the scriptures,[25] he sought Rosenzweig's cooperation. Shortly before, Rosenzweig had expressed doubts about the possibility of an entirely new translation,[26] but the idea of revising Luther seemed tempting. One major obstacle, however, was the state of his health, as the lateral sclerosis that was to end his life four years later was already considerably advanced. As Buber later recalled:

I had a feeling that my suggestion at once pleased and disturbed him. Later on I came to understand his reaction. Though he no longer expected death within the next few weeks or months, as he had done during the first stage of his illness, he had given up measuring his life in long periods. Here he was being offered, and therefore considered equal to, participation in a project which, as he recognized much sooner than I, would involve several years of intensive work. It meant adopting a different calculus of the future.[27]

Although Rosenzweig was unable to do more than point to keys on a typewriter to indicate his revisions of the initial drafts prepared by Buber, he agreed to the collaboration. But one serious problem became quickly apparent. In 1921, Rosenzweig had anticipated it in a letter to Gershom Scholem:

Only one who is profoundly convinced of the impossibility of translation can really undertake it. Not by any means of the impossibility of translation in general (that isn't the case at all; rather, all life beyond one's own soul is conditioned by the possibility of this miracle, as you so rightly call it), but of the impossibility of the particular translation he is about to embark on. This special impossibility is different in every case. In this case [the translation of "Grace After Meals" by Rosenzweig] its name is: Luther.[28]

Luther was an obstacle because he and other translators had transformed German into an unmistakably "Christian" language. To build upon his version of the Bible would only compound the problem. The only alternative was to begin anew from the original Hebrew in the hope of freeing German from its Christian overlay.

Buber had translated his Hasidic tales in a free and metaphorical way, but he had long since left the *Jugendstil* of his prewar years behind. Rosenzweig had also attacked paraphrasing translations in his epilogue to the hymns of Yehuda Halevi, where he sided with Nietzsche in his celebrated controversy with Ulrich von Wilamowitz-

Moellendorff. Both men were thus at one in their philosophies of translation and were able to collaborate without difficulty. Despite Rosenzweig's illness, the first volume, entitled *Das Buch im Anfang* (Genesis) appeared in late 1925 with nineteen subsequent volumes promised to follow. At the fourth memorial meeting for Rabbi Nobel at the *Lehrhaus* Buber read selections to general acclaim. During the course of their common effort, Buber and Rosenzweig's friendship had reached the point where they were able to use the familiar *du* form in addressing each other,[29] a significant step in any German relationship, but more so in the context of Buber's I-Thou philosophy. They continued to work steadily until Rosenzweig's death on December 10, 1929, by which time chapter 53 of the book of Isaiah had been completed.[30] Shortly after, the publishing responsibility was assumed by Schocken *Verlag,* which took over Lambert Schneider in 1931. Buber worked on the translation alone during the early Nazi years until he left for Palestine in 1938 to take a professorship in social philosophy at the Hebrew University, the same year the Schocken *Verlag* was closed by the Nazis. By that time Buber had reached the book of Proverbs. He resumed the task in the middle 1950s and worked until 1961 when he was eighty-three. With the publication in that year of the two books of Chronicles, the extraordinary undertaking was finally finished only four years before Buber's death.

In the late twenties and early thirties, the principles underlying the translation, many of them anticipated in the epilogue to Rosenzweig's Yehuda Halevi, were spelled out in a series of accompanying essays and enriched by Buber's interpretive work on the Bible. In opposition to Moses Mendelssohn,[31] the Enlightenment advocate of a Jewish rationalism compatible with German culture, who had tried more than a century before to turn the Hebrew original into contemporary German, Buber and Rosenzweig sought to preserve the original tongue in its new setting. Like Hölderlin in his translations from Greek,[32] they tried to remain as literally faithful as possible to the first language in order to break through the encrusted conventional idiom of modern German. All previous translations were like layers of a palimpsest covering the pristine word beneath, rather than allowing it to reemerge as a transfigured German. Centuries of theological and historical glosses on the sacred text had further obscured the original language, which needed no interpretation beyond itself. Theirs was to be a "postcritical" translation that avoided any pedantic mediation between the reader and the holy word.

At the root of this approach were two crucial premises, both religious in nature. First, Buber and Rosenzweig assumed that the Old

Testament was the mediated word of God, a unified and internally co-herent verbal expression of His encounter with the Jewish people. Nei-ther a code of law nor a body of abstract moral teachings, the Bible was a Voice in an existential, dialogic relationship between a divine I and a mundane Thou. The text had originally been spoken before it became Holy Writ; therefore, it should be read out loud rather than silently. In this way it would bear witness to the eternal presence of the Almighty, whose power to speak in the here and now was thwarted only by the inattentiveness of his listeners.

Secondly, they, or at least Rosenzweig, assumed that there had been one original *Ursprache,* a pre-Babel pure speech in which name and thing were identical.[33] Translation promised to restore the area of original universality preserved in the two languages in question, a gnos-tic expectation expressed in the Kabbalah.[34] The utopian hope of re-constituting this lost *Ursprache* was not entirely groundless if God were understood to be eternally present. "Every translation," Rosenzweig confidently asserted, "is a messianic act, which brings redemption nearer."[35] By Hebraicizing German, Buber and Rosenzweig hoped to alienate their readers from the pedestrian discourse of their quotidian lives, thereby expanding their openness to divine speech.

A number of techniques were employed to achieve this goal. In their choice of words, Buber and Rosenzweig sought the etymologi-cal origins of the Hebrew terms and tried to find as close an equivalent in German as possible. Instead of rendering the same Hebrew word in different contexts by a variety of German synonyms, they used the same word throughout. God's name they rendered in pronominal form as *Ich, Er* or *Du* to emphasize the presence of a partner in a conversation. Men-delssohn's decision to call God *"Der Ewige"* (the eternal one) they re-jected because it underemphasized the presentness of the dialogue. If at all possible, they chose the more concrete and sensuous word over its abstract alternative. Original symbols and images were retained in as lit-eral a form as could be done. Buber and Rosenzweig also tried to ap-proximate the rhythmic pattern of the original text, which they equated with the phrasing of normal speech. This meant a textual articulation based less on standard punctuation than on "breathing colons," corre-sponding to the breathing capacities of the speaking voice, which writ-ten German had long since abandoned.

The result was a curious mixture of poetry and prose, which was too irregular to be the former in any traditional sense, but too ele-vated and mannered to be the latter. To take one frequently discussed example, they chose the German word *"Künder"* instead of *"Prophet"* for the Hebrew *"Nabi"* despite its overly aesthetic connotations; their reason was that *"Prophet"* had acquired a prognosticating sense that the Hebrew with its meaning of announcer had lacked.[36] But despite this type of reasoning, critics were divided over the extent of their artificial poeticizing of the text.[37] The authors were themselves uncertain. In 1925, Rosenzweig had written that "poetry is the mother tongue of the human race—we shouldn't deny the wisdom of Hamann and Herder."[38] But two years later he wrote to Buber that anyone who expects a work of art from them will be disappointed, as elegance is only a byproduct of their literalist goal.[39] And when Buber was mildly chided by Gershom Scholem for writing a text that looked as if it asked to be sung rather than recited, he replied that the Bible was prose not poetry, but that prose could reach a level much higher than normal discourse.[40] Their basic defense was that however artificial the result might sound to the modern ear, they were being faithful to the Hebrew original.

On the whole, this argument and the translation itself were positively received, although disagreements among various experts over specific word choices were common and continue to this day.[41] There were, however, a few dissenters, such as Emanuel Bin Gorion (Berditschewski), who had fundamental disagreements.[42] The most far-reaching critique, however, appeared in the *Frankfurter Zeitung*, the most prominent newspaper of the enlightened, liberal Jewish bourgeoisie.[43] Its author was Siegfried Kracauer, who was to become well known many years later in the English-speaking world for his books on film.[44] At the time of his attack on the translation, however, he was primarily recognized as leading *feuilleton* writer for the *FZ*, who wrote on a wide variety of cultural subjects from the Tiller Girls to urban architecture.[45] Although the newspaper for which he worked was liberal, Kracauer was a man of the so-called Weimar "homeless left," who counted among his close friends Ernst Bloch, Walter Benjamin, Leo Lowenthal, and Theodor Wiesengrund Adorno. Like many of the unaffiliated leftist intellectuals of this period, he came from a Jewish background, but he had little use for traditional Judaism. His uncle, with whom Kracauer had lived from a very early age, was the historian of the Frankfurt Jewish community,[46] and his household seems to have been relatively pious. But like many of his generation—he was born in 1889, eleven years after Buber and three after Rosenzweig—Kracauer felt oppressed by the inadequate combination of German patriotism and conventional religiosity that characterized much of the assimilated Jewish community. For a short while, he seems to have taken the Jewish Renaissance around Rabbi Nobel seriously, at least enough to contribute to the *Festschrift* in the Rabbi's honor in 1921 and to teach a course that winter at the Frankfurt *Lehrhaus* with Fritz Edinger on contemporary religious and political movements.[47] There is evidence as well to show that he found Buber's personality a compelling one in the same year.[48] He also had a brief flirtation with the work of Kierkegaard,[49] which had stimulated Buber to a great extent. These, however, were only fleeting episodes in an intellectual development that resisted attempts to find panaceas for the emptiness of modern cultural life.[50] Like Ginster, the hero of a semi-autobiographical novel of the same name published anonymously by Kracauer in 1928,[51] he was always a marginal figure afraid of any communal identification or positive ideology. In short, Kracauer was the very model of that estranged, negative, rootless intellectual so characteristic of the Weimar period.

On January 25, 1926, the *FZ* carried a short notice of the translation by Kracauer, which was essentially hostile. In thanking a reader who had written a letter of complaint to the newspaper, Buber described Kracauer as having "the resentment of a man who feels himself slighted, whose better knowledge has been frequently and privately expressed."[52] He then added that he understood that Kracauer would respond to a storm of criticism by writing a "so-to-say reparation article," although he was skeptical about its appearance. The expected piece did appear later in April, but it was anything but an act of contrition.[53] Buber's *ad hominen* explanation of the first notice fell far short of the truth as Kracauer made clear his case against *Das Buch im Anfang*.

He began by situating the translation in the context of the general return to fundamentalist religious practice in the postwar years when the liberal historicism of Troeltsch and neo-Kantianism of Ritschl had been discredited. In Christian circles, Karl Barth was its unnamed leader.[54] The Frankfurt *Lehrhaus* and the Yehuda Halevi translation had foreshadowed this attempt to move from the level of abstract theological theory to direct *Lebenspraxis*. The new Bible was not intended as a work of art, as some critics had argued, but as a means of restoring a lost religious immediacy. Thus aesthetic criteria were far less important in judging the translation than epistemological ones. Here the fundamental question of the Bible as spoken word of God was crucial, as Buber and Rosenzweig had argued.

Having acknowledged the purpose of the translation, Kracauer then turned to what he considered its inadequate means. Because the Bible could not be approached solely in historical or aesthetic terms, the rationale that lay behind Rudolf Borchardt's recent translation of *The Divine Comedy* into medieval German, the German of Dante's contemporaries, could not hold.[55] This type of archaicizing did not render the Bible more immediately accessible to the modern reader, which after all was Buber and Rosenzweig's purpose. Yet the opposite strategy, reducing the original language to the vulgar speech of the contemporary everyman, was equally fallacious; the truth, Kracauer argued, did not reside in the status quo and, by extension, in its conventional language. Luther's Bible, on the other hand, was written at a time of cultural, social and political efflorescence. It served as a weapon against the papist use of the Vulgate, and was thus an instrument of a broadly grounded revolutionary movement, which signalled a rising era in German history. It thus arose out of a constellation of factors that were now absent.

In contrast to Luther's effort, the new translation had no roots in social, economic, or political tendencies; in fact, it grew out of a conviction that spiritual regeneration was possible apart from mundane considerations. If it had any political implications, they were reactionary and privatizing. The I-Thou relationship between God speaking through his prophets and the individual reader left little room for real social solidarity. Words like *Erdvolk* and *Künder* were reminiscent of the mythologizing neoromanticism of Wagner and other *Völkisch* thinkers who vacillated between a heroic individualism and the populist call for instant community. This latter impulse, Kracauer implied, was repeated in Buber's Zionism.[56]

Moreover, without any historical exegesis, the Bible was like an art-for-art's-sake product that could only be aesthetic in appeal, despite the translators' intentions. Instead of speaking to the real existential situation of modern Jewry, the translation represented a flight into an ideological pseudo-alternative. In short, there was no room for a third undertaking beyond Luther's translation, which had emerged out of a period of cultural-social-political wholeness, and subsequent philological exegesis, the only possible approach in an era of essential meaninglessness such as ours.

Kracauer finished his critique with a point that would underlie the entire corpus of his subsequent work: seeking truth through a return to religious or metaphysical immediacy was a vain endeavor "because the entrance into the truth is now in the profane."[57] From his earliest studies of the cultural debris of Weimar life—detective novels, popular biographies, the cinema and its following—to his last explorations into history, the "waiting room" before the metaphysical inner sanctum,[58] Kracauer would devote himself to the sphere of the profane. As a "rag-picker in the dawn of a revolutionary day,"[59] to borrow Walter Benjamin's felicitous phrase, he acted on the assumption that truth and existence were not now one, but that the fragments of our shattered culture were the only place where anticipations of a new truth might be found.

To Buber and Rosenzweig, however, this oversensitivity to

the historical present meant an inattentiveness to the divine presence
that was perpetually in potential existence. In *The Star of Redemption,*
Rosenzweig had singled out the Jews as the "eternal people" who had
escaped the historical developments of other nations.[60] Hostile to historicism, he and Buber also had little patience with any really future-
orientated religiosity, despite their stress on the messianic side of Judaism.[61] Thus in their reply to Kracauer, which was printed in the *FZ*
on May 18, 1926,[62] they defended their choice of *Künder* rather than
Prophet because of their hostility to the apocalyptic implications of the
latter word. *Prophet* suggested a foreteller of a future already shaped,
which meant man's existential need to choose was undermined (a charge,
it might be noted in passing, Buber laid against Marx as well).[63] Neither
the past nor the future was determining; only the present, the lived moment really mattered. History, in either the past or the future, was not
the realm of providential intervention. God was wholly outside of the
world, although He was in relation to it.[64]

On all other charges, Buber and Rosenzweig were equally
defensive. The times, they argued, were not completely closed to the
Bible, as Kracauer assumed, no matter how far the process of disenchantment had gone. "The times are passive," they wrote, "the word is
active."[65] Kracauer was equally wrong in seeing their choice of uncom-
mon words and use of alliteration and repetition as Wagnerian in origin;
all they were doing was following the Hebrew original. For Kracauer to
label such words as *Erdvolk* neoromantic was nonsense; the League of
Nations would look in vain for a better term to describe its basic goal.
Furthermore, Kracauer's reliance on the Luther translation was misplaced, as Luther had been far too heavily indebted to his Greek and
Latin predecessors; in addition, Kracauer had overemphasized the Lutheran dominance of German society since the Reformation, thereby
missing the Catholic contribution which they themselves retained in
certain of their name choices. As for the charge of archaicizing, they
were merely following a trend for getting old names right that Nietzsche
had exemplified by his calling Zoroaster "Zarathustra." In short, Kracauer was really arguing against the original text, not its translation.

In addition to his public rebuttal, Kracauer also received another rebuke from within the ranks of the Frankfurt *Lehrhaus.* On May
7th, Ernst Simon, the young coeditor with Buber of *Der Jude* and a leading religious Zionist, wrote a long and heated letter defending Buber
and Rosenzweig.[66] After reminding Kracauer that during the early days
of the *Lehrhaus* he too had called for a "sociology of metaphysical communication," Simon went on to challenge Kracauer on a number of specific points, with the general complaint that Kracauer had always cho-

sen the least generous of possible alternatives. First, he pointed to the significance of Rosenzweig's illness, but not to play on Kracauer's sympathy, which he dismissed as a sentimentalism unworthy of Rosenzweig's courage. The illness was meaningful, Simon argued, in another sense: the extraordinary suffering Rosenzweig had endured with such strength meant that he had possible access to a sphere of reality denied to the rest of us. Kracauer was too hasty in extrapolating from his own experience of meaninglessness to everyone else.

Secondly, although Buber's Zionism was not directly tied by Kracauer to the charge of *völkisch* neoromanticism, the reader is led to make this connection. To do so, however, is to slander the real nature of Buber's Zionism, which was universalist and antinationalist. In fact, at the Twelfth Zionist Congress in Karlsbad,[67] Buber had strongly opposed Jabotinsky's call for a Jewish Legion and sponsored a motion calling for fraternal cooperation with the Palestinian Arabs. Third, and worse still, these anti-Zionist remarks, which coincide with a current campaign in the *FZ* against Zionism, are grounded in a complete ignorance of Hebrew, which is best demonstrated in Kracauer's remarks on names. Whereas previous translators had captured only the sounds of the original Hebrew names, Buber and Rosenzweig have restored the meanings as well. Finally, it was irresponsible to keep the reader uninformed of Kracauer's incompetence in Hebrew; in fact, the opposite conclusion was invited by Kracauer's praise of the scientific nature of the translation, as if he could legitimately judge it.

Kracauer was quick to reply to Simon, but unfortunately the letter has not survived in his *Nachlass* or in Simon's own files. However, we can piece together some of his arguments from Simon's second letter of May 17th, which has been preserved. Kracauer claimed that his personal admiration for Rosenzweig and his courage was enormous, and he had meant him no slight; what he had found objectionable was the implied attempt to unite truth and existence in an unmediated way. As for the Zionist issue, he clearly felt that the *völkisch* description was appropriate despite factional disputes within the movement. And finally, he argued that Simon's other points were bagatelles that did not touch the central issue of his critique, the lack of social awareness in the religious revival.

Simon's counterrebuttal clarified the issues still further. Kracauer, he argued, was wrong to posit a stark alternative between an absolute identity of truth and existence, on the one hand, and a complete separation, on the other. The relationship between truth and existence was certainly complicated and mediated, but it was Kracauer, not the *Lehrhaus* people, who was oversimplifying it by positing an absolute nonidentity. This was further demonstrated by his refusal to see any connection between Rosenzweig's life and his work, which had caused many of his readers—and here Simon quoted a letter from an unnamed Christian theologian—to infer that Kracauer had a personal grudge against Rosenzweig. Secondly, the argument that Simon had ignored the main point of Kracauer's critique in order to focus on bagatelles missed the fact that Simon had accepted the sociological criticism at the beginning of his letter. The points he chose to stress were not mere trifles, as the misunderstanding about truth and existence demonstrated. If there was a danger in collapsing the two prematurely, there was an equal hazard in retreating from the actual choices and responsibilities of living men into the realm of the radical theoretician who worships overarching objective forces. Finally, Kracauer had called for close attention to the current connotations of certain words, but he had disregarded his own injunction in insisting on the link between Zionism and *völkisch* thought. As everybody knows, the word *völkisch* is the sole property of the antisemites, and it is no light matter to put Buber, who has struggled against all forms of nationalism, in the same camp with Jabotinsky, his avowed adversary.

With this parting shot, the quarrel between Kracauer and the *Lehrhaus* circle ended, at least as far as I have been able to determine. But the echoes of the dispute continued to reverberate for some time. As I have already noted, Kracauer was personally close to Walter Benjamin and Theodor W. Adorno, both of whom were keenly interested in problems of language and translation. Benjamin, himself a translator of numerous French works into German, had written an introduction to his version of Baudelaire's *Tableaux parisiens* in 1923 called "The Task of the Translator."[68] In his recent memoir, Scholem has called it "a high point of his openly theologically orientated period in linguistic philosophy," adding that Benjamin considered it his "credo" and was bitterly disappointed when it received little attention.[69] In the essay, Benjamin presented a case strikingly similar to Rosenzweig's in several respects. In fact, in *After Babel,* George Steiner juxtaposed Rosenzweig and Benjamin as if they were arguing virtually the same position.[70] Like Rosenzweig, Benjamin endorsed the Kabbalistic notion of an *Ursprache* that translation can help us to regain:

all suprahistorical kinship of languages rests in the intention underlying each language as a whole—an intention, however, which no single language can attain by itself but which is realized by the totality of their intentions supplementing each other: pure language.[71]

Benjamin also argued for a literal rather than free translation as the best means to attain this goal:

A real translation is transparent; it does not cover the original, does not block its light, but allows the pure language, as though reinforced by its own medium, to shine upon the original all the more fully. This may be achieved, above all, by a literal rendering of the syntax which proves words rather than sentences to be the primary element of the translator. For if the sentence is the wall before the language of the original, literalness is the arcade.[72]

And finally, like Rosenzweig and Buber, he saw the Bible as the most translatable of all texts because its meaning was perfectly expressed in its language:

Where a text is identical with truth or dogma, where it is supposed to be "the true language" in all its literalness and without the mediation of meaning, this text is unconditionally translatable. In such a case translations are called for only because of the plurality of languages. Just as, in the original, language and revelation are one without any tension, so the translation must be one with the original in the form of the interlinear version, in which literalness and freedom are united. For to some degree all great texts contain their potential translation between the lines; this is true to the highest degree of sacred writings. The interlinear version of the Scriptures is the prototype or ideal of all translation.[73]

But despite these significant areas of agreement, there was one fundamental point of divergence. Whereas Buber and Rosenzweig saw the Bible as an act of direct communication between a divine I and a human Thou, Benjamin minimized the importance of the receiving reader: "no poem is intended for the reader, no picture for the beholder, no symphony for the listener."[74] Anticipating the recent French critics Roland Barthes and Jacques Derrida,[75] he implicitly differentiated between speech and *écriture,* whose divorce he traced back to the time novels replaced storytelling.[76] This event was rooted in the waning of what Benjamin called experience *(Erfahrung),* which could not be regained by fiat, religious or otherwise. Thus the primary intention of the Buber-Rosenzweig translation, to contribute to a reawakening of Jewish life on the most immediate, existential level, was something Benjamin did not share. In fact, as early as 1915, Benjamin had vehemently criticized the glorification of concrete *Erlebnis* (lived experience) in Buber's philosophy.[77] And during one of the many conversations with Scholem over Palestine in the following year, he had said Zionism should abandon three of its orientations: "the agricultural tendency, the race ideology, and the Buberian blood and experience argumentation."[78] Thus, not surprisingly, he rejected the major premise of the translation: no empathetic rapport between the Biblical *Künder* and the attentive listener, whatever his historical circumstances, could be assumed possible in the present era. The chasm between speech and writing was not capable of being bridged by naïvely restoring the original Hebrew. Indeed, Benjamin felt that recapturing the spoken word was not the way to overcome linguistic alienation; there was no easy return to an Edenic unity of name and thing in which meanings were perfectly expressive of a deliberate intention. In short, for Benjamin God was not eternally present, although the telos of translation was the possibility of His messianic return.[79]

With these reservations already implicit in the 1923 essay—and possibly discussed directly with Rosenzweig in the interview Benjamin had the previous year[80]—it is not surprising that his reaction to the translation was essentially negative. On May 29, 1926 he wrote to Scholem, then in Jerusalem, that Kracauer's critique "appears to me, as far as I can go without knowing Hebrew, simply decisive; moreover, [it] adopts many of the things I had told him verbally on this theme."[81] In a later letter to Scholem,[82] whose opinion of the translation was somewhat more positive,[83] Benjamin raised the issue again, beginning with the admission that "I don't need to say that I myself, not to mention Kracauer, cannot be regarded as competent in this matter." He then went on to explain his qualms:

I have no idea who or what at this time might be justly interested in a translation of the Bible into German. Isn't this translation ultimately a highly questionable exhibition of things which, being exhibited, immediately disavow themselves in the light of this German—particularly at a time when the contents of Hebrew are being discussed anew, when German on the other hand is in a rather problematic state, and especially when fruitful mutual relations between the two seem only latently possible, if at all?

What this highly convoluted question espressed was Benjamin's strong sense of the historical inappropriateness of the translation at that time in German and Jewish history. Precisely which criticisms in the Kracauer essay were borrowed from Benjamin is hard to say with certainty, but it is clear that both men shared a fundamental skepticism about the basic premises of the *Lehrhaus* religious renaissance. In the early thirties, Benjamin would move away from his Jewish concerns, although never entirely,[84] and under the influence of his new friendship with Bertolt Brecht move towards a fitful kind of Marxism. Although Kracauer was still troubled by the messianic residues he saw in his friend's thinking until the end,[85] and had little use for Brecht's brand of Marxism, it is clear that both men shared a fundamental antipathy to the antihistorical Jewish existentialism they saw at the root of the translation.

The same can be said of Theodor Adorno, who wrote his *Habilitationsschrift* on Kierkegaard in the late 1920s, in which parallel criticisms were made.[86] Many years later, when the Kracauer article was

republished in a collection of his work called *Das Ornament der Masse,*
Adorno wrote to his friend that he totally shared its arguments.[87] He
acknowledged that the same complaints had motivated his recent attack
on *Existenzphilosophie* in *The Jargon of Authenticity.*[88] Although Heidegger was the major target of the book, Buber came in for his share of
responsibility for the jargon's current vogue:

> Ever since Martin Buber split off Kierkegaard's view of the existential from Kier-
> kegaard's Christology, and dressed it up as a universal posture, there has been a
> dominant inclination to conceive of metaphysical content as bound to the so-
> called relation of I and Thou. This content is referred to the immediacy of life.
> . . . In this process, nothing less is whisked away than the threshold between the
> natural and the supernatural. . . . Buber's style of existentialism draws its tran-
> scendence, in a reversed *analogia entis,* out of the fact that spontaneous relation-
> ships among persons cannot be reduced to objective poles. This existentialism
> remains the *Lebensphilosophie* out of which it came, in philosophical history, and
> which it abnegated: it overelevates the dynamism of mortality into immortality.[89]

Thus almost forty years after the original debate Adorno was fighting
the same existentialist enemy Kracauer had seen lurking behind the
translation. His complaint against Buber's destroying the threshold between the natural and the supernatural paralleled Kracauer's criticism
of the translation's collapse of history and eternity. Where the parallel
ended, however, was the charge of nebulous and loose language, which
Kracauer had not and could not have brought against the translation,
but which Adorno did level against Heidegger and his followers with
some justification.

   With the passage of time, certain of the basic issues in the
debate have been resolved, or at least can no longer be presented in the
same way. When the final volume of the translation appeared in March
1961, a party was held in Buber's Jerusalem home to mark the event.
Gershom Scholem, Ernst Simon, and Hugo Bergmann all made com-
memorative addresses.[90] While there was doubtless an air of celebration, a note of melancholy could not be avoided. As Scholem reminded
his listeners, the audience for whom the translation was intended had
ceased to exist. Baldly put, the God of the Jews no longer spoke German. The translation had been "the tombstone of a relationship that was
extinguished in unspeakable horror."[91] In the face of this sad truth,
Scholem saw a source of hope in an intention he imputed to Buber and
Rosenzweig, which was to persuade the German reader to return to the
Hebrew original. But although this had in fact been an ancillary goal of
the translators,[92] it was clearly far less ambitious than that utopian re-
constitution of a divine *Ursprache* that had animated Rosenzweig, and

the young Walter Benjamin, in the early 1920s. Their goal was an inter-linear translation of the Bible, not merely a return to the Hebrew.[93] Like much else in the Jewish renaissance promoted by the *Lehrhaus,* it fell victim to the history that Rosenzweig, and to a lesser extent Buber, had wanted to deny. The times proved far less passive than they had thought, the word much less active. Kracauer's skeptical warning against a purely spiritual answer to the cultural crisis was confirmed in the most appall-ing way imaginable. And with the creation of the state of Israel in 1948, Rosenzweig's notion of the Jewish people as outside of history received its final refutation. Moreover, with Hebrew once again a language of everyday life, its pretensions to a unique status closer to the *Ursprache* than other languages was called into question.

What then of Kracauer's other basic charge against the trans-lation that had so incensed Ernst Simon, the allegedly *völkisch* taint on Buber's Zionism? Here what seemed more than a spiritual answer to the Jewish dilemma was at stake, but was it the correct answer? Simon was surely right in chiding Kracauer for his failure to distinguish between Buber's humanitarian, nonchauvinist Zionism and the anti-Arab nation-alism of a Jabotinsky. Later, Buber would reaffirm the sentiments he ex-pressed at the Twelfth Zionist Congress by joining Brith Shalom and then Ichud, both movements for reconciliation with the Arabs to which Si-mon also belonged.[94] And yet, as George Mosse has recently reminded us,[95] there were unmistakable signs of *völkisch* thinking in Buber's work, especially in his irrationalist and mystical celebration of Hasidism. The translation was not entirely free of its influence, however Buber may have protested otherwise. The contemporary reader of at least the opening volumes cannot help hearing echoes of a linguistic style whose connotations are faintly disturbing. Zionism, especially in the nonna-tionalist meaning Buber gave it, is certainly much more than the Jewish version of *völkisch* thought, and yet there are unsettling residues that remain unpurged to this day.[96]

Finally, what can one say about the more general issue of existence and truth raised by the debate of the 1920s? Obviously this is a vast and complex problem that cannot be adequately spelled out, let alone settled, in this space. Only a few observations can be offered in place of a real analysis. During the 1960s, when Buber's I-Thou philos-ophy was at its height of popularity in America, a variety of efforts was made to reenchant our alienated world and achieve the immediacy and fulfillment denied by modern civilization. On the fringes of the political New Left, but unjustly equated with it, were a whole range of fads and cults—encounter groups, drugs, astrology, occultism, eastern mysti-cism, sexual freedom leagues—that attempted in one way or another to unite truth and existence in an unmediated way. What Adorno labeled the "jargon of authenticity" attacked alienation while leaving its social sources unexplored.

To equate these phenomena with the Buber-Rosenzweig translation of the Bible would of course be criminal; the prodigious learning and devotion to scholarly standards demonstrated by Buber and Rosenzweig, Rosenzweig's transcendence of physical suffering, the frequent power and beauty of the translation itself are all light years away from the nirvana-mongering of much of the counterculture. However difficult it may be to define, there is still a difference between genuine religion and pseudoreligiosity. And yet, an attenuated link does exist, which Kracauer's critique helps us to see. The confidence with which Buber and Rosenzweig set out to translate the Bible, that messianic act aimed at moving us closer to primal speech, was certainly misplaced. Babel is still very much with us, not only linguistically but socially as well. No attempt to transform one of these realities can hope to succeed without transforming the other,[97] for the identity of truth and existence is not a matter of words alone.

But even if this were the case, there is a potential danger in the very search for an *Ursprache,* which is shared by all forms of gnostic hubris. Benjamin was aware of this threat when he noted in his discussion of Hölderlin's translations: "the gates of language thus expanded may slam shut and enclose the translator with silence."[98] George Steiner echoed this worry in the final paragraph of *After Babel,* with which I will now myself conclude:

The Kabbalah, in which the problem of Babel and the nature of language is so insistently examined, knows of a day of redemption on which translation will no longer be necessary. All human tongues will have re-entered the translucent immediacy of that primal, lost speech shared by God and Adam. . . . But the Kabbalah also knows of a more esoteric possibility. It records the conjecture, no doubt heretical, that there shall come a day when translation is not only unnecessary but inconceivable. Words will rebel against men. They will shake off the servitude of meaning. They will "become only themselves, and as dead stones in our mouths." In either case, men and women will have been freed forever from the burden and the splendor of the ruin at Babel. But which, one wonders, will be the greater silence?[99]

13.

Adorno and Kracauer: Notes on a Troubled Friendship

E very man strives to rescue the most valua-ble part of his ephemeral existence from the flow of time, to expose it and somehow to eternalize it. What is alive in him should not become a victim of the hour and sink into oblivion, but if possible survive the fleeting day and still have an effect in the most distant future. . . . The more conscious of personality the man is, the more the drive towards eternalization grasps his whole [being]. . . . In friendship, these basic desires are fulfilled.[1]

In these sentences from one of his earliest essays, "On Friendship,"[2] Siegfried Kracauer lay bare one of the central motivations underlying his life's work: to rescue the contingent from the flux of time and redeem it from oblivion. Here it was expressed in terms of personal immortality, but elsewhere in his large and checkered corpus of writings, the same theme reappeared in other, more impersonal guises. Most obviously, it was expressed in the title of Kracauer's second film study, *Theory of Film: The Redemption of Physical Reality*,[3] but as he himself came to recognize while writing his final book, *History: The Last Things Before the Last*, it was a Leitmotif of his entire career.[4] The desire, however, to identify what was worthy of redemption and to find the means to achieve it created a chronic tension in his work, which was never fully resolved. For along with his desire to redeem went an equally great need to debunk, expose, and criticize. And even more significantly, it was shadowed by a fear that final totalizations meant reification and closure. What I have described elsewhere[5] as the "extraterritorial" nature of Kracauer's life and work prevented him from ever achieving the "re-

First published in *Salmagundi* (Winter 1978), vol. 40.

demption" on a personal level for which he so clearly yearned, however that elusive word may be defined.

At the beginning of his career, of course, this frustration could not be fully anticipated. In fact, the passage quoted above shows that the young Kracauer believed in at least one potential avenue of escape from unredeemed contingency: a friendship between two strongly defined personalities. Through such a friendship, rooted in a Platonically erotic attraction, the isolation and ephemerality of individual existence might be suspended. Although the independence of each partner would be preserved, the interaction between them would work to transcend the limitations of their separate beings. Or at least so Kracauer asserted during the fateful year of 1917 when "On Friendship" was composed.

1917 was of course a year of no small significance in European history, and it is a matter of some note that Kracauer was able to forget the events around him long enough to muse on the eternal characteristics of friendship. "Where ties to the polis disappear," Kracauer's editor Karsten Witte points out, "thinking about friendship increases."[6] To a German in 1917, it may well have appeared as if the political community were in crisis, especially if he were an opponent of the war effort, as was Kracauer. But that Kracauer saw no hope for a new polis in the revolutionary rumblings to the east set him apart from many who shared his antipathy to Wilhelmian society. In the long run, Kracauer has been vindicated, at least as far as that revolution went, but his pessimism from the first shows how apolitical his hopes for redemption always tended to be. Even during the 1920s, when he moved toward an uneasy endorsement of the Weimar left, he still remained skeptical of easy political solutions to the crisis of his society. However concerned he may have become with social issues during those years, he never lost his hope that personal friendship might provide one route of escape. In both of the semi-autobiographical novels he wrote before his exile from Germany, *Ginster* and *Georg,*[7] friendship plays a crucial role. And much later, in the culminating work of his career on history, he paused to acknowledge the importance of a friendship in his own life.[8]

Among the subtypes Kracauer singled out for special mention in his essay of 1917 was a friendship between two partners of significantly different ages. For the younger friend, such a relationship provides a model for his aspirations as well as a sober reminder of their possible limits. He is able to reveal his inner desires and fears to the older partner without expecting or demanding a reciprocal revelation in return. The more mature friend enjoys as compensation the role of mentor, helping to nurture the best impulses in a developing soul. His major reward, however, is the continued stimulus to his creative powers provided by contact with youth. The eternal inclination of the young to ask fundamental questions lifts him out of the deadening routine of everyday life and returns him to the center of his existence. There were to be sure sources of potential difficulty in such an asymmetrical friendship, most notably in the awkwardness of communicating feelings which might arouse shame, as in discussions of erotic experiences. But on the whole, Kracauer implied, the advantages could be greater, especially if such a bond contributed to that eternalization of their personalities for which all men strive.

Kracauer's hopes and doubts about such a friendship are of more than academic interest. For it was at this very time in his life that perhaps his most important friendship began with a boy who was 14 years his junior, Theodor Wiesengrund Adorno. By examining the course and conclusion of this friendship, we will come to a better understanding of the way in which such relationships can contribute to that revocation of contingency for which Kracauer yearned. But, as we shall see, it was achieved by an ironic reversal of his expectations.

As Adorno later remembered it,[9] he was still a secondary school student at the end of World War I when a mutual friend of his parents and Kracauer's uncle brought them together. In 1918, Adorno was only 15, whereas Kracauer was already 29 and embarked on a career as an architect. Kracauer's intellectual interests went far beyond those of the normal architect, and he and the precocious Adorno found a great deal to talk about. Soon they started regular Saturday afternoon meetings devoted to a careful analysis of Kant's *Critique of Pure Reason.* "I don't exaggerate in the least," Adorno later admitted,

when I say that I owe more to those readings than to my academic teachers. Extraordinarily gifted as a pedagogue, he brought Kant to speech for me. From the beginning I learned under his guidance to see the work not only as epistemological, as an analysis of the conditions of scientifically valid judgments, but as a type of coded writing in which the historical status of the spirit could be read, and in so doing, something of the truth could be won.[10]

From Kracauer, Adorno continued, he learned one of the major premises of his later work: to look at philosophy as a conflicting "force field" of objective-ontological and subjective-idealist moments, which revealed its meaning as much through its discontinuities and silences as its positive assertions. Kracauer was especially sensitive, Adorno remembered, to the expressions of suffering that he found submerged in philosophical texts. "Although in no way sentimental," Kracauer appeared to Adorno as "a man without a skin. . . . much in him was reactive; philosophy was not ultimately a medium of self-assertion."[11]

The memoir from which these remarks are quoted was part of a tribute Adorno composed when Kracauer turned 75 in 1964, after more than 45 years of their friendship. By then, however, their relationship had substantially altered, as Adorno matured from Kracauer's pupil to an autonomous intellectual whose fame overshadowed his former teacher's. As might be expected, the shift in their respective roles was greeted by Kracauer, this "man without a skin," with some ambivalence. There was, however, little, if any, public acknowledgment of the growing tension between them. The barbs in Adorno's birthday tribute were submerged in the generally positive and appreciative tone of the piece. When it was followed only two years later by an obituary notice,[12] critical reflections were fewer still and even more subtly hidden. Kracauer, for his part, contented himself with a brief swipe at Adorno's *Negative Dialectics* in his final work, *History: The Last Things Before the Last.*[13] But otherwise their growing estrangement remained hidden from public scrutiny. In his *Nachlass,* however, Kracauer preserved his extensive correspondence with Adorno, as well as detailed memoranda of two meetings between them in 1960 and 1964, which document the sources and intensity of their dispute. An angry Kracauer clearly wanted the story to be told some day. It is worthwhile accommodating this wish, as intellectual issues of the highest order were intertwined with the personal dimensions of their dispute. By bringing to light this hitherto unknown controversy, I hope to clarify these issues and contribute to our understanding of these two extraordinary men.

From Adorno's reminiscence of his early years as Kracauer's pupil, it is possible to recreate some of the potential sources of their last controversy, although it is likely that Adorno's memory was colored by the current issues between them. As Adorno remembers him, Kracauer extended his antipathy toward idealists and especially toward Hegel into a general prejudice against philosophical thought as a whole. Although Kracauer maintained a critical distance from irrationalist intuitionism, to Adorno his thinking was "actually always more perception *(Anschauung)* then thought."[14] This meant a healthy distrust of abstract systematizers, whom Kracauer dubbed "hundred percent thinkers," but it also led to an unhealthy incapacity to think dialectically. For Kracauer, Adorno recalled, tended to overemphasize the particular givens of the world, which he was at a loss to negate theoretically. The result was a certain defenselessness against reification.

In the early years of their friendship, however, the sharpness of this critique seems to have been absent, as Adorno eagerly absorbed Kracauer's distrust of coherent, systematic philosophy, a distrust shared by his other older mentor, Walter Benjamin.[15] With Kracauer and Benjamin, Adorno found a great deal to question in totalistic, positive philosophies, including the Hegelian Marxism introduced by Georg Lukács in *History and Class Consciousness* in 1923.[16] These qualms are evident in the correspondence between Kracauer and Adorno in 1930,[17] after Kracauer left Frankfurt for Berlin to take over the *Frankfurter Zeitung's feuilleton* bureau in that city. Adorno was busily working on a study of Kierkegaard for his *Habilitation* while Kracauer was concerned with the reception of his recently published book on the crisis of Germany's white collar workers, *Die Angestellten.*[18]

On May 12th, Adorno described the methodological approach of his study as hovering somewhere between Benjamin's and Lukács', using the strengths of one to counter the weaknesses of the other. After beginning with some disparaging remarks on Lukács's pre-Marxist essay on Kierkegaard in *Soul and Form,* Adorno turned to *History and Class Consciousness,* which he said made his hair stand on end and broadcast an insufferable Heidelberg local color that was only a step away from Karl Mannheim. What he disliked in particular was Lukács' abstract use of the concept of ideology, which he said was handled in an overly deductive and schematic way. Although he admitted there were a number of excellent places in the book, he objected to its inherently idealistic attempt to deduce proletarian consciousness from the allegedly objective role of the proletariat as the subject and object of history. What he most liked about the book was its consistent historical emphasis, which he found lacking in the work of Walter Benjamin. In fact, he reproached the introduction to Benjamin's study on Baroque tragedy, *Ursprung des deutschen Trauerspiels,* for being alienated from history and ultimately beholden to a kind of mythological Platonism.

Kracauer replied on May 25, 1930, expressing his eagerness to see Adorno's Kierkegaard study and spelling out his own methodology which he called a "material dialectics" as opposed to the dialectical materialism of contemporary orthodox Marxism. The latter, he argued, was the "last offshoot of total philosophy," while what he wanted to do was separate materialism "from this guarantee and hold it up to the machine-gun-fire of the finest intuitions." These intuitions were of a reality that defied subsumption under general categories. Even Benjamin, Kracauer contended, lacked the sufficient "élan for reality," which had prevented him from grasping the essence of Kracauer's method in *Die Angestellten.*

On the following day, Adorno wrote back enthusiastically of his agreement with Kracauer's concept of material dialectics, which he said sounded very similar to what he had called "intermittent dialectics" in his Kierkegaard study. He explained this approach as a dialectics

that refuses to rigidify into a closed mode of thought, being broken up
instead by incursions of a reality that it cannot include. This was a dialectics that "held its breath," to borrow Kierkegaard's phrase, and constantly began anew. All of his debates over Marxism, he contended, turn
on this point. Kracauer was correct in rejecting a closed dialectical concept with its ultimately idealistic totality concept. Thus, although he
disagreed with Kracauer on certain specific questions, such as the chances
for meaningful social change at that historical moment, Adorno fully
shared his suspicion of an idealistic identity theory with its belief in the
unity of subject and object. His hostility to Lukács anticipated his similar position in *Negative Dialectics* over thirty years later. Kracauer had
been making the same points as early as 1926.[19]

In more personal terms, the letters of the late Weimar years
also demonstrate the level of intimacy of the two friends. Adorno discussed his budding relationship with Gretel Karplus, whom he was to
marry in 1937, and asked for Kracauer's opinion.[20] He brooded over his
chances for a successful *Habilitation* and complained about his rivalry
with a mutual friend, Leo Lowenthal, in the ranks of the Frankfurt *Institut für Sozialforschung.*[21] Kracauer responded with details of his new
life in Berlin, mentioning among other things a disappointing meeting
with Brecht, whose theoretical acumen he disparaged.[22] In later years,
Adorno complained about the reception of his inaugural lecture once
he was habilitated in 1931, singling out Karl Mannheim's surmise that
he had gone over to the Vienna Circle as only the stupidest of many
stupid responses.[23] Possibilities of Kracauer contributing to the new *Institut* journal were discussed, with Adorno lamenting that his hands were
tied by Lowenthal, whom he described as "king of the desert" *(Wüsten-
könig)* at the *Institut.*[24]

On occasion, friction would appear in the correspondence,
as when Kracauer complained that Adorno had wrongly accused him of
borrowing his ideas from someone else, which evoked the reply that
Kracauer was unnecessarily defensive when confronted with the slightest criticism.[25] On the whole, however, the letters of these years reveal
an enormous amount of intellectual comradeship and personal affection, which suggests the friendship was fulfilling, at least in large measure, the expectations and hopes of Kracauer's 1917 essay. Appro-
priately, when Adorno's Kierkegaard study finally appeared on the very
day of Hitler's assumption to power in 1933, it bore the simple dedication: "To my friend, Siegfried Kracauer."[26]

Kracauer responded with a very generous review of the book
entitled "The Unveiled Kierkegaard,"[27] which began with a frank acknowledgment of his personal relationship with its author. As might be

expected, he endorsed Adorno's accusation of a hidden idealism in Kierkegaard as well as his attempt to find a correlation between Kierkegaard's stress on *Innerlichkeit* and the contemporary fetish of the interior of bourgeois homes. He also singled out for special praise Adorno's method, which he compared to Benjamin's, as particularly well suited for the exposure of the residues a work leaves behind in history despite its author's intentions. Kracauer's encomium, however, went unread, as the loss of his job with the *Frankfurter Zeitung* and hasty departure from Germany in March 1933 prevented its publication.

With his forced exile, Kracauer's friendship with Adorno began subtly and gradually to change with intellectual as well as personal consequences. From a position of prestige and influence as one of Germany's leading cultural arbiters, he was reduced to free-lance writing in an alien environment in Paris, where his circumstances progressively declined. Adorno, on the other hand, was able to retain a residence in Germany for several years more without any apparent harassment, although he spent a good deal of time abroad at Oxford as an associate of Merton College. During those years his ties with the *Institut für Sozialforschung,* newly resettled in New York, grew stronger and in 1938 he made the decision to follow it to America. His personal ties with Max Horkheimer, the *Institut's* director, had always been close, and moving to New York strengthened them considerably. It was at about the same time that he began to distance himself to some extent from Walter Benjamin, whose work on Baudelaire and the Paris of the nineteenth century he criticized in a now well-known exchange of letters.[28] Like Kracauer, Benjamin had moved to Paris and was in serious financial difficulty. Adorno's ability to aid Benjamin through his influence at the *Institut* helped to redefine their relationship, the former pupil gaining the upper hand. The implications of this shift have been the source of a widespread controversy that need not concern us now.[29]

What is of importance is the parallel readjustment of Adorno's relationship to Kracauer, a process further complicated by the fact that, unlike Benjamin, Kracauer never received significant help from the *Institut.* For reasons that are not entirely clear, Horkheimer and Kracauer had never been on good terms.[30] In 1930, when Adorno wrote to Kracauer that Horkheimer had felt slighted by his not having received a copy of *Die Angestellten,* Kracauer caustically replied that Horkheimer had not been interested while it was being written and he saw no reason to remember him now.[31] Three years later, Adorno wrote that he had assumed control of the philosophy section of the *Zeitschrift für Sozialforschung's* review columns, which meant that he could offer Kracauer a chance to bury the hatchet with the *Institut* by writing a review of Ernst Cassirer's new book on the Enlightenment.[32] Kracauer, however, refused the invitation, as he did a subsequent one to do a general review of French social novels.[33]

In later years, however, Kracauer's financial situation worsened to the point that any source of income was welcome. So, swallowing his pride, which may have been further damaged by a mixed review Adorno gave his book on Offenbach in 1937,[34] he attempted to do work for the *Zeitschrift*. Ultimately, however, nothing came of his efforts. In 1937, he discussed a collaborative project with Adorno and Benjamin on "Mass Art and Monopoly Capitalism," which the *Institut* rejected as too costly.[35] In 1938, he submitted a piece on totalitarian propaganda, which Adorno liked but wanted to revise. Kracauer, always sensitive to criticism, balked at Adorno's suggestions, which he claimed would lead to the overexplanation of phenomena in conceptual terms and the dissolution of the concreteness of his analysis. When Adorno insisted, he withdrew the essay in disgust, writing to his friend that "you have not really edited my manuscript, but used it as the basis of a new work."[36]

Despite these setbacks, Kracauer still held out hope for *Institut* aid. In his last desperate years in Paris, he repeatedly beseeched the *Institut* to help him obtain an affidavit to expedite his immigration to America. Ultimately, following a number of false starts, the necessary papers were arranged, and Kracauer sailed from London to New York in 1941, after writing Adorno and Friedrich Pollock, the *Institut's* associate director, of his urgent need for work once he arrived.[37] In financial difficulties of its own during this period, the *Institut* could offer nothing substantial, but Kracauer had better luck with the Museum of Modern Art, which was interested in his film work, and disaster was averted. During the next half decade, his connection with the Museum and a succession of foundation grants allowed him to stay afloat while completing his first major work in English, *From Caligari to Hitler*, published in 1947.

Coincidentally, Adorno was also writing on film at this time, specifically on its use of music, in collaboration with the composer Hanns Eisler. It is a mark of the continued vitality of his friendship with Kracauer that, despite the strains of the late thirties, he requested help in dealing with this medium and Kracauer eagerly agreed.[38] Although they found new things to argue about, especially Kracauer's acceptance of English as a proper language in which to write,[39] the two friends remained on generally warm terms until the 1960s. In 1951, for example Kracauer wrote to Lowenthal that he "was very proud of Teddie"[40] after reading a positive review of his *Minima Moralia* in *Der Monat*. After Adorno returned permanently to Germany in 1953, Kracauer made several trips which included meetings between the two friends, although he never contemplated following Adorno's move. By the 1960s, Adorno was a dominant figure in German intellectual life as the director of the reconstituted Frankfurt *Institut für Sozialforschung*. Partly through his influence, Kracauer's novel *Ginster,*[41] which had originally appeared anonymously, was now published with its author's name affixed. In addition, two collections of Kracauer's essays, *Das Ornament der Masse* and *Strassen in Berlin und Anderswo,*[42] were also published, bringing to the attention of modern German readers classics of the Weimar *feuilleton* and helping to revive an interest in Kracauer's work in general. In thanks, Kracauer dedicated the first collection to Adorno, returning the compliment of three decades before.

Adorno's influence on the reception of Kracauer's work went beyond his aid in its republication; he helped Kracauer choose the title for *Das Ornament der Masse* (the name of one of the essays therein) and persuaded him to drop the last chapter of *Ginster,* which he felt had "coquetted with positivity."[43] In addition, he sponsored a *Diplomarbeit* on Kracauer by a student, Erika Lorenz, which Kracauer found enormously flattering.[44] When she failed to turn it into a full-fledged doctoral dissertation for personal reasons, he was disappointed and remarked half-jokingly to Adorno that he couldn't understand "why dissertations should always be on Tillich."[45] But nonethless it was clear that Kracauer was finally receiving some of the attention in his native Germany that had eluded him since his departure in 1933, and, as in the similar case of Walter Benjamin, Adorno was in part responsible. The most important function of friendship, as Kracauer had defined it in his 1917 essay, seemed to be fulfilled: Adorno was helping Kracauer achieve a modest degree of immortality.

But paradoxically, as all this was happening, the latent tensions in their intellectual positions finally emerged to poison the last years of their relationship. Kracauer in particular came to question the continued basis of their friendship, and even doubted Adorno's intentions in trying to keep his (Kracauer's) reputation alive. Adorno, more secure in the knowledge of his own success and needing less reassurance about his ultimate fame, seems to have reacted with bewilderment and regret. The issues between them came to a head when Adorno wrote his 75th birthday tribute, "The Whimsical Realist," but serious conflict, both intellectual and personal, had broken out in 1960 at a meeting they had in Switzerland. Both men were working on the major books they saw as their intellectual testaments, summarizing a life's work: Adorno on *Negative Dialectics* and Kracauer on *History:The Last Things Before the Last.* On August 12, 1960 at the Hotel Sonnenheim in Berguen, they met to discuss their projects. The argument between them apparently became so heated that Kracauer later took the time to write an extensive memorandum detailing the points at issue, as he was later to do for another meeting in 1964. Although summarized in very brief form in *History: The Last Things Before the Last,* the full extent of his quarrel with Adorno could not be known until his *Nachlass* was partially opened a few years ago. Because these memoranda have never been published, I will quote from them at some length. Without Adorno's own version of the events, it is difficult to have a fully rounded sense of the encounter, but it can be assumed that much of his rebuttal appeared in the birthday tribute that so outraged Kracauer.

The memorandum of August 12, 1960, is divided into three sections: "Concept of Utopia," "Dialectics vs. Ontology," and "Ideology and Sociology." Throughout all three, certain fundamental charges against Adorno recur again and again: excessive formalism, indifference to the concrete, and an arrogant disregard for the internal contradictions of his position. Kracauer began the first section by immediately stating his reservations concerning Adorno's use of Utopia:

I argued that he uses this concept in a formal way, as a borderline concept *(Grenzbegriff)* which at the end invariably emerges like a *Deus ex Machina.* In my opinion, I told him, Utopian thought makes sense only if it assumes the form of a vision or intuition with a definite content of a sort.

Kracauer was arguing here for a position close to that of a mutual friend, Ernst Bloch, whose notion of "concrete utopia" also stressed the importance of fleshing out utopian desires. This was a view very different from that held by Adorno and his colleagues in the Frankfurt School, who often talked about a *Bildverbot* or prohibition on the picturing of utopia underlying their Critical Theory. In the 1960s Horkheimer was to justify it by invoking the Jewish refusal to name God or picture paradise,[46] but it had always been a premise of Critical Theory. Adorno remained true to this position, although according to Kracauer's memorandum:

'1. was inclined to admit the justice of my argument. He says—of course, he would—that he will deal with the concept of Utopia in future, more systematic and elaborate works. His intention is then to show that the concept of Utopia is a *vanishing* concept when besieged; it vanishes if you want to spell it out.

Kracauer clearly found this solution insufficient, but it would be difficult to find a truly concrete utopian vision in his own work despite his insistence on its importance. Still, one must admit the force of his argument against the way in which essentially empty utopian ideals often serve Adorno as the Archimedean point from which the current non-utopian present is measured and found wanting.[47]

In the second, much longer section of the memorandum entitled "Dialectics vs. Ontology," Kracauer began by recapitulating Adorno's current thinking on the problem:

He rejected any ontological stipulations in favor of an infinite dialectics which penetrates all concrete things and entities, and, taking its clue from what they may reveal, works its way through them in a process which has no goal outside the movement itself and no direction that could be stated in terms other than those immanent in that movement.

Kracauer then detailed his critical response to this position, a response that later readers of *Negative Dialectics* were often to share:

I told Teddie that many of his articles concocted this way made me just dizzy; that I had often the feeling that other interpretations might be as conclusive as his, or even more so; that his whole dialectics seemed inseparable from a certain arbitrariness to me; and that, in sum, my dizziness was presumably caused by the complete absence of content and direction in these series of material evaluations.[48]

Kracauer pressed his point by returning to his earlier criticism of Adorno's use of utopia:

I related this argument against his dialectics to my statement on the formality, the emptiness of his Utopian concept: indeed, if the movement he unchains gravitated toward a Utopian goal, it still remains unoriented throughout because the term "Utopia," as used by him, is nothing but a conceptual stopgap.

As Kracauer presented it, Adorno answered in the following way:

Teddie's response showed that he was struck (although he is a skilled enough debater not to show it). My objections, said he, reveal that I still cling to obsolete, ontological habits of thought in requesting that something fixed must be given, postulated or desired. No sooner does one fall into this common error than the consequence is a ready-made "system" starting from the vision or postulate and passing above the concrete material of things and entities instead of *through* them. And he insisted that, contrary to ontological bias, the truth, as revealed through this immanent processing of concretions, is always "hovering" *(schwebend)*. As for my reproach of dizziness, arbitrariness, etc., he declares that there is after all a definite outlook in his writings which, of course, is accessible only to those absorbing his production in its entirety. He demands, in fact, that the student should understand each meaning from the contexts of what he, Teddie, has written (and will write in the future). Then, Teddie seems to believe, the student cannot but experience the substance behind it all and get the sense of direction I am missing.

In composing his memorandum, Kracauer thought of a response which had eluded him at the time of the debate and included it in parentheses:

I could have answered him, but did not so, that, since his dialectics consists of an unending sequence of concrete moments and each moment is supposed to be interpreted in depth, the sum total of these moments is unattainable. Which means that the reader familiar with all of Teddie's writings will feel exactly as insecure and dizzy as one who has read only part of Teddie's output. The emphasis lying on the movement from moment to moment, more samples of the same may increase the impression of the movement punctuated by "hovering truths," but are extremely unlikely to endow it with the substance it deliberately negates as sheer movement.

Instead of this objection, Kracauer used another which was derived from his work on the cinema:

I compared Teddie's dialectics with a film made up exclusively of close-ups. Such a film is of course imaginable, I said; but the close-ups of which it consists would be completely undefined and hence puzzling rather than revealing, were they not every now and then interrupted by "establishing" shots relating them to the reality with which we are all confronted after all and thus defining, however tentatively, their approximate position. Otherwise expressed, the radical immanence of the dialectical process will not do; some ontological fixations are needed to imbue it with significance and direction.

Kracauer's phrase "the reality with which we are all confronted after all" is not one Adorno was likely to have received without question, concerned as he always was with negating that reality, but Kracauer presented him with another opening to respond:

I spoke of "ontologischen Wuerfen" [ontological directions] within this context and remarked that Hegel's dialectics moved toward, or implied, an ontological end. This was a bit careless of me, for Teddie, knowing my lifelong aversion to Hegel, immediately exploited the situation by saying that Hegel never committed the sin of orienting the dialectical process toward anything "objective" outside that process.

As Kracauer recalls it, Adorno was nonetheless taken with his remarks about Hegel:

Thereupon he admitted that ontological elements might indeed be needed—but only in the form of hypostatized elements, not as eternal truths. Well, I replied, no one has spoken of eternal truths; rather, what is required is a dialectics between the endless, purely immanent movement—Teddie's procedure—and an ontological stipulation outside it, a "Schau" which, itself, may, or should not assume a definite character.

What this "Schau" or "look" into a reality deeper than the dialectical course of history might reveal, however, Kracauer did not attempt to say. Instead, he called upon an unexpected ally:

Exploring further my advantage, I cited *Benjamin* against Teddie. Does not Benjamin, I continued, time and again feel himself bound by visions of partial ontological truths? And does he not orient his penetrations of concrete entities toward these messianic visions which are rich in content, as indeed Utopian ideas should be in order to carry meaning? Here I had Teddie trapped. True, he tamely criticized Benjamin for not being the perfect dialectician à la Hegel and Teddie himself (who invokes the Hegel of his making as a sort of protective cover and shield), but on the other hand, he could not well deny Benjamin's strength as an autonomous thinker and undermine his position.

Kracauer then drew what he called a graph to illustrate the similarity of his position to Benjamin's, as compared to Adorno's. In it, he portrayed Adorno's position in terms of a complete divergence between dialectics and ontology, whereas both he and Benjamin recognized the necessity of some relationship.

Although he did not spell it out here, the one significant difference between his position and Benjamin's was Kracauer's lack of confidence in the ultimate interpenetrability of the utopian-ontological and dialectical-historical spheres. In *History: The Last Things Before the Last,* he spelled out what he called a "side-by-side" principle, which forces us to assume "that the two aspects of truths exist side by side, relating to each other in ways which I believe to be theoretically undefinable. Something like an analogy may be found in the 'complementarity principle' of the quantum physicists."[49] But he and Benjamin presented a common front against Adorno's ontological agnosticism:

Both Benjamin and I coinciding [sic] in not accepting immanent dialectics. I subtly implied that we are engaged in terms of substances. We think under a sort of ontological compunction, Utopian or not, whereas Teddie is, indeed, free-hovering and does not feel any such compunction.

Kracauer finished this section of his memorandum on a note of triumph, as well as with a sarcastic afterthought:

At this point, I believe, Teddie was at the end of his rope. I am sure, however, he will not admit this to himself but immediately manage to believe that all my thoughts are in reality his own, annex these thoughts, which he already considers his property, to his "system" and pass them off as the natural outgrowth of the latter. As Benjamin said: he grabs everything he is told, digests it and its consequences and then takes over.

The final section of the memorandum on "Ideology and Sociology" began with an equally querulous tone:

The formality and possessiveness of Teddie's mind flagrantly show in the way he relates the ideological to the sociological dimension. In all his articles or books he invariably traces the aesthetic or conceptual characteristics of some entity—a poem, a philosophical viewpoint, or the like—to the social situation from which that entity (historically) arises, but does so in a manner which unmistakingly reveals his complete unconcern for the material nature of society, past or present, and for the means of improving our social condition. His sociological concepts are much too wide to be able to characterize any social reality; they are just leftovers, never revised, from his Marxist past.

Kracauer, who by this time had jettisoned whatever Marxist past he may have had, was reluctant to admit that the Marxism still present in Adorno's worldview was anything but a liability. This was especially the case with one concept, which Adorno consistently used in his work, "bürgerlich" or bourgeois:

Ontological thinking, ideology-formation, etc.—all this he lays on to the "bürgerlich" Warengesellschaft [commodity society], which he makes also responsible for the "Verdinglichung" [reification] of specific values, abstractness in our approach to the world, unjustified relativism, and the loss of substance in general. I asked him to define his concept of "bürgerlich." He said it goes beyond Capitalism proper, covering the "Tauschgesellschaft" [exchange society] with its exchange of goods. It goes without saying that, on some other occasion, he declared Aristotle's Politeia with its emphasis on Moderation and the middle way etc. resulted from bourgeois mentality. (!) What are the counterconcepts, I further asked. The feudal society, the primitive horde, and so on, he answered. Whereupon I gave him to understand that his concept of "bürgerlich" is much too wide to define the social forces which may account for this or that intellectual or artistic phenomenon.

Kracauer finished his recollection of the meeting by making a point that he would later expand in History: The Last Things Before the Last[50] where he attacked the premise that any one historical period was unified:

Without realizing that he proceeds from this assumption [the unity of the historical period], Teddie contended that he was in complete agreement with me and had already dealt with the issue I raised in one of his essays. To repeat it, he grabs everything. In order to prove [to] him how alienated he is from all substances, intellectual or social, he pretends to penetrate and set moving, I told him: You curse the "bürgerlich Gesellschaft," reject Communism, frown down on Social Democracy, etc.: what do you suggest should be done in terms of social change, other institutions? His (pitiable) answer was: I know and say what is bad; is this not enough?

Clearly, to Kracauer as to other critics of Adorno further to the left in the later 1960s, it was not. But once again, there is little in Kracauer's own writing during these years to suggest his answers were any more concrete than Adorno's.

Four years later, from July 15 to July 21, 1964, the two friends met once again, this time in Frankfurt, to thrash out the same problems. In a somewhat shorter memorandum than the first, written in Zurich on

July 27 and 28, Kracauer once again detailed the points separating them.
Adorno had stressed the *"Zeitbedingtheit"* (temporally conditioned)
character of his thought, warning Kracauer against abstract generalities.
He had disparaged Kracauer's penchant for the concrete with characteristic Hegelian arguments, but to little effect. He had chastised Kracauer for believing in "ideological shelterlessness"[51] at a time when
ideologies were still rampant, drawing Kracauer's response that one might
live without ideology—"the relation of Sancho Panza to Don Quixote."[52] And predictably Adorno had raged against Kracauer's writing in
English, a practice Kracauer continued to defend while attacking Adorno's style as "obtrusive, not transparent."

The major part of the memorandum, however, dealt once
again with Adorno's *Negative Dialectics,* which Kracauer found no less
deficient than before. Kracauer began with a recapitulation of Adorno's
central thesis. Although repeating much of his description from the first
memorandum, it bears quotation because of its further elaboration of
some of the points therein.

He wants to disengage Hegelian dialectics from its ontological roots: the identity
principle and of course the Zeitgeist are dropped. What remains is the dialectical
movement as such, based on the (still Hegelian) view that each significant historical phenomenon (a work of art, a social situation, etc.) is a configuration of
elements—or conceptual trends—which point both backward and forward. As
concrete phenomenon it is not a static unit, a self-contained gestalt, but a mirage-
like entity which, because of its inherent limitations, is bound to show negative
and positive facets. Interpretation consists in bringing them into the open (by
dissolving the seeming unit) and thus making the entity appear as a phase (or a
densification) of the conceptual process.

Kracauer then asked, "now why negative dialectics?" From conversing
not only with Adorno, but also with Adorno's colleague Karl Heinz Haag,
he wrote that Teddie:

wants to seize on precisely those phenomena which Hegel throws overboard or
disparages (hence "negative") because they are undigestible to him—i.e., cannot
be incorporated into the movement toward the Absolute, do not coincide with
the general materializing in the concrete. In other words, with T. *et al.* the process is not a unified movement with an ontological goal but a series of intermittent processes involving articulate and perhaps unconnected entities. T.'s intention is to explode the Hegelian identity philosophy and dwell on the phenomena
in the resultant gaps or ruins. Obviously he too believes in the identity of the
particular and the general, but to him the general is no [word obscured] something that can be systematized. There is no absolute for T. that would yield a
world view in the form of a system.

Kracauer finished his memorandum with some acid comments:

(1) T's negative dialectics hangs in mid-air. The term "negative" would acquire full meaning only if it were conceived in the light of my side by side principle. But in retaining the Hegelian dialectical method, T. is undoing again his destruction of Hegel; he reconnects, dialectically, what he had better keep apart. So his advance has a retrogressive character.

(2) T. pretends to eliminate all ontological residues. Does he? His invariable references to a Utopian state of things certainly denote something ontological, something absolute.

(3) T. wants to eat his cake and have it. His *negative dialectics is a fraud.* [Italics in original]

With the dust scarcely settled from this heated encounter, Adorno sent Kracauer a copy of the article he had written in commemoration of his 75th birthday. It had just appeared in *Neue Deutsche Hefte*[53] after having first been broadcast on the Hessischer Rundfunk earlier in the year. Although ostensibly a tribute, the essay contained several critical reflections that echo his position in the debate recorded in Kracauer's memoranda. Adorno began with an appreciative recollection of his adolescent indebtedness to Kracauer, which we have discussed earlier. He then characterized Kracauer's general method as anti-idealist and ultimately antiphilosophical, quoting a 1923 remark of Benjamin to that effect. The medium of Kracauer's thought, he argued, was experience, although not in a positivist or empiricist sense. In connection with this observation, he mentioned Kracauer's debt to Simmel and Scheler as well as his early training as an architect. The materialist impulse of his thought, Adorno continued, necessarily led Kracauer to social issues, but always with a certain skeptical moderation. He quoted Kracauer's remark that he had been the "derrière-garde of the avant-garde" during his Berlin years and mentioned his identification with Charlie Chaplin, as well as his critical stance toward thinkers such as Buber who sought eternal values.[54]

Turning to his work on film, Adorno praised Kracauer for being among the first to decipher the social significance of the medium. But he implied that Kracauer's later work on the immanent dialectic of film was inferior by comparison and he spoke disparagingly of Kracauer's "tolerance" for commercial film. Adorno then commented on Kracauer's more strictly sociological work, especially *Die Angestellten,* and remarked on his ambivalence toward empirical techniques. He followed with a long paragraph on Kracauer's "most meaningful achievement," *Ginster,* which "hovered in the no man's land between novel and biography."[55] He compared Kracauer to Lichtenberg as the author of a *roman philosophique* and praised him for cropping the last chapter of the work from its republication because of its overly affirmative tone.

He ended his discussion of *Ginster* by saying that it was a pity that Kracauer had abandoned the German language he could use so well for English.

This last remark was a continuation of a complaint Kracauer had heard before, but Adorno's next allegation was new. Kracauer, he argued, had begun a subtle shift in his thinking during the last years of the Weimar period that expressed an acceptance of the desirability of happiness in the present world. "He who has no skin," he wrote of his friend, "allows armor to grow."[56] Kracauer's new strategy of accommodation was evident in his second, unpublished novel, *Georg,* but it became dominant only during his American exile: "emigrants who had no friends standing in solidarity with them had to capitulate in order to live."[57] The result, Adorno suggested, was a kind of "identification with the aggressor," an explanation borrowed from Anna Freud he was later to use in Benjamin's case as well.[58]

In the final two pages of the essay, pages he would later stress to Kracauer as containing the essence of his argument, Adorno attempted to spell out the implications of Kracauer's "whimsical realism." Kracauer's fixation on things in the world Adorno traced back to his troubled and anxiety-ridden childhood which nurtured his desire for fixed realities. People having failed Kracauer, Adorno argued, he sought stability in the realm of physical reality. "The primacy of the optical in him was not the cause, but the consequence of his relation to the world of things. In the treasure of motives of his thought, one would look in vain for protest against reification."[59]

Despite this parting barb, Kracauer's initial reactions were positive. On October 15, he wrote to Adorno that the piece showed all the old affinities and antagonisms, but that he learned a great deal from it, both about Adorno and himself. The article, he reflected, would help him to a better "self-objectification." He finished by offering to correct some minor factual errors that had crept into the piece should Adorno wish to republish it elsewhere. This being his intention, Adorno replied warmly on October 28 that he was gratified by Kracauer's response and would welcome any corrections.

Shortly thereafter, on November 3, Kracauer wrote back in a letter whose tone was far different from that of his previous note. After listing a number of specific factual mistakes, Kracauer indignantly challenged Adorno's assertion that he had become a conformist seeking happiness during his American period. As evidence against the charge he adduced his staunch opposition to American sociological techniques, especially quantitative ones. Furthermore, there was no possible link between his alleged conformity and any success he might have had as a writer, as Adorno had implied, for his most critical works, especially *Die Angestellten* and *Ginster*, were the most widely acclaimed. As for Adorno's charge that *Georg* had demonstrated the beginnings of his shift toward conformity, he reminded Adorno that its hero had to leave his newspaper job because of his leftist leanings. Nor could a conformist bias be found in *From Caligari to Hitler*, a work which Adorno had mysteriously neglected to treat in his piece.[60] After listing several other minor errors of fact, Kracauer finished by arguing that Adorno had wrongly deprecated his ability to tie the particular and the universal together, a problem he would deal with in his forthcoming book in history.

A surprised Adorno replied on November 13, acknowledging most of the minor factual errors, but holding fast to his contention that Kracauer had indeed changed in a conformist direction. This had been one of the central experiences of their friendship, so Adorno recalled. As for Kracauer's decision to seek happiness in the present world, Adorno quoted a sentence from *Georg* which he argued endorsed that view. The source of Kracauer's shift, he now admitted, was not his success, but the pressures of the migration. The reason he had neglected to discuss the Caligari book was his ignorance of the technology of film. What really troubled him now, however, was the sudden shift in Kracauer's tone in his second letter. Why was Kracauer so anxious to determine the way his work was received? A really valuable work, Adorno claimed, lives on more through its criticism than its simple acceptance. When he was a student Kracauer had once applied an expression of the poet Mörike to him, that he was too *"sehrhaft"* (roughly translatable as too earnest), which could now be applied to Kracauer himself.

Kracauer doggedly responded on the 21st without yielding any ground. A lack of technical expertness was no reason, he complained, to have ignored *From Caligari to Hitler*. As for the charge that he wanted to manipulate the image of his work he argued that he played the pilot only to help avoid a friend making errors in print. And the general charge of conformity he still vigorously denied.

Although this was the last of the direct exchanges on the article which have been preserved in Kracauer's *Nachlass*, there was one final burst of acrimony between them the following February and March concerning Kracauer's *Theory of Film*.[61] Adorno began by criticizing the book for lacking a sociological dimension, which Kracauer answered by insisting that the history of film did indeed have an immanent development that could be traced on its own. Adorno disputed this point in his rejoinder, and added the assertion that Kracauer's indiscriminate desire to "redeem" physical reality had an inevitably affirmative dimension. By now the two friends were bitter rivals reiterating fixed positions and refusing to yield any ground on the issues dividing them. When Kracauer died on November 26 of the following year, it appeared as if they were no closer to an intellectual or personal reconciliation.

Kracauer's ultimate ploy in their battle was his collecting the correspondence and memoranda used in this account in a special file in his *Nachlass*. And to make sure no doubt would be left in the mind of anyone finding it, he affixed the following note to a copy of Adorno's "The Whimsical Realist": "this emotionally laden, slanderous article of TWA who does not shrink from telling falsehoods." Adorno had been correct when he accused Kracauer of trying to manipulate his image for posterity; or more precisely, Kracauer would not allow Adorno to do so himself through his article. Kracauer's hostility toward "The Whimsical Realist" was, as we have seen, derived in large measure from his belief that Adorno had twisted the truth in order to blacken his memory. But an even more basic motivation underlay his displeasure, which was revealed by a note he added to his July 27–28, 1964, memorandum, at which time he had known about Adorno's intention to write the article, but had not yet seen it. "In writing the article," Kracauer complained, "T. obviously reckons that I'll belong among the forgotten men." In other words, that long-held hope for friendship as the antidote to personal contingency was now proving to be vain in Kracauer's mind, even at the very time when one might suppose he would have thought it fulfilled.

Ironically, however, Kracauer's early expectations were not entirely betrayed, even though his friendship with Adorno did not live up to his idealized image of what a perfect friendship should be. In fact, it might be argued that the very dissolution of their relationship contributed to whatever modest immortality Kracauer may achieve. For the record of that dissolution, preserved in Kracauer's *Nachlass* and presented in this essay must surely add to the stature of his intellectual reputation. Many of the points he made against *Negative Dialectics* and Adorno's approach in general must be acknowledged as serious obstacles for anyone anxious to defend the Frankfurt School's legacy. Can one preserve the dialectical impulse of Hegel's method without some ontological underpinnings, idealist, materialist, or otherwise? Has Adorno introduced a hidden ontology despite himself, and one which he has not really been able to defend? Can Adorno hold to a Hegelian notion of concreteness as that which is complexly mediated and situated in a force-field of dialectical relations, while at the same time denying the coherence of the totality in which the concrete is embedded? Does his hostility to the more conventional notion of concrete as particular, contingent, and irreducible to conceptual categorizing, the view underlying Kracauer's approach, inevitably lead to that formalism and indifference to real history of which Kracauer accuses him? Does utopia function in his thought as an empty and elusive *deus ex machina* introduced when the implications of his hostility to ontology become too difficult to handle? Although Kracauer's own solutions to these problems were by no means always superior to Adorno's, especially because of his tendency to posit the need for ontology without spelling out what it actually is, it must be acknowledged that he asked many of the tough questions that Adorno's version of Critical Theory must struggle to answer.

But in conclusion, it might be said that in an unexpected way, Adorno's position has itself been justified. For it is in the very history of his troubled friendship with Kracauer that the power of his vision of a negative dialectics can be appreciated. Theirs was a bond which did not result in easy reconciliations or a falsely positive consensus. Instead, it culminated in the series of conflicts, sometimes petty but more often not, which this article has traced. And in so doing, it demonstrated that real friendships may well fail to transcend or escape the contradictions of society, as the young Kracauer had hoped, but instead realize their true value through the relentless exposure of those contradictions on the levels of personal and intellectual interaction.

14.

The Political Existentialism of Hannah Arendt

The news of Hannah Arendt's sudden and unexpected death on December 4, 1975, was greeted with an outpouring of deeply felt shock and grief that made abundantly clear her extraordinary stature in our intellectual life. Personal tributes appeared by many of our most distinguished cultural figures, among them Mary McCarthy, Robert Lowell, Hans Morgenthau, William Phillips, Leonard Krieger, Maurice Cranston, and Hans Jonas.[1] Symposia were organized to honor her memory at The New School and Bard College. The aura of acrimony that had dogged her reputation since the ugly furor over her Eichmann book in 1963 was dispelled, at least temporarily, in a general wave of good feeling that has yet to end. Clearly Hannah Arendt had made a mark on the cultural life of her adopted country the rival of any made by other intellectual migrants from fascist tyranny.

But precisely what that mark was her mourners could not easily say. Again and again, they puzzled over what Morgenthau called "the impossibility of categorizing Hannah Arendt according to prevailing classifications,"[2] often concluding with Cranston that she was "altogether *hors categorie,* a unique intellectual mixture of the reactionary and the revolutionary."[3] That she was a true "original,"[4] to borrow yet another formulation from one of her eulogizers, has in fact been long recognized and indeed accounted a virtue by her admirers, who see it as evidence of creativity and a refusal to wear ideological blinders. Although there has always been a minority position arguing that she was more confused and eclectic than truly original, the more common feeling, if one can generalize about these things, was that her noncategorizability was a source of strength rather than weakness. The joy of reading

First published in *Partisan Review* (1978), 45(3).

Hannah Arendt's not always pellucid prose lay, in fact, in the expectation of finding fresh insights into old problems, an expectation rarely disappointed.

Just how idiosyncratic Hannah Arendt was can be gleaned from a brief glance at her intellectual career in this country. She first came to prominence in 1951 with the publication of *The Origins of Totalitarianism,* by some accounts her masterpiece despite its rough handling by more conventional historians in subsequent years.[5] With hindsight, the book now can be seen as more than merely an historical-philosophical analysis of one of the key problems of our century; it was also a monument of the Cold War because of its relentless equation of Communism and Nazism as the two subtypes of the totalitarian genus. Because of her insistence that Communism could only follow out its historical logic and grow increasingly oppressive and imperialist, the book was eagerly received by defenders, conservative and liberal alike, of the American democratic system. Her credentials as an upholder of traditional American virtues were given additional support by her later insistence in *On Revolution*[6] that our version of that phenomenon was superior to the French in a number of important respects, including its relative indifference to social issues. Clearly, as Jonas would recall at her funeral, her gratitude as an emigré experiencing American political practice first hand had "decisively shaped her political thinking," so that the American Republic, at least in its ideal state, would always hold a special place in her affections. Not surprisingly, in the one book-length study of her thought preceding her death, Margaret Canovan concluded that she was best understood as a "Republican . . . in the old eighteenth-century sense of a partisan of public freedom."[7]

But as readers of *On Revolution,* as well as her earlier theoretical studies *The Human Condition* and *Between Past and Future,*[8] could easily see, her vision of what constituted the ideal republic was deeply at odds with current American practice. For Hannah Arendt, at least in the majority of her writings, only direct and not representative democracy was the institutional setting for the exercise of true freedom. It was this emphasis on what became fashionable in the 1960s as "participatory democracy" that more than anything else accounts for her discovery by a new constituency in those years, the nascent New Left. In fact, at Berkeley, as political theorist Norman Jacobson remembers it,[9] the Free Speech Movement was deeply influenced by her work during its formative period before the Left reread its Marx. At approximately the same time, her heterodox treatment of the Eichmann case[10] and her allegation of unwitting Jewish complicity in the holocaust cost her much support in the more traditionally liberal American Jewish community. On both Vietnam and Watergate, she took positions that identified her more and more closely with the left, especially as her most frequent forum was *The New York Review of Books*.[11] And yet at the same time she spoke out against the romanticization of the Third World then so popular in New Left circles and continued to hold to many non-leftist beliefs, a striking example being her insistence that private property was a necessary bulwark in the defense of liberty. Thus by her death, she had managed alternately to inspire and infuriate almost all sectors of the political spectrum, remaining still an enigma whose elusive and unpredictable mind continued to confound attempts to pigeonhole it.

But even enigmas can be unraveled and it is perhaps not too much to expect that with the passage of time it will be easier to make out the contours of her intellectual career and give her work a coherence it may have lacked to her contemporaries, especially those who saw her solely in the American context. She now, after all, belongs to history and with the perspective that history should offer, it may be easier to see her whole. To do so will, of course, entail a more thorough understanding of her intellectual biography than is now possible with the materials available. One obvious starting point would be her deep and ambiguous involvement with Jewish issues, which sparked her first work on Rahel Varnhagen[12] and clearly colored much of the rest. As Benjamin Schwartz demonstrated some years ago,[13] her controversial attitudes towards the Jewish question were very much of a piece with her historical and theoretical work. It will, however, still take more time for the dust to settle from the *Eichmann in Jerusalem* controversy to approach this problem with the proper distance, so I will not attempt to go beyond Schwartz's account now.

What I would prefer to do instead is focus on another context in which Hannah Arendt's work must be placed, that of the *Existenzphilosophie* which many commentators have seen as her starting point. What I will argue is that to a remarkable degree this point of origin defined her attitudes well after she had apparently moved beyond it. She often, of course, gratefully acknowledged her indebtedness to Heidegger and Jaspers. In a *Partisan Review* essay written in 1946, in which she posed and answered the question "What is Existenz Philosophy?",[14] Hannah Arendt made clear her conviction that the tradition beginning with Schelling and Kierkegaard and culminating in her teachers of the 1920s was *the* philosophy of the modern age. The French existentialists, Sartre in particular, were excluded from this judgment, although in later years she would find much to admire in Merleau-Ponty. Even though she made no reference to the political implications of *Existenzphilosophie,* with hindsight one can see that many of the themes made explicit in her subsequent work on politics were developed in strictly philosophical terms in the essay. Her distaste for the Hegelian-Marxist tradition, indeed for rationalism in general, her stress on the importance of new beginnings out of nothing, her belief in the role of deeds as opposed to pure contemplation, her agreement with Jaspers' stress on intersubjective communication as the source of a new humanism, her insistence that philosophy must transcend historicism, all of these were to figure prominently in her political theorizing. So too was her persistent reliance on the etymological significance of a word to explain its "real" meaning, which was a favorite ploy of Heidegger in particular. The explicit politicization of *Existenzphilosophie* was to come somewhat later in 1958 with *The Human Condition*, the most ambitious of her theoretical works, but all the ingredients were there in her postwar essay.

Perhaps what made her reluctant to spell it out was the memory of previous attempts to derive political conclusions from existentialism in the Weimar era. In addition to her teacher Heidegger, whose political adventures were confined to a brief, sorry period after the Nazi era began, the "political existentialists" of the 20s included Carl Schmitt, Ernst Jünger and Alfred Bäumler.[15] Because all of them, to one degree or another, have been seen by most historians as having prepared the way for fascism, it is not surprising that Hannah Arendt, so outspoken in her criticism of totalitarianism, would shun their company. There can in fact be little question that she found much of their thought intolerable. Thus, she wrote against the celebration of violence in Jünger,[16] and criticized Schmitt's emphasis on sovereignty and his glorification of movements rather than parties.[17] She was equally opposed to their view of politics as the continuation of war by other means, having instead a far more benign reading of the public realm as an arena of pluralist cooperation. She also admitted that the *völkisch* excesses of Heidegger's collaborationist period were "mythologizing confusions,"[18] although she refrained from linking his philosophy as a whole with his sympathy for fascism as did another of his former students, Herbert Marcuse.

And yet despite these criticisms, Hannah Arendt's political philosophy can justly be situated in the political existentialist tradition of the 1920s, albeit as one of its "tender" rather than "tough" variants. To stress this link is useful not because it establishes some sort of guilt by association, but rather because it provides the historical context in which her apparently uncategorizable position begins to make sense. On the most general level, it allows us to see the broad movement of which she was a part, a movement which asserted the primacy of the political realm over society, culture, economics, or religion as the arena in which man's most quintessentially human quality, his capacity for freedom, could be realized. In opposition to the typical nineteenth-century tendency to downgrade politics to a function of socioeconomic trends, which appeared in such widely different theories as classical economics, Saint-Simonian socialism, corporatist conservatism, Durkheimian sociology and Marxism (although as I shall argue shortly, with questionable support from the founder himself), a reaction set in during the early years of this century. Its leaders included Pareto and Mosca in Italy, the Action Française clique in France, and the political existentialists in Germany. On a practical level, a similar reassertion of the relative autonomy of politics can be seen in Lenin and the Italian Fascists.

Although Hannah Arendt's definition of the political cannot be simply equated with that of her predecessors, she nonetheless shared with them a strong desire to rescue politics from the debased state into which much nineteenth-century thought had cast it. Although she claimed that she had no preference between the life of the mind, the *vita contemplativa,* and the life of practice, the *vita activa,* Hannah Arendt significantly devoted virtually all of her intellectual gifts to an exploration of the latter realm.[19] In *The Human Condition,* the *locus classicus* of her position, she divided the *vita activa* into three subcategories: labor, work, and action. In the first, man is understood as an *animal laborans* whose existence is consumed by a never-ending cycle of reproducing the conditions of his survival. Labor is endless, repetitive, tied to biological necessity, and without permanent residue. Higher on the scale of human activities is work in which man is understood as *homo faber.* Here man leaves the purely biological level by violently transforming his environment through the creation of man-made products. The model is man as isolated craftsman leaving behind him more or less permanent artifacts which constitute what Hannah Arendt calls the "world." The third category, action, is the highest of the three for here men engage in the activity which is most ennobling: the public interaction through speech which is the essence of freedom. The life of action, best exemplified by the Greek *polis,* where free men interacted on the basis of absolute equality, is an end in itself. The remembrance of noble political deeds, which the political community preserves, is a higher goal than even the preservation of life. The individual man is not the measure of all things as humanists since Protagoras have wrongly assumed: the "world," which is the product of *homo faber,* and the earthly immortality produced by the remembrance of the *polis* should be seen as higher values instead.

In attempting to liberate political action from its subordination to other modes of the *vita activa,* Hannah Arendt, like the political existentialists of the twenties, was anxious to assure its utmost possible autonomy. Thus, she saw politics not merely as irreducible to socioeconomic forces, but also as unhampered by all normative or instrumental constraints as well, a position often known as "decisionism." As its own end, politics should not be conceived as a means to anything else whether it be domination, wealth, public welfare, or social justice: in short, *politique pour la politique.* Or as Bäumler once put it, "Action does not mean 'deciding in favor of' . . . for that presupposes that one knows in favor of what one is deciding; rather action means 'setting off in a direction'. . . . It is really secondary to decide in favor of something that I have come to know."[20] For Bäumler's "setting off in a direction," Hannah Arendt substitutes "the sheer capacity to begin,"[21] but the meaning is essentially the same. The existentialist roots of her position are clear in her discussion of Heidegger's stress on nothingness in her 1946 essay:

The peculiar fascination, which the thought of the Nothing has exercised on modern philosophy, is not simply characteristic of Nihilism. If we look at the problem of Nothing in our context of a philosophy revolting against philosophy as pure contemplation, then we see it as an effort to become "Master of Being" and thereby to question philosophically in such a manner that we progress immediately to the deed; thus the thought that Being is really the Nothing has a tremendous advantage. Basing himself on this, Man can imagine himself, can relate himself to Being that is given, no less than the Creator before the creation of the world, which, as we know, was created out of nothing.[22]

Although she was far less certain about the will as the motor of political action than the decisionists were, Miss Arendt shared their yearning to free politics from all extraneous considerations: "Action, to be free, must be free from motive on one side, from its intended goal as a predictable effect on the other."[23] In so arguing she seemed to conclude that action should be free of even purely political goals (e.g., persuading one's opponents) as well as nonpolitical ones, which is characteristic of the binds into which she sometimes fell. Politics is also different, she argued, from violence, which is always instrumental in nature. It is moreover unlike authority, which relies on the coercion, albeit legitimized, of religion, tradition, or other nonpolitical factors. In fact, authority was a Roman invention, the Greek *polis* having operated on the principle of persuasion rather than coercion.[24] If politics has any analogy outside itself, it is to the performing arts where virtuosity is its own ephemeral end. "The theater is the political art par excellence; only there is the political sphere of human life transposed into art. By the same token, it is the only art whose sole object is man in his relationship to others."[25]

Among the most significant constraints on politics which Hannah Arendt and the political existentialists alike found objectionable is rationalism. In her reading of the Greek experience, it is Socrates who introduced an illegitimately rationalist element where none had previously existed. The "public space" of the *polis* was one in which a plurality of views and opinions were tolerated and discussed without any attempt to distinguish among them according to transcendent criteria of truth or falsehood, rationality or irrationality. The search for truth was always done in isolation; politics was the realm of intersubjective opinion. In celebrating the political experience of the pre-Socratic Greeks, Hannah Arendt paralleled Heidegger's resurrection of the pre-Socratic philosophers with his concomitant denigration of *Logos*. In so doing, she arrived at a type of "positive" freedom very different from that dangerous identification of freedom with rational necessity so abhorred by liberal opponents of the term such as Sir Isaiah Berlin.[26] Like Rousseau, Hegel, Marx, Lukács, and other "positive" freedom proponents, she disliked the privatized, internal "negative" alternative stemming from Christianity and defended by liberalism, but she refused to accept their positing of a congruence between general and particular wills or interests. Freedom, she maintained, is the opposite of necessity, not its handmaiden. Pluralism, not unity, is the precondition for its maintenance. Montesquieu and Tocqueville were among the few modern theorists whose recognition of this reality ties them to the pre-Socratic Greeks.

Not surprisingly, one of her major philosophical heroes was Lessing, whose defiant embrace of relativism she praised.[27] For the same reason, Jaspers' psychology of *Weltanschauungen* with its justification for universal relativism earned him high marks.[28] Acting in the name of reason, she contended, is applying the criterion of *homo faber* to the realm of action because it entails the positing of an essential model to follow. Like the existentialists, she was anxious to avoid adopting a normative view of essential man; only the "human condition," not human nature, can be meaningfully discussed. Whether Platonic or Cartesian, Kantian or Hegelian, a philosophy that tries to introduce rational considerations into the *vita activa's* highest mode, political action, is in the service of oppression.

Finally, Hannah Arendt drew on the political existentialist tradition in viewing history as an illegitimate source of constraints on freedom. In her 1946 essay, she applauded Husserl's success in freeing modern philosophy from "the fetters of historicism."[29] Here a possible analogy with Burke suggested by Margaret Canovan fails to hold, for although she shared Burke's appeal to artifice over nature, she lacked his sense of the historical concreteness of specific liberties, which were really privileges passed down from generation to generation. To a significant extent, political existentialism was directed against the prevailing historicist orthodoxy, bourgeois or Marxist, which dominated German thought from the time of Herder to the 1920s. The argument that everything must be dissolved in the solvent of history, whose dead hand weighs on the living present, seemed unnecessarily oppressive to an existentialist mentality proclaiming the permissibility and possibility of everything. What makes Hannah Arendt's version of the revolt against history novel is that it was directed not only against history understood as the working out of laws or trends outside of human control, an understanding which combined both religious and natural scientific impulses, but also against the alternative view that history is made by men. This latter assumption, which stems from Vico and informed Marxism, was objectionable to her because it reflects the view of man as *homo faber* creating a world of useful products rather than that of man as free actor. Vico's humanistic stress on the creative origins of history, so Hannah Arendt argued, mirrors the early modern world's new confidence in the power of technology, which involves the domination of nature and hence violence.

Miss Arendt's faith in the possibility of cutting through the restraining bonds of the past makes one of the more controversial aspects of her analysis of totalitarianism less obscure, if still difficult to support. Although she treated Nazism and Stalinism in solely systemic terms as the incursion of the most automatic processes of society into the political realm, she nonetheless argued that totalitarianism operates on the premise that men can be made entirely anew. In other words, for the Enlightenment's belief in the infinite perfectibility of man, totalitarianism substitutes an infinite degradability. Underlying both, however, is a common disregard for the intractibility of historical conditioning and the limits of human nature. That Hannah Arendt accepted the premise that totalitarianism does indeed represent a remaking of man in wholly new terms, which is best shown in the concentration camps,[30] illustrates her scorn for the historical limitations resisting such a total transformation. Like the existentialists, she tended to believe in unlimited human malleability with little regard for historical constraints, even if at times she came to share the existentialists' grudging acknowledgment of the power of "situation" to qualify that freedom.

Hannah Arendt's animus toward society, history, reason, utilitarianism, and essentialism all coalesced in what Canovan calls her "continuous dialogue"[31] with Marx, an interchange that justifies more than cursory comment. Like the political existentialists, she sought a way to transcend the left-right, socialism-capitalism alternatives bequeathed by the nineteenth century, and in so doing go beyond Marxism. In her reply to Gershom Scholem's attack on *Eichmann in Jerusalem,* she wrote: "I came late to an understanding of Marx's importance because I was interested neither in history nor in politics when I was young. If I can be said to 'have come from anywhere,' it is from the tradition of German philosophy."[32] Precisely when she began to read Marx seriously is difficult to determine, but what is clear is that she absorbed a now old-fashioned interpretation of Marx which she tenaciously defended until her death. It is the Marx of the Second International, which is still current in orthodox Communist circles, although scarcely anywhere else. As she stated in *Between Past and Future,* the separation of Marx from Engels' interpretation of him, "an opinion current among Marx scholars,"[33] is one she rejected. Since she wrote those words, the "opinion" has become the new orthodoxy with commentators like Lichtheim, Avineri, Schmidt, Rubel, Fetscher, and McClellan[34] endorsing the insight Lukács and Korsch had in the early 1920s. Although there are some residual difficulties, such as explaining why Marx allowed Engels to publish the unfortunate *Anti-Dühring* without apparent objection, the weight of evidence brought to light in the past decade makes her insistence indefensible.

Yet to abandon it would undermine what is essentially the Marxist straw man she attacked. In her last years, she was willing to grant the possibility of an "early" and "late" Marx,[35] although the publication of the *Grundrisse* has served to call that distinction into question, just as it has reinforced the Marx-Engels gap.

By holding on to what can be called a discredited view of Marx, she was able to accuse him of several basic failings. First, although recognizing that Marx restored the predominance of the *vita activa,* she argued that he raised the wrong one of its modes to the highest status: that of man as *animal laborans,* whose sole concern is the reproduction of the conditions for biological survival. This means that Marx in her understanding is best categorized as a *Lebensphilosoph* in the tradition of Nietzsche and Bergson.[36] That is, his highest value is life itself, rather than the "world" of crafted artifacts or the remembrance of great deeds in the public realm:

Within a completely "socialized mankind," whose sole purpose would be the entertaining of the life process—and this is the unfortunately quite unutopian idea that guides Marx's theories—the distinction between labor and work would have completely disappeared; all work would have become labor because all things would be understood, not in their worldly, objective quality, but as results of living labor power and functions of the life process.[37]

There is, of course, something to be said for the contention that Marx glorified labor in a way that reduced other human activities to aspects of the labor process. But what must be understood is that for Marx labor was far more than the reproduction of the conditions necessary for biological survival. It entailed precisely what Miss Arendt designated as work: the creation of a world of objects through man's interaction with nature. It is thus incorrect to state the Marx's goal was the reduction of work to labor when what he wanted was the overcoming of the reified quality of objectification under capitalism, not objectification *per se.* As her treatment of reification as a necessary component in all fabrication indicates, she failed to perceive the crucial distinction Marx makes between objectification and reification. In fact, she mistranslated *Vergegenständlichung* (objectification) as reification,[38] whereas that word is more correctly the translation of *Verdinglichung.* Rather than championing *animal laborans,* Marx was a believer in the power of man as a *homo faber,* as Avineri has shown in the chapter he devotes to that concept.

However, Hannah Arendt might have conceded this point and still argued that Marx's work was pernicious because of its reduction of politics to the socioeconomic realm. In several places in her writing, she contended that Marx wanted the public realm to "wither away" with the triumph of socialism.[39] This familiar argument is unfortunate for two reasons. First, the phrase "withering away" was used by Engels in his *Anti-Dühring ("der Staat wird nicht 'abgeschafft,' er stirbt ab")*[40] and not by Marx, who consistently used the term *Aufhebung* instead. As is well known, *Aufhebung* implies preservation as well as cancellation and transcendence. Secondly, even if one accepts Engels' formula as representing his friend's thought, the phrase "withering away" refers to the state, not politics as a whole. That the two need not be equated is clear in Hannah Arendt's own call for the replacement of the sovereign nation-state by a federated system of councils, which of course would foster political life.[41] What Marx wanted was the transcendence of the Hegelian distinction between civil society and the state, bourgeois "man" and the citizen, not the reduction of the state to society or the political citizen to natural man. Although one may share Hannah Arendt's skepticism about reconciling these oppositions under communism, it is simply misleading to chastise Marx for sociological reductionism. Moreover, and this is the third argument against her, there are abundant passages in Marx's concrete historical writings, most notably in *The Eighteenth Brumaire,* where he recognizes the relative autonomy of the political sphere at certain moments in history. That he was far more cynical about its serving as the arena for public freedom before the end of capitalism is another matter; what is crucial to note is that his image of man, either in the present or in some communist future, was far more than that of *animal laborans.*

Hannah Arendt's blindness on this point was reflected in her inexplicable neglect of twentieth-century Marxist theoreticians such as Gramsci, Korsch, Pannekoek, and Lefebvre, who have found in Marx's work a philosophy of *praxis* rather than a theory of economic determinism. That she was perhaps somewhat aware of this potential in Marxism can be argued from her very positive attitude toward Rosa Luxemburg, whose endorsement of the council movement and criticism of the Bolsheviks she applauded. But her grasp of the history of Marxist theory must be judged uncertain as she neglected to acknowledge the extent to which Rosa Luxemburg was still beholden to the economism of her Orthodox opponents in the Second International. In fact, Rosa Luxemburg's polemic with Lenin must be understood not merely as a critique of his dictatorial methods, but also as a warning against seizing the political initiative before economic conditions are ripe. Margaret Canovan fails to go beyond the misunderstanding of her subject when she writes: "Much of *On Revolution* is strongly reminiscent of the views of Rosa Luxemburg: the emphasis on the spontaneity of revolution as against theories of historical necessity or professional planning."[42] What she misunderstands is that the spontaneity Rosa Luxemburg championed meant the unforced combination of objective and subjective factors produced by the logic of capitalism and raising the consciousness of the working class. It did not mean a purely subjectivist, political intervention into the course of history. One cannot imagine Rosa Luxemburg praising the American Revolution in the way that Hannah Arendt did in *On Revolution:* "the course of the American Revolution tells an unforgettable story and is apt to teach a unique lesson: for this revolution did not break out but was made by men in common deliberation and on the strength of mutual pledges."[43] Although it is true that she emphasized the subjective factor in revolutions far more than her less radical counterparts in the Second International, Rosa Luxemburg never succeeded in reconciling this side of her theory with her equally firm commitment to mechanical materialism.[44] In this sense, she was a transitional figure and Miss Arendt would have done better to seek allies among more recent theoreticians of *praxis.*

There is one final point to be made about Hannah Arendt's "continuous dialogue" with Marx, which concerns one of her major preoccupations, the question of violence. In her lexicon, it will be recalled, violence is understood as inherently nonpolitical because of its instrumental character. It is conceptually distinct from power, which involves men acting without coercion on the basis of equality, although in practice power and violence often exist together. In *Between Past and Future* (1961), she berated Marx for assuming violence is the midwife of history:

To Marx . . . violence or rather the possession of the means of violence is the
constituent element of all forms of government; the state is the instrument of the
ruling class by means of which it oppresses and exploits, and the whole sphere
of political action is characterized by the use of violence.[45]

**But by the time of _Crises of the Republic_ (1972), she had reversed her-
self entirely and now claimed Marx in support of her distinction:**

The strong Marxist rhetoric of the New Left coincides with the steady growth of
the entirely non-Marxian conviction, proclaimed by Mao Tse-Tung, that "Power
grows out of the barrel of a gun." To be sure, Marx was aware of the role of
violence in history, but this role was to him secondary.[46]

**Sartre, she goes on to argue, is thus far closer to Sorel and Fanon than
he is to Marx because of his endorsement of political violence.**

    **What is important about this reversal is not the fact that she
was guilty of a self-contradiction, which is inevitable in such a large body
of work, but rather the warning it provides to follow her reasoning in
this area with an eye open for other inconsistencies. They are in fact
not hard to find. In her discussion of _homo faber,_ Miss Arendt argued
that the violence done to the natural material fashioned into a human-
ized product is necessarily entailed in any act of fabrication. In what is
normally seen as the political realm, the chief act of fabrication is that
of the secure founding of a polity, which provides the public space necessary for the exercise of freedom. In _On Revolution,_ she emphasized
the necessity of such a foundation for a stable society, which is one reason she preferred the American to the French Revolution. The prototype of all foundings is that of Rome, which she first described in _Be-
tween Past and Future_ as free of violence:**

Like the Romans, Machiavelli and Robespierre felt founding was the central political action . . . but unlike the Romans, to whom this was an event of the past,
they felt that for this supreme "end" all "means," and chiefly the means of violence, were justified. They understood the act of founding entirely in the image
of making. . . . [It is] because of his rediscovery of the foundation experience
and his _reinterpretation_ of it in terms of the justification of (violent) means for a
supreme end, that Machiavelli may be regarded as the ancestor of modern revolutions. [Italics added][47]

**By _On Revolution,_ however, she realized that the Roman experience of
founding also had a violent element expressed in the legend of Romulus's slaying of Remus.[48] But her uneasiness about overemphasizing the
violent nature of the act of founding led her to observe:**

It was perhaps because of the inner affinity between the arbitrariness inherent in
all beginnings, and human potentialities for crime that the Romans decided to

derive their descendence not from Romulus, who had slain Remus, but from Aeneas.[49]

Although she admitted that even Aeneas had been involved in a war with the native Italians, she excused this by saying that according to Virgil, his war was fought to undo the earlier war against Troy. The point of this argument is that even the foundation of Rome harkened back to an earlier tradition, but what comes through far clearer is the affinity between beginnings and violence.

What makes this point worth stressing is that such an affinity serves to muddy her distinction between violence and politics, the latter having been defined over and over again in terms of the capacity to begin. By *Crises of the Republic,* the confusion was total as she wrote:

A characteristic of human action is that it always begins something new, and this does not mean that it is ever permitted to start *ab ovo,* to create *ex nihilo.* In order to make room for one's own action, something that was there before must be removed or destroyed, and things as they were before are changed.[50]

Thus the watertight separation between violence and politics proves in the end to be porous, and we are left with the age-old suspicion that the violence at the origin of a polity lingers beneath the surface however legitimate its foundation may appear to later generations.

If, then, one can say that Hannah Arendt's grasp of Marx, her chief polemical rival, was uncertain, and that her distinction between politics and violence is less than convincing, how satisfactory was the remainder of her political theory? Can her brand of "tender" political existentialism be said to have surmounted the difficulties encountered by her "tough" predecessors in the 1920s? Was she merely a proselytizer for what Benjamin Schwartz has dubbed "the religion of politics," or did she provide what Margaret Canovan calls "both a new and noteworthy example of political thought, and also a demonstration that that genre is by no means dead."[51] The short answer, at least for this writer, is that despite the obvious breadth of her knowledge and the unquestionable ingenuity of her mind, the political thought of Hannah Arendt is ultimately as problematic as her historical scholarship. Built on a foundation of arbitrary definitions and questionable, if highly imaginative, interpretations of history and previous political thought, her system is vulnerable to many of the objections that led to the shipwreck of her political existentialist predecessors.

A chief source of this failure is what Canovan recognizes as the "lop-sided" quality of her theory. That is, in trying to restore the relative autonomy of politics in the face of sociological reductionism and the growing domination of society itself, she left herself vulnerable to a number of obvious charges. By locating freedom and equality exclusively in the political realm, she condemned *by definition* the nonpolitical to eternal inequality and oppression.[52] As she frankly conceded, the *polis,* her favorite prototype of a political community, was made possible by the institution of slavery which liberated the full citizens of Athens from the household, which was ruled by necessity. In the modern world, where slavery is harder to justify, private property is the *sine qua non* for political participation. The obviously class-oriented nature of this argument is mitigated only marginally by Hannah Arendt's admission that:

Our problem today is not how to expropriate the expropriators, but, rather, how to arrange matters so that the masses, dispossessed by industrial society in capitalist and socialist systems, can regain property.[53]

What makes this statement untenable is the assumption that the masses once had sufficient property to free them for political action, which they should now "regain." What makes it even more objectionable is that she provided no means whatsoever to help in this reappropriation, for in *On Revolution,* she categorically stated that: "Nothing, we might say today, could be more obsolete than to attempt to liberate mankind from poverty by political means; nothing could be more futile and more dangerous."[54]

The modern unleashing of economic forces which might serve as a precondition for the universalizing of private property she equated with the victory of wealth over property, by which she meant the glorification of productivity, consumption, and abundance rather than a stable and secure holding in the world. Although one can sympathize with her criticism of unbounded economic growth as an answer to social dilemmas, without at least some expansion of the wealth of society, no universalization of private property is even remotely possible. Because of her general hostility to the world of *animal laborans,* she failed to give a convincing social and economic basis to her political utopia.

The result is that Hannah Arendt left herself vulnerable to the charge of elitism, even though she rejected the label in *On Revolution:*

My quarrel with the "elite" is that the term implies an oligarchic form of government, the domination of the many by the rule of a few. From this, one can only conclude—as indeed our whole tradition of political thought has concluded—that the essence of politics is rulership and that the dominant political passion is the passion to rule or to govern. This, I propose is profoundly untrue.[55]

What makes this defense implausible is that even granting the possibility of an isonomic interaction among the members of a political élite, it is disingenuous to call the relationship between those happy few and the rest of the population anything but hierarchical and elitist. It would be little consolation for the masses on the bottom of the heap, as little as it must have been for Athenian slaves, to be reassured that their inferiority was incidental to the "essence, the very substance of their [masters'] lives, which is freedom."[56] It would be even less to hear that their oppression cannot be justly called political, because *by definition* politics cannot oppress. What is nonpolitical, she argued, need not concern itself with equality: "It may be that ancient political theory, which held that economics, since it was bound up with the necessities of life, needed the rule of masters to function, was not so wrong after all."[57]

Hannah Arendt's insensitivity to this issue is captured at its most perverse in her observation that the failure to confront the question of slavery in the American Revolution was a key source of its "success," when it is clear that that "success" has been mocked by that neglect ever since.[58] One can only surmise an unfeeling disdain for the nonpolitical masses, which is also reflected in *ex cathedra* statements such as:

The hidden wish of poor men is not "To each according to his needs," but "To each according to his desires." And while it is true that freedom can come only to those whose needs have been fulfilled, it is equally true that it will escape those who are bent upon living from their desires.[59]

What is questionable in this passage is not the defensible insight that unlimited desires can produced unintended misery, but rather the assumption that the ethic of infinite wants is a function of poverty, as if rich men through the centuries have known when to stop when their "needs" were satisfied. The poor are not so much the source of the consumption ethic as its worst victims, especially under an advanced capitalism so dependent on the perpetual creation of new desires. How we are to distinguish between legitimate needs and illegitimate wants is, of course, another matter, and one which Hannah Arendt's work never attempts to address.

But even if one were to accept Hannah Arendt's pessimism about extending the free life of the *polis* beyond a select few, there are still considerable difficulties in her normative description of political action. Both conceptually and historically, her view of politics as a performing art utterly uncorrupted by extraneous considerations is without foundation.Conceptually, as we have seen earlier, her stress on the

importance of beginnings in action led her perilously close to the de-
structive violence she was at pains to distinguish from the truly political. Moreover, there is a further irony in the fact that the very "aestheticization of politics" she championed may well have a special affinity
for violence, as her friend Walter Benjamin warned during the fascist
era.[60] Similarly, her frequent insistence on birth, or "natality" as she insisted on calling it, as the prototype of these beginnings ties action to
the rhythms of the natural world, which she usually denigrated as the
sphere of the *animal laborans*.[61] Likewise, her assertion that politics
and utilitarianism are incompatible is undercut by her acknowledge-
ment that the men of the *polis* did have an implicit goal beyond the
sheer joy of political participation: the achievement of worldly immortality through the performance of glorious and memorable deeds.[62] Such
an admission, of course, begs an important question, for how can the
criteria used to establish what are "glorious and memorable deeds" escape being nonpolitical themselves?

Hannah Arendt failed to ask this question because of the implicit existentialist premises of her argument. Thus in 1946 *Partisan Review* essay on *Existenzphilosophie,* she asserted that without a secure,
objective reality, a Being, in which truth can be said to reside, the only
suitable response is a kind of heroism: "The hero's gesture has not ac-
cidentally become *the* pose of philosophy since Nietzsche; it requires
heroism to live in the world as Kant left it."[63] Later in that piece, she
endorsed Jaspers' call for an "unconditioned deed that invokes
transcendence"[64] as the way to assert man's freedom in "extreme situations." All that was missing was her subsequent insistence that the only
arena in which such "unconditioned deeds" can be performed is the political, and that was not far behind when she argued:

This "deed" arising out of extreme situations appears in the world through communication with others, who as my fellows and through the appeal to our common reason guaranteed the universal; through activity it carries out the freedom
of Man in the world and becomes thereby "a seed, though perishing, of the
creation of a world."[65]

To a political existentialist, glory and heroism may seem self-evident
values indistinguishable from the political life itself, but others who have
entered the public realm for less self-centered and melodramatic reasons may well demur. Although one might accept the notion of the banality of evil, to assume that banality is itself evil is another matter. Indeed, one might wonder if Hannah Arendt had not adopted some of the
Prussian values a Berlin Jew struggling with her own identity might absorb through a kind of "identification with the aggressor," just as Rahel

Varnhagen surrounded herself with a salon of powerful and worldly gentiles a century before.

Such an *ad hominem* speculation, however, is not even necessary to undercut her argument, for this can be done from some of her own insights in other contexts. Thus, as she stressed in *The Origins of Totalitarianism,* one of the most sinister characteristics of totalitarian systems, best shown in the Nazi attitude towards the Jews, is their indifference to utilitarian considerations. A politics that is oblivious to the means-ends continuum and the consequences of its actions risks descending into the realm of fantasy in which the inexorable logic of an ideology can justify even self-destructive behavior. The "expressive" moment of politics need not be seen as the absolute negation of the instrumental.

Similarly, Hannah Arendt's insistence that rationalism and the search for truth have no place in the public realm left her, as it did the political existentialists of the 1920s, with no defense against an untruthful, self-deceptive politics, whose consequences she recognized in her essay on the Pentagon Papers.[66] Having earlier concluded that "our ability to lie—but not necessarily our ability to tell the truth—belongs among the few obvious, demonstrable data that confirm human freedom" and accordingly that there was an "undeniable affinity of lying with action, with changing the world—in short with politics,"[67] she was essentially defenseless against the charge that the totalitarian politics of the "big lie" and her own vision of an ideal politics were curiously alike. Her attempt to argue that factual as opposed to theoretical truth provided an outer limit on the practice of lying because of the stubborn irreversibility of facts was a weak resolution to this problem for she admitted that "contingent" facts are "never compellingly true."[68] Once again her reliance on idiosyncratic definitions—the search for truth, she tells us, is an isolated, singular activity, whereas the essence of politics is discursive, intersubjective opinion-sharing—led her into dangerous waters.

If examined historically, her examples of pure political action prove equally uncertain. Thus, as Schwartz has pointed out, she never reflected on the source of the Socratic turn away from the life of the *polis* in the name of reason: "Is it possible," he asks, "that, living as closely as they did to the 'public space' of the Athenian assembly, they were aware that the public realm offers no escape from the self-interest, lowly intrigues, and what seems to have been the manipulations of some of those whom they called sophists?"[69] When it comes to Machiavellian *virtu* Hannah Arendt offered no real evidence to show that its pursuit remained unsullied by the more mundane issues of Renaissance politics. Similarly, in her discussion of the American Revolution, she admitted that the major activity of the founding fathers was the creation of a constitution, which, by her definition, puts them under the sign of *homo faber*. Indeed, all legislation, as she saw it, is nonpolitical because of its constitutive function. Finally, her appeal to the councils, soviets, and *Räte* as examples of man's persistent desire for a public space in which to speak and act in the hope of attaining worldly immortality, although not without its virtues, can only be judged as historically inaccurate. Workers' councils, as the name implies, were designed from the very first to seize economic power at the factory site itself. Nonetheless, Hannah Arendt chastised the councils for betraying the purely political goal she assigned them:

The fatal mistake of the councils has always been that they themselves did not distinguish clearly between participation in public affairs and administration or management of things in the public interest. In the form of workers' councils, they have again and again tried to take over the management of the factories, and all these attempts have ended in dismal failure.[70]

But in *Crises of the Republic,* after reiterating her belief that collective ownership is a contradiction in terms, she conflated workers' management and the political role of the councils:

In Yugoslavia we have the "system of self-management" in the factories, a new version of the old "workers' councils," which, incidentally, also never became part of orthodox socialist or communist doctrine—despite Lenin's "all power to the *soviets.*"[71]

Thus, the "fatal mistake" of mixing economics and politics seems not so fatal after all, and once again the absolute purity of the political proves an unworkable myth. Her search for an historical embodiment of Jaspers' "extreme situation" in which "unconditional deeds" were committed was ultimately fruitless.

With all of these failings, it might seem as if the object of all the recent eulogizing may well be as forgotten in a few years as Alfred Bäumler or Carl Schmitt is today. Even the tempered admiration of Margaret Canovan may seem premature when Hannah Arendt's role as a latter-day political existentialist is put in its proper perspective. And yet, although the burden of my argument would seem to endorse this prediction, my intuition is that she will have a somewhat higher reputation among future intellectual historians than her predecessors now enjoy. First, because of her unerring instinct for the issues that excite public controversy, her place is secure in any history of the New York intellectual community over the last quarter century. The furor over the Eichmann book alone justifies her centrality in any account of the intellectual migration of Central European Jews to America, as has in fact been recognized in H. Stuart Hughes' recent *The Sea Change.*[72] She will also have an inevitable role in any history of Cold War ideology because of her seminal role in establishing the category of totalitarianism to cover systems of both the left and right. And paradoxically, she will also have to be included in accounts of the New Left for her theoretical legitimation of its political existentialist impulse, even though its aestheticization of politics ultimately led to an excess she came to deplore.

Secondly, the type of political theorizing in which she engaged will continue to serve for many as a welcome bulwark against the engulfing tide of political science, as well as a reminder that the political need not be reduced to the question "who governs?"[73] Although it is questionable to identify the free interaction Hannah Arendt applauded with some ideal political community and damn the rest as society (just as it is inaccurate to condemn all sociology as anti-interactionist), there is real value in arguing that wherever one may find what she calls political action, it is inappropriate to subsume it under the same categories used to explain processes or structures. Uncoerced, symmetrically organized communication which leads to the creation of shared meanings is not equivalent to the technical, instrumental, utilitarian relations that characterize so much of human interaction.

The fruitfulness of this distinction, which is one of the healthier legacies of the hermeneutic and existentialist movements, is perhaps most apparent in the work of Jürgen Habermas, the leading member of the Frankfurt School's second generation. Habermas' debt to Hannah Arendt has rarely been noticed, but in both *Strukturwandel der Öffentlichkeit* and *Theorie und Praxis,* he cited *The Human Condition* with approval, crediting it (along with the work of Hans-Georg Gadamer) for calling his attention to the Aristotelian distinction between *techne* and *praxis.*[74] Without rigidly absolutizing the difference between politics and society, Habermas has pursued the foundations of the type of communicative interaction Miss Arendt endorsed by drawing on a combination of philosophical sources from Hegel to Wittgenstein. He has, however, avoided the *politique pour la politique* dilemma by linking communicative competence in an undistorted speech situation to an emancipatory cognitive interest that embraces all men, not merely a political elite. Unlike Hannah Arendt, Habermas has been keenly aware of the social preconditions which may make such a utopian communicative situation possible. As he wrote in a review of *On Revolution:*

We can meaningfully discuss the conditions of political freedom only in connection with an emancipation from domination. This category of domination must not separate political force *(Gewalt)* from social power *(Macht),* but instead must show them as they both are: as repression. Under conditions of social dependency the best right to political freedom remains ideology. On the other hand, Hannah Arendt insists with good reason that the realization of welfare does not correspond to the emancipation from domination.[75]

Hannah Arendt must also be praised for her attempt to rescue the notion of freedom from its purely "negative" interpretation, although she was wrong to deny the moment of "freedom from" in any more embracing definition of that term. To have a non-Marxist theorist stress the importance of ending political alienation and realize that an intersubjective definition of freedom has something to be said for it is a refreshing change from the conventional state of affairs. As all observers have noted, Hannah Arendt was difficult to place along any normal left-right political axis (as in certain respects the political existentialists were as well), which means that reading her works requires a healthy suspension of received notions about our range of choices. And lastly, Miss Arendt will continue to be consulted by students of our era because of her frequently trenchant analyses of topical issues, many of which transcend the limitations of her more basic theoretical position.

But having allowed these strengths, what must finally be recognized is that the version of the human condition on which all her work rested will simply not wash. Despite her intention to restore the proper notion of freedom, Hannah Arendt's stubborn insistence on the split between society and polity undermined whatever hope her theory might have had for illuminating the conditions under which that freedom could be realized. Political existentialism was an obfuscating ideology in the 1920s, and one not entirely blameless in the rise of fascism; it must be judged no less of an ideology half a century later, although luckily its potential to blight our lives is far smaller than it was when Hannah Arendt, ironically fleeing from fascism, first succumbed to its dangerous charms.

15.

Remembering Henry Pachter

My first encounter with Henry Pachter came, characteristically enough, through an angry letter to the editor. I had just published a review in *Commentary* of Istvan Deak's *Weimar Germany's Left-Wing Intellectuals.* The year was 1969 and *Commentary* had yet to take its turn to the right. So I was permitted, with full awareness of the parallels often drawn between Weimar and the America of that era, to praise Deak's sympathetic account of the *Weltbühne* circle's rejection of the Republic in its waning years. It was my first foray into the heady world of New York intellectual journalism, in fact only my second piece in print, and so I was both flattered and distressed by the indignant response it aroused in so distinguished a reader as Professor Pachter. His personal stake in the historical episode involved had been, to put it mildly, much greater than my own, and it seemed to him the height of irresponsibility to defend the *Weltbühne's* abandonment of a democratic government, however imperfect, in the name of an illusory proletarian revolution. In my response, I tried to argue that by the early 1930s and the suspension of parliamentary government by Hindenberg, it was no less an illusion to believe a moderate solution to the crisis of Weimar was probable. But Professor Pachter remained stubbornly unconvinced, and in yet another letter to the editor, which concluded with a reference to his own youthful radicalism, he forthrightly expressed his opinion of my political acumen: "I failed to see the difference then because I was young and inexperienced in politics. But if Mr. Jay, with all the benefit of hindsight, still does not understand the difference, he should not write about political affairs."

Such a peroration, needless to say, was not designed to spark

First published in *Salmagundi* (Spring-Summer 1981), vol. 52–53.

a friendship, but one soon did develop nonetheless. In October 1971, both of us delivered papers to the New School's conference on Weimar Culture, a remarkable gathering of notable exiles and those, like myself, who studied them. The general air of the meeting was celebratory, perhaps even a touch complacent. The survivors of the migration had now truly earned Peter Gay's characterization of their status before 1933 as outsiders who had become insiders. Professor Pachter, however, recoiled from what he perceived as the puffery of the proceedings. Mocking Karl Mannheim's celebrated comparison of Weimar and Periclean Athens, he told the increasingly uneasy audience:

Perhaps the Weimar Republic was not a Periclean Age after all, but the age of Marlene Dietrich. We were no great innovators, we were innovators on a small scale. We did not generate the great idea that might have led us out of the impasse in our social, economic, and political plight. Far from "freely floating," we were being floated and coaxed and pushed. We were a generation of first-rate mediocrities; never have there been so many brilliant failures, so many excellent second-raters.

Impressed by his iconoclastic vigor (and relieved·to see that his testiness was not reserved for benighted defenders of the Weimar Left alone) I sought him out. We had a spirited and useful discussion, what in diplomatic circles is often called a "frank exchange of views," centering on the work I was then doing on the Frankfurt School. Professor Pachter's estimation of its achievement was somewhat less positive than my own, but I was deeply impressed by his willingness, even eagerness, to argue with an open mind on the issues involved. In my book on the subject, which appeared eighteen months later, I was happy to incorporate several of his points.

But, soon after, I discovered that he had much more to say about the subject than had been possible standing outside the New School that October afternoon. In a long and detailed letter, he scolded me for not having dealt in greater depth with the *Institut Für Sozialforschung's* first decade, when its links with Weimar's organized Left, most importantly the Communist Party, were still strong. In particular, he wanted to impress upon me how vital Karl Korsch had been in the *Institut's* early years, a fact that surviving *Institut* members had downplayed in their interviews. As for Horkheimer and the Frankfurt School properly speaking, he had only scorn:

The windings of Horkheimer's brains which you follow so faithfully are of no interest to the history of philosophy (even in the *Institut* sense of Ph.) and the whole enterprise was a failure, ideologically as you note yourself and in other respects too. Your book convinced me that Adorno and Horkheimer were literati of a peculiar kind which was even more remote from real life (even or *erst recht* if by real one means some Hegelian march of the world spirit) than ordinary bohemians. I am also struck by the lack of rigor in Horkheimer's philosophy. Your quotes, without exception, are pronouncements on what a desirable philosophy would look like, but nothing has been developed in any philosophical manner. Horkheimer was a guru who spoiled Adorno's real talents and Marcuse's later success came from his existentialist sources rather than from the Institut's philosophy.

These were sentiments, needless to say, I was not prepared to share, but I felt gratified that my account had generated so impassioned and extensive a reaction in someone whose opinion I valued. I was even more appreciative of another letter he wrote, this one for publication to *The New Republic,* protesting against a particularly inane and uninformed review of my book written, for mysterious reasons, by their poetry editor. It was enjoyable, for a change, to have the considerable power of his indignant wrath on my side.

    When I began my next subject, which also dealt with a German refugee he had known personally, Siegfried Kracauer, I did not wait for its completion before soliciting his views. Instead, I paid a visit, on an especially hot and muggy New York summer day, to his apartment on West 106th Street. We shared a very profitable few hours and my understanding of Kracauer's life and work was considerably deepened. I was especially happy to receive an approving letter from Henry, as he now called himself to me, when my first Kracauer article appeared in *Salmagundi*'s tenth anniversary issue in 1975–76. Consistent with his general attitude toward the migration, he singled out what he saw as my demonstration of "the tragedy of [Kracauer's] existence, best represented in the egregious failure of his last work."

    Aside from some later, less substantively interesting correspondence, these were the personal interactions I enjoyed with Henry Pachter, most of which were unfortunately epistolary rather than immediate because of the physical distance between us. Inconsequential as they may appear, I offer them for what should be seen as their emblematic character. For I am certain they were typical of other such relationships between Henry and members of my generation, for example Marshall Berman, Douglas Kellner, and Stephen Eric Bronner, for whom Henry also had a special importance. He was always more to us than the remote author of countless articles and a slew of books on subjects as diverse as the Cuban missile crisis, Nazi language, and Renaissance philosophy. For although he clearly had no use for the extremist wing of the New Left and indeed often fulminated against it, he was nonetheless anxious to share his experiences and views with those young radicals he felt were willing to learn from them. While it would be imprecise to call his attitude avuncular (at least none of my uncles was ever as acerbic and feisty), he felt a special responsibility to those of us trying to make sense of the history through which he himself lived. As he wrote to me in another letter, which was devoted to clarifying a relatively minor point about Lukács, "I wish to make you aware of this historical note since you are writing on the period and I am much concerned about the numerous misinterpretations one can read because people don't have access to the feel and smell of the period."

It must, however, have been a source of no small ambivalence for him to see that the attitudes of his youth, which in many ways he had outgrown, were not merely of historical interest, but also in part an inspiration to members of my generation. Henry clearly felt a certain pride in having been there and knew his value as a witness; as he wrote in a critique of Kellner's work on Korsch in *Telos,*

There is always a certain discrepancy between the personal recollections of participants in an historical action, and the historians (I am one myself) who must work on papers which are mere sediments of the whirling matter in the agitated waters of history. In the present case, memory is able to correct the shadowy evidence of the papers.

But ironically, his political evolution away from his leftist past, an evolution that he shared with so many other emigrés, meant that he resisted full identification with it. Thus, for the Kellner critique he resurrected the pseudonym he had first used during his days in Paris in the 1930s, Henri Rabasseire, in order to speak freely of his personal involvement in Korsch's ultraleft Communist faction. Although more than a half century had passed, he was apparently made anxious by the possible repercussions of such a disclosure, as if it were still the heyday of McCarthyism. Using a *nom de plume* was perhaps added insurance that Henry Pachter, the defender of liberal democracy both present and past, would not be mistaken for Heinz Paechter, the young *enragé* of a bygone era. Here, ironically, it might be noted in passing, he shared the same fears that dominated the later years of Max Horkheimer, who labored in vain to cover over his radical youth at a time when its rediscovery was a stimulus to contemporary admirers.

For those of us who were spared the agonies of Henry's generation, it would be presumptuous in the extreme to pass judgment on the complex reasons underlying this attitude. But it can perhaps be legitimately accounted a source of some sadness, for it exemplifies in a small way the costs of emigration, the dislocation in both senses of the word produced by the flight of Weimar culture. What Adorno in *Min-*

ima Moralia calls the "damaged lives" of his fellow emigrés took many forms. As Henry's sour reflections on the "failures" of the Frankfurt School, Kracauer, and the other "excellent second-raters" of his generation demonstrate, he was especially sensitive, perhaps exaggeratedly so, to the promises thwarted by the wrenching experience of migration. There may, in fact, have been some special significance in the pseudonym Rabasseire, with its echoes of the French word for discounting, although one can only conjecture. In his own case, the shortcircuiting of his active political career in his mid-twenties seems to have been particularly painful. As he once put it with a certain wistfulness in discussing his role in *Dissent,* "in practice . . . *Dissent* has been an ideological gadfly rather than a political animal, and to that extent I am engaged in American politics." But gratifying as this may have been on a certain level, it surely could not have been a complete substitute for that more immediate political engagement he had experienced in Weimar.

What that engagement must have meant to Henry came through in the special intensity that infused his interaction with politically inclined intellectuals of my generation. His deep concern for the current implications of what we wrote, his fierce determination to set the record straight when he thought we had gotten it wrong, and his willingness to call us to account when he detected irresponsible political posturing in our writing all bear witness to the high seriousness with which he took the practical effects of intellectual activity. At a time when many intellectuals seem willing to recloister themselves away from the political arena, his is a voice whose absence will be registered with a special keenness. I am certain I speak for many when I say how deeply I will miss those remarkable letters, incisive, sharp-tongued, combative, and written with an uncompromising integrity, that were Henry's special gift to both public and private intellectual life. The significant audience for whom we write has been immeasurably diminished by the loss of this one, unique reader.

Notes

Introduction

1. Roland Barthes, *Critical Essays*, trans. Richard Howard (Evanston: 1972), p. xi.

2. "Alienation Effects," *Midstream* (October 1972), 18(8): 72. In order to preserve the original state of the essays, I have resisted the temptation to make more than cosmetic changes in the texts or update the notes.

3. Another example is the essay I wrote for the memorial conference on Marcuse at the University of California, San Diego in March 1980. Published as "Anamnestic Totalization: Reflections on Marcuse's Theory of Remembrance" in *Theory and Society* (January 1982), 11(1), it would have been included in this collection had it not already served as the basis for the chapter on Marcuse in *Marxism and Totality: The Adventures of a Concept from Lukács to Habermas* (Berkeley, 1984).

4. Wolf Lepenies, "Transformation and Storage of Scientific Traditions in Literature," in *Literature and History*, eds. Leonard Schulze and Walter Wetzels (New York, 1983), p. 37–63.

5. *Ibid.*, p. 62.

6. *Midstream* (December 1969), 15(10).

7. Norman O. Brown, *Life Against Death: The Psychoanalytical Meaning of History* (New York, 1959), p. 318. Shortly after this passage was brought to my attention, I had the opportunity to talk with Professor Brown. When I tried to apologize for not having acknowledged it, he generously replied that he had forgotten about the phrase himself. In any event, it is gratifying to have the chance now to bring its provenance to light.

8. "Marcuse's Utopia," *Radical America* (April 1970),4(3); "Metapolitics of Utopianism," *Dissent* (July-August 1970), 17(4); "How Utopian is Marcuse?," *The Revival of American Socialism: Selected Papers of the Socialist Scholars Conference*, ed. George Fischer (New York, 1971).

9. *The Revival of American Socialism*, p. xii.

10. Theodore Draper, "The Specter of Weimar," *Social Research* (Summer 1972), 39(2) this volume contains other papers from the conference by Walter Laqueur, Henry Pachter, Wolfgang Sauer, Ivo Frenzel, Geoffrey Barraclough and Hans Morgenthau, as well as my own on "The Frankfurt School's Critique of Marxist Humanism."

11. *Tekla; Teori och klasskamp* (August 1982), 12/13. I am grateful to Lisbet Rausnig for having translated Anders Ramsay's introduction to the article, in which its function as a counterweight to Therborn is made clear. Therborn's "The Frankfurt School" first appeared in the *New Left Review* (September/October 1970), no. 63.

12. "Cultural Transplants," *Commentary* (March 1970), 49(3).

13. *Perspectives in American History* (Cambridge, Mass., 1972), vol. 6.

14. Review of Radkau, *Die deutsche Emigration in den USA: Ihr Einfluss auf die amerikanische Europapolitik 1933–1945* (Düsseldorf, 1971) in the *Journal of Modern History* (June 1973), 45(2).

15. *Telos* (Summer 1974), no. 20.

16. James Schmidt, "Critical Theory and the Sociology of Knowledge: A Response to Martin Jay," *Telos* (Fall 1974), 21:168–80.

17. "Crutches versus Stilts: A Reply to James Schmidt on the Frankfurt School," *Telos* (Fall 1974), no. 22; James Schmidt, "Reification and Recollection: Emancipatory Intentions and the Sociology of Knowledge," *Canadian Journal of Political and Social Theory* (Winter 1978), 2(1).

18. "The Concept of Totality in Lukács and Adorno," *Telos* (Summer 1977), no. 32. Paul Piccone and Andrew Arato reply in the same issue to this piece and to my "Further Considerations on Western Marxism," also in the same issue.

19. Seyla Benhabib, "Modernity and the Aporias of Critical Theory," *Telos* (Fall 1981), no. 49, and *Critique, Norm and Utopia: On the Normative Foundations of Critical Theory* (New York, 1985).

20. The remark is from Horkheimer's 1940 essay, "Authoritarian State" and is quoted by Schmidt on p. 179 of his essay.

21. See also the critique by Richard Kilminster, *Praxis and Method: A Sociological Dialogue with Lukács, Gramsci and the Early Frankfurt School* (London, 1979), p. 208.

22. For an example of the former position, see Zoltan Tar, *The Frankfurt School: The Critical Theories of Max Horkheimer and Theodor W. Adorno* (New York, 1977), which I reviewed in *Central European History* (March 1979), 12(1). For an example of the latter, see Douglas Kellner, "The Frankfurt School Revisited: A Critique of Martin Jay's "The Dialectical Imagination," *New German Critique* (Winter 1975), vol. 4.

23. For useful discussions of their attitudes, see Rudolf J. Siebert, "Fromm's Theory of Religion," *Telos* (Winter 1977–78), no. 34; "Horkheimer's Sociology of Religion," *Telos* (Winter 1976-77), no. 30; and "Adorno's Theory of Religion," *Telos* (Winter 1983–84), no. 58.

24. "Anti-Semitism and the Weimar Left," *Midstream* (January 1974), 20(1). For a suggestive extension of its argument, see John Murray Cuddihy, *The Ordeal of Civility: Freud, Marx, Lévi-Strauss and the Jewish Struggle with Modernity* (New York, 1979), p.153 f.

25. "Frankfurter Schule and Judentum; Die Antisemitismusanalyse der Kritischen Theorie," *Geschichte und Gesellschaft* (1979), 5(4).

26. *New German Critique* (Winter 1980), vol. 19.

27. Leo Lowenthal, *Mitmachen wollte ich nie: Ein autobiographisches Gespräch mit Helmut Dubiel* (Frankfurt, 1980), p. 156.

28. It appeared in *Telos* (Fall 1980), no. 45, although one of the articles intended for it, Sandor Radnoti's "Mass Culture," was not ready until issue 48 (Summer 1981). Perhaps it is appropriate to mention here as well another *Festschrift* for a former *Institut für Sozialforschung* figure to which I was privileged to contribute: that for Kurt Martin (Mandelbaum) in *Development and Change* (October 1979), 10(4).

29. An American edition is now being published by Transaction Press.

30. Wolfgang Bonss and Axel Honneth, eds., *Sozialforschung als Kritik: Zum sozialwissenschaftlichen Potential der Kritischen Theorie* (Frankfurt, 1982).

31. Helmut Dubiel, *Wissenschaftsorganisation und politische Erfahrung: Studien zur Frühen Kritischen Theorie* (Frankfurt, 1978), translation forthcoming from M.I.T. Press; Alfons Söllner, *Geschichte und Herrschaft: Studien zur materialistischen Sozialwissenschaft 1929–1942* (Frankfurt, 1979).

32. See, for example, Wolfgang Bonss, *Die Einübung des Tatsachenblicks: Zur Struktur und Veränderung empirischer Sozialforschung* (Frankfurt, 1982), p. 192

33. "Positive and Negative Totalities: Implicit Tensions in Critical Theory's Vision of Interdisciplinary Research," *Thesis Eleven* (1981), vol. 3.

34. Jürgen Habermas, "Einleitung zum Vortrag von Martin Jay," in *Adorno-Konferenz 1983*, eds. Ludwig von Friedeburg and Jürgen Habermas (Frankfurt, 1983), p. 353.

35. "Adorno in America," *New German Critique* (Winter 1984), vol. 31.

36. "The Loss of George Lichtheim," *Midstream* (October 1973), 19(8).

37. The essays from the conference were published as *Varieties of Marxism*, ed. Shlomo Avineri (The Hague, 1977); my own contribution was also published in *Telos* as "The Concept of Totality in Lukács and Adorno."

38. "The Extraterritorial Life of Siegfried Kracauer," *Salmagundi* (Fall 1975–Winter 1976), vol. 31–32.

39. "Politics of Translation—Siegfried Kracauer and Walter Benjamin on the Buber-Rosenzweig Bible," *Leo Baeck Yearbook* (London 1976), vol. 21.

40. "Adorno and Kracauer—Notes on a Troubled Friendship," *Salmagundi* (Winter 1978), vol. 40.

41. Margaret Canovan, *The Political Thought of Hannah Arendt* (New York, 1974).

42. Marcuse, "The Struggle Against Liberalism in the Totalitarian View of the State," *Negations: Essays in Critical Theory,* trans. Jeremy J. Shapiro (Boston, 1968), p. 31f; Habermas, *Theory and Practice,* trans. John Viertel (London, 1974), p. 266.

43. It was published as the opening part of "Hannah Arendt, Opposing Views," *Partisan Review* (1978), 45(3), without the footnotes, which are included in the version below.

44. Elisabeth Young-Bruehl, *Hannah Arendt: For Love of the World* (New Haven, 1982).

45. Young-Bruehl discusses this controversy on p. 359. It grew out of the journal's treatment of *Eichmann in Jerusalem* in 1963.

46. Botstein and I had another exchange in the *Partisan Review* letters column in (1979), 46(2). Other critiques included Gerard P. Heather and Matthew Stolz, "Hannah Arendt and the Problem of Critical Theory," *The Journal of Politics* (February 1979), 41(1), which elicited a rebuttal from John Forester, "Hannah Arendt and Critical Theory: A Critical Response," *The Journal of Politics* (February 1981), 43(1), and a counterrebuttal by Stolz and Heather, "Reply to Professor Forester" in the same issue; James T. Knauer, "Motive and Goal in Hannah Arendt's Concept of Political Action," *The American Political Science Review* (September 1980), 74(3), which also included critiques of the Arendt interpretations of Habermas and Kirk Thompson; and Stan Draenos, "The Totalitarian Theme in Horkheimer and Arendt," *Salmagundi* (Spring 1982), vol. 56.

47. "Hannah Arendt: Opposing Views," p. 368.

48. *Ibid.,* p. 379.

49. Knauer, p. 724; Heather and Stolz, "Reply to Professor Forester," p. 204.

50. *Partisan Review* (1979) 46(2):312.

51. Draenos, p. 167.

52. Mildred Bakan, "Hannah Arendt's Concepts of Labor and Work," in *Hannah Arendt: The Recovery of the Public World,* ed. Melvyn A. Hill (New York, 1979), p. 63.

53. Hannah Arendt, *The Life of the Mind* (New York 1978), 2:172f.

54. Stephen J. Whitfield, *Into the Dark: Hannah Arendt and Totalitarianism* (Philadelphia, 1980), p. 194.

55. See Carl Schmitt, *The Concept of the Political,* trans. with intro. by George Schwab (New Brunswick, N.J., 1976). Although the concept was different in the two cases to some extent, it is significant that both Arendt and Schmitt spoke of "the political" rather than politics in a more mundane sense. In my essay, I noted that Schmitt was a virtually forgotten figure, which now seems no longer to be the case. For my reflections on his career and recent attempts to whitewash it, see my review of Joseph W. Bendersky, *Carl Schmitt: Theorist for the Reich* (Princeton, 1983), *Journal of Modern History* (September 1984), 56(3).

56. The former is held, for example, by Botstein and Knauer, whereas the latter is defended by Heather and Stolz.

57. Young-Bruehl reports (p. 80) the source of the animosity between Arendt and Adorno as the latter's snub of her first husband Günther Stern's work on music in the 1920s. There is a small measure of irony in the fact that in 1983, the winner of the city of Frankfurt's Adorno Prize was none other than Günther Anders, who had been known as Stern when he was married to Arendt. Adorno's original remark, "in psychoanalysis, nothing is true except the exaggerations," was made in *Minima Moralia: Reflections from Damaged Life,* trans. E.F.N. Jephcott (London, 1974), p. 49.

58. Pachter, 'Heidegger and Hitler: The Incompatibility of Geist and Politics," in *Weimar Etudes* (New York, 1982). For Pachter's reminiscences of his friendship with Arendt and her second husband, see his "On Being in Exile" in the same collection, p. 326f.

59. "Remembering Henry Pachter," *Salmagundi* (Spring-Summer 1981), vol. 52–53; it was published after a much fuller memoir by Robert Boyers, who writes at length of Pachter's relation to *Salmagundi.*

60. H. Stuart Hughes, "Social Theory in a New Context," in *The Muses Flee Hitler: Cultural Transfer and Adaptation, 1930–45,* eds. Jarrell C. Jackman and Carla M. Borden (Washington, 1983), p. 120. See also Hughes's earlier study *The Sea Change: The Migration of Social Thought, 1930–1945* (New York, 1975).

61. The first volume was published in Munich in 1983 and was devoted to "Stalin und die Intellektuellen und andere Themen." The Society for Exile Studies also published a substantial newsletter in March 1984, edited by Ernst Loewy of Frankfurt. Among the most important recent books are Anthony Heilbut, *Exiled in Paradise: German Refugee Artists and Intellectuals in America from the 1930s to the Present* (New York, 1983) and Lewis A. Coser, *Refugee Scholars in America: Their Impact and Their Experiences* (New Haven, 1984).

1. The Metapolitics of Utopianism

1. *Marcuse: Cet Inconnu, La Nef* (January–March 1969), 36.

2. Herbert Marcuse, *An Essay on Liberation* (Boston, 1969), p. 22.

3. See, for example, Marcuse, "Contributions to a Phenomenology of Historical Materialism" (1928), published in English in *Telos* (Fall 1969), no. 4.

4. For a discussion of this problem see Alfred Schmidt, "Existential-Ontologie

und historischer Materialismus bei Herbert Marcuse," *Antworten auf Herbert Marcuse,* ed. Jürgen Habermas (Frankfurt, 1968).

    5. *One-Dimensional Man: Studies in the Ideology of Advanced Industrial Society,* (Boston, 1964), pp. 153–54.

    6. "The Struggle Against Liberalism in the Totalitarian View of the State," *Negations: Essays in Critical Theory,* (Boston, 1969), pp. 31–42.

    7. *Being and Nothingness,* trans. Hazel Barnes (New York, 1966), p. 364.

    8. *Negations,* pp. 135–36.

    9. "On Hedonism," *Negations,* p. 198.

    10. *Eros and Civilization* (Boston, 1955), p. 213.

    11. Marcuse, *Five Lectures* (Boston, 1970), p. 41.

    12. *Illuminations: Essays and Reflections,* trans. Harry Zohn (New York, 1968).

    13. See Alfred Schmidt, *Der Begriff der Natur in der Lehre von Marx* (Frankfurt, 1962).

    14. *Negations,* p. 238.

    15. In *Eros and Civilization* (pp. 214–15), he writes: "The death instinct operates under the Nirvana principle: it tends toward that state of 'constant gratification' where no tension is felt. . . . If the instinct's basic objective is not the termination of life but of pain—the absence of tension—then paradoxically, in terms of the instinct, the conflict between life and death is the more reduced, the closer life approximates the state of gratification. . . . As suffering and want recede, the Nirvana principle may become reconciled with the reality principle. The unconscious attraction that draws the instincts back to an 'earlier state' would be effectively counteracted by the desirability of the attained state of life."

    16. Hans Heinz Holz, *Utopie und Anarchismus: Zur Kritik der Kritischen Theorie Herbert Marcuses* (Cologne, 1968); George Lichtheim, "From Marx to Hegel: Reflections on Georg Lukács, T. W. Adorno, and Herbert Marcuse," *Triquarterly* (Spring 1968), no. 12.

    17. Herbert Read, "Rational Society and Irrational Art," *The Critical Spirit: Essays in Honor of Herbert Marcuse* ed. Kurt Wolff and Barrington Moore, Jr. (Boston, 1967).

    18. *Illuminations,* p. 244.

    19. When Marcuse first stressed the ontological centrality of labor in one of his early Heideggerian essays, his attitude toward play was less favorable than in *Eros and Civilization.* In play, he argued, the sway of the objective world over the free subject is suspended. Thus, unlike labor, play produces no permanent objectifications. It has no essential duration, existing in the "inbetween" separating true *praxis.* Nor does it express man's essentially historical nature. "First and only in labor," he wrote, "does man become historically real and win his specific place in historical occurrence." ("Über die philosophischen Grundlagen des Wirtschaftswissenschaftlichen Arbeitsbegriffs," *Archiv für Sozialwissenschaft und Sozialpolitik* [June 1933], 69(3):279.) Using his own reasoning against him, it might therefore be argued that his recent praise of play as a superior alternative to labor indicates an ahistorical strain in his thinking. I think it is more important to note that Marcuse's discovery of *Homo Ludens* in his recent work occurred against the background of his life-long conviction of the ontological importance of labor. This allows him to see play as resolving contradictions, as he once argued labor did, rather than creating new ones, as is the case when play is understood as related to what Habermas calls "symbolically-mediated interaction."

    20. *Reason and Revolution: Hegel and the Rise of Social Theory* (Boston, 1966), p. 78.

21. *Technik und Wissenschaft als "Ideologie"* (Frankfurt, 1968).
22. *Reason and Revolution,* p. 75.
23. *Technik und Wissenschaft als "Ideologie,"* p. 46.
24. Hannah Arendt, *The Human Condition* (Chicago, 1958), pp. 155–61.

2. The Frankfurt School's Critique of Marxist Humanism

1. The beginning of the "Hegel renaissance" is often traced back to Wilhelm Dilthey's *Die Jugendgeschichte Hegels* in 1906.
2. Merleau-Ponty uses this term in *Les Aventures de la Dialectique* (Paris, 1955). The relevant chapter has been translated into English in *Telos* (Fall 1970), no. 6.
3. Michel Crouzet first used this term and George Steiner picked it up in his *Language and Silence* (New York, 1967).
4. Perhaps the best definition of the term, and certainly the earliest, can be found in Marx's own writings. In the *Economic and Philosophic Manuscripts,* he wrote:

Communism as a fully developed naturalism is humanism and as a fully developed humanism is naturalism. It is the definite resolution of the antagonism between man and nature. It is the true solution of the conflict between existence and essence, between objectification and self-affirmation, between freedom and necessity, between individual and species. It is the solution of the riddle of history, and knows itself to be this solution.

(*Karl Marx: Early Writings,* trans. and ed. T. B. Bottomore [New York, 1963], p. 155.)
5. Lenin himself developed a strong interest in Hegel's *Logic* during World War I, but little of this filtered down to Bolshevik ideology in the subsequent years. On this question, see Raya Dunayevskaya, "The Shock of Recognition and the Philosophic Ambivalence of Lenin," *Telos* (Spring 1970), no. 5.
6. The Hungarian revolution in 1956 was the most important political stimulus of the discussion.
7. Reprinted in *Revisionism: Essays on the History of Marxist Ideas,* ed. Leopold Labedz (New York, 1962).
8. June 5, 1969. The article is unsigned, but Lichtheim is surely the author.
9. "A Critique of the Frankfurt School," *New Left Review* (September-October 1970), no. 63.
10. *Ibid.,* p. 70.
11. For Althusser's polemic against Marxist Humanism, see his *For Marx,* trans. by Ben Brewster (New York, 1970), pp. 219–47.
12. Therborn, "A Critique of the Frankfurt School," p. 77.
13. Marcuse has been the special target of this allegation. See, for example, Alasdair MacIntyre, *Herbert Marcuse: an Exposition and a Polemic* (New York, 1970), and Hans Heinz Holz, *Utopie und Anarchismus: Zur Kritik der kritischen Theorie Herbert Marcuses* (Cologne, 1968).
14. Therborn, "A Critique of the Frankfurt School," p. 79. Elsewhere in his essay, Therborn perceptively notes that the Frankfurt School concentrated on exchange rather than alienation or reification as the fundamental relation of capitalism. He fails, however, to draw the implications of this difference for the rest of his analysis. The dialectic of the Enlightenment was disliked by Horkheimer and Adorno precisely because it assumed the identity of interchangeable atoms in the social as well as natural universe. As will be made clearer below, hostility toward identity theory underlay the Frankfurt School's critique of humanism. Reification and alienation, which are humanist concepts, are by no means the same as the concept of exchange as the central reality of capitalist society.

15. New York, 1961. This volume contained the first complete edition of Marx's *Economic and Philosophic Manuscripts* to reach a wide audience in this country.

16. New York, 1965.

17. "Neue Quellen zur Grundlegung des historischen Materialismus," *Die Gesellschaft* (August 1932), 9(8).

18. New York, 1941.

19. "Socialist Humanism?," *Socialist Humanism,* ed. by Erich Fromm (New York, 1965), p. 111–13.

20. This became the name of the Frankfurt School's theoretical position after the publication of Horkheimer's essay "Traditionelle und kritische Theorie," *Zeitschrift für Sozialforschung* (1937), 6(2).

21. Therborn's admission that "comparatively little space has been devoted to Adorno" in his essay (p. 95) helps explain why he neglects the distance between Critical Theory and Marxist Humanism.

22. "Adorno—ein Philosoph des realen Humanismus," *Neue Rundschau* (1969), 80(4).

23. Horkheimer, "Bemerkungen zur philosophischen Anthropologie," *Zeitschrift für Sozialforschung* (1935), 4(1); Marcuse, "The Concept of Essence," *Negations: Essays in Critical Theory* trans. by Jeremy J. Shapiro (Boston, 1968), originally *Zeitschrift für Sozialforschung* (1936), 5(1).

24. Therborn, "A Critique of the Frankfurt School", p. 77.

25. "Über die philosophischen Grundlagen des wirtschaftwissenschaftlichen Arbeitsbegriff," *Archiv für Sozialwissenschaft und Sozialpolitik* (June 1933), 69(3).

26. See, especially, pp. 272ff.

27. *Man for Himself* (New York, 1947), p. 89ff.

28. *Dämmerung* (Zurich, 1934), p. 181. Accordingly, Horkheimer and Adorno were not convinced when Marx talked about the reconciliation of man and nature (see note 4) when in the same essay he would also write:

Industry is the actual historical relationship of nature, and thus of natural science, to man. If industry is conceived as the *exoteric* manifestation of the essential human *faculties,* the *human* essence of nature and the *natural* essence of man can also be understood. . . . nature, as it develops through industry, though in an *alienated* form, is truly *anthropological* nature. [Italics in original.]

(*Ibid.*, pp. 163–64).

29. *Negative Dialektik* (Frankfurt, 1966), p. 189.

30. *Technik und Wissenschaft als 'Ideologie'* (Frankfurt, 1969).

31. *History and Class Consciousness,* trans. by Rodney Livingstone (Cambridge, Mass., 1971), p. 237.

32. This was an integral part of the Frankfurt School's interpretation of fascism. See Horkheimer's *Eclipse of Reason* (New York, 1947) and Horkheimer and Adorno, *Dialektik der Aufklärung* (Amsterdam, 1947).

33. See, for example, Mihailo Marković, "Humanism and Dialectic," *Socialist Humanism,* ed. Erich Fromm, p. 85.

34. To be fair to Lukács, however, it is necessary to mention that his book contains a rejection of static philosophical anthropology:

By transforming philosophy into "anthropology," [Feuerbach] caused man to become frozen in a fixed objectivity and thus pushed both dialectics and history to one side. And precisely this is the great danger in every "humanism" or anthropological point of view. For if man is made the measure of all things, and if with the aid of that assumption all transcendence is to be eliminated without man himself being measured against this criterion, without applying the same "standard" to himself or—more exactly—without making man himself dialectical, then man himself is made into an absolute and he simply puts himself in the place of those transcendental forces he was supposed to explain, dissolve and systematically replace. (pp. 186–87)

Yet elsewhere in the text of *History and Class Consciousness,* Lukács permits himself to talk of a conception of nature as one in which

we can clearly discern the ideal and the tendency to overcome the problems of a reified existence. "Nature" here refers to authentic humanity, the true essence of man liberated from the false, mechanizing forms of society; man as a perfected whole who has inwardly overcome, or is in the process of overcoming, the dichotomies of theory and practice, reason and the senses, form and content; man whose tendency to create his own forms does not imply an abstract rationalism which ignores concrete content; man for whom freedom and necessity are identical. (pp. 136–37)

35. See chapter 1 above.

36. *Kierkegaard: Konstruktion des Aesthetischen,* 3d ed. (Frankfurt, 1962).

37. *Minima Moralia: Reflexionen aus dem beschädigten Leben* (Frankfurt, 1951), p. 80.

38. Adorno's study of Husserl, *Zur Metakritik der Erkenntnistheorie* (Stuttgart, 1956), which was written mostly during the 1930s, makes this point very frequently. It also appears in much of his cultural criticism. For example, in his study of Veblen, Adorno wrote: "As the reflection of truth, appearances are dialectical; to reject all appearance is to fall completely under its sway, since truth is abandoned with the rubble without which it cannot appear." (*Prisms,* trans. Samuel and Shierry Weber [London, 1967], p. 84).

39. *Prisms,* p. 106.

40. The first philosophical book Horkheimer ever read was Schopenhauer's *Aphorismen zur Lebensweisheit,* which Pollock gave him when they were in Brussels together before World War I. (Source: interview with Horkheimer in Montagnola, Switzerland, in March 1969).

41. Theodor W. Adorno, Else Frenkel-Brunswik, Daniel J. Levinson, and R. Nevitt Sanford (New York, 1950).

42. Letter from Horkheimer to Lowenthal, October 31, 1942 (in Lowenthal's personal collection).

43. His essays in the *Zeitschrift für Sozialforschung* have recently been translated and collected in *The Crisis of Psychoanalysis* (New York, 1970).

44. Boston, 1955.

45. Neil McInnes, "From Marx to Marcuse," *Survey* (Winter 1971), 16(1):153.

46. *Der Begriff des Unbewussten in der tranzendentalen Seelenlehre* (Ph.D. disc., University of Frankfurt, 1927).

47. Interview with Horkheimer in March 1969.

48. Frieda Reichmann had been Leo Lowenthal's personal analyst during the mid-twenties. He was, in fact, the first *Institut* figure to develop a serious interest in Freud.

49. See his article "Geschichte und Psychologie," *Zeitschrift für Sozialforschung* (1932), 1(1). Fromm remembers the change coming "only after the *Institut* had been for some time in New York, and maybe since I began to write *Escape from Freedom.*" Horkheimer then "became a defender of orthodox Freudianism, and considered Freud as a true revolutionary because of his materialistic attitude toward sex. . . . Horkheimer was also on very friendly terms with Horney in the first years of his stay in New York, and did not then defend orthodox Freudianism. It was only later that he made this change. . . . I assume partly this had to do with the influence of Adorno" (letter from Fromm to me dated May 14, 1971).

50. Letter from Horkheimer to Lowenthal dated October 31, 1942, in Lowenthal's files.

51. Fromm, it should be noted parenthetically, has always resented his inclusion in this group. See, for example, his remarks in Richard I. Evans, *Dialogue with Erich Fromm* (New York, 1966), p. 58.

52. In his *Die Entwicklung des Christusdogmas,* first published in *Imago* (1930), vol. 16, and translated as *The Dogma of Christ* (New York, 1963), Fromm spoke of the "character matrix common to all members of the group." By the time he wrote *Escape from Freedom* (New York, 1951), he was using the term "social character" to describe "a selection of traits, *the essential nucleus of the character structure of most members of a group which has developed as the result of the basic experiences and mode of life common to that group.*" (Italics in the original, p. 239 in English version entitled *Fear of Freedom* [London, 1942].)

53. "Social Science and Sociological Tendencies in Psychoanalysis" (unpublished paper dated April 26, 1946, p. 6, in Lowenthal's personal collection).

54. "Sociology and Psychology," first in *Sociologica* (Frankfurt, 1955), then in *New Left Review,* 46 (November-December 1967) and 47 (January-February 1968). The quotation appears on p. 85 in no. 47.

55. *One-dimensional Man: Studies in the Ideology of Advanced Industrial Society* (Boston, 1964).

56. Letter from Horkheimer to Lowenthal, December 31, 1950 (in Lowenthal's personal collection). Many years later, and without knowing about this letter, Hans Mayer, the distinguished Marxist literary critic, wrote an essay on Adorno which closed with the following words: "He succeeded in not becoming an adult, without remaining infantile." The words were, in fact, Adorno's own and were originally applied to his teacher Alban Berg. Mayer thought they were applicable to Adorno himself. (*Der Repräsentant und der Märtyrer; Konstellationen der Literatur* [Frankfurt, 1971],p. 168.)

57. "Schopenhauer Today," *The Critical Spirit: Essays in Honor of Herbert Marcuse* ed. by Kurt H. Wolff and Barrington Moore, Jr. (Boston, 1967), p. 67.

3. The Frankfurt School in Exile

1. *Fluchtlingsgespräche* (Frankfurt, 1961), p. 112.

2. Frankfurt, 1951.

3. New York, 1947.

4. The German spelling of *Institut* will be used throughout, although in America it called itself the International Institute of Social Research or simply the Institute of Social Research.

5. The first use of this term appeared in Horkheimer's essay "Traditionelle und kritische Theorie," *Zeitschrift für Sozialforschung* (henceforth *ZfS*), (1937), vol. 6.

6. For the clearest examples of this concern, see Horkheimer's "Egoismus und Freiheitsbewegung," *ZfS,* (1938), vol. 7, and Marcuse's "On Hedonism," reprinted in *Negations: Essays in Critical Theory* trans. Jeremy J. Shapiro (Boston, 1968).

7. *Reason and Revolution: Hegel and the Rise of Social Theory* (New York), p. 322.

8. *Minima Moralia,* p. 80.

9. *Ibid.,* p. 428.

10. "Walter Benjamin zum Gedächtnis" (unpublished, 1942). A copy can be found in Friedrich Pollock's personal collection.

11. *Ibid.,* p. 143.

12. See his "Theses on the Philosophy of History," *Illuminations: Essays and Reflections* trans. Harry Zohn (New York, 1968), p. 263.

13. "Autoritärer Staat," p. 158.

14. *Ibid.,* p. 149.

15. *Ibid.,* p. 160.

16. *Eclipse of Reason,* p. 184.

17. *Studien über Autorität und Familie* (Paris, 1936).

18. New York, 1941.

19. "Sozialpsychologischer Teil," *Studien über Autorität und Familie.*

20. See his discussion of the study in *Social Character in a Mexican Village* (with Michael Maccoby) (Englewood Cliffs, 1970), pp. 24–25.

21. Boston, 1955; epilogue.

22. "Social Science and Sociological Tendencies in Psychoanalysis" (unpublished manuscript, April 27, 1946, in Leo Lowenthal's personal collection). A German version can be found in Max Horkheimer and Theodor W. Adorno, eds., *Sociologica II: Reden und Vorträge* (Frankfurt, 1962).

23. *Ibid.,* p. 6.

24. Memorandum by Adorno on the Labor Project, November 3, 1944, pp. 43–55, in Paul Lazarsfeld's personal collection.

25. Herbert H. Hyman and Paul B. Sheatsley, " 'The Authoritarian Personality'—A Methodological Critique," in Richard Christie and Marie Jahoda, eds., *Studies in the Scope and Method of the Authoritarian Personality* (Glencoe, Ill., 1954), p. 109.

26. *The Authoritarian Personality* (New York, 1950), 2:747.

27. *Eclipse of Reason,* pp. 105–7.

28. *Eros and Civilization,* p. 41. The choice of the term is explained because "under its rule society is stratified according to the competitive economic performances of its members."

29. Letter in Lowenthal's collection, January 22, 1957. All of the letters cited below can be found in this collection, which has recently been deposited in the Houghton Library at Harvard.

30. For an example of the ignorance of his work in America, see the obituary which appeared in *The New York Times* a day after his death on August 8, 1969. Adorno's philosophical work is almost entirely ignored in an article which devotes more than half of its space to an obscure analysis he once made of jitterbugging.

31. "Tradition, Ecology, and Institution in the History of Sociology," *Daedalus* (Fall 1970), 99(4):776.

32. Letter to author from Fromm, May 14, 1971.

33. Letter from Lazarfeld to Theodore Abel, February 5, 1946, in Lowenthal's collection.

34. Über Jazz," *ZfS* (1936), vol. 5, and "Perennial Fashion-Jazz," *Prisms,* trans. Samuel and Shierry Weber (London, 1967).

35. "Scientific Experiences of a European Scholar in America," in Donald Fleming and Bernard Bailyn, eds., *The Intellectual Migration, 1930–1960* (Cambridge, 1969).

36. *Prisms,* pp. 97–98.

37. For a discussion of its effects, see Richard Christie, "Authoritarianism Reexamined," in Christie and Jahoda, *Studies.*

38. See, for example, Horkheimer's article, "Egoismus und Freiheitsbewegung," for an analysis of the sadomasochistic elements in Jacobin politics during the French revolution.

39. Edward Shils, "Authoritarianism: 'Right' and 'Left,' " in Christie and Jahoda, *Studies.*

40. The most extensive and notorious treatment of this concept appeared in Marcuse's essay, "Repressive Tolerance" in Herbert Marcuse, Barrington Moore, Jr., and Robert Paul Wolff, *Critique of Pure Tolerance* (Boston, 1965). The earliest formulation appeared in Fromm's "Die gesellschaftliche Bedingtheit der psychoanalytische Therapie," *ZfS* (1935), vol. 4.

41. Letter from Horkheimer to Lowenthal, February 18, 1950. Although not published until 1947, *Dialektik der Aufklärung* was written primarily in the years before Horkheimer became director of the scientific division of the American Jewish Committee in 1944. Presumably, Horkheimer would have included it in his work before the "interim."

42. Letter from Horkheimer to Lowenthal, February 16, 1949.

43. John R. Everett, review of *Eclipse of Reason,* in *The Journal of Philosophy* (1948), 45:605.

44. "I.B.M. Plus Reality Plus Humanism—Sociology," *Saturday Review* (May 1954), p. 54. Mills, it might be added, could not read German and was thus unfamiliar with the bulk of the *Institut's* theoretical work.

45. I am indebted to Richard Gillam of Stanford, who is working on a biography of Mills, for bringing this contact to my attention.

46. Lowenthal's studies of biographies in popular magazines are mentioned in *White Collar: The American Middle Class* (New York, 1951) at several points, but Mills' other works seem to have been written without much awareness of the Frankfurt School's theory.

47. Princeton, 1961.

48. See, for example, Paul Lazarsfeld, Bernard Berelson, Hazel Gaudet, *The People's Choice* (New York, 1948).

49. Here the concept of reification, which Lukács had done so much to revive in *History and Class Consciousness,* and the notion of the fetish were the major mediating categories between the socioeconomic analysis of late capitalism and contemporary culture.

50. For a more extensive treatment of this issue, see my *The Dialectical Imagination: A History of the Frankfurt School and the Institute of Social Research, 1923–1950* (Boston, 1973).

51. "Art and Mass Culture," *Studies in Philosophy and Social Science* (1941), 9:292.

52. "Die Auffassung Dostojewskis im Vorkriegsdeutschland," *ZfS* (1934), vol. 3.

53. "Über Jazz."

54. "L'oeuvre d'art à l'époque da sa reproduction mécanisée," *ZfS* (1936), vo. 5; translated in *Illuminations.*

55. *ZfS* (1941), vol. 9.

56. Conversation with Professor Riesman, Cambridge, Massachusetts, in May 1971.

57. See, for example, *Individualism Reconsidered, and Other Essays* (Glencoe, 1954) p. 187, and *The Lonely Crowd* (in collaboration with Reuel Denney and Nathan Glazer) (New Haven, 1950), p. 239.

58. Reprinted in *Against the American Grain* (New York, 1962). In 1958, MacDonald defended Lowenthal's argument that the "counterconcept of Kitsch is art" in an exchange of letters with Harold Rosenberg in *Dissent* (Summer and Autumn 1958).

Adorno's work was less widely discussed because most of it appeared in German. One of the few references appeared in Rolf Meyersohn and Elihu Katz, "Notes on a Natural History of Fads," in Eric Larrabee and Rolf Meyersohn, eds., *Mass Leisure* (Glencoe, 1958). Adorno's piece on jazz in *Prismen* is cited on page 315.

59. The only reference I have seen is in Arnold Hauser, "Popular Art and Folk Art," *Dissent* (Summer 1958), p. 233. Hauser, of course, was an emigré from Central Europe and could read German.

60. Englewood Cliffs, N.J., 1961; reissued, Palo Alto, Calif., 1968.

61. A shortened version of the television study appeared in Bernard Rosenberg and David Manning White, eds., *Mass Culture: The Popular Arts in America* (Glencoe, 1957). The astrology paper was published as "The Stars Down to Earth: The Los Angeles Times Astrology Column: A Study in Secondary Superstition," *Jahrbuch für Amerikastudien* (Heidelberg, 1957), vol. 2.

62. "Perennial Fashion-Jazz."

63. Letter from Adorno to Lowenthal, September 22, 1955.

64. "Scientific Experiences of a European Scholar in America," p. 347.

65. "Historical Perspectives of Popular Culture," in Rosenberg and White, eds., *Mass Culture.*

66. See, for example, Herbert J. Gans, "Popular Culture in America: Social Problem in a Mass Society or Social Asset in a Pluralist Society?" in Herbert S. Becker, ed., *Social Problems, A Modern Approach* (New York, 1966).

67. Italics added. "Ideas, Intellectuals, and Structures of Dissent," in Philip Rieff, ed., *On Intellectuals* (New York, 1970), p. 121. Nettl accepts Bramson's analysis in *The Political Context of Sociology* uncritically.

68. For an exposition of that methodology in English, see Horkheimer, "Notes on Institute Activities," *Studies in Philosophy and Social Science* (1941), 9.

69. See, for example, his critique of Shils, "A Dissent from the Consensual Society," in Hendrik M. Ruitenbeek, ed., *Varieties of Modern Social Theory* (New York, 1963). He dismisses Shil's argument that critics of mass culture are likely to be ex-Marxists by saying: "So what? Ex-Marxists are likely to be critical minds. That is what made them first Marxists and then ex" (p. 273).

70. "Daydreams and Nightmares: Reflections on the Criticism of Mass Culture," *Sewanee Review* (1957), vol. 65.

71. Gans, "Popular Culture in America," p. 573.

72. "Society," *Salmagundi* (1969–1970), 10–11:249, translation corrected.

73. "Über den affirmativen Charakter der Kultur," *ZfS* (1937), vol. 6, reprinted in *Negations.*

74. "Cultural Criticism and Society," *Prisms,* pp. 23–25.

75. Letter from Horkheimer to Lowenthal, June 2, 1942.

76. Letter from Horkheimer to Lowenthal, December 30, 1955.

77. See, for one out of many examples, Neil McInnes, "From Marx to Marcuse," *Survey* (1971), vol. 16.

78. For a discussion of the activists, see George Mosse, *Germans and Jews* (New York, 1970), and Lewis D. Wurgaft, "The Activist Movement: Cultural Politics in the German Left, 1914–1933" (Ph.D. diss., Harvard, 1970). Walter Benjamin wrote a critique of the Activists in "The Author as Producer," *New Left Review* (1970), no. 62.

79. *A Critique of Pure Tolerance* (1968 ed.), p. 122 (italics in original).

80. Paul Breines, "Marcuse and the New Left in America," in Jürgen Habermas, ed., *Antworten auf Herbert Marcuse* (Frankfurt, 1968), p. 137.

81. See, for example, Robert W. Marks, *The Meaning of Marcuse* (New York,

1970), and Alasdair MacIntyre, *Herbert Marcuse: An Exposition and a Polemic* (New York, 1970).

82. Conversation with Professor Marcuse, San Francisco, May 1971.

83. Boston, 1964.

84. Boston, 1955. For a discussion of the implications of Marcuse's attitude toward the Oedipus Complex, see Sidney Lipshires, "Herbert Marcuse: From Marx to Freud and Beyond" (Ph.D. diss., University of Connecticut, 1971).

85. He made this explicit in his essay on "The Obsolescence of the Freudian Concept of Man," *Five Lectures,* trans. Jeremy J. Shapiro and Shierry Weber (Boston, 1970).

86. See note 40.

87. See, for example, Paul Mattick, "The Limits of Integration," in Barrington Moore, Jr., and Kurt Wolff, eds., *The Critical Spirit: Essays in Honor of Herbert Marcuse* (Boston, 1967).

88. The most recent of these is Paul Piccone and Alexander Delfini, "Marcuse's Heideggerian Marxism," *Telos* (1970), no. 6.

89. It is important to note that Marcuse was ambivalent about technology and its effects, not simply hostile, as some of his critics have suggested. See, for example, his first treatment of the problem in "Some Social Implications of Modern Technology," *Studies in Philosophy and Social Science* (1941), vol. 9.

90. *Ibid.,* p. 425.

91. Letter from Horkheimer to Lowenthal, April 13, 1951.

92. Frankfurt, 1967.

93. Chicago, 1955.

94. Letter from Horkheimer to Lowenthal, September 9, 1956.

95. For a discussion of the debate in English, see Anon., "Dialectical Methodology, Marx or Weber: The New 'Methodenstreit' in Postwar German Philosophy," *The Times Literary Supplement* (March 12, 1970).

96. See, for example, his interview in *Der Spiegel* (January 5, 1970).

97. This was made clear in a public letter he sent to the S. Fischer Verlag shortly before agreeing to publication, and in the prefatory remarks in *Kritische Theorie.*

98. This is the admission Göran Therborn, a follower of Louis Althusser, makes in his generally hostile analysis of the Frankfurt School, "A Critique of the Frankfurt School," *New Left Review* (1970), 63:87.

99. Breines, "From Guru to Spectre: Marcuse and the Implosion of the Movement," in Paul Breines, ed., *Critical Interruptions; New Left Perspectives on Herbert Marcuse* (New York, 1970), p. 14.

100. See, for example, his review of Charles Reich's *The Greening of America* in *The New York Times* (November 6, 1970).

101. In addition to Sidney Lipshires, who has already been mentioned, Alan Graubard and Paul Robinson, both of Harvard, wrote dissertations on Marcuse. Robinson's was published as *The Freudian Left* (New York, 1969). The books by Marks and MacIntyre have already been cited (note 81).

102. Conversation with Professor Marcuse, San Francisco, May 1971.

103. Leiss and Ober also contributed to *Critical Interruptions.*

104. Habermas' *Knowledge and Human Interests* and *Towards a Rational Society* have recently been translated into English, as have Schmidt's *The Concept of Nature in Marx* and Wellmer's *The Critical Theory of Society.*

105. Letter from Horkheimer to Lowenthal, February 2, 1943.

106. Review of *The Intellectual Migration* and *The Bauhaus* by Hans Wingler in *Commentary,* 49 (1970).

107. William Jordy, "The Aftermath of the Bauhaus in America: Gropius, Mies, and Breuer," in Fleming and Bailyn, eds., *The Intellectual Migration,* p. 488.

108. See Jordy's article for evidence of its extent.

109. *Die Neue Sachlichkeit* (Frankfurt, 1970).

110. Zurich, 1934; pp. 216–19.

111. This type of critique was, of course, a constant theme of Weimar intellectual life. The Frankfurt School was somewhat unique, however, in applying it within a leftist framework. For a discussion of the modernist-antimodernist debate during these years, see Fritz K. Ringer, *The Decline of the German Mandarins* (Cambridge, 1969).

4. The Frankfurt School's Critique of Karl Mannheim and the Sociology of Knowledge

1. Conversation with Kurt H. Wolff, Cambridge, Massachusetts, May 1971.

2. Max Horkheimer, "Ein neuer Ideologiebegriff?," *Archiv für die Geschichte des Sozialismus und der Arbeiterbewegung* (1930), vol. 15.

3. Among the other articles were Herbert Marcuse, "Zur Wahrheitsproblematik der soziologischer Methode," *Die Gesellschaft* (1929), 6(2); Karl August Wittfogel, "Wissen und Gesellschaft. Neuer deutsche Literatur zur Wissenssoziologie," *Unter dem Banner des Marxismus* (1931), 6(1); Theodor W. Adorno, "The Sociology of Knowledge and its Consciousness," *Prisms,* trans. Samuel and Shierry Weber (London, 1967) first appeared as "Über Mannheims Wissensoziologie," *Aufklärung* (April 25, 1953) vol. 2; Max Horkheimer, "Ideologie und Handeln," in *Soziologische Forschung in unseren Zeit. Leopold von Wiese zum 75. Gebürtstag,* ed. Karl Gustav Specht (Cologne and Opladen, 1951); and "Ideology" in *Aspects of Sociology,* by the Frankfurt Institute for Social Research, trans. John Viertel (Boston, 1972).

4. See, for example, Max Horkheimer, "Bemerkungen zur philosophischen Anthropologie," *Zeitschrift für Sozialforschung* (1935), 6(1). A postwar member of the *Institut,* Kurt Lenk, has continued the attack. See his *Von der Ohnmacht des Geistes: Darstellung der Spätphilosophie Max Schelers* (Tübingen, 1959) and "Geist und Geschichte. Ein Beitrag zum Geschichtsdenken Max Schelers," *Kölner Zeitschrift für Soziologie und Sozialpsychologie* (1956) vol. 8. I am indebted to Volker Meja for bringing Lenk's work to my attention.

5. George Lichtheim in *The Concept of Ideology* (New York, 1967), p. 40, calls it the "positivists' rejoinder to *History and Class Consciousness.*" Mannheim's response to Lukács was primarily over his treatment of ideology. The section of his book on utopia might be seen as an answer to Ernst Bloch's *Geist der Utopie,* which appeared in 1918, although Mannheim never mentions this work in his book. I owe this suggestion to a conversation with Hans Mayer in Milwaukee in November 1973.

6. David Kettler, "Sociology of Knowledge and Moral Philosophy: The Place of Traditional Problems in the Formation of Mannheim's Thought," *Political Science Quarterly* (1967), vol. 82; "Culture and Revolution: Lukács in the Hungarian Revolution of 1918," *Telos* (Winter 1971), no. 10.

7. Mannheim, "Über die Eigenart kultursoziologische Erkenntnis," discussed in Kettler, "Sociology of Knowledge and Moral Philosophy."

8. Mannheim, "Eine soziologische Theorie der Kultur und ihrer Erkennbarkeit," discussed in Kettler, "Sociology of Knowledge and Moral Philosophy."

9. Werner Stark, *The Sociology of Knowledge* (Glencoe, Ill., 1958).

10. For Mannheim's indebtedness to Troeltsch, see his essay on "Historicism," in *Essays on the Sociology of Knowledge,* ed. Paul Kecskemeti (New York, 1952).

11. For a history of historicism, see Georg G. Iggers, *The German Conception of History* (Middletown, Conn., 1968).

12. Kettler has also argued that Mannheim adjusted his remarks to his audience in a way that might well have earned the Frankurt School's distrust (letter from Kettler to me, January 17, 1974).

13. Mannheim, *Ideology and Utopia*, trans. Louis Wirth and Edward Shils (New York, 1936), p. 310.

14. Fritz Ringer, *The Decline of the German Mandarins* (Cambridge, 1969), pp. 425f; Maurice Mandelbaum, *The Problem of Historical Knowledge; An Answer to Relativism* (New York, 1938), pp. 67f.

15. See, for example, Paul Kecskemeti, Introduction to Mannheim, *Essays on the Sociology of Knowledge* (London, 1952), p. 7; and H. Stuart Hughes, *Consciousness and Society* (New York, 1958), p. 424. Felix Gilbert has gone as far as linking Mannheim to Carl Schmitt as common advocates of decisionism. See his article "Political Power and Academic Responsibility: Reflections on Friedrich Meinecke's *Drei Generationen deutscher Gelehrtenpolitik*," in *The Responsibility of Power*, ed. Leonard Krieger and Fritz Stern (Garden City, New York, 1969), p. 437.

16. Mannheim, *Essays on Sociology and Social Psychology*, ed. Paul Kecskemeti (New York, 1953).

17. *Ideology and Utopia*, p. 93.

18. *Ibid.*, p. 253.

19. Mannheim, "Historicism," p. 96.

20. Karl Popper, *The Poverty of Historicism* (London, 1957), *passim*.

21. Lukács, "Die deutsche Soziologie zwischen dem ersten und dem zweiten Weltkrieg," *Aufbau* (1946), vol. 2, and *Die Zerstörung der Vernunft* in *Werke*, vol. 9 (Neuwied, 1961); for a defense of Mannheim, see M. A. Hodges, "Lukács on Irrationalism," in *Georg Lukács, The Man, his Work and his Ideas*, ed. G. H. R. Parkinson (New York, 1970), pp. 104f.

22. See note 3.

23. The most important of these was "Beiträge zu einer Phänomenologie des historischen Materialismus," *Philosophische Hefte* (1928), 1(1); for a critique of his efforts, see Alfred Schmidt, "Existential-Ontologie und historischer Materialismus bei Herbert Marcuse," *Antworten auf Herbert Marcuse*, ed. Jürgen Habermas (Frankfurt, 1968).

24. See, for example, Max Horkheimer, "Zum Problem der Wahrheit, *Zeitschrift für Sozialforschung* (1935), 4(3).

25. *Ideology and Utopia*, pp. 248–63.

26. Marcuse, "Zur Wahrheitsproblematik . . . ," p. 369.

27. Marcuse, "The Struggle against Liberalism in the Totalitarian View of the State," *Negations: Essays in Critical Theory* trans. Jeremy J. Shapiro (Boston, 1968), pp. 31f.

28. Horkheimer, "Traditionelle und kritische Theorie," *Zeitschrift für Sozialforschung* (1937), 6(2).

29. See chapter 2 above.

30. For an example of this position, see Theodor W. Adorno, *Negative Dialectics*, trans. E. B. Ashton (New York, 1973), p. 41, where it is argued, "If a stroke of undeserved luck has kept the mental composition of some individuals not quite adjusted to the prevailing norms—a stroke of luck they have often enough to pay for in their relations with their environment—it is up to these individuals to make the moral and, as it were, representative effort to say what most of those for whom they say it cannot see or, to do justice to reality, will not allow themselves to see."

31. Walter Benjamin, "The Author as Producer," *New Left Review* (July-August 1970), no. 62.

32. Mannheim, *Man and Society in the Age of Reconstruction* (London, 1940); Adorno's review essay, which was an expansion of an earlier, unpublished critique of Mannheim written in 1937, is cited in note 3.

33. Adorno, *Prisms*, p. 37.

34. *Ibid.*, p. 38.

35. *Ibid.*, p. 48.

36. See note 3. Adorno was the unidentified author of the essay.

37. Adorno, *Prisms*, p. 34.

38. *Aspects of Sociology*, p. 190. This point is particularly interesting when seen in contrast to Hannah Arendt's contemporaneously published *The Origins of Totalitarianism*, where ideology plays a key role in her analysis of Nazism.

39. *Ibid.*, p. 199.

40. Marcuse, *One-dimensional Man: Studies in the Ideology of Advanced Industrial Society* (Boston, 1964); Habermas, *Technik und Wissenschaft als "Ideologie"* (Frankfurt, 1968).

41. Adorno, *Negative Dialectics*, p. 148.

42. Habermas, *Knowledge and Human Interests*, trans. Jeremy J. Shapiro (Boston, 1971).

43. Marcuse, *Negations*, pp. 147–48.

44. Adorno, *Negative Dialectics*, pp. 197–98.

45. *Ibid.*, p. 141.

46. Walter Benjamin, "Theses on the Philosophy of History," *Illuminations*, trans. Harry Zohn (New York, 1968), pp. 259–60. Benjamin, it should be noted, was not endorsing a view of inevitable progress; indeed, his point was the very opposite. But his emphasis on the angel's desire to make whole what is smashed, a desire thwarted by the onrushing force of the wind of progress, expresses the still powerful hope for redemption in his work and that of his Frankfurt School colleagues.

5. Anti-Semitism and the Weimar Left

1. Franz Neumann, *Behemoth; the Structure and Practice of National Socialism, 1933–1944* (New York, 1944), p. 121.

2. *Ibid.*, p. 551.

3. George Mosse, *The Crisis of German Ideology* (New York, 1964); Peter J. G. Pulzer, *The Rise of Political Anti-Semitism in Germany and Austria* (New York, 1964); Paul Massing, *Rehearsal for Destruction: A Study of Political Anti-Semitism in Imperial Germany* (New York, 1949); Peter Viereck, *Metapolitics: The Roots of the Nazi Mind* (New York, 1941).

4. Edmund Silberner, *Sozialisten zur Judenfrage* (Berlin, 1962) and George Lichtheim, "Socialism and the Jews," in *Collected Essays* (New York, 1973). The most appalling cases in Lichtheim's study, it should be noted, are non-Marxist leftists such as Proudhon and Fourier.

5. Sir Isaiah Berlin, "The Life and Opinions of Moses Hess," in *On Intellectuals*, ed. Philip Rieff (Garden City, N.Y., 1970).

6. For a recent treatment of the role of Jews during the first years of the republic, see Werner T. Angress, *Deutsches Judentum in Krieg und Revolution, 1916–1923; Schriftenreihe Wissenschaftlicher Abhandlungen des Leo Baeck Institut*, 25 (Tübingen, n.d.).

7. Letter from Friedrich Pollock to me, Montagnola, Switzerland, March 24, 1970.

8. Letter from Felix J. Weil to me, Ramstein, Germany, June 1, 1969.

9. Geoffrey Barraclough, "Mandarins and Nazis, Part I," *New York Review of Books* (October 19, 1972), "The Liberals and German History, Part II," *NYRB* (November 2, 1972), and "A New View of Germany History, Part III," *NYRB* (November 16, 1972).

10. Baton Rouge, La., 1971.

11. Barraclough, "The Liberals and German History," p. 37.

12. *Niewyk*, p. 29.

13. *Ibid.*

14. *Ibid.*

15. For a recent treatment of the Central Association during the Wilhelminian era, see Ismar Schorsch, *Jewish Reactions to German Anti-Semitism, 1870–1914* (New York and Philadelphia, 1972).

16. Erich Matthias, "Das Sozialdemokratische Partei Deutschlands," in Erich Matthias and Rudolf Morsey, eds., *Das Ende der Parteien* (Düsseldorf, 1960).

17. *Niewyk*, p. 221.

18. *Commentary* (October 1970), 50(4).

19. Istvan Deak, *Weimar Germany's Left-wing Intellectuals* (Berkeley and Los Angeles, 1968).

20. *Commentary* (March 1971), 51(3).

21. Deak, p. 24; for a recent treatment of the role of Jews in the intellectual life of Weimar see Wolfgang Sauer, "Weimar Culture: Experiments in Modernism," *Social Research* (Summer 1972), 34(2).

22. Angress, *Deutsches Judentum* p. 304.

23. Hans-Helmuth Knütter, *Die Juden und die deutsche Linke in der Weimarer Republik* (Düsseldorf, 1972).

24. An English translation has recently appeared as "Moses Hess and the Problem of the Idealist Dialectic," *Telos* (Winter 1971), no. 10.

25. Werner T. Angress, *Stillborn Revolution: The Communist Bid for Power in Germany, 1921–1923* (Princeton, 1963), pp. 314–77.

26. Quoted in *ibid.,* p. 340.

27. For an analysis of the changing composition of the *Mittelstand* in Weimar, see Herman Lebovics, *Social Conservatism and the Middle Classes in Germany, 1914–1933* (Princeton, 1969), pp. 3–48.

28. Hannah Arendt, "Walter Benjamin, 1892–1940," introduction to Walter Benjamin, *Illuminations: Essays and Reflections,* trans. Harry Zohn (New York, 1968).

29. For a description of her attitude toward the Jewish question, see J. P. Nettl, *Rosa Luxemburg* (London, 1969), abridged ed., p. 517.

6. The Jews and the Frankfurt School: Critical Theory's Analysis of Anti-Semitism

1. Max Horkheimer, *Notizen 1950 bis 1969 und Dämmerung Notizen in Deutschland,* ed. Werner Brede, intro. Alfred Schmidt (Frankfurt am Main, 1974). *Dämmerung* was first published under the pseudonym Heinrich Regius in Zurich in 1934. It was translated along with the notes of 1950–1969 under the title *Dawn and Decline* (New York, 1978).

2. *Dawn and Decline,* p. 43.

3. *Studien über Autorität und Familie* (Paris, 1935).

4. The Marcuse article appeared in the *Zeitschrift für Sozialforschung* (1934), 3(1):161–95; the Lowenthal in the *Zeitschrift für Sozialforschung* (1937), 6(3):295–345. In the latter, footnote 1 on p. 330 quotes a remark Hamsun made about Jews, but makes no comment about it. Lowenthal had written earlier for Jewish periodicals and about Jewish issues, but when he joined the Institute, he left this interest behind. Marcuse, in his long career, never discussed Jewish issues or anti-Semitism.

5. "Fragmente über Wagner," *Zeitschrift für Sozialforschung* (1939), 7(1-2):1– 49; *Versuch über Wagner* (Frankfurt am Main, 1952).

6. "Die Juden und Europa," *Zeitschrift für Sozialforschung* (1939), 7(1-2). Originally Horkheimer had not wanted to use this title for the essay, only the last ten pages of which actually deals with the Jews. He was persuaded to do so by Adorno, according to the recollection of Gershom Scholem, *Walter Benjamin, Geschichte einer Freundschaft* (Frankfurt am Main, 1975), p. 278. Horkheimer later felt embarrassed by this essay with its frequently quoted phrase, "he who does not wish to speak of capitalism should also be silent about fascism," and chose to omit it from his collection *Kritische Theorie*, 2 vols., ed. Alfred Schmidt (Frankfurt am Main, 1969).

7. Scholem, *Walter Benjamin*, pp. 276–78.

8. This pattern is discussed, *inter alia*, in Robert Wistrich, "German Social Democracy and the Problem of Jewish Nationalism, 1897–1917," *Yearbook of the Leo Baeck Institute* (1976), 20:109–42; Donald L. Niewyk, *Socialist, Anti-Semite, and Jew: German Social Democracy Confronts the Problem of Anti-Semitism, 1918–1933* (Baton Rouge, 1971).

9. See, for example, "Über die deutschen Juden," in *Kritik der Instrumentellen Vernunft. Aus den Vorträgen und Aufzeichenung seit Kriegsende*, ed. Alfred Schmidt (Frankfurt am Main, 1967), originally published in 1961. For a discussion of Horkheimer's later turn toward Jewish themes, see Eva G. Reichmann, "Max Horkheimer the Jew: Critical Theory and Beyond," *Yearbook of the Leo Baeck Institute* (1974), 29:181–95, and Julius Carlebach, *Karl Marx and the Radical Critique of Judaism* (London, 1978).

10. In an interview with *Der Spiegel* (January 5, 1970), 24, Horkheimer claimed that Critical Theory's refusal to name the "other" was derived from the Jewish taboo on naming God or picturing paradise.

11. In 1939 a prospectus was drafted for such a project; it was published in the *Studies in Philosophy and Social Science* (the short-lived English language successor to the *Zeitschrift für Sozialforschung*) (1941), 9(1):124–43.

12. *Behemoth: The Structure and Practice of National Socialism, 1933–44*, rev. ed. (New York, 1944).

13. For a discussion of Neumann's conflict with Pollock over State Capitalism, see Martin Jay, *The Dialectical Imagination: A History of the Frankfurt School and the Institute of Social Research, 1923–50* (Boston, 1973), pp. 162–67.

14. *Behemoth*, p. 122.

15. *Ibid.*

16. *Ibid.*, p. 121.

17. *Ibid.*

18. Interview with Leo Lowenthal, Berkeley, Ca., August, 1968. In the 1939 prospectus for a study of anti-Semitism, the *Institut* wrote: "While frank disgust for the anti-Semitism of the government is revealed among the German masses, the promises of anti-Semitism are eagerly swallowed where fascist governments have never been attempted" (p. 141).

19. *Behemoth*, p. 551. This attitude was characteristic of the SPD, to whose left wing Neumann had belonged during the Weimar Republic. See Niewyk, p. 217.

20. "Anxiety and Politics," *The Democratic and Authoritarian State: Essays in Political and Legal Theory,* ed. Herbert Marcuse (New York, 1957), p. 286.

21. For a discussion of Fromm's work with the *Institut,* see *The Dialectical Imagination,* chapter 3.

22. For a discussion of the American Labor Project, see *The Dialectical Imagination,* pp. 224–26.

23. (New York, 1949). According to Ismar Schorsch, "After twenty-five years, Massing's penetrating and judicious study . . . remains unsurpassed." See "German Antisemitism in the Light of Post-war Historiography," *Yearbook of the Leo Baeck Institute* (1974), 19:262.

24. Nathan W. Ackerman and Marie Jahoda, *Anti-Semitism and Emotional Disorder: A Psychoanalytic Interpretation* (New York, 1950) and Bruno Bettelheim and Morris Janowitz, *Dynamics of Prejudice: A Psychological and Sociological Study of Veterans* (New York, 1950). For a brief discussion of these works, see *The Dialectical Imagination,* pp. 235–37).

25. *Prophets of Deceit* (New York, 1949); *The Authoritarian Personality* (New York, 1950).

26. *Prophets of Deceit,* p. 140. The theoretical underpinnings of the code were spelled out more clearly in Adorno, "Freudian Theory and the Pattern of Fascist Propaganda," in *Psychoanalysis and the Social Sciences,* ed. Geza Roheim (New York, 1951).

27. *Prophets of Deceit,* p. 88.

28. *The Authoritarian Personality,* p. 605.

29. *Ibid.,* p. 653.

30. *Ibid.,* p. 638. Here it is argued that the proletarian anti-Semite is likely to identify the Jew with the bourgeois agent of capitalism, while the bourgeois anti-Semite tends to see the Jew as a "misfit bourgeois" who does not belong to modern society. The study's sample was essentially middle-class, but the earlier labor project had given evidence of the former tendency.

31. *Ibid.,* pp. 759–60.

32. *Ibid.,* p. 671.

33. *Ibid.,* p. 608.

34. *Dialectic of Enlightenment,* tr. John Cumming (New York, 1972); Lowenthal was the coauthor of the first three of the seven sections of this chapter.

35. *The Authoritarian Personality,* p. 607.

36. For an analysis, see *The Dialectical Imagination,* chapter 8; Susan Buck-Morss, *The Origin of Negative Dialectics: Theodor W. Adorno, Walter Benjamin and the Frankfurt Institute* (New York, 1977), pp. 59–62, 178–80, and Christian Lenhardt, "The Wanderings of Enlightenment," in *On Critical Theory,* ed. John O'Neill (New York, 1976).

37. One of the book's first reviewers, Heinz L. Matzal, found it the least convincing section. See *Philosophischer Literaturanzeiger* (1949), vol. 1. In subsequent discussions of the Frankfurt School's work, it has not been prominently featured. Carlebach is an exception, and his attitude is generally hostile. See note 4.

38. *Dialectic of Enlightenment,* p. 173.

39. *Ibid.,* p. 175.

40. *Ibid.*

41. *Ibid.*

42. See especially the theoretical introductions to *Studien über Autorität und Familie* and Marcuse's essay cited in note 4.

43. *Dialectic of Enlightenment,* p. 168. They also argued, in a manner anticipating Hannah Arendt's well-known analysis in *The Origins of Totalitarianism* of 1951,

that the nineteenth-century Jews had sold their political rights and power for economic security. Accordingly, when the nation-state ceased to protect them in the era of mass politics, they were entirely vulnerable to attack (pp. 171–72).

44. *Ibid.*, p. 169.
45. *Ibid.*, p. 171.
46. *Ibid.*, p. 172.
47. *Ibid.*, p. 199.
48. *Ibid.*, p. 175. In a letter Horkheimer wrote to Lowenthal on July 5, 1946, he talked of the mistrust the peasant had of the urban manipulator of language, which he called partly justified. "This distrust," Horkheimer continued, "is an element of anti-Semitism itself, and the Jew who manipulates language so easily is not free from guilt in the prehistory of what you explain as the fascist handling of language. Here, too, the Jew is the pioneer of capitalism" (Lowenthal collection, Berkeley, California).
49. *Ibid.*, p. 186.
50. *Ibid.*, p. 185.
51. *Ibid.*, p. 187.
52. *Ibid.*, p. 189.
53. *Ibid.*, p. 193.
54. *Negative Dialectics*, trans. E. B. Ashton (New York, 1973).
55. *Dialectic of Enlightenment*, pp. 199–200.
56. *Ibid.*, p. 200.
57. *Ibid.*, p. 207.
58. *Ibid.*
59. "The State of Israel" in *Dawn and Decline*, pp. 206–7. See also, the aphorism entitled "End of the Dream" on pp. 221–22.
60. Franz Rosenzweig, *The Star of Redemption*, trans. William Hallo (New York, 1970).
61. See note 10.
62. For example, see Zoltan Tar, *The Frankfurt School: The Critical Theories of Max Horkheimer and Theodor W. Adorno* (New York, 1977), and Arnold Künzli, *Aufklärung und Dialektik* (Freiburg, 1971). They reduce negative dialectics to Adorno's belated guilt over his earlier rejection of Judaism, produced by his surviving the Holocaust, rather than seeing it as an expression of his (and Horkheimer's) positive identification with the Jews.
63. In "Elements of Anti-Semitism," Horkheimer and Adorno wrote, "from the outset there has always been an intimate link between anti-Semitism and totality" (p. 172). This critical attitude toward totality, a term that frequently appeared in their other writings in a more positive light, was indicative of a general shift away from what might be called the Lukácsian tenor of their early work. Instead of using totality in a completely positive sense, they began to recognize its ambiguous relationsip with totalitarianism. For more on this issue, see Martin Jay, "The Concept of Totality in Lukács and Adorno," *Telos* (Summer 1977), 32:117–37 and *Varieties of Marxism*, ed. Shlomo Avineri (The Hague, 1977).
64. *Dialectic of Enlightenment*, p. 207.

7. Introduction to a *Festschrift* for Leo Lowenthal on His Eightieth Birthday

1. Zoltan Tar, *The Frankfurt School: The Critical Theories of Max Horkheimer and Theodor W. Adorno* (New York, 1977), p. 17.

2. Phil Slater, *Origin and Significance of the Frankfurt School; A Marxist Perspective* (London, 1977); Paul Connerton, *The Tragedy of Enlightenment; An Essay on the Frankfurt School* (Cambridge, 1980); Alfons Söllner, *Geschichte und Herrschaft; Studien zur materialistischen Sozialwissenschaft, 1929–1942* (Frankfurt, 1979); Francesco Apergi, *Marxismo e ricerca sociale nella Scuola di Francoforto* (Florence, 1977).

3. *The Essential Frankfurt School Reader*, ed. with intros. by Andrew Arato and Eike Gebhardt (New York, 1978), pp. 529, 118.

4. Helmut Dubiel, *Wissenschaftsorganisation und politische Erfahrung; Studien zur frühen Kritischen Theorie* (Frankfurt, 1978).

5. Herbert Marcuse, *The Aesthetic Dimension: Toward a Critique of Marxist Aesthetics* (Boston, 1978), p. vii.

6. See the bibliography of Lowenthal's works in *Telos* (Fall, 1980), no. 45.

7. Leo Lowenthal, *Mitmachen Wollte Ich Nie; Ein Autobiographisches Gespräch mit Helmut Dubiel* (Frankfurt, 1980). In addition to the interviews, this volume contains several very interesting letters between Lowenthal and a variety of figures in his life, including Franz Rosenzweig, Siegfried Kracauer, Walter Benjamin, Theodor W. Adorno, and Max Horkheimer.

8. Burkhardt Lindner and W. Martin Lüdke, eds., *Materielen zur asthetischen Theorie Theodor W. Adorno; Konstruktion der Moderne* (Frankfurt, 1980).

9. The translation is taken from the slightly revised version in *Erzählkunst und Gesellschaft; Die Gesellschaftsproblematik in der deutschen Literatur des 19.Jahrhunderts*, intro. by Frederic C. Tubach (Neuwied, 1971).

10. Herbert Marcuse, *Negations: Essays in Critical Theory*, trans. Jeremy J. Shapiro (Boston, 1968).

11. Georg Lukács, *The Historical Novel*, trans. Hannah and Stanley Mitchell (London, 1962).

12. *Ibid.*, p. 226. For a more recent view closer to Lowenthal's, see W. D. Williams, *The Stories of C. F. Meyer* (Oxford, 1962), p. 20.

13. See, for example, Marianne Burkhard, *Conrad Ferdinand Meyer* (Boston, 1978), chapter 9.

14. For Lowenthal's views on naturalism, see "Individuum und Gesellschaft in Naturalismus," in *Notizen zur Literatursoziologie* (Stuttgart, 1975). This article was originally written in the later 1930s for the *Zeitschrift*, but was not published until 1975.

15. Lowenthal, *Mitmachen Wollte Ich Nie*, p. 217.

16. See, for example, the tribute to him on his 70th birthday in the *Berkeley Journal of Sociology* (1971–72), vol. 16.

8. Positive and Negative Totalities: Implicit Tensions in Critical Theory's Vision of Interdisciplinary Research

1. Helmut Dubiel, *Wissenschaftsorganisation und politische Erfahrung; Studien zur frühen Kritischen Theorie* (Frankfurt, 1978); Alfons Söllner, *Geschichte und Herrschaft; Studien zur materialistischen Sozialwissenschaft 1929–1942* (Frankfurt, 1979). These works are the products of an ongoing collective project on Critical Theory, whose other members include Wolfgang Bonss, Manfred Gangl, Norbert Schindler and Klaus Schubert. The model of *Darstellung* and *Forschung*, it should be noted, has seemed to some survivors of the Frankfurt School overly schematic. See, for example, Marcuse's skeptical remarks in Silvia Bovenschen u.a., *Gespräche mit Herbert Marcuse* (Frankfurt, 1978), pp. 16–17. Leo Lowenthal in conversation with the author has agreed with Marcuse's position.

2. The phrase "dictatorship of the director" appears in Carl Grünberg's address at the dedication of the *Institut* in 1924. See his "Festrede gehalten zur Einweihung des Instituts für Sozialforschung an der Universität Frankfurt a. M. am 22 Juni 1924," *Frankfurter Universitätsreden* (Frankfurt, 1924), 20:7.

3. Söllner, p. 36.

4. Horkheimer, "Die Gegenwärtige Lage der Sozialphilosophie und die Aufgaben eines Instituts für Sozialforschung," *Frankfurter Universitäetsreden* (Frankfurt, 1931), 37:11.

5. *Studien über Autorität und Familie* (Paris, 1936).

6. Habermas, "The Inimitable *Zeitschrift für Sozialforschung*: How Horkheimer Took Advantage of a Historically Oppressive Hour," *Telos* (Fall 1980), 45:117.

7. For a discussion of this split, chapter 3.

8. For a general discussion of the Institute's work on anti-Semitism, see chapter 6.

9. Söllner, p. 188. The difference between the terms "theory" and "philosophy" is a significant one for Marxism. Many Marxists have understood their task as the overcoming of philosophy, which generally meant German Idealism, through the creation of a science of society. To those Western Marxists who rejected the purely scientific image of Marxism, the term "theory" was often used to register continuity with the critical elements in traditional philosophy. In his essay "Philosophy and Critical Theory," Marcuse was still reluctant to collapse the two. "Like philosophy," he wrote, Critical Theory "opposes making reality into a criterion in the manner of complacent positivism. But unlike philosophy, it always derives its goals only from present tendencies of the social process": *Negations, Essays in Critical Theory,* trans. Jeremy J. Shapiro (Boston, 1968), p. 143. It was precisely when Horkheimer and his colleagues despaired of locating negative tendencies in the present social process that they began to defend the validity of philosophy per se once again. See, for example, Horkheimer's essay of 1939, "The Social Function of Philosophy," reprinted in *Critical Theory: Selected Essays*, trans. Matthew J. O'Connell and others (New York, 1972).

10. Lukács, *History and Class Consciousness: Studies in Marxist Dialectics,* trans. Rodney Livingstone (Cambridge, Mass., 1971), p. 27.

11. Colletti, *From Rousseau to Lenin: Studies in Ideology and Society,* trans. John Merrington and Judith White (London, 1972); Therborn, "The Frankfurt School," in *Western Marxism: A Critical Reader,* ed. *New Left Review* (London, 1977).

12. For a discussion of Western Marxist uses of the *verum-factum* principle, see Martin Jay, "Vico and Western Marxism," in *Giambattista Vico: New Studies and Recent Interpretations,* ed. Giorgio Tagliacozzo, vol. 2, (New York, 1981).

13. Dubiel, p. 40.

14. Horkheimer, "Ein neuer Ideologiebegriff?" *Grünberg Archiv* (1930) vol. 15; reprinted in Horkheimer, *Sozialphilosophische Studien,* ed. Werner Brede (Frankfurt, 1972).

15. Horkheimer, "Traditional and Critical Theory," in *Critical Theory,* pp. 237–38.

16. Adorno, "The Actuality of Philosophy," *Telos* (Spring 1977), no. 31.

17. Adorno to Kracauer, May 29, 1931, and June 8, 1931; in Kracauer, *Nachlass* Schiller National Museum, Marbach am Neckar.

18. Susan Buck-Morss, *The Origin of Negative Dialectics; Theodor W. Adorno, Walter Benjamin, and the Frankfurt Institute* (New York, 1977).

19. Adorno, "The Actuality of Philosophy," p. 120.

20. *Ibid.,* p. 126.

21. *Ibid.,* p. 127.
22. *Ibid.*
23. *Ibid.,* p. 128.
24. *Ibid.,* p. 129.
25. *Ibid.,* p. 131.
26. *Ibid.,* p. 126.
27. *Ibid.,* p. 127.
28. *Ibid.,* p. 131.
29. *Ibid.,* p. 127.
30. *Ibid.,* p. 130.
31. Horkheimer, "Notes on Institute Activities," *Studies in Philosophy and Social Science* (1941), 9(1):123; for an interpretation that stresses the Benjaminian quality of these remarks, see David Held, *Introduction to Critical Theory: Horkheimer to Habermas* (Berkeley, 1980), p. 189.
32. Adorno to Benjamin, November 10, 1938, in *Aesthetics and Politics: Debates Between Bloch, Lukács, Brecht, Benjamin, Adorno,* ed. *New Left Review* (London, 1977), p. 129.
33. Benjamin's enthusiasm for Surrealism is registered in his essay of 1929, "Surrealism: The Last Snapshot of the European Intelligentsia," in *Reflections: Essays, Aphorisms, Autobiographical Writings,* trans. Edmund Jephcott, ed. with intro. by Peter Demetz (New York and London, 1978). Adorno's distaste for Surrealism is manifested many places in his work; see especially "Looking Back on Surrealism," in *The Idea of the Modern in Literature and the Arts,* ed. Irving Howe (New York, 1967). In his "A Portrait of Walter Benjamin," in *Prisms: Cultural Criticism and Society,* trans. Samuel and Shierry Weber (London, 1967), Adorno wrote disapprovingly, "His aim was not merely for philosophy to catch up to surrealism, but for it to become surrealistic" (p. 239).
34. Adorno, "A Portrait of Walter Benjamin," p. 235.
35. Adorno, "Sociology and Psychology," *New Left Review* (November-December 1967), no. 46; and *New Left Review* (January-February 1968), no. 47, p. 74 in no. 46.
36. *Ibid.,* p. 78.
37. Buck-Morss, p. 182. The Koenigstein position refers to talks the two friends had in that German town in the fall of 1929.
38. Adorno, Introduction to *The Positivist Dispute in German Sociology,* Adorno et al., trans. Glyn Adey and David Frisby (London, 1976), p. 39.
39. Adorno, "Sociology and Empirical Research," in *ibid.,* p. 77.
40. *Ibid.,* 79.
41. Adorno, Introduction, in *ibid.,* p. 12.
42. Therborn, "Jürgen Habermas: A New Eclecticism," *New Left Review* (May–June 1971), no. 67.
43. One might also note the impact of the method on more recent Marxist cultural criticism. Fredric Jameson, for example, clearly draws on it in *Fables of Aggression: Wyndham Lewis, the Modernist as Fascist* (Berkeley, 1979), where he defends his use of several unintegrated approaches by claiming that "the methodological eclecticism with which such a project can be reproached is unavoidable, since the discontinuities projected by these various disciplines or methods themselves correspond to objective discontinuities in their object (and beyond that, to the very fragmentation and compartmentalization of social reality in modern times)" (p. 6).

9. Adorno in America

1. Paul Lazarsfeld, "An Episode in the History of Social Research: A Memoir," *The Intellectual Migration: Europe and America, 1930–1960,* Donald Fleming and Bernard Bailyn (Cambridge, 1969), p. 301.

2. Theodor W. Adorno, "Scientific Experiences of a European Scholar in America," *The Intellectual Migration,* p. 342.

3. Lazarsfeld, p. 313. For an account of the failure written from Lazarsfeld's perspective, see David E. Morrison, "Kultur and Culture: The Case of Theodor W. Adorno and Paul F. Lazarsfeld," *Social Research* (Summer 1978), 45(2):331–55.

4. Adorno, *Minima Moralia: Reflections from Damaged Life,* trans. E. F. N. Jephcott (London, 1974), p. 22.

5. Adorno, *Gesammelte Schriften,* (Frankfurt, 1977).

6. *Ibid.,* p. 698.

7. *The New York Times,* August 7, 1969. It is held up to ridicule in Hans Mayer, *Der Repräsentant und der Martyrer: Konstellationen der Literatur* (Frankfurt, 1971), p. 145; Martin Jay, "The Frankfurt School in Exile," *Perspectives in American History* (1972), 6:356; and Zoltan Tar, *The Frankfurt School: The Critical Theories of Max Horkheimer and Theodor W. Adorno* (New York, 1977), p. 11.

8. Robert Craft, "A Bell for Adorno," *Prejudices in Disguise* (New York, 1974), p. 94.

9. Edward Shils, "Daydreams and Nightmares: Reflections on the Criticism of Mass Culture," *Sewanee Review* (Autumn 1957), 65(4):587–608; Leon Bramson, *The Political Context of Sociology* (Princeton, 1961); Herbert J. Gans, "Popular Culture in America: Social Problem in a Mass Society or Social Asset in a Pluralist Society?" in *Social Problems, A Modern Approach,* ed. Herbert S. Becker (New York, 1966).

10. This in particular was Shils' argument, which paid no attention to the hedonist dimension of Critical Theory.

11. Tar, p. 118.

12. George Friedman, *The Political Philosophy of the Frankfurt School* (Ithaca, 1981), p. 32.

13. Irving Wohlfahrt, "Hibernation: On the Tenth Anniversary of Adorno's Death," *Modern Language Notes* (December 1979), 94(6):980–81. Wohlfahrt, who studied with Adorno in the 1960s and wrote one of the first introductions to him in English (the short "Presentation of Adorno" in *New Left Review* [January 1968], no. 46), is a far more sensitive analyst of his work, and that of Benjamin, than either of the two previously cited authors. He ends this compact but very insightful piece by reversing its generally critical direction and warning against "blaming the messenger [Adorno] for the news" (p. 982).

14. Dagmar Barnouw, " 'Beute der Pragmatisierung': Adorno und Amerika," in *Die USA und Deutschland: Wechselseitige Spieglungen in der Literatur der Gegenwart,* ed. Wolfgang Paulsen (Bern, 1976). The author teaches in the German Department of Brown University in America, so perhaps the essay can be taken as another example of the American response to Adorno rather than a German reading of it.

15. *Ibid.,* p. 76.

16. Adorno, *Prisms: Culture Criticism and Society,* trans. Samuel and Shierry Weber (London, 1967), p. 98.

17. For a good discussion of this issue, see Egbert Krispyn, *Anti-Nazi Writers in Exile* (Athens, Ga., 1978).

18. The correspondence between them, which can be found in the Kracauer

Nachlass in the Schiller National Museum in Marbach am Neckar, contains many examples of their differing views of English.

19. Eugene Lunn, *Marxism and Modernism: An Historical Study of Lukács, Brecht, Benjamin, and Adorno* (Berkeley, 1982), p. 209.

20. Adorno, "Scientific Experiences of a European Scholar in America," pp. 369–70. H. Stuart Hughes is one of the few observers who has noted the validity of Adorno's remarks about his debt to America. See his *The Sea Change: The Migration of Social Thought, 1930–1965* (New York, 1975), pp. 150f. He points out how frequently American terms enter his vocabulary in the writings done after his return, terms like "healthy sex life," "some fun," "go-getters," "social research," "team," "middle range theory," "trial and error," "administrative research," "common sense," "fact finding," "statement of fact," "case studies," "facts and figures," "nose counting," and "likes and dislikes" (p. 166).

21. Adorno, "Scientific Experiences of a European Scholar in America," p. 367.

22. See, for example, his remarks that "the greatest fetish of cultural criticism is the notion of culture as such. . . . Only when neutralized and reified, does Culture allow itself to be idolized. Fetishism gravitates towards mythology." *Prisms,* pp. 23–24.

23. See, in particular, Marcuse, "The Affirmative Character of Culture," *Negations: Essays in Critical Theory,* trans. Jeremy J. Shapiro (Boston, 1968); the first use of the term came in Horkheimer's "Egoismus und Freiheitsbewegung," *Zeitschrift für Sozialforschung* (1936), 5(2):161–231.

24. Lunn, p. 208.

25. Adorno, "Scientific Experiences of a European Scholar in America," p. 367.

26. Joachim Radkau, *Die deutsche Emigration in den USA: Ihr Einfluss auf die amerikanische Europapolitik 1933–1934* (Düsseldorf, 1974). Radkau includes the *Institut für Sozialforschung* in his general indictment because of their psychologization of social problems. But he notes that Adorno's "Scientific Experiences" essay has a "skeptical and pessimistic undertone" that sets it apart from other emigré memoirs (p. 13).

27. Adorno, "Scientific Experiences of a European Scholar in America," p. 370. The desire of the returning *Institut* members to contribute to political enlightenment is expressed in a letter Horkheimer sent to Lowenthal on April 13, 1951, in which he wrote:

We stand here for the good things: for individual independence, the idea of the Enlightenment, science freed from blinders. When Fred [Pollock] reports to me that you and other friends see the type of empirical social science we are conducting here as in many ways conventional, I am convinced that you would be of another opinion could you see the thing with your own eyes. . . . As much as I yearn for pure philosophical work again, as much as I am determined to take it up again under the right conditions and devote myself solely to it, so much do I also know that effectiveness here, either for the education of students or for ourselves, is not lost. (Lowenthal archive).

28. Adorno, "Zur gegenwärtigen Stellung der empirischen Sozialforschung in Deutschland," in *Empirische Sozialforschung: Meinungs- und Marktforschung Methoden und Probleme: Schriftenreihe des Instituts zur Förderung öffentlicher Anglegenheiten e.V.* (Frankfurt, 1952).

29. See for example, Friedrich Pollock, ed. *Gruppenexperiment: Ein Studienbericht: Frankfurter Beiträge zur Soziologie,* vol. 2 (Frankfurt, 1955).

30. Adorno, *Gesammelte Schriften,* 10.2.

31. Adorno et al., *The Authoritarian Personality* (New York: 1950), 2:976.

32. The proceedings of the conference were collected as *Freud in der Gegenwart: Frankfurter Beiträge zur Soziologie,* (Frankfurt, 1957), vol. 6. The Institute's purpose in sponsoring this conference were expressed in a letter Horkheimer sent to Lowenthal on January 20, 1956:

I participate in the affair—on the urgent request of Mitscherlich—because such an event in Germany means a restrengthening of enlightened cultural forces, because young people in general no longer know of these things, but should be led through them, because the jurists in regard to the new formation of the penal code, the ministers and pedagogues in regard to the new teaching code should be reminded of these things, because psychiatry to a great extent is a scandal. I am very aware of the risks brought by such an undertaking, but it belongs to the things that justify my being here. (Lowenthal archive).

33. For an overview of the Frankfurt School's changing attitude toward this issue, see chapter 6.

34. See, for example, his remark in *Introduction to the Sociology of Music,* trans. E. B. Ashton (New York, 1976), that "it is different in America, where one meets scientists who must strain even to imagine experiencing music otherwise than by radio. The culture industry has become much more of a second nature than thus far on the old continent" (p. 231).

35. C. Wright Mills, "I.B.M. Plus Reality Plus Humanism-Sociology," *Saturday Review* (May 1954), p. 54.

36. Kuspit actually went earlier, from 1957 to 1960. See his "Theodor W. Adorno: A Memoir," *Chateau Review* (1983), 6(1):20–24.

37. Paul Breines, ed., *Critical Interruptions: New Left Perspectives on Herbert Marcuse* (New York, 1970). In 1968, Breines had written an essay on "Marcuse and the New Left in America," in Jürgen Habermas, ed., *Antworten auf Herbert Marcuse* (Frankfurt, 1968), in which he noted that "Horkheimer, Adorno, Benjamin and the perspectives developed in the *Institut für Sozialforschung* remain all but unknown" in America (p. 137).

38. See, for example, the work of Ben Agger, "On Happiness and Damaged Life," in John O'Neill, ed., *On Critical Theory* (New York, 1976); and "Dialectical Sensibility I: Critical Theory, Scientism and Empiricism," *Canadian Journal of Political and Social Theory* (Winter 1977) 1(1):1–30; "Dialectical Sensibility II: Towards a New Intellectuality," *Canadian Journal of Political and Social Theory* (Spring-Summer 1977) 1(2):47–57.

39. Fredric Jameson, "Adorno: or, Historical Tropes," *Salmagundi* (Spring 1967), 5:3–43.

40. Jameson, *Marxism and Form: Twentieth-Century Dialectical Theories of Literature* (Princeton, 1967), pp. 58–59.

41. George Steiner, *Language and Silence: Essays on Language, Literature, and the Inhuman* (New York, 1967).

42. George Lichtheim, "From Marx to Hegel," *Triquarterly* (Spring 1978) 12:5–42; republished in *From Marx to Hegel* (New York, 1971), where the citation appears on p. 21.

43. Lichtheim, *From Marx to Hegel,* p. viii. For an overview of Lichtheim's career, which discusses his links with Critical Theory, see chapter 10.

44. Martin Jay, "The Permanent Exile of Theodor W. Adorno," *Midstream* (December 1969), 15(10):62–69.

45. Russell Jacoby, review of Adorno, *Aufsätze zur Gesellschaftstheorie,* in *Telos* (Fall 1970), 6:343–48. For a general account of *Telos* and its debt to Critical Theory, see John Fekete, "*Telos* at 50," *Telos* (Winter 1981–1982), 50:161–71.

46. Russell Jacoby, "Marcuse and the New Academics: A Note on Style," *Telos* (Spring, 1970) 5:188–190; "Marxism and the Critical School," *Theory and Society* (1974), 1:231–38; "Marxism and Critical Theory: Martin Jay and Russell Jacoby," *Theory and Society* (1975), 2:257–63; review of Phil Slater, *Origin and Significance of the Frankfurt*

School in *Telos* (Spring 1977), 31:198–202; review of Zoltan Tar, *The Frankfurt School* in *Sociology and Social Research* (1978), 63:168–71; review of George Friedman, *The Political Philosophy of the Frankfurt School* in *Telos* (Fall 1981), 49:203–15.

47. Dick Howard, review of *Jargon der Eigentlichkeit*, in *Telos* (Summer 1971), 8:146–49; Susan Buck-Morss, "The Dialectic of T. W. Adorno," *Telos* (Winter 1972), 14:137–44.

48. *Telos* (Spring 1970), no. 5, table of contents.

49. *The New Left Review* did publish a two-part translation of Adorno's "Sociology and Psychology" in numbers 46 (November-December 1967) and 47 (January-February 1968), but its first extended analysis of *Critical Theory* was the Althusserian attack of Göran Therborn, "Frankfurt Marxism: A Critique," in number 63 (September-October, 1970), pp. 65–89. My essay, "The Frankfurt School's Critique of Marxist Humanism," *Social Research* (Summer 1972), 34(2):285–305 was in part a rebuttal to Therborn.

50. Martin Jay, *The Dialectical Imagination: A History of the Frankfurt School and the Institute of Social Research, 1923–1950* (Boston, 1973); Phil Slater, *Origin and Significance of the Frankfurt School: A Marxist Perspective* (London, 1977); Tar, *The Frankfurt School*; O'Neill, ed., *On Critical Theory*; David Held, *Introduction to Critical Theory: Horkheimer to Habermas* (Berkeley, 1980); Friedman, *The Political Philosophy of the Frankfurt School*; Paul Connerton, *The Tragedy of Enlightenment: An Essay on the Frankfurt School* (Cambridge, 1980); Andrew Arato and Eike Gebhardt, eds., *The Essential Frankfurt School Reader* (New York, 1977); and *The New Left Review*, ed., *Aesthetics and Politics: Debates Between Bloch, Lukács, Brecht, Benjamin, Adorno* (London, 1977). For an overview of the American reception of Critical Theory, see Douglas Kellner and Rick Roderick, "Recent Literature on Critical Theory," *New German Critique* (Spring-Summer 1981), 23:141–70.

51. Susan Buck-Morss, *The Origin of Negative Dialectics: Theodor W. Adorno, Walter Benjamin and the Frankfurt Institute* (New York, 1977). See also her "Piaget, Adorno, and the Possibilities of Dialectical Operations," in Hugh J. Silverman, ed. *Piaget, Philosophy and the Human Sciences* (Atlantic Highlands, N.J., 1980).

52. David Gross, "Lowenthal, Adorno, Barthes: Three Perspectives on Popular Culture," *Telos* (Fall 1980), 50:122–40; Martin Jay, "The Concept of Totality in Lukács and Adorno," *Telos* (Summer 1977), 30:117–37; and in Shlomo Avineri, ed., *Varieties of Marxism* (The Hague, 1977); Martin Jay, "Adorno and Kracauer: Notes on a Troubled Friendship," *Salmagundi* (Winter 1978) 40:42–66; reprinted below as chapter XIII.

53. Richard Wolin, *Walter Benjamin: An Aesthetic of Redemption* (New York, 1982); Lunn, *Marxism and Modernism*.

54. Axel Honneth, "Adorno and Habermas," *Telos* (Spring 1979), 39:45–61. See the response in the same issue by James Schmidt, "Offensive Critical Theory? Reply to Honneth," pp. 62–70.

55. Murray Bookchin, *The Ecology of Freedom* (Palo Alto, Ca., 1982); "Finding the Subject: Notes on Whitebook and 'Habermas Ltd.,'" *Telos* (Summer 1982), 52:78–98.

56. Joel Whitebook, "Saving the Subject: Modernity and the Problem of the Autonomous Individual," *Telos* (Winter 1981–1982), 50:94.

57. Gillian Rose, *The Melancholy Science: An Introduction to the Thought of Theodor W. Adorno* (London, 1978), pp. 146f. She continues the attack on Habermas in *Hegel Contra Sociology* (London: Athlone, 1981), pp. 33f, but now her perspective is closer to Hegel than to Adorno, whom she also accuses of regressing back to a form of neo-Kantianism.

58. See, for example, Jean Cohen, "Why More Political Theory?," *Telos* (Sum-

mer 1979), 40:70–94, and Seyla Benhabib, "Modernity and the Aporias of Critical Theory," *Telos* (Fall 1981), 49:39–59. Although these writers are by no means uncritical supporters of Habermas, they clearly find his version of Critical Theory an advance over Adorno's.

59. See, for example, the review of Colletti's *Marxism and Hegel* by Ben Agger in *Telos* (Summer 1975), 24:191. See also the chapter on Della Volpe and Colletti in my *Marxism and Totality: The Adventures of a Concept from Lukács to Habermas* (Berkeley, 1984).

60. See, for example, Russell Jacoby, *Dialectic of Defeat: Contours of Western Marxism* (Cambridge, 1981).

61. Michael T. Jones, "Constellations of Modernity: The Literary Essays of Theodor W. Adorno" (Ph.D. diss., Yale University, 1978); Lambert Zuidervaart, "Refractions: Truth in Adorno's Aesthetic Theory" (Ph.D. diss., University of Amsterdam, 1981 (Zuidervaart is a Canadian); the best essay in English on Adorno's aesthetic theory is Richard Wolin, "The De-Aestheticization of Art: On Adorno's *Aesthetische Theorie,*" *Telos* (Fall 1979) 41:105–127. See also Robert Lane Kauffmann, "The Theory of the Essay: Lukács, Adorno, and Benjamin," (Ph.D. diss., University of California, San Diego, 1981), and J. N. Mohanty, "The Concept of Intuition in Aesthetics Apropos a Critique by Adorno," *The Journal of Aesthetics and Art Criticism* (1980), 39:39–45.

62. Russell Berman, "Adorno, Marxism and Art," *Telos* (Winter 1977–1978, 34:157–66; Peter Uwe Hohendahl, "Autonomy of Art: Looking Back at Adorno's *Aesthetische Theorie,*" *German Quarterly* (1981), 54:133–148, and *The Institution of Criticism* (Ithaca, 1982).

63. Frank Lentricchia, *After the New Criticism* (Chicago, 1980), p. xii.

64. Ronald Weitzman, "An Introduction to Adorno's Music and Social Criticism," *Music and Letters* (July 1971), 102(3):287–98; Donald B. Kuspit, "Critical Notes on Adorno's Sociology of Music and Art," *Journal of Aesthetics and Art Criticism* (1975), 33:321–77; Wesley Blomster, "Sociology of Music: Adorno and Beyond," *Telos* (Summer 1976), 28:81–112; Rose Rosengard Subotnik, "Adorno's Diagnosis of Beethoven's Late Style: Early Symptoms of a Fatal Condition," *Journal of the American Musicological Society* (Summer 1976), 29(2):242–75; "Why is Adorno's Music Criticism the Way It Is?," *Musical Newsletter,* (Fall 1977) 7(4):3–12,; "The Historical Structure: Adorno's 'French Model' for Nineteenth-Century Music," *Nineteenth-Century Music* (July 1978), 2(1):36–60; "Kant, Adorno, and the Self-Critique of Reason: Toward a Model for Music Criticism," *Humanities in Society* (Fall 1979), 2(4):353–86, and James L. Marsh, "Adorno's Critique of Stravinsky," *New German Critique* (Winter 1983), 28:147–69. One might also add two articles by the Hungarian-born sociologist, now living in Australia, Ferenc Fehér, because they were written for American journals: "Negative Philosophy of Music—Positive Results," *New German Critique* (Winter 1975), 4:99–111, and "Rationalized Music and its Vicissitudes (Adorno's Philosophy of Music)," *Philosophy and Social Criticism* (1982), 9(1):42–65. Compare this rather paltry collection of essays with the German reception of Adorno's musicological works, a bibliography of which can be found in Burkhardt Lindner and W. Martin Lüdke, eds. *Materielien zur ästhetische Theorie Th. W. Adornos Konstruktion der Moderne* (Frankfurt, 1979, pp. 543f. For the reception in several other European countries, see the essays in *Adorno und die Musik,* ed. Otto Kolleritsch (Graz, 1977). See also Anne G. Mitchell Culver, "Theodor W. Adorno's Philosophy of Modern Music, Evaluation and Commentary," (Ph.D. diss., University of Colorado, 1973).

65. Charles Rosen, *Arnold Schoenberg* (Princeton, 1975), which does not even list anything by Adorno in the bibliography. Rosen gave a hostile paper on "Adorno and

Stravinsky" at the Adorno conference at the University of Southern California in 1979, but it was not included in the proceedings published in *Humanities in Society* (Fall 1979), 2(4). Adorno's influence can, however, be seen in Gary Schmidgall, *Literature as Opera* (New York, 1977), especially in the chapter on Berg's *Wozzeck.*

66. Carl Dalhaus, *Esthetics of Music,* trans. William Austin (Cambridge, 1982), p. 101.

67. Craft, p. 92.

68. Andreas Huyssen, "Introduction to Adorno," *New German Critique* (Fall 1975),6:3–11; Diane Waldman, "Critical Theory and Film: Adorno and 'The Culture Industry' Revisited," *New German Critique* (Fall 1977), 12:39–60; Stanley Aronowitz, *The Crisis in Historical Materialism: Class, Politics and Culture in Marxist Theory* (South Hadley, Mass., 1981); Douglas Kellner, "TV, Ideology, and Emancipatory Popular Culture," *Socialist Review* (1979), 45:13–53; "Network Television and American Society: Introduction to a Critical Theory of Television, *"Theory and Society* (January 1981) 10(1):31–62; "Kulturindustrie und Massenkommunikation. Die Kritische Theorie und ihre Folgen," in Wolfgang Bonss and Axel Honneth, eds. *Sozialforschung als Kritik: Zum Sozialwissenschaftlichen Potential der Kritischen Theorie* (Frankfurt 1982); Philip Rosen, "Adorno and Film Music: Theoretical Notes on Composing for the Films," *Yale French Studies* (1980), 60:157–182; Miriam Hansen, "Introduction to Adorno, 'Transparencies on Film' (1966)" *New German Critique* (Fall/Winter, 1981–82) 24/25:186–98; Mattei Calinescu, *Faces of Modernity: Avant-Garde, Decadence, Kitsch* (Bloomington, 1977); Jon Brenkman, "Mass Media: From Collective Experience to the Culture of Privatization," *Social Text* (Winter 1979), 1:94–109; Thomas Andrae, "Adorno on Film and Mass Culture," *Jump Cut* (May 1979) vol. 20: For still more recent considerations, see J. Frow, "Mediation and Metaphor. Adorno and the Sociology of Art." *Clio* (1982), 12:57–66, and Patrick Brantlinger, *Bread and Circuses: Theories of Mass Culture and Social Decay* (Ithaca: 1983), chap. 7.

69. Adorno, "Culture Industry Reconsidered," *New German Critique* (Fall 1975) 6:12–19; "Transparencies on Film," *New German Critique* (Fall/Winter 1981–82), 24/25:199–205.

70. Bruce Brown, *Marx, Freud, and the Critique of Everyday Life: Toward A Permanent Cultural Revolution* (New York, 1973); Russell Jacoby, *Social Amnesia* (Boston, 1975).

71. Christopher Lasch, *Haven in a Heartless World* (New York, 1977); *The Culture of Narcissism* (New York, 1979).

72. Joel Kovel, *A Complete Guide to Therapy* (New York, 1977); *The Age of Desire: Reflections of a Radical Psychoanalyst* (New York, 1981).

73. See, for example, Jessica Benjamin, "The End of Internalization: Adorno's Social Psychology," *Telos* (Summer 1977), 32:42–64; "Authority and the Family Revisited: or, a World Without Fathers," *New German Critique* (Winter 1978), 13:35–57; "Die Antinomien des patriarchalischen Denkens: Kritische Theorie und Psychoanalyse," in Bonss and Honneth; Mark Poster, *Critical Theory of the Family* (New York, 1978).

74. Pier Aldo Rovatti, "Critical Theory and Phenomenology," *Telos* (Spring 1973), 15:25–40. Rovatti is an editor of *Aut Aut* and heavily influenced by the phenomenological Marxism of Enzo Paci, which also had a strong impact on Piccone. See, for example, his "Beyond Identity Theory" in O'Neill, in which he attacks the Frankfurt School for its lack of appreciation for Husserl.

75. Paul Piccone, "The Crisis of One-Dimensionality," *Telos* (Spring 1978), 35:43–54; "The Changing Function of Critical Theory," *New German Critique* (Fall 1977),

12:29–37. Piccone's point is that the system is so well-established now that it can tolerate, indeed even generate, pockets of "artificial" negativity that nonetheless function to stabilize it.

76. Fred R. Dallmayr, "Phenomenology and Critical Theory: Adorno," *Cultural Hermeneutics,* 3:367–405; *Twilight of Subjectivity: Contributions to a Post-Individualist Theory* (Amherst, 1981). It might also be noted that another philosophical target of Adorno's, Wittgenstein, has been defended in precisely the same way. According to H. Stuart Hughes, "in Adorno's failure to come to grips with the *Philosophical Investigations,* an enormous intellectual opportunity was missed—the chance to associate two of the finest intelligences of the century in the enterprise of bridging the philosophical traditions which Wittgenstein's death had cut off in midcourse" (*The Sea Change,* p. 167).

77. Dallmayr, "Phenomenology and Critical Theory: Adorno," p. 395.

78. Herman Mörchen, *Adorno und Heidegger—Untersuchung einer philosophischen Kommunikationsverweigerung* (Stuttgart, 1981).

79. Jean-Francois Lyotard, "Adorno as the Devil," *Telos* (Spring 1974), 19:128–37.

80. See, for example, James Miller, "Some Implication of Nietzsche's Thought for Marxism," *Telos* (Fall 1978), 37:22–41 and Rose, pp. 18f. Another common theme that some commentators have claimed links Adorno and Derrida is the importance of Husserl as a target of their work. It would, in fact, be very interesting to compare Adorno's *Metakritik der Erkenntnistheorie* with Derrida's *Speech and Phenomena: and Other Essays on Husserl's Theory of Signs,* trans. David B. Allison (Evanston, 1973).

81. Terry Eagleton, *Walter Benjamin: Or Towards a Revolutionary Criticism* (London, 1981), p. 141.

82. Michael Ryan, *Marxism and Deconstruction: A Critical Articulation* (Baltimore, 1982).

83. *Ibid.,* p. 75.

84. Hubert L. Dreyfus and Paul Rabinow, *Michel Foucault: Beyond Structuralism and Hermeneutics* (Chicago, 1982), p. xii.

85. Tom Long, "Marx and Western Marxism in the 1970's," *The Berkeley Journal of Sociology* (1980), 25:36.

86. Horkheimer and Adorno, *Dialectic of Enlightenment,* trans. John Cumming (New York, 1972), p. 231.

87. Foucault, *Power/Knowledge: Selected Interviews and Other Writings 1972-1977,* ed. Colin Gordon, trans. Colin Gordon et al. (New York, 1980), p. 145.

88. Jameson, "Reification and Utopia in Mass Culture," *Social Text* (Winter 1979), 1:130–48. See also his further reflections on these issues in *The Political Unconscious: Narrative as a Socially Symbolic Act* (Ithaca, 1981); and his "Reflections in Conclusion" to *Aesthetics and Politics.*

89. Jameson, "Reification and Utopia in Mass Culture," p. 148.

90. Habermas, "Modernity versus Postmodernity," *New German Critique* (Winter 1981), 22:3–14.

91. Habermas, "The Entwinement of Myth and Enlightenment," *New German Critique* (Spring/Summer 1982), 26:13–30.

92. See, for example, Peter Uwe Hohendahl, review of Buck-Morss in *Telos* (Winter 1977–78), 34:185.

93. As the examples cited above demonstrate, his American reception has been confined almost entirely to academic circles. But a glimmer of a slightly more popular appreciation may perhaps be discerned in the fact that a play entitled "The Dialectic of Enlightenment" by Daryl Chin was produced off-Broadway in New York in 1982. The play

seems to have borrowed only the title from Horkheimer and Adorno's work. But surely there is some significance in the fact that the reviewer for *The Village Voice,* Roderick Mason Faber, could assume enough recognition of the authors to pun on one of their names in his negative review, which was called "Adore? No."

94. See Rose, p. 13.

95. Adorno, "Die Wunde Heine," in *Noten zur Literatur, Gesammelte Schriften* 2 (Frankfurt, 1974), p. 100.

96. Harvey Gross, "Adorno in Los Angeles: The Intellectual in Emigration," *Humanities in Society* (Fall 1979), 2:350.

11. The Extraterritorial Life of Siegfried Kracauer

1. Kracauer's *Nachlass* was deposited in 1973 in the Schiller National Museum in Marbach am Neckar. All letters quoted in the text can be found there, although I consulted the correspondence with Leo Lowenthal in Professor Lowenthal's own collection in Berkeley, California. I am deeply indebted to Dr. Werner Volke and the staff of the Schiller National Museum for their courtesy and helpfulness during my stay in Marbach.

2. The only instance of "success" I have found is in the article by Hans G. Helms entitled "Der wunderliche Kracauer," *Neues Forum* (June-July 1971), p. 27, where Kracauer's age in 1964 is said to be 70, when it was in fact 75.

3. Kracauer to Adorno, November 8, 1963. The other correspondents with whom he discussed his "chronological anonymity" were Erika Lorenz, Michel Ciment, and Hans Kohn. Unless otherwise indicated, the letters were written in German and translated by me.

4. Theodor W. Adorno, "Siegfried Kracauer Tot," *Frankfurter Allgemeine Zeitung* (December 1, 1966), p. 20.

5. Peter Gay, *Weimar Culture: The Outsider as Insider* (New York, 1968), chapter 4.

6. Adorno, "Siegfried Kracauer Tot."

7. Asja Lacis, *Revolutionär im Beruf; Berichte über proletarisches Theater, über Meyerhold, Brecht, Benjamin, und Piscator,* ed. Hildegard Brenner (Munich, 1971), p. 62.

8. Conversation with Professor Mayer, Milwaukee, Wisconsin, November 30, 1973.

9. Conversation with Professor Arnheim, Cambridge, Massachusetts, December 21, 1973.

10. His most notable work was a two-volume *Geschichte der Juden in Frankfurt a. M. (1150–1824)* published posthumously in 1925 and 1927 with the editorial help of his widow, Hedwig. He was supported by the Jewish Community of Frankfurt in this endeavor.

11. "Gedanken über die Freudschaft," in *Gabe Herrn Rabbiner Dr. Nobel zum 50. Geburtstag* (Frankfurt, 1921). This was the second part of an essay whose first part appeared as "Über die Freundschaft," *Logos* (Tubingen, 1917/18, 7(2). Both parts were published by Suhrkamp in 1972.

12. "Die Bibel auf Deutsch," *Frankfurter Zeitung* (henceforth *FZ*) (April 17 and 28, 1926); reprinted in *Das Ornament der Masse* (Frankfurt, 1963). Buber and Rosenzweig answered the attack in the *FZ* on May 18, 1926; their essay is reprinted in *Die Schrift und ihre Verdeutschung* (Berlin, 1936), pp. 276ff. Kracauer also attacked Zionism in a 1922 article entitled "Die Wartenden," reprinted in *Das Ornament der Masse,* p. 112.

13. *Die Entwicklung der Schmiedekunst in Berlin, Potsdam und einigen*

Städten der Mark vom 17. Jahrhundert bis zum Beginn des 19. Jahrhunderts (Worms, 1915).

14. *Ginster, Von ihm selbst geschrieben* (Berlin, 1928); 2d ed. *Ginster* (without final chapter), (Frankfurt, 1963); 3d ed. (with final chapter), (Frankfurt, 1973), published as vol. 7 of *Schriften* with his other novel, *Georg.*

15. Theodor W. Adorno, "Der wunderliche Realist," *Noten zur Literatur III* (Frankfurt, 1965), p. 87.

16. These have been collected as *Strassen in Berlin und anderswo* (Frankfurt, 1964).

17. "Georg Simmel," *Logos* (1920), 9(3); reprinted in *Das Ornament der Masse; Soziologie als Wissenschaft, Eine erkenntnistheoretische Untersuchung* (Dresden, 1922); reprinted in vol. 1 of *Schriften* (Frankfurt, 1971).

18. Georg Lukács, *Die Theorie des Romans* (Berlin, 1920), cited on page 13 of *Soziologie als Wissenschaft* (1971 ed.). Kracauer reviewed this book twice, in *Die Weltbühne* (September 1, 1921), 17(35), and *Neue Blatter für Kunst und Literatur* (October 4, 1921), 4(1).

19. *Ibid.,* p. 29. The term, of course, was originally Hegel's.

20. He attacked Scheler's turn to Catholicism in "Katholizismus und Relativismus," *FZ* (November 19, 1921); reprinted in *Das Ornament der Masse.*

21. Modris Eksteins, "The Frankfurter Zeitung: Mirror of Weimar Democracy," *Journal of Contemporary History* (1971), 6(4):5. Kracauer himself wrote an article on Leopold Sonnemann for the *Encyclopedia of the Social Sciences,* vol. 14 (London, 1934).

22. Benno Reifenberg (1892–1970) was trained as an art historian. He joined the *FZ* in 1919 and became its *feuilleton* director in 1924. In 1930–32, he was the head of its Paris bureau. After the war, he was a founder and leading writer for *Die Gegenwart.*

23. "Die Kleinen Ladenmädchen gehen ins Kino," reprinted in *Das Ornament der Masse.*

24. Kurt Pinthus, "Quo Vadis—Kino?" cited in Karsten Witte's excellent *Nachwort* to Kracauer's *Kino* (Frankfurt, 1974), p. 266.

25. Walter Benjamin treated the early years of the *feuilleton* in Paris in his unfinished *Passagenarbeit;* see the selection in his *Charles Baudelaire: A Lyric Poet in the Era of High Capitalism,* trans. Harry Zohn (London, 1973), pp. 27–34.

26. Carl Schorske, "Politics and the Psyche in *fin-de-siècle* Vienna; Schnitzler and Hofmannstahl," *American Historical Review* (July, 1961), 116(4):935. For a more recent appraisal of the role of the *feuilleton* in Vienna, see Allen Janik and Stephen Toulmin, *Wittgenstein's Vienna* (New York, 1973).

27. "Über Arbeitsnachweise," reprinted in *Strassen in Berlin und Anderswo,* and "Das Ornament der Masse," reprinted in the collection with the same title.

28. Asja Lacis, *Revolutionär im Beruf,* p. 63. The crucial article was "Der Mann mit dem Kinoapparat," *FZ* (May 19, 1929), reprinted in *Kino.*

29. *Die Angestellten: Aus dem neuesten Deutschland,* 1st and 2d ed. (Frankfurt, 1930); 3d ed. (Allensbach and Bonn, 1959), with an intro. by Erich Peter Neumann; 4th ed. (Berlin, 1970); 5th ed. in vol. 1 of *Schriften* (Frankfurt, 1971), and as separate book with review by Walter Benjamin appended.

30. One of the chapters in *Die Angestellten* is called "Asyl für Obdachlose," which echoes the phrase "transzendentale Obdachlosigkeit," a frequent refrain in *Die Theorie des Romans.*

31. Hans Fallada, *What Now, Little Man?,* trans. E. Sutton (London, 1933).

32. R. S. and H. M. Lynd, *Middletown . . . Contemporary American Culture* (London, 1929).

33. *Die Angestellten*, p. 316 in *Schriften I*.

34. Kracauer to Adorno, May 25, 1930.

35. See the bibliography in Fritz Croner, *Soziologie der Angestellten* (Cologne, 1962).

36. Leo Lowenthal has remarked on this aspect of the Adorno-Kracauer friendship. In a letter to Adorno on December 10, 1962, Kracauer speaks of "reawakening the old Platonic eros" in connection with the writer Alexander Kluge. Before the war, Kracauer's closest friend was Otto Heinebach, who was the model for the character named Otto in *Ginster*. He died in the fighting. (Letter from Lili Kracauer to Hans G. Helms, March 10, 1970).

37. Kracauer to Lowenthal, January 3, 1964.

38. "Aufruhr der Mittelschichten," *FZ* (December 10 and 11, 1931); reprinted in *Das Ornament der Masse*.

39. "Die Wissenschaftskrise," *FZ* (March 8 and 22, 1923); reprinted in *Das Ornament der Masse*, p. 208.

40. Helms has stressed this in his essay on Kracauer.

41. *Ginster*, 2d ed., p. 48.

42. Theodor W. Adorno, "Der wunderliche Realist," p. 98.

43. *Die Angestellten*, p. 212 in *Schriften I*.

44. Walter Benjamin, "Politisierung der Intelligenz," reprinted in *Die Angestellten*, 5th ed. not in *Schriften*, p. 118.

45. Among the reviews are the following: Kracauer review of Bloch's *Thomas Münzer als Theologe der Revolution* in *FZ* (August 2, 1922); Kracauer of Benjamin's *Ursprung des deutschen Trauerspiels* and *Einbahnstrasse* in *FZ* (July 15, 1928), reprinted in *Das Ornament der masse*, Kracauer of Adorno's *Kierkegaard: Konstruktion des Aesthetischen*, written for *FZ*, but not printed because of the Nazi takeover; Bloch of Kracauer's *Die Angestellten* in *Neue Rundschau* (December 1930), 41(12), and in *Erbschaft dieser Zeit* (Frankfurt, 1962); Benjamin of Kracauer's *Die Angestellten* (see note 44); Benjamin of Adorno's *Kierkegaard* in *Vossische Zeitung* (April 2, 1933); and Adorno of Kracauer's *Jacques Offenbach und das Paris seiner Zeit* in *Zeitschrift für Sozialforschung* (1937), 6(3).

46. See, for example, Benjamin's complaint to Gershom Scholem that many of the ideas in Kracauer's critique of the Buber-Rosensweig translation of the bible were his. Letter to Scholem, March 29, 1926, in Walter Benjamin, *Briefe*, ed. Gershom Scholem and Theodor W. Adorno, 2 vols. (Frankfurt, 1966), p. 429. Many of the same ideas were later to play a prominent role in Adorno's attack on Heidegger in *Jargon of Authenticity*, trans. Kurt Tarnowski and Frederic Will (Evanston, Ill., 1973), as Adorno acknowledged in a letter to Kracauer (July 22, 1963).

47. Quoted in Adorno, "Der wunderliche Realist," p. 86.

48. *Der Detektiv-Roman; Ein philosophischer Traktat* in *Schriften I*; for references to Kierkegaard, see pp. 107–9.

49. Bloch to Kracauer, June 6, 1926. I am indebted to Karsten Witte for drawing my attention to the lost manuscript underlying the Lukács debate.

50. *Die Angestellten*, p. 216.

51. Kracauer to Bloch, June 29, 1926.

52. Lili Kracauer to Hans G. Helms, June 19, 1970.

53. Bloch to Kracauer, April 29, 1931; Kracauer to Bloch, May 29, 1932. The review appeared in the *FZ* on April 5, 1932.

54. In a letter to Adorno, written on December 21, 1930, Kracauer wrote of a meeting with Brecht: "Once the conversation turned to theoretical matters, one had the

feeling of talking with a school boy *(Obertertianer)*. The craziest is that some people are taken in by this inverted Romanticism, whose brutality is possible only in a national socialist country. For Benjamin I have explanations, for others I don't." In a letter to Bloch on July 5, 1934, he made sarcastic remarks about Benjamin's trip to his "God" in Denmark (where Brecht was in exile) and said that Kafka would be astonished to learn that his work was so close to Brecht's and Communism (as Benjamin had asserted).

55. See note 44. Kracauer's appreciation is expressed in a letter to Erika Lorenz. October 22, 1961.

56. *Ibid.*, 122. Benjamin did not choose the phrase "rag-picker" idly. It was a key concept in his understanding of nineteenth-century Paris and Baudelaire, who wrote a prose-poem about the figure. See Benjamin, *Charles Baudelaire: A Lyric Poet in the Era of High Capitalism*, pp. 19–20, 79–80.

57. See notes 2 and 15. Helms demonstrates how the recent publication history of Kracauer's works, especially the first German translation of *From Caligari to Hitler* and the second edition of *Ginster*, helped mute his earlier radicalism.

58. Joseph Roth, *Briefe, 1911–39*, ed. with intro. by Hermann Kesten, (Cologne, 1970), p. 175.

59. *Die Angestellten*, p. 207.

60. *Ibid.,* p. 304.

61. Kracauer to Adorno, July 22, 1930.

62. Letters from Tucholsky to Kracauer, March 4, 1927, and Ossietzky to Kracauer, July 7, 1929. Tucholsky, who lived in Paris, was very enthusiastic about Kracauer's descriptions of Parisian life. Ossietzky wrote positively about *Ginster.*

63. Kracauer to Erika Lorenz, March 31, 1962.

64. See notes 12 and 16.

65. On December 8, 1934, Mann wrote to Kracauer that "the high literary qualities of your grand picture of society have not failed to make their impression on me." See Karsten Witte, *Nachwort to Schriften*, vol. 7, p. 505.

66. The article, a review of an American film, was called "The Charlatan as President." It has been reprinted in *Kino*, pp. 221–23.

67. Benjamin, *Briefe*, vol. 2, p. 62.

68. Kracauer, *History: The Last Things Before the Last* (New York, 1969), p. 83.

69. Kracauer, *Jacques Offenbach und das Paris seiner Zeit* (Amsterdam, 1937); 2d ed. as *Pariser Leben. Jacques Offenbach und seine Zeit* (Munich, 1962); *Jacques Offenbach ou le secret du Second Empire*, with a preface by Daniel Halévy (Paris, 1937); *Orpheus in Paris: Offenbach and the Paris of his Time*, trans. Gwenda David and Eric Mosbacher (London, 1939). The English edition dropped Kracauer's forward without explanation.

70. *Orpheus in Paris*, p. 289.

71. *Ibid.*

72. See note 25.

73. See note 45.

74. Conversation with Henry Pachter, New York, September 4, 1973; Pachter was on the same ship as Kracauer.

75. Kracauer to Adorno, March 28, 1941.

76. Kracauer to Pollock, March 28, 1941.

77. Conversation with Bernard Karpel, New York, September 7, 1973.

78. Appended to *From Caligari to Hitler: A Psychological History of the German Film* (Princeton, New Jersey, 1947).

79. *Ibid.*, p. 289.
80. *Ibid.*, p. 305.
81. "Über die Aufgabe des Filmkritikers," *FZ* (May 23, 1932); reprinted in *Kino*,
p. 9.
82. "Die kleinen Ladenmädchen gehen ins Kino," in *Das Ornament der Masse*,
p. 279.
83. *From Caligari to Hitler*, p. 6. This position marked his approach as early as "Die Kleinen Ladenmädchen gehen ins Kino," where he wrote: "the idiotic and unreal film fantasies are the *day dreams of society* . . ." (p. 280, italics in original).
84. Ernst Kris, *German Radio Propaganda* (New York, 1944). Kracauer's social psychological approach to fascist behavior also links him to the work done by his friends at the *Institut für Sozialforschung* that led to *The Authoritarian Personality* (New York, 1950).
85. *From Caligari to Hitler*, p. 250.
86. Eric Rohde, *Tower of Babel: Speculations on the Cinema* (London, 1966),
p. 86.
87. *Die Angestellten*, p. 287. For a Marxist discussion of Kracauer's critique of the *Neue Sachlichkeit*, see Helmut Lethen, *Die Neue Sachlichkeit* (Frankfurt, 1970), esp. pp. 102–5. He attacks Kracauer for remaining a "free-floating intellectual" despite himself. Kracauer's distrust of groups is in fact clearly evident as early as his 1922 essay "Die Gruppe als Ideenträger," reprinted in *Das Ornament der Masse*.
88. *From Caligari to Hitler*, p. 165.
89. *Ibid*, p. 272.
90. Among the reviews were Seymour Stern in the *Los Angeles Daily News* (May 10, 1947) and *The New Leader* (June 28, 1947); Eric Bentley in *The New York Times Book Review* (May 18, 1947); Arthur Schlesinger, Jr., in the *Nation* (July 26, 1947); Richard Griffith in *New Movies*. (Summer 1947), 22(4); Franklin Fearing in *Hollywood Quarterly* (July 1947),2(4); David T. Bazelon in *Commentary* (August 1947), 4(2); Iris Barry in *The New Republic* (May 19, 1947), 116(20); Hans Sahl in *The Modern Review* (August 1947); Herman G. Weinberg in *Sight and Sound* (Summer 1947); Karl W. Hinckle in *Etc., A Review of General Semantics* (Winter 1948), 5(2); and L. M. Hanks, Jr. in *The Journal of Aesthetics and Art Criticism* (December 1947), 6(2). Robert Warshow wrote a letter to *The New Leader* on August 9, 1947, defending Kracauer against Stern's attack.
91. Adorno, "Der wunderliche Realist," p. 105.
92. Peter Gay's *Weimar Culture* follows Kracauer's judgments closely, but David Stewart Hull's *Film in the Third Reich: A Study of the German Cinema, 1933–1945* (Berkeley, 1968), is far more critical, calling Kracauer's major thesis "preposterous" (p. 3). I. C. Jarvie, *Towards a Sociology of the Cinema* (London, 1970), and Dieter Prokop, *Materialien zur Theorie des Films, Aesthetik, Soziologie, Politik* (Munich, 1971) are equally hostile. For a detailed and wide-ranging defense of Kracauer, see Michael Schröter, *Über Siegfried Kracauers Filmtheorie—zugleich ein Beitrag zur angewandten Psychoanalyse* (unpub. Diplomarbeit, Free University of Berlin, 1972).
93. Lotte H. Eisner, *The Haunted Screen*, trans. R. Greaves (London, 1969).
94. *Satellite Mentality: Political Attitudes and Propaganda Susceptibilities of Non-Communists in Hungary, Poland and Czechoslovakia* (New York, 1956).
95. "The Challenge of Qualitative Content Analysis," *The Public Opinion Quarterly* (Winter 1952–53), 16(4).
96. Kracauer to Erika Lorenz, October 22, 1961.
97. Kracauer to Leo Lowenthal, October 26, 1955; Adorno, "Der wunderliche Realist," p. 100. For an implicit endorsement of Kracauer's position, see George Steiner's

essay on Nabokov, significantly entitled "Extraterritorial," in *Extraterritorial: Papers on Literature and the Language Revolution* (London, 1972).

98. Pauline Kael, "Is There a Cure for Film Criticism? Or, Some Unhappy Thoughts on Siegfried Kracauer's *Theory of Film: The Redemption of Physical Reality,*" reprinted in *I Lost It at the Movies* (Boston, 1965), p. 260.

99. Kracauer to Leo Lowenthal, October 20, 1956. (Original in English).

100. Kracauer to Leo Lowenthal, August 16, 1958. (Original in English).

101. Kracauer to Leo Lowenthal, October 29, 1960.

102. "Die Photographie," *FZ* (October 28, 1927), reprinted in *Das Ornament der Masse;* "Der historische Film," *National-Zeitung Basel* (May 9, 1940); reprinted in *Kino;* "Abstrakter Film," *FZ* (March 13, 1928), reprinted in *Kino.*

103. "Abstrakter Film," p. 47. Still, it would be erroneous to deny that Kracauer also criticized *The Cabinet of Doctor Caligari* for what Paul Rotha called its "studio constructivism," that is, a violation of film's inherently realistic character. (*From Caligari to Hitler,* p. 76)

104. See, for example, his remarks on the relationship between the capitalist production process, the rationalization of the world, and the Tiller Girls precision dancing act in "Das Ornament der Masse," pp. 53–55.

105. Adorno to Kracauer, February 5, 1965; Kracauer responded on March 3, 1965, arguing that film did have an immanent development apart from its social function. For a vigorous defense of the essential unity of the two books, see Michael Schröter's *Diplomarbeit.*

106. My discussion of the history of film criticism relies in large measure on V. F. Perkins, *Film as Film: Understanding and Judging Movies* (London, 1972) and Andrew Tudor, *Theories of Film* (London, 1974).

107. Rudolf Arnheim, *Film as Art* (Berkeley and Los Angeles, 1957); Paul Rotha, *The Film Till Now* (New York, 1950); Vachel Lindsay, *The Art of the Moving Picture* (New York, 1970); and Béla Balázs, *Theory of the Film* (London, 1952).

108. V. F. Perkins, *Film as Film,* p. 11.

109. André Bazin, *Qu'est-ce que le Cinema?,* 4 vols. (Paris, 1958, 1959, 1961, and 1962); English trans. of vols. 1 and 2 as *What is Cinema?* (Berkeley and Los Angeles, 1967 and 1971).

110. André Bazin, *What is Cinema?* vol. 1, p. 12.

111. Tudor argues that Eisenstein should not be seen as the high priest of formalism, although this has frequently been the case.

112. Kracauer, *Theory of Film,* pp. 215–31; Bazin, *What is Cinema?,* vol. 1, pp. 76–124.

113. See note 9.

114. *Theory of Film,* p. 15.

115. *Ibid.,* p. 305.

116. *Ibid.,* p. 17.

117. *Ibid.,* pp. 60–74.

118. *Ibid.,* p. 286.

119. *Ibid.,* p. 295.

120. *Ibid.,* p. 301. For a similar argument, see the 1926 essay "Kult der Zerstreuung," reprinted in *Das Ornament der Masse,* p. 315–16.

121. *Ibid.,* pp. 265–70.

122. *Ibid.,* p. 309.

123. *Ibid.,* p. 309. Schröter makes the interesting point that the implications

of Kracauer's film theory are anarchistic (p. 44). This jibes with Kracauer's self-description in his letter to Bloch of June 29, 1926, which Schröter could not have seen.

124. Walter Benjamin, *Illuminations: Essays and Reflections*, ed. with intro. by Hannah Arendt, trans. Harry Zohn (New York, 1968). Kracauer himself had advanced a similar argument in "Kult der Zerstreuung" in 1926.

125. Herbert Read in *British Journal of Aesthetics* (April 1962), 2(2); Rudolf Arnheim, in *Journal of Aesthetics and Art Criticism* (1963), 21; republished as "Melancholy Unshaped" in *Toward a Psychology of Art* (Berkeley and Los Angeles, 1972).

126. See note 9.

127. Arnheim, "Melancholy Unshaped," p. 180.

128. *Ibid.,* p. 186.

129. *Ibid.,* p. 191.

130. See note 98.

131. *Ibid.,* p. 244.

132. *Ibid.,* pp. 245–46.

133. *Ibid.,* p. 259.

134. Parker Tyler, *Sex Psyche Etcetera in the Film* (New York, 1969); George W. Linden, *Reflections on the Screen* (Belmont, Cal., 1970); Gunther Engels, "In der Zwangsjacke der Theorie," *Saarbrückner Zeitung* (January 30/31, 1965); for Perkins and Tudor, see note 105.

135. Pauline Kael, "Is There a Cure for Film Criticism," p. 245.

136. In *Theory of Film* (New York, 1960), Kracauer does talk about some of Fellini's earlier films, especially *The Nights of Cabiria* and *La Strada,* but he sees them in the context of neorealism. He also speaks highly of Buñuel, but it is the postsurrealist Buñuel of *Land Without Bread* and *Los Olvidados.* Bergman is mentioned only in passing, but Kracauer tries to save him for his thesis by saying that the "down-to-earth attitude" of certain characters in *The Seventh Seal* "in a measure acclimatize(s) the film to the medium (p. 308). Resnais, Godard, and Antonioni had not yet made enough of a mark to be considered in the book. But we do know from his later correspondence that he considered Resnais's *Last Year at Marienbad* a pretentious bore. (Kracauer to Michel Ciment, May 23, 1965).

137. *Theory of Film,* p. 169–70.

138. "Die Wartenden," *FZ* (March 12, 1922); reprinted in *Das Ornament der Masse,* p. 108–9.

139. Arnheim, "Melancholy Unshaped," p. 183.

140. *Theory of Film,* p. 306.

141. Andrew Sarris, "Notes on the Auteur Theory in 1962," *Film Culture* (1962–63), vol. 27. Pauline Kael also ridiculed Sarris in "Circles and Squares: Joys and Sarris" in *I Lost It at the Movies.*

142. Christian Metz, *Language et Cinéma* (Paris, 1971); Peter Wollen, *Signs and Meaning in the Cinema* (London, 1969).

143. Helmut Günther, review of *Ginster* in *Welt und Wort* (1964), vol. 3.

144. Erika Lorenz, *Siegfried Kracauer als Soziologe* (Diplomarbeit, Johann Wolfgang Goethe Universitat, Frankfurt, 1962). Adorno informed Kracauer of her decision to leave West Germany in a letter of January 10, 1964.

145. See note 15.

146. The unsigned Kirkus review of February 15, 1969, called the book "passé and muddled," ill-informed on contemporary writings in the philosophy of history and in need of "a dose of analytic rigor." Iggers' review was in the *American Historical Review*

(February 1970), 75(3); he called the book "a real gem," although he took issue with its interpretation of Marc Bloch.

147. J. H. Hexter to Sheldon Meyer, April 26, 1967; Werner Kaegi's praise was quoted in a letter from Lili Kracauer to Sheldon Meyer, December 11, 1969. Other letters favorable to Kracauer's essay on "Time and History" came from Karl Löwith (January 20, 1964), H. I. Marrou (April 20, 1964), Arnold Hauser (February 2, 1964), and Erwin Panofsky (March 16, 1964).

148. *History: The Last Things Before the Last,* p. 163. Proust's work also played a crucial role in *Theory of Film;* Michael Schröter has a number of illuminating observations on its significance (pp. 59f).

149. Wilhelm Dilthey, *Pattern and Meaning in History: Thoughts on History and Society,* ed. with intro. by H. P. Rickman (New York, 1961), p. 106.

150. Adorno, "Der wunderliche Realist," p. 100. This accusation infuriated Kracauer.

151. Lili Kracauer to Hans G. Helms, June 19, 1970.

152. Adolph Lowe, "Thoughts on Siegfried Kracauer," delivered at his funeral in New York, November 27, 1966, now in the *Nachlass.*

153. Kracauer to Leo Lowenthal, October 29, 1966.

154. The chapters are as follows: "Nature," "The Historical Approach," "Present Interest," "The Historian's Journey," "The Structure of the Historical Universe," "Ahaseurus, or the Riddle of Time," "General History and the Aesthetic Approach," and "The Anteroom."

155. Kracauer to Leo Lowenthal, February 16, 1961.

156. All of these are collected in *Das Ornament der Masse,* with the exception of "Der verbotene Blick," which appeared in the *FZ* (April 9, 1925) and is reprinted in *Strassen in Berlin und anderswo.* (Letter from Erika Lorenz to Kracauer, February 2, 1962).

157. *History: The Last Things Before the Last,* p. 4.

158. *Ibid.,* p. 5.

159. *Ibid.,* p. 123.

160. *Ibid.,* p. 134.

161. *Ibid.,* p. 131.

162. *Ibid.,* p. 138.

163. *Ibid.,* p. 136.

164. *Ibid.,* p. 25.

165. *Ibid.,* p. 67.

166. *Ibid.,* p. 68.

167. *Ibid.,* p. 92.

168. Walter Benjamin, *Ursprung des deutschen Trauerspiels* in *Schriften,* vol. 1 (Frankfurt, 1955). In a review of Kurt Breysig's *Vom geschichtlichen Werden,* vol. 2 *(Die Macht des Gedankens in der Geschichte),* which is contained in the Kracauer *Nachlass* under the category "Old German Manuscripts," Kracauer made a similar critique of induction as the sole mode of historical knowledge. Although no date is affixed, the review appears to be from the Weimar period.

169. *History: The Last Things Before the Last,* p. 101.

170. Robert K. Merton, *On the Shoulders of Giants: A Shandean Postscript* (New York, 1965). Kracauer communicated his admiration to Merton in a letter, which Merton deeply appreciated. (Letter from Merton to Lili Kracauer, June 28, 1968).

171. In German in *Zeugnisse, Theodor W. Adorno zum sechzigsten Gebürtstag,* ed. Hermann Schweppenhäuser and Rolf Tiedemann (Frankfurt, 1963); in English in

History and Theory, Beiheft 6 (Middletown, Conn., 1966); in Italian in *Tempo Presente* (1965).

172. *History,* p. 157.

173. Erwin Panofsky, *Renaissance and Renascences in Western Art* (Stockholm, 1960); George Kubler, *The Shape of Time: Remarks on the History of Things* (New Haven 1962); Henri Focillon, *The Life of Forms in Art* (New York, 1963). During the writing of *History,* Kracauer corresponded on several occasions with Panofsky and Kubler, who had been Focillon's student.

174. Hans Robert Jauss, *Zeit und Erinnerung in Marcel Proust's "A la recherche du temps perdu,"* (Heidelberg, 1955). See also Jauss's *Literaturgeschichte als Provokation* (Frankfurt, 1970), p. 195–96, for positive remarks on Kracauer.

175. Kracauer to Lévi-Strauss, December 18, 1963 (original in English).

176. Lévi-Strauss to Kracauer, December 23, 1963 (original in English).

177. Kracauer to Marrou, May 18, 1964 (original in English). Kracauer was indebted to Marrou's *De la connaissance historique* (Paris, 1962) and to several of his articles on historical method.

178. Walter Benjamin, "Theses on the Philosophy of History," in *Illuminations.*

179. *History: The Last Things Before the Last,* p. 155.

180. *Ibid.,* p. 162. Kracauer's point is repeated in Roger Shattuck's recent Modern Masters Series study, *Proust* (London, 1974), p. 119.

181. The essay in which many of these ideas are most clearly adumbrated is "Die Wartenden," *FZ* (March 12, 1922); reprinted in *Das Ornament der Masse.*

182. Hans-George Gadamer, *Wahrheit und Methode* (Tübingen, 1960).

183. *History: The Last Things Before the Last,* p. 199–200.

184. *Ibid.,* p. 195.

185. *Ibid.,* p. 217.

186. *Ibid.,* p. 14.

187. *Ibid.,* p. 219.

188. Parker Tyler, *Sex Psyche Etcetera in the Film,* p. 122.

189. Conversation with Professor Kristeller, New York, September 5, 1973.

190. Louis Althusser, *For Marx,* trans. Ben Brewster (London, 1969), pp. 134–37. Althusser's discussion is not specifically on Marx here, but on the dialectical notion of time in a play by Bertalozzi. In *Reading Capital,* written with Etienne Balibar, trans. Ben Brewster (New York, 1970), Althusser specifically deals with the concept of nonhomogeneous time in Marx himself (pp. 99f).

191. Benjamin, *Theses on the Philosophy of History,* p. 263.

192. Gershom Scholem, "Walter Benjamin," *The Leo Baeck Institute Yearbook* (New York, 1965). On May 23, 1965, Kracauer wrote to Scholem that he shared his view on Benjamin's Marxism, adding "I once had a very heated argument with him in Berlin over Benjamin's slavish masochistic attitude *(Haltung)* toward Brecht."

193. Kracauer to Tiedemann, February 21, 1966. To Lowenthal, he had complained years before of Benjamin's tendency toward "messianic dogmatism." (Letter of January 6, 1957.)

194. *Durch die Wüste,* 1964).

195. Kracauer to Bloch, June 17, 1963.

196. Kracauer, "Zwei Deutungen in zwei Sprachen," in *Ernst Block zu Ehren; Beiträge zu seinem Werk,* ed. Siegfried Unseld (Frankfurt, 1965).

197. *Ibid.,* p. 146.

198. Stefan Zweig, *Triumph und Tragik des Erasmus von Rotterdam* (Vi-

enna, 1934). Kracauer's distaste for Zweig's type of biography was expressed in his 1930 piece "Die Biographie als neubürgerliche Kunstform," reprinted in *Das Ornament des Masse.*

199. Georg Lukács, *The Historical Novel,* trans. Hannah and Stanley Mitchell (Boston, 1963), pp. 266–69. For a discussion of the Zweig-Lukács dispute, see Albert William Levi, *Humanism and Politics* (Bloomington, Indiana, 1969).

200. Theodor W. Adorno, *Negative Dialectics,* trans. E.B. Ashton (New York, 1973).

201. *History: The Last Things Before the Last,* p. 201.

202. *Ibid.,* pp. 200 and 206.

203. *Ibid.,* p. 200.

204. Arnheim, "Melancholy Unshaped," p. 191.

205. Adorno, "Der wunderliche realist," p. 107.

12. Politics of Translation: Siegfried Kracauer and Walter Benjamin

1. *Die Schrift,* zu verdeutschen unternommen von Martin Buber gemeinsam mit Franz Rosenzweig, 15 vols., Berlin 1926–61.

2. Gershom Scholem, "At the Completion of Buber's Translation of the Bible," in *The Messianic Idea in Judaism and Other Essays in Jewish Spirituality* (New York, 1971), p. 318.

3. This judgment is based on the personal communications of several German friends. No popular edition of the translation has yet appeared. That the translation was intended to be read outside Jewish circles is evidenced by Rosenzweig's letter to Buber of July 29, 1925: "By the Bible, the Christian today understands only the New Testament [and] something of the psalms, which he does not think belong for the most part to the Old Testament. Thus we will be missionaries." Martin Buber, *Briefwechsel aus sieben Jahrzehnten,* vol. 2, 1918–1938 (Heidelberg, 1973), p. 232.

4. Walter Kaufmann, "Buber's Religious Significance," in *The Philosophy of Martin Buber,* ed. Paul Arthur Schilpp and Maurice Friedman (La Salle, Ill., 1967), p. 671. Solomon Liptzin praised it for being "universally acclaimed as a miracle of fidelity and beauty." *Germany's Stepchildren* (Cleveland and New York, 1944), pp. 255–56.

5. He admits the influence in the article cited above. Coincidentally, Rosenzweig had supported Nietzsche in his philological conflict with Wilamowitz-Moellendorf many years before. See his *Kleinere Schriften* (Berlin, 1937), pp. 200–3. Another recent translator to follow the precepts laid down by Buber and Rosenzweig is William W. Hallo, who translated Rosenzweig's *The Star of Redemption* (London, 1971); see his remarks in the translator's preface, p. vii.

6. George Steiner, *After Babel: Aspects of Language and Translation* (London, 1975).

7. Uriel Tal, *Christians and Jews in Germany: Religion, Politics, and Ideology in the Second Reich, 1870–1914,* trans. Noah Jonathan Jacobs (Ithaca, 1975).

8. Ismar Schorsch, *Jewish Reactions to German Anti-Semitism, 1870–1914* (New York, 1972); Arnold Paucker, "Zur Problematik einer jüdischen Abwehrstrategie in der deutschen Gesellschaft," in *Juden im Wilhelmischen Deutschland, 1890–1914.* Ein Sammelband herausgegeben von Werner Mosse unter Mitwirkung von Arnold Paucker (Tübingen, 1976) Schriftenreiher wissenschaftlicher Abhandlungen des Leo Baeck Instituts 33. Paucker had earlier made a similar case for the Weimar era in *Der jüdische Abwehrkampf gegen Antisemitismus und Nationalsozialismus in den letzten Jahren der Weimarer Republik* (Hamburg, 1969), Hamburger Beiträge zur Zeitgeschichte IV.

9. Istvan Deak, *Weimar Germany's Left-wing Intellectuals: A Political History of the Weltbühne and its Circle* (Berkeley, 1968); George L. Mosse, *Germans and Jews: The Right, the Left and the Search for a "Third Force" in Pre-Nazi Germany* (New York, 1970).

10. Carl Schorske, "Politics and Patricide in Freud's *Interpretation of Dreams,*" *The American Historical Review* (April 1973), 78(2), and "Politics and Psyche in *fin-de-siècle* Vienna: Schnitzler and Hofmannstahl," *The American Historical Review* (July 1961), 66(4).

11. Peter Gay, *Weimar Culture: The Outsider as Insider* (New York, 1968, p. 70f.).

12. Martin Buber and Franz Rosenzweig, *Die Schrift und Ihre Verdeutschung* (Berlin, 1936); see also Hans Kohn, *Martin Buber. Sein Werk und seine Zeit,* 2d ed., with *Nachwort* by Robert Weltsch, Veröffentlichung des Leo Baeck Instituts (Cologne, 1961); Else Freund, *Die Existenzphilosophie Franz Rosenzweigs,* 2d ed. (Hamburg, 1959); Ernst Simon, "Martin Buber und das deutsche Judentum," in *Deutsches Judentum. Aufstieg und Krise,* ed. Robert Weltsch, Veröffentlichung des Leo Baeck Instituts (Stuttgart, 1963); James Muilenberg, "Buber as an Interpreter of the Bible," Nahum N. Glatzer, "Buber as an Interpreter of the Bible," and the Kaufmann essay cited above, all in *The Philosophy of Martin Buber,* ed. Schilpp and Friedman; Maurice S. Friedman, *Martin Buber: The Life of Dialogue* (New York, 1955); Nahum N. Glatzer, introduction to *Biblical Humanism: Eighteen Studies by Martin Buber* (London, 1968); Nahum N. Glatzer, *Franz Rosenzweig: His Life and Thought* (New York, 1953); and Grete Schaeder, *The Hebrew Humanism of Martin Buber,* trans. Noah J. Jacobs (Detroit, 1973).

13. *Die Geschichten des Rabbi Nachman* (Frankfurt, 1906), and *Die Legende des Baalschem* (Frankfurt, 1908).

14. Hans Kohn, *Martin Buber,* p. 369.

15. For a history of the *Lehrhaus,* see Nahum N. Glatzer, "The Frankfort Lehrhaus," in *LBI Year Book* vol. 1 (1956), and Erich Ahrens, "Reminiscences of the Men of the Frankfurt Lehrhaus," in *LBI Yearbook,* vol. 19 (1974).

16. Cohen had retired from Marburg in 1912 and assumed a position at the Hochschule für die Wissenschaft des Judentums in Berlin. His last years until his death in 1918 were spent in working out a Jewish philosophy, which Rosenzweig found compelling in certain respects. See his *Einleitung* to Hermann Cohen, *Jüdische Schriften* (Berlin, 1924).

17. Franz Rosenzweig, *Hegel und der Staat* (Berlin, 1920). The dissertation was completed in 1914, but its publication was delayed by the war. For biographical details on Rosenzweig's life, see Glatzer, *Franz Rosenzweig: His Life and Thought.*

18. For a discussion of this event, see Alexander Altmann, "Franz Rosenzweig and Eugen Rosenstock-Huessy: An Introduction to Their 'Letters on Judaism and Christianity,'" *The Journal of Religion* (October 1944), 24(4). In 1916 Rosenstock-Huessy sent Rosenzweig a copy of his *Angewandte Seelenkunde,* which spells out his so-called "speech-thinking."

19. Franz Rosenzweig and Eugen Rosenstock-Huessy, *Judaism Despite Christianity* (Alabama 1969). For an introduction to Rosenstock-Huessy, see Harold Stahmer, *Speak That I May See Thee* (New York, 1968). For a discussion of similar theories of speech from Schelling on, see Freund, pp. 132–40.

20. "Das neue Denken," *Kleinere Schriften.*

21. There were, however, some differences, especially over the place of Jewish law. See Rosenzweig's "Die Bauleute," in *Kleinere Schriften.* For an excellent short survey of these differences and other aspects of their relationship, see Alexander Altmann,

"Theology in Twentieth-Century German Jewry," in *LBI Year Book,* vol. (1956). According to Ernst Simon, Rosenzweig became increasingly observant during his last years "because the 'cruel blessing' of his illness no longer permitted him such transcending of the law, of which in principle he approved." (Letter of Simon to the author, October 30, 1975.)

    22. See note 5. For an interesting commentary on the background to its composition, see Arthur A. Cohen, "Franz Rosenzweig's *The Star of Redemption:* An Inquiry into its Psychological Origins," *Midstream* (February 1972), 18(2).

    23. "Tischdank," *Jüdische Bücherei* 22 (Berlin, 1920).

    24. Jehuda Halevi, *Zweiundneunzig Hymnen und Gedichte,* trans. with an epilogue by Franz Rosenzweig (Konstanz, 1924).

    25. Martin Buber, *Briefwechsel,* vol. 2.

    26. See his letter to Buber, January 25, 1925, in Franz Rosenzweig, *Briefe,* ed. Edith Rosenzweig in collaboration with Ernst Simon (Berlin, 1935), p. 527, and his letter to Eugen Mayer, December 30, 1925, in Glatzer, *Franz Rosenzweig: His Life and Thought.*

    27. Glatzer, *Franz Rosenzweig: His Life and Thought,* p. 149.

    28. *Ibid.,* pp. 100–1. In 1925 Rosenzweig wrote an essay on this topic entitled "Luther und die Schrift," *Kleinere Schriften;* fragments in English appear in Glatzer. Grete Schaeder argues that the difference between the two translations appears to be far less obvious today than it was in the 1920s (Schaeder, p. 353).

    29. Rosenzweig to Buber, September 1925, in Buber, *Briefwechsel,* vol. 2, p. 238. The invitation came after Rosenzweig sent Buber a poem which is reprinted in Glatzer, *Franz Rosenzweig: His Life and Thought,* p. 151.

    30. Shortly before his death, Rosenzweig was cheered by the news that Leo Baeck had persuaded his B'nai B'rith lodge to buy 12,000 copies of the Pentateuch translation. See Leo Baeck, *Von Moses Mendelssohn zu Franz Rosenzweig. Typen jüdischen Selbstverständnisses in den letzten beiden Jahrhunderten* (Stuttgart, 1955), p. 48.

    31. For a discussion of Mendelssohn's translation, see Alexander Altmann, *Moses Mendelssohn: A Biographical Study* (University, Alabama, 1973).

    32. For a discussion of Hölderlin's translation work, see Steiner, *After Babel,* pp. 322–33. Steiner mentions Walter Benjamin's debt to Hölderlin, but it is probable that Buber and Rosenzweig were equally influenced by his example. Or more precisely, they were influenced by his attempt to remain faithful to the original Greek and not by the Christian overtone in his translations, which Rosenzweig criticized in his 1921 letter to Scholem cited in note 28.

    33. In *The Star of Redemption* Rosenzweig talked of a "language prior to language" (p. 109), adding that language "includes the end, for even as the individual language of today, or as the language of the individual, it is dominated by the ideal of coming to a perfect understanding which we visualize as the language of mankind" (p. 110). One of Rosenzweig's major complaints against the idealism he had once followed was its subordination of language to logic.

    34. In *Major Trends in Jewish Mysticism* (London, 1955), Gershom Scholem writes: "Language in its purest form, that is, Hebrew, according to the Kabbalists, reflects the fundamental spiritual nature of the world; in other words, it has mystical value. Speech reaches God because it comes from God" (p. 17). Elsewhere in his text, Scholem discusses the thirteenth-century Spanish Kabbalist Abraham Abulafia, whose investigation of the mysteries of the divine name was based on this language mysticism (p. 133). It is significant to note that whereas the medieval Kabbalists equated Hebrew with the divine language, their modern followers argue for an *Ursprache* located somewhere between or beyond all known tongues, including Hebrew. Although Benjamin "half-jokingly" referred to Hebrew as the *Ursprache* on one occasion, he did not share the Kabbalist position. See

Gershom Scholem, *Walter Benjamin, Die Geschichte einer Freundschaft* (Frankfurt, 1975), p. 53.

It should also be mentioned, as Glatzer stresses in his foreword to *The Star of Redemption*, that Schelling had believed in a primary, common language, and that Rosenzweig was impressed with Schelling's critique of Idealism.

35. Quoted in Steiner, *After Babel*, p. 244.

36. Buber and Rosenzweig, *Die Schrift und ihre Verdeutschung*, p. 289.

37. For an attack on these grounds, see Emanuel Bin Gorion (Berditschewski), "Eine neue Verdeutschung der Bibel," in *Ceterum Recenseo. Kritische Aufsätze* (Tübingen, 1929). For a defense, see Hans Kohn, *Martin Buber*, p. 263.

38. Franz Rosenzweig, "Die Schrift und das Wort," in *Kleinere Schriften*, p. 140. Rosenzweig's evocation of Hamann and Herder, who were among the founders of linguistic relativism, should not be taken as an endorsement of their general position.

39. Rosenzweig to Buber, September 2, 1927, in Glatzer, *Franz Rosenzweig: His Life and Work*, p. 161.

40. Buber to Scholem, May 24, 1926, in Buber, *Briefwechsel*.

41. See, for example, the criticisms in Muilenberg, "Buber as an Interpreter of the Bible."

42. See note 37. Berditschewski was the son of the celebrated Hebrew essayist and fiction writer, Micha Josef Bin-Gorion. In addition to his critique of the aestheticizing tendency of the translation, Berditschewski accused the translators of frequent inconsistencies in their name and word choices, as well as of ignoring the centuries of biblical scholarship that could not be naïvely brushed aside. He defended the continuing validity of the Luther Bible and castigated the new one as superfluous.

43. For a recent study of the *Frankfurter Zeitung*, see Modris Eksteins, "The *Frankfurter Zeitung*: Mirror of Weimar Democracy," *Journal of Contemporary History* (1971), 6(4). Ernst Simon writes that the *FZ* was "Über dem Strich liberal, unter dem Strich marxistisch." (Letter to the author, October 10, 1975.) The "Strich" or line in question separated the political columns of the paper from the *feuilleton* section, which was at the bottom of the page.

44. Siegfried Kracauer, *From Caligari to Hitler: A Psychological History of the German Film* (Princeton, 1947); and *Theory of Film: The Redemption of Physical Reality* (New York, 1960); for an intellectual biography of Kracauer, see chapter 11, and Karsten Witte, 'Introduction to Siegfried Kracauer's 'The Mass Ornament,' " *New German Critique* 5 (Spring 1975).

45. Many of these articles have been collected in *Strassen in Berlin und Anderswo* (Frankfurt, 1964); *Das Ornament der Masse* (Frankfurt, 1963); and *Kino, Essays, Studien, Glossen zum Film*, ed. Karsten Witte (Frankfurt, 1974).

46. Isidor Kracauer, *Geschichte der Juden in Frankfurt a.M. (1150–1824)*, 2 vols. (Frankfurt, 1925 and 1927).

47. "Gedanken über die Freudschaft," in *Gabe Herrn Rabbiner Dr. Nobel zum 50. Geburtstag* (Frankfurt, 1921). The course is mentioned in Glatzer, "The Frankfort Lehrhaus," p. 111.

48. Letter from Kracauer to Leo Lowenthal, undated, between letters of December 16 and 19, 1921, in the collection of Leo Lowenthal, Berkeley, California.

49. See his *Der Detektiv-Roman*, written between 1922 and 1926 but first published in his *Schriften*, vol. 1 (Frankfurt, 1971). There was a revival of interest in Kierkegaard directly after the war, with Barth, Gogarten, Jaspers, Grisebach, and Heidegger among its leaders.

50. His most trenchant critique of premature attempts to resolve the meta-

physical crisis of modern life appeared in "Die Wartenden," *Frankfurter Zeitung*, March 12, 1922; reprinted in *Das Ornament der Masse*.

51. *Ginster*, most recently reprinted in *Schriften*, vol. 7 (Frankfurt, 1973).

52. Buber to Leopold Marx, February 9, 1926, *Briefwechsel*, vol. 2, p. 245.

53. "Die Bibel auf Deutsch," *Frankfurter Zeitung*, April 27 and 28, 1926; reprinted in *Das Ornament der Masse*.

54. On the neo-orthodox revival, see Gustav Krüger, "The Theology of Crisis,'" in *European Intellectual History Since Darwin and Marx*, ed. W. Warren Wager (New York, 1966).

55. For a discussion of the Borchardt translation, see Steiner, *After Babel*, pp. 338–41.

56. Rosenzweig's far cooler attitude toward Zionism Kracauer chose to ignore. He also refrained from remarking on the emphasis on the Jewish "blood-community" in *The Star of Redemption*, which one recent commentator has invidiously compared to Gobineau's racist theories. See Trude Weiss-Rosmarin, "The Light Still Shines Forth," *Judaism* (Summer 1972), 21(3): 371.

57. "Die Bibel auf Deutsch," in *Das Ornament der Masse*, p. 186. Benjamin also stressed the profane in a similar manner; see his "Theologischpolitisches Fragment," in *Schriften*, vol. 1, ed. Theodor W. Adorno and Gretel Adorno with help from Friedrich Podszus (Frankfurt, 1955). This piece, although undated, was written in 1920 or 1921. See Scholem, *Walter Benjamin. Die Geschichte einer Freundschaft*, p. 117.

58. *History: The Last Things Before the Last* (New York, 1969).

59. Walter Benjamin, "Politisierung der Intelligenz; Zu S. Kracauer *Die Angestellten*," reprinted in Siegfried Kracauer, *Die Angestellten* (Frankfurt, 1971), p. 122.

60. For an excellent discussion of Rosenzweig's attitudes toward history, see Alexander Altmann, "Franz Rosenzweig on History," in *Studies in Religious Philosophy and Mysticism* (London, 1969).

61. See Altmann, *ibid.*, pp. 286–87 for Rosenzweig's views on the future and the Kingdom of God.

62. "Die Bibel auf Deutsch; Zur Ewiderung," in *Die Schrift und ihre Verdeutschung* (this is a slightly expanded version of the reply in the *FZ*).

63. For a discussion of Buber's attitude toward Marx, see Glatzer, "Buber as an Interpreter of the Bible," p. 373.

64. Buber's attitude toward God's relation to the world was derived from the Kabbalistic notion of "the exile of *Shekinah*." According to the *Zohar*, the late thirteenth-century masterpiece of Spanish Kabbalism, evil in the world was understood as a division between the *En-Sof*, God's hidden essence, and his Glory immanent in creation, which was the *Shekinah*. Ending this division or "exile," as it was called, meant the reconciliation of God and his Glory, which could be aided by the piety of mankind. This reunification was called *yihud*. For Buber, God was both transcendent and potentially immanent in the world, both Being and Becoming. Man was a coworker with God in bringing about *yihud* through living religiously, but the world was still unredeemed. In this sense, he was opposed to pantheism, as was Rosenzweig with his critique of Hegelian immanentism. For a discussion of the *Shekinah*, see Friedmann, *Martin Buber: The Life of Dialogue*, pp. 17, 20, 53, 71, and 154–58. This negative attitude toward history is preserved in the work of Emmanuel Levinas, the leading Jewish existentialist in France today, who is especially indebted to Rosenzweig. See Charles McCollester, "The Philosophy of Emmanuel Levinas," *Judaism* (Summer 1970), 19(3): 351. There are also significant parallels with Paul Tillich's well-known notion of *kairos*.

65. "Die Bibel auf Deutsch. Zur Erwiderung," p. 291.

66. In the Kracauer *Nachlass,* deposited in the Schiller National Museum, Marbach am Neckar.

67. Buber's address is printed as "Nationalism" in his *Israel and the World: Essays in a Time of Crisis* (New York, 1948). For a recent discussion of Buber's Zionism, see Stephen Poppel, "Martin Buber: The Art of the Unpolitical," *Midstream* (May 1974), 20(5).

68. Walter Benjamin, "The Task of the Translator," reprinted in *Illuminations: Essays and Reflections,* ed. with intro. by Hannah Arendt, trans. Harry Zohn (New York, 1968). See also "Über Sprache überhaupt und über die Sprache des Menschen," in Walter Benjamin, *Schriften,* vol. 2, ed. Theodor W. Adorno and Gretel Adorno with help from Friedrich Podszus (Frankfurt, 1955). See also Hans Heinz Holz, "Philosophie als Interpretation. Thesen zum theologischen Horizont der Metaphysik Benjamins," *Alternative* (October–December 1967), 56/57, for a secondary account of his linguistic theory, which drew upon a number of sources, including the Kabbalah. Scholem had studied the Kabbalah's teachings on language for his dissertation and served as Benjamin's mentor in this area. See Scholem, *Walter Benjamin. Die Geschichte einer Freundschaft,* p. 118.

69. *Ibid.,* p. 153. Stefan Zweig was one of the few to take notice of the introduction, but only to ridicule it. Interestingly, his negative article appeared in the *Frankfurter Zeitung,* with the result that Benjamin was furious at Kracauer for reneging on an earlier promise to give the review to someone else. See his letter to Scholem of June 13, 1924, reprinted in *ibid.*

70. *After Babel,* pp. 244 and 276. Another possible parallel, which Steiner does not draw, can arguably be found between Rosenzweig's theory of translation and that of Stefan George. For a discussion of this possibility, which Rosenzweig himself rejected, see Hans Liebeschütz, "Jewish Thought and Its German Background," in *LBI Year Book,* vol. 1 (1956), p. 235.

71. "The Task of the Translator," p. 74. The religious underpinnings of Benjamin's theory are not as immediately apparent in this quotation as in the following:

One might, for example, speak of an unforgetable life or moment even if all men had forgotten it. If the nature of such a life or moment required that it be unforgotten, that predicate would not imply a falsehood but merely a claim not fulfilled by men, and probably also a reference to a realm in which it *is* fulfilled: God's remembrance. Analogously, the translatability of linguistic creations ought to be considered even if men should prove unable to translate them (p. 70).

72. *Ibid.,* p. 79.

73. *Ibid.,* p. 82.

74. *Ibid.,* p. 69. The same antisubjectivism is manifested in a remark Benjamin made in a letter, which Hannah Arendt quotes in her introduction (p. 49): language was not the gift of speech, but rather "the world essence . . . from which speech arises." Benjamin's hostility to subjectivism was such that Adorno once wrote that "in all his phrases, Benjamin conceived the downfall of the subject and the salvation of man as inseparable." ("A Portrait of Walter Benjamin," in *Prisms,* trans. Samuel Weber and Shierry Weber [London, 1967], p. 231). In the same essay, Adorno points to another crucial difference between Benjamin and Buber and Rosenzweig: "For him philosophy consisted essentially in commentary and criticism, and language as the crystallization of the 'name' took priority over its function as bearer of meaning and even of expression. . . . He transposed the idea of the sacred text into the sphere of enlightenment, in which, according to Scholem, Jewish mysticism itself tends to culminate dialectically. His 'essayism' consists in treating profane texts as though they were sacred" (p. 234). This last remark invites comparison with the final sentence of Kracauer's review quoted above (pp. 208).

75. For a discussion of *écriture* in the work of Derrida and Barthes, see Jonathan Culler, *Structuralist Poetics: Structuralism, Linguistics, and the Study of Literature* (London, 1975), pp. 131f. Their critique of a "metaphysics of presence" in traditional literary criticism also echoes the attack Kracauer and Benjamin made against the translation as the speech of God. It might also be noted that although some structuralists (and Noam Chomsky) are also interested in linguistic universals, they find them on a different level of language from either Benjamin or Buber and Rosenzweig. Whereas the latter were interested in names and words, the former seek formal and grammatical regularities. It also seems as if Benjamin later adopted a utopian belief in the possibility of ending the estrangement between speech and writing through a revolution in society and the media. Hans Magnus Enzensberger has more recently developed this line of reasoning in "Constituents of a Theory of the Media," in *The Consciousness Industry; on Literature, Politics, and the Media*, selected with a postscript by Michael Roloff (New York, 1974).

76. "The Storyteller: Reflections on the Works of Nicolai Leskov," in *Illuminations*.

77. For examples of Benjamin's hostility to Buber, see Gershom Scholem, *Walter Benjamin. Die Geschichte einer Freundschaft*, pp. 22, 38, 40, 41, 42. His relations with Buber, although strained, never reached the breaking point. In 1927 he wrote an essay on his trip to Russia for Buber's journal *Die Kreatur* ("Moskau," *Die Kreatur*, 2 [1]).

78. *Ibid.*, p. 41.

79. It should be noted that Benjamin did share Buber and Rosenzweig's hostility to the idea of a progressive, evolutionary achievement of the Kingdom (or a Marxist utopia). See his "Theses on the Philosophy of History," *Illuminations*.

80. Benjamin to Scholem, December 30, 1922, in Walter Benjamin, *Briefe*, ed. Gershom Scholem and Theodor W. Adorno, vol. 1 (Frankfurt, 1966).

81. *Ibid.*, p. 429.

82. Benjamin to Scholem, September 18, 1926, *Briefe*, vol. 1, p. 432.

83. For Scholem's view of the translation, see his letter to Buber, April 27, 1926, in Buber, *Briefwechsel*, vol. 2, pp. 252–53, a letter that Buber called "the only serious criticism" he had yet received; and his essay in *The Messianic Idea in Judaism*. Scholem was himself a frequent translator from Hebrew to German, and also influenced by Hölderlin's literalist method (see his *Walter Benjamin. Die geschichte einer Freundschaft*, p. 106). Scholem's own complex relations with Buber and Rosenzweig, including his well-known quarrel with Buber over Hasidism, cannot be treated here. For a brief discussion, see Jochanan H. A. Wijnhoven, "Gershom G. Scholem: The Study of Jewish Mysticism," *Judaism* 19, 4 (1970), 19(4). For Rosenzweig's attitude toward Scholem, whom he called a "nihilist" motivated by the "resentment of an ascetic," see his letters to Rudolf Hallo of May 12, 1921, and March 27, 1922, in his *Briefe* (see note 26). See also Scholem's review of the 1930 edition of *The Star of Redemption*, reprinted in *The Messianic Idea in Judaism*.

84. For Benjamin's unresolved attitude towards Judaism and Zionism, see Scholem, *Walter Benjamin. Die Geschichte einer Freundschaft*, passim. As late as 1938 he continued to invoke "God's word" in opposition to the speech of man in an unmetaphorical way (*ibid.*, p. 260).

85. See his letters of January 6, 1957, to Leo Lowenthal and February 21, 1966, to Rolf Tiedemann in the Kracauer *Nachlass*.

86. Theodor W. Adorno, *Kierkegaard. Konstruktion des Aesthetischen*, rev. ed. (Frankfurt, 1966). Adorno's attitude toward Benjamin's theory of translation seems to have been ambivalent. He read "The Task of the Translator" before it was published (see his

Über Walter Benjamin [Frankfurt, 1970], p. 68) and appears to have been impressed. But in later years, he was wary of Benjamin's stress on names rather than concepts. See his letter to Benjamin of November 10, 1938, translated in *The New Left Review* (September–October 1973), 81: 71.

87. Adorno to Kracauer, July 22, 1963, in Kracauer *Nachlass.* Kracauer praised Adorno's *Jargon of Authenticity* for showing Heidegger's relation to the "basest dirt *(Dreck)"* and for its attack on Buber. (Kracauer to Adorno, November 22, 1963). For a recent discussion of the similarities and the differences between Heidegger and Rosenzweig, see Karl Löwith, *Nature, History and Existentialism and Other Essays in The Philosophy of History,* ed. with intro. by Arnold Levinson (Evanston, Ill., 1966).

88. Theodor W. Adorno, *The Jargon of Authenticity,* trans. Knut Tarnowski and Frederic Will (London, 1973).

89. *Ibid.,* pp. 16–17. In his essay on Benjamin cited in note 74, Adorno wrote, "an Existentialist overlord had the effrontery to defame him as being 'touched by demons,' as though the suffering of a person dominated and estranged by the mind should be considered his metaphysical death sentence, merely because it disturbs the all-too-lively I-Thou relationship" (p. 232).

90. The proceedings have been preserved in a special printing in Tel Aviv entitled *An einem denkwürdigen Tag,* which I have been unable to obtain. For a summary, see Schaeder, pp. 350f.

91. Scholem, "At the Completion of Buber's Bible Translation," p. 318. Characteristically, Scholem mixed his praise of the translation with subtle criticisms. For example, he said he preferred the "urbanity" of the later volumes to the "fantaticism" of the earlier ones.

92. Rosenzweig had said so in his *Nachwort* to *Yehuda Halevi,* and Buber agreed with Scholem when he made the statement. (Letter from Scholem to the author, October 20, 1975). Grete Schaeder also endorses this view, p. 351.

93. As mentioned in note 34, the medieval Kabbalists considered Hebrew the *Ursprache* itself, whereas this does not seem the case with their twentieth-century descendants.

94. See Martin Buber, Judah L. Magnes, and Moses Smilansky, *Palestine, a Bi-National State* (New York, 1946).

95. George L. Mosse, "The Influence of the Volkish Idea on German Jewry," in *Germans and Jews* (London, 1971). For another treatment of this question, see Eugene Lunn, *Prophet of Community. The Romantic Socialism of Gustav Landauer* (Berkeley, 1973). Lunn stresses the benign aspects of *völkisch* thought shared by the close friends, Buber and Landauer. It might also be mentioned in their defense that the Nazis had no use for the translation. In *Meyer's Lexikon,* 8th ed. (Leipzig, 1937), vol. 2, p. 207, the work was characterized as one "in which the German language is raped by being fitted into Hebrew rhythms and its bombastic expressions" (quoted in Albert H. Friedland, *Leo Baeck: Teacher of Theresienstadt* [New York, 1968], p. 203).

96. For a recent discussion of chauvinism on the Israeli right, see Bernard Avishai, "Israel Letter: The New Trap," *New York Review of Books* (October 30, 1975), 22(17).

97. A recognition of the interaction between society and language is at the heart of Jürgen Habermas' recent work in which a secularized version of the *Ursprache* is manifested in his heuristic stress on an ideal speech situation without distorted communications of any kind.

98. Benjamin, "The Task of the Translator," p. 81.

99. *After Babel,* p. 474. Although Steiner takes the gnostic argument for an

Ursprache very seriously, his sympathies are clearly on the side of linguistic diversity, as evidenced by his defense of Benjamin Whorf's unfashionable theory of linguistic relativism against Chomsky.

13. Adorno and Kracauer: Notes on a Troubled Friendship

1. Siegfried Kracauer, *Über die Freundschaft* (Frankfurt, 1971), p. 47. There are echoes of Georg Simmel's views on friendship throughout the essay, although Simmel was more pessimistic about fully reciprocal friendships in the modern world. See his remarks in his *Soziologie* (1908), reprinted in *The Sociology of George Simmel*, ed. and trans. by Kurt M. Wolff (New York, 1950), pp. 324–26.

2. Although written as one essay, "On Friendship" appeared in two parts as "Über die Freundschaft, *Logos* (1917–18), 7(2), and "Gedanken über Freundschaft," in *Gabe Herrn Rabiner Dr. Nobel zum 50. Geburtstag* dargebracht von Martin Buber et al. (Frankfurt, 1921).

3. *Theory of Film: the Redemption of Physical Reality* (New York, 1960).

4. *History: The Last Things Before the Last* (New York, 1969), p. 4.

5. See chapter 12.

6. Karsten Witte, "Nachwort" to Kracauer, *Über die Freundschaft,* p. 99.

7. Both of these novels are collected in the 7th volume of Kracauer's *Schriften* (Frankfurt, 1973).

8. *History: The Last Things Before the Last,* p. 157.

9. "Der wunderliche Realist," *Noten zur Literatur III* (Frankfurt, 1965), p. 83.

10. *Ibid.,* pp. 83–84.

11. *Ibid.,* p. 85.

12. "Siegfried Kracauer Tot," *Frankfurter Allgemeine Zeitung* (December 1, 1966), p. 20.

13. *History: The Last Things Before the Last,* p. 201.

14. "Der wunderliche Realist," p. 88.

15. For a discussion of Benjamin's influence on Adorno, see Susan Buck-Morss, *The Origins of Negative Dialectics: Theodor W. Adorno, Walter Benjamin and the Frankfurt Institute* (New York, 1977).

16. For a discussion of Adorno's critique of Lukács, see Martin Jay, "The Concept of Totality in Lukács and Adorno," *Telos* (Summer 1977), vol. 32.

17. The correspondence and all other unprinted material used in this paper are deposited in the Schiller National Museum in Marbach am Neckar.

18. First published in 1930, *Die Angestellten* has most recently appeared as the 5th volume of Kracauer's *Schriften* (Frankfurt, 1971).

19. For further evidence of Kracauer's hostility to Lukács, see his letters of May 27 and June 29, 1926, to Ernst Bloch, quoted in chapter 12.

20. Adorno to Kracauer, September 3, 1927; Kracauer reserved judgment on the grounds of ignorance in his letter of February 18, 1928.

21. Adorno to Kracauer, May 20, 1927.

22. Kracauer to Adorno, December 21, 1930, quoted in chapter 12.

23. Adorno to Kracauer, May 29, 1931, and June 8, 1931.

24. Adorno to Kracauer, June 8, 1931; Adorno mentioned Alfred Sohn-Rethel as another friend whose work he wanted to introduce to the *Zeitschrift,* but could not. The "desert" in Adorno's description was the review section of the *Zeitschrift,* which Lowenthal controlled.

25. Adorno to Kracauer, August 6, 1930; the accusation that caused Kracauer

to bristle was that he had allegedly borrowed Benjamin's idea of houses as dreams of the collective will in his piece on "Die Arbeitsnachweise," reprinted in Kracauer, *Strassen in Berlin und Anderswo* (Frankfurt, 1964).

26. Adorno, *Kierkegaard; Konstruktion des Aesthetischen* (Tübingen, 1933).

27. "Der enthüllte Kierkegaard" (n.d.); in the Kracauer *Nachlass*.

28. An English translation of these letters can be found in *New Left Review* (September–October 1973), vol. 81.

29. For a discussion of the controversy, see Martin Jay, *The Dialectical Imagination: A History of the Frankfurt School and the Institute of Social Research, 1923–1950* (Boston, 1973), chapter 6.

30. Conversation with Leo Lowenthal, Berkeley, California, September 18, 1973. One source of their estrangement, Lowenthal remembers, was Kracauer's refusal to write about the *Institut* in the *feuilleton* columns of the *Frankfurter Zeitung*.

31. Kracauer to Adorno, May 25, 1930.

32. Adorno to Kracauer, January 12, 1933.

33. Kracauer to Adorno, January 21, 1933; Kracauer to Leo Lowenthal, January 14, 1934 and February 27, 1934.

34. *Zeitschrift für Sozialforschung* (1937), 6(3).

35. The initial idea, which was Adorno's, was to have Benjamin write on film, Kracauer on architecture, and Adorno on jazz; see Adorno to Kracauer, January 27, 1937. Kracauer agreed, but apparently failed to define his project in a way acceptable to the *Institut*. Adorno wrote back on February 11, 1937, saying the collaboration was no longer possible.

36. Kracauer to Adorno, August 20, 1938; Kracauer to Horkheimer, August 20, 1938.

37. Kracauer to Adorno, March 28, 1941; Kracauer to Pollock, March 28, 1941.

38. Adorno to Kracauer, December 22, 1942; Kracauer to Adorno, January 5, 1943. The book ultimately appeared as *Composition for Film* (New York, 1947), but Adorno did not affix his name to the title page because of his fear of being associated with the Communist Eisler.

39. Kracauer to Adorno, January 5, 1943, and the Kracauer memorandum of July 15–21, 1964, are just two of many places where this issue was raised.

40. Kracauer to Lowenthal, August 13, 1951.

41. *Ginster* was first republished in Frankfurt in 1963, without the final chapter, and then ten years later with it.

42. *Das Ornament der Masse* (Frankfurt, 1963); *Strassen in Berlin und Anderswo* (Frankfurt, 1964). I am indebted to Karsten Witte for pointing out to me that Adorno's role in the renewed interest in Kracauer must be put in some perspective. Kracauer had been friends with Peter Suhrkamp himself since the 1930s and did not need Adorno's intervention to gain access to his publishing house. Moreover, it must not be forgotten that Adorno's *Institut für Sozialforschung* never saw fit to invite Kracauer to lecture to its students, which was not the case with the group of scholars around the "Poetics and Hermeneutics" circle in Giessen and Konstanz, led by Hans Robert Jauss. Finally, it should be noted that Adorno's role in determining which works of Kracauer should be republished was a somewhat clouded one, as the case of *Ginster's* last chapter demonstrates.

43. Adorno, "Der wunderliche Realist," p. 99.

44. Erika Lorenz, *Siegfried Kracauer als Soziologe* (Diplomarbeit, Johann Wolfgang Goethe Universität, Frankfurt, 1962).

45. Kracauer to Adorno, January 16, 1964.

46. Max Horkheimer, "Auf das andere Hoffen," *Der Spiegel* (January 5, 1970).

47. For a discussion of the problematic nature of the Frankfurt School's Archimedean point, chapter 4.

48. In *Negative Dialectics,* Adorno attempted to meet this accusation in a section entitled "Vertiginousness":

A dialectics no longer "glued" to identity will provoke either the charge that it is bottomless—one that ye shall know by its fascist fruits—or the objection that it is dizzying. In great modern poetry, vertigo has been a central feeling since Baudelaire; the anachronistic suggestion often made to philosophy is that it must have no part in any such thing. . . . The decisions of a bureaucracy are frequently reduced to Yes or No answers to drafts submitted to it; the bureaucratic way of thinking has become the secret model for a thought allegedly still free. But the responsibility of philosophical thought in its essential situations is not to play this game. . . . To insist on the profession of a standpoint is to extend the coercion of conscience to the realm of theory . . . a cognition that is to bear fruit will throw itself to the objects *a fond perdu.* The vertigo which this causes is an *index veri;* the shock of inconclusiveness, the negative as which it cannot help appearing in the frame-covered, never-changing realm, is true for untruth only (pp. 31–33).

Adorno's defense of dizziness is reminiscent of Hegel's well-known remark in the *Preface* to the *Phenomenology of Spirit* (without the concluding reference to repose): "The true is thus the bacchanalian whirl in which no member is not drunken; and because each, as soon as it detaches itself, dissolved immediately—the whirl is just as much transparent and simple repose."

49. Kracauer, *History; The Last Things Before the Last,* p. 199–200.

50. *Ibid.,* p. 67.

51. Adorno's quarrel with Kracauer on this point had two dimensions. First, he argued with Kracauer's assumption in *Theory of Film* that an era of postideological thinking had been reached, a myth he equated with the end-of-ideology school fashionable in the 1950s. There were still many ideologies operative in our allegedly disenchanted world, Adorno insisted. And second, he contested Kracauer's assumption that this cooling off of ideological thinking was an unequivocally positive development, for it entailed a decline in nonideological theoretical thinking as well. In other words, the alleged end of ideology really meant an end to the type of critical theory that could transcend the givens of the status quo. What Kracauer had applauded as "ideological shelterlessness" (a term Kracauer had in fact borrowed from Lukács's *Theory of the Novel* as early as the 1920s) Adorno saw as a misguided effort to achieve a nontheoretical realism, which meant a regression to predialectical thinking.

52. In *History; The Last Things Before the Last,* Kracauer expanded on his identification with Sancho Panza.

53. *Neue Deutsche Hefte* (September–October 1964), vol. 101.

54. For a discussion of Kracauer's critique of Buber, which Adorno saw as an anticipation of his critique of existentialism in *Jargon of Authenticity,* see chapter 12.

55. Adorno, "Der wunderliche Realist," p. 98.

56. *Ibid.,* p. 101.

57. *Ibid.,* p. 102.

58. Adorno, intro. to Walter Benjamin, *Briefe,* ed. Gershom Scholem and Theodor W. Adorno, 2 vols. (Frankfurt, 1966), 2: 16.

59. Adorno, "Der wunderliche Realist," p. 107.

60. The mystery, Karsten Witte suggests in a letter to the author (November 9, 1976), might be resolved if one recalls that the version of *Caligari* probably read by Adorno was the first German translation, which was a severely abridged one lacking most of Kracauer's social analysis of the films.

61. Adorno to Kracauer, February 5, 1965; Kracauer to Adorno, March 3, 1965; Adorno to Kracauer, March 17, 1965.

14. The Political Existentialism of Hannah Arendt

1. Mary McCarthy, "Saying Good-by to Hannah," *The New York Review of Books* (January 22, 1976), 22(21 and 22); Robert Lowell, "On Hannah Arendt," *The New York Review of Books* (May 13, 1976), 23(8); Hans Morgenthau, "Hannah Arendt, 1906–1975," *Political Theory* (February 1976, 4(1); William Phillips, "Hannah Arendt and Lionel Trilling,." *Partisan Review* (January–February, 1977), 43(1); Leonard Krieger, "The Historical Hannah Arendt," *Journal of Modern History* (December 1976), 48(4); Maurice Cranston, "Hannah Arendt," *Encounter* (March 1976), 46(3); Hans Jonas, "Hannah Arendt, 1906–1975," *Social Research* (Spring 1976), 43(1).

2. Morgenthau, p. 6.

3. Cranston, p. 56.

4. Krieger, p. 672.

5. For a good summary of the historical inadequacies of *The Origins of Totalitarianism,* see Margaret Canovan, *The Political Thought of Hannah Arendt* (New York, 1974), chapter 2. Canovan admits that the book "fails as history," but tries to salvage it by saying "it succeeds as reflection" in the manner of Burke's *Reflections on the Revolution in France* (p. 48). For a defense of its worth, which admits its historical flaws, see Bernard Crick, "On Rereading *The Origins of Totalitarianism,"* *Social Research* (Spring 1977), 44(1).

6. *On Revolution* (New York, 1963).

7. Canovan, p. 15.

8. *The Human Condition* (Chicago, 1958); *Between Past and Future* (Cleveland, 1963). Further elaborations of her position can be found in *Men in Dark Times* (New York, 1968), *On Violence* (New York, 1970) and *Crises of the Republic* (New York, 1972).

9. Conversation with Norman Jacobson, Berkeley, June 22, 1976.

10. *Eichmann in Jerusalem* (New York, 1963).

11. Actually, her role at the *New York Review* was somewhat equivocal. As Philip Nobile reports in *Intellectual Skywriting: Literary Politics and The New York Review of Books* (New York, 1974), p. 75, her 1969 essay "On Violence" was seen as a counterweight to more radical pieces by New Left figures such as Jerry Rubin because of its critique of left-wing violence. But by and large, she became increasingly identified with the leftish *New York Review* circle in the internecine warfare that split the New York intellectual community, as evidenced by the fact that she stopped contributing to its arch rival, *Commentary,* which came to attack her work from a more conservative perspective. See Nathan Glaser, "Hannah Arendt's America," *Commentary,* (September 1975), 60(3).

12. *Rahel Varnhagen: The Life of a Jewess,* trans. Richard and Clara Winston (London, 1957).

13. Benjamin I. Schwartz, "The Religion of Politics," *Dissent* (March–April 1970), 17(2).

14. *Partisan Review* (Winter 1946), 13(1).

15. For a discussion of political existentialism, see Christian Graf von Krockow, *Die Entscheidung. Eine Untersuchung über Ernst Jünger, Carl Schmitt, Martin Heidegger* (Stuttgart, 1958); Herbert Marcuse, "The Struggle Against Liberalism in the Totalitarian View of the State," *Negations: Essays in Critical Theory,* trans. Jeremy J. Schapiro (Boston,

1968); and George Schwab, *The Challenge of the Exception: An Introduction to the Political Ideas of Carl Schmitt between 1921 and 1936* (Berlin, 1970).
16. *The Origins of Totalitarianism,* p. 328.
17. *Ibid.,* p. 166; *Between Past and Future,* p. 240. However, she expressed a great deal of respect for Schmitt, "whose very ingenious theories about the end of democracy and legal government still make arresting reading." (*The Origins of Totalitarianism,* p. 339.)
18. "What is Existenz Philosophy?" p. 51. In her tribute to Heidegger on his eightieth birthday, *New York Review of Books* (October 1971), 17(6), she was much more charitable to the "error" he committed in the 1930s. In the same article, she makes clear the power of his influence over her own development in the Weimar years.
19. At the time of her death, she was writing a three-volume study to be called *The Life of the Mind,* sections of which appeared posthumously in *The New Yorker* under the title "Thinking" (November 21, 25, and December 5, 1977).
20. Alfred Bäumler, *Männerbund und Wissenschaft* (1934), p. 108; quoted in Marcuse, pp. 33–34.
21. *Between Past and Future,* p. 169.
22. "What is Existenz Philosophy?," p. 36. She did, however, on occasion acknowledge the limits on boundless change and the importance of durability, permanence, and stability. For a discussion of these qualities in her work, see Leroy A. Cooper, "Hannah Arendt's Political Philosophy: An Interpretation," *The Review of Politics* (April 1976), 38(2): 147, 163–67.
23. *Between Past and Future,* p. 151.
24. It is typical of Hannah Arendt's selective reading of the classical world that she ignores almost entirely the role of such Greek founders of authority as Solon and Lycurgus, whom she mentions only rarely and in passing.
25. *The Human Condition,* p. 167.
26. Isaiah Berlin, *Four Essays on Liberty* (Oxford, 1969); for a defense of "positive freedom," see C. B. Macpherson, "Berlin's Division of Liberty," *Democratic Theory: Essays in Retrieval* (Oxford, 1973). Berlin, however, recently called *The Human Condition* the most overrated book of the past 75 years. (Quoted in *Newsweek,* February 7, 1977, p. 72).
27. *Men in Dark Times,* pp. 3–33.
28. *Ibid.,* pp. 84–86.
29. "What is Existenz Philosophy?," p. 36.
30. *The Origins of Totalitarianism,* p. 437.
31. Canovan, p. 13. Sheldon Wolin describes Marx as "that thinker who exercized a profound fascination for Hannah Arendt, part attraction, part repulsion." "Hannah Arendt and the Ordinance of Time," *Social Research,* (Spring 1977), 44(1).
32. "Eichmann in Jerusalem; An Exchange of Letters between Gershom Scholem and Hannah Arendt," *Encounter* (January 1964), 22(1): 53.
33. *Between Past and Future,* p. 21.
34. George Lichtheim, *Marxism: An Historical and Critical Study* (New York, 1961); Shlomo Avineri, *The Social and Political Thought of Karl Marx* (Cambridge, 1968); Maximilien Rubel, *Marx Critique du Marxisme* (Paris, 1974); Alfred Schmidt, *Der Begriff der Natur in der Lehre von Marx* (Frankfurt, 1962); Iring Fetscher, *Karl Marx und das Marxismus* (Munich, 1967); David McClellan, *Karl Marx: His Life and Thought* (London, 1973). There is, of course, an alternative argument in the work of Della Volpe, Colletti, Althusser and their followers, but it is not as convincing. Moreover, Hannah Arendt would

derive little comfort from Althusser's argument that politics was a relatively autonomous sphere in Marx's thinking.

35. *On Revolution,* p. 58.

36. *The Human Condition,* p. 375; *Crises of the Republic,* p. 171.

37. *The Human Condition,* p. 78.

38. *Ibid.,* p. 89.

39. *Between Past and Future,* p. 18; *Crises of the Republic,* p. 124.

40. *Anti-Dühring,* 3d English ed. (Moscow, 1962), p. 385; quoted and discussed in Avineri, pp. 202–3.

41. *On Revolution,* pp. 268–69; *Crises of the Republic,* pp. 230–31.

42. Canovan, p. 100. For another Arendtian reading of Luxemburg, see Ernst Vollrath, "Rosa Luxemburg; Theory of Revolution," *Social Research* (Spring, 1973), 40(1). An interesting critique of this position can be found in Norman Geras, *The Legacy of Rosa Luxemburg* (London, 1976), p. 133–41.

43. *On Revolution,* p. 215.

44. For two recent treatments of Rosa Luxemburg that make this point, see Andrew Arato, "The Second International: A Re-examination," and Dick Howard, "Re-reading Luxemburg," both in *Telos* (Winter 1973–74), no. 18.

45. *Between Past and Future,* p. 22.

46. *Crises of the Republic,* p. 113.

47. *Between Past and Future,* p. 139.

48. *On Revolution,* p. 31.

49. *Ibid.,* p. 210.

50. *Crises of the Republic,* p. 5.

51. Canovan, p. 4.

52. Leroy Cooper argues against the watertight separation of politics from everything else by alleging that "she observes that freedom 'animates and inspires *all* human activities' " (p. 172). But the whole passage from which this quotation is taken (*Between Past and Future,* p. 169) suggests otherwise. It reads in full: "What usually remains intact in the epochs of petrifaction and foreordained doom is the faulty of freedom, the sheer capacity to begin, which animates and inspires all human activities and is the hidden source of production of all great and beautiful things. But so long as this source remains hidden, freedom is not a worldly, tangible reality; that is, it is not political. Because the source of freedom remains present even when political life has become petrified and political life impotent to interrupt automatic processes, freedom can so easily be mistaken for an essentially nonpolitical phenomenon." Cooper has confused her views on "the faculty of freedom" and the "source of freedom" with freedom itself.

53. *Crises of the Republic,* p. 214.

54. *On Revolution,* p. 110.

55. *Ibid.,* p. 280.

56. *Ibid.*

57. *The Origins of Totalitarianism,* p. 498.

58. In her discussion of slavery in *On Revolution* (pp. 65ff), she does acknowledge that "the absence of the social question from the American scene was, after all, quite deceptive" because of slavery, but she never really questions the consequences of this deception.

59. *Ibid.,* p. 136.

60. Walter Benjamin, "The Work of Art in the Era of Mechanical Reproduction," *Illuminations: Essays and Reflections,* ed. with an introduction by Hannah Arendt,

trans. Harry Zohn (New York, 1968), p. 244. For a discussion of a recent manifestation of aesthetized politics, see Martin Jay, "The Politics of Terror," *Partisan Review* (January 1971), 38(1). For a more sympathetic appraisal of the role of beauty in her political theory, see J. Glenn Gray, "The Winds of Thought," *Social Research* (Spring 1977), 44(1).

61. The difficulty of avoiding some appeal to naturalism as a justification for a normative preference is shown in Miss Canovan's remark that Hannah Arendt "is prepared to agree, as we have seen, that to a large extent in modern times politics *has* been merely an offshoot of society, but that she takes to be a peculiarity of the period rather than part of *the order of nature* (p. 119, last italics added).

62. Canovan only partly sees the implications of this definition of politics when she writes:

Hannah Arendt constantly refers to Achilles, the "doer of great deeds and speaker of great words"; and whatever Achilles' eloquence in the assembly his fame rests, of course, upon his deeds in battle. Indeed "great deeds," in the context of the ever-warring Greek *polis,* has an inescapable connotation of personal military valour that seems to suggest that if we are to find more recent parallels, the appropriate place to look might be the Wild West (p. 62).

What distinguished Homeric Greece from the American West was the eponymous nature of its epic heroes, who were understood to embody communal values rather than purely individual ones.

63. "What is Existenz Philosophy?," p. 41.

64. *Ibid.,* p. 53.

65. *Ibid.,* p. 52.

66. "Lying in Politics," in *Crises of the Republic.*

67. "Truth and Politics," in *Between Past and Future,* rev. ed. (New York, 1968), pp. 250 and 258.

68. "Lying in Politics," p. 206.

69. Schwartz, p. 151.

70. *On Revolution,* p. 277. Eric Hobsbawm shows the futility of her purely political definition of the councils in his acute review of *On Revolution* reprinted in his *Revolutionaries: Contemporary Essays* (New York, 1973).

71. *Crises of the Republic,* p. 216.

72. H. Stuart Hughes, *The Sea Change: The Migration of Social Thought, 1930–1965* (New York, 1974).

73. As Hanna Fenichel Pitkin points out in *Wittgenstein and Justice* (Berkeley, 1972), p. 215, by making a substantive of "the political," Arendt was trying to distinguish it from politics as it is normally understood.

74. Jürgen Habermas, *Strukturwandel der Öffentlichkeit* (Frankfurt, 1962), pp. 14 and 30; *Theory and Practice,* trans. John Viertel (London, 1974), p. 286. Another theorist on the left whose work shows Hannah Arendt's influence is Sheldon Wolin; see especially *Politics and Vision* (Boston, 1960) and "Hannah Arendt and the Ordinance of Time."

75. Jürgen Habermas, *Kultur und Kritik: Verstreute Aufsätze* (Frankfurt, 1973), p. 369.

Author Index

Subject Index